From Partition to Brexit

Manchester University Press

From Partition to Brexit

The Irish Government and Northern Ireland

DONNACHA Ó BEACHÁIN

Manchester University Press

Published by Manchester University Press
Altrincham Street, Manchester M1 7JA

www.manchesteruniversitypress.co.uk

British Library Cataloguing-in-Publication Data
A catalogue record for this book is available from the British Library

ISBN   978 0 7190 8583 3   hardback
ISBN   978 1 5261 3295 6   paperback

First published 2019

Typeset
by Toppan Best-set Premedia Limited
Printed in Great Britain
by Bell & Bain Ltd, Glasgow

Do Karolina agus Gaia le grá

Contents

Glossary

Áras an Uachtaráin	Official residence of the President of Ireland
Ard fheis(eanna)	Party conference(s)
Birmingham Six	Six men sentenced to life imprisonment in 1975 for bombings in Birmingham. Their convictions were quashed by the Court of Appeal in 1991
Black and Tans	An armed British military force recruited to augment the Royal Irish Constabulary during the 1919–1921 War of Independence. It acquired a particularly negative reputation during the conflict
B-Specials	A quasi-military reserve police force in Northern Ireland, composed almost exclusively of Protestants, established in 1920 and disbanded in 1970
Bunreacht na hÉireann	The Irish Constitution, passed by referendum in 1937
Ceann comhairle	Speaker of parliament
Chequers	The country home of the United Kingdom's Prime Minister
CIÉ	Córas Iompair Éireann – the statutory body responsible for most public transport in the Republic of Ireland
Clár(acha)	Programme(s), usually referring to those produced for party conferences
Comhairle na dTeachtaí	'Council of Deputies' in the Irish language. A short-lived body established in 1924 composed of those surviving members of the second Dáil

	who had taken the anti-Treaty side, and all Sinn Féin deputies elected subsequently. It effectively dissolved shortly after Fianna Fáil was established in 1926
Cumann	Party branch (used by Fianna Fáil and Sinn Féin)
Dáil Éireann	Lower house of parliament
DFA	Department of Foreign Affairs
Downing Street	Usually refers to No. 10 Downing Street, the official residence of the United Kingdom's Prime Minister. Consequently, it is sometimes used as a metonym for the UK Government
DSD	Downing Street Declaration
DUP	Democratic Unionist Party
ECHR	European Court of Human Rights
ERA	External Relations Act
EEC	European Economic Community
FCÁ	An Fórsa Cosanta Áitiúil (Second Line Reserve of the Irish Army)
FCO	Foreign and Commonwealth Office
FPR	Forum for Peace and Reconciliation
Free State	Refers to the Irish Free State, which existed between 1922 and 1937. It was replaced by 'Ireland' in the 1937 Constitution
Garda(í) Síochána	Irish police
GFA	Good Friday Agreement
GHQ	General Headquarters
H-Blocks	A prison in Northern Ireland for paramilitary prisoners from 1971 to 2000. Officially called Her Majesty's Prison Maze
HMG	His/Her Majesty's Government (refers to British Government)
INC	Irish National Caucus
INLA	Irish National Liberation Army
IRA	Irish Republican Army
IRB	Irish Republican Brotherhood
Iveagh House	Location of the Irish Department of Foreign Affairs
Leinster House	Building in which the houses of the Oireachtas meet

Loyalism	Generally associated with a strongly unionist position and those more disposed to use violence against Catholics
MEP	Member of the European Parliament
MI5	Military Intelligence, Section 5. Britain's domestic counter-intelligence and security agency
MI6	The foreign intelligence agency of the British Government (officially known as the Secret Intelligence Service)
MLA	Member of Legislative Assembly (Northern Ireland)
MoD	Ministry of Defence (UK)
MP	Member of Parliament
NAI	National Archives of Ireland
NATO	North Atlantic Treaty Organization
NAUK	National Archives of the United Kingdom
NICRA	Northern Ireland Civil Rights Association
NIO	Northern Ireland Office
NORAID	Irish Northern Aid Committee. An Irish-American fundraising organisation founded in 1969
O/C	Officer Commanding
Officials	The Official IRA, a term that originates with the republican movement split in December 1969. During the 1970s, it was also occasionally employed to refer to the Sinn Féin wing that supported the Official IRA
Oireachtas	Collective term for both houses of parliament
Orange Order	An anti-Catholic religious/political organisation established in 1795, which enjoys a mass membership amongst unionists and loyalists
PDs	Progressive Democrats
PRONI	Public Record Office of Northern Ireland
Provisionals	The Provisional IRA, a term that originates with the republican movement split in December 1969. 'Provisional Sinn Féin' was employed to refer to the party that supported the Provisional IRA but this description fell out of general use during the 1980s and was replaced simply by 'Sinn Féin'

PR-STV	Proportional Representation/Single Transferable Vote
PUP	Progressive Unionist Party
Republican	Generally associated with a strongly anti-partitionist position and frequently treated as synonymous with those who support the use of force to end partition
RTÉ	Raidió Telefís Éireann (national broadcaster)
RUC	Royal Ulster Constabulary
SAS	Special Air Services, an undercover wing of the British Army
SDLP	Social Democratic and Labour Party
Seanad	Upper house of parliament
Section 31	A section of the 1960 Broadcasting Act that enabled the Irish Government to prohibit the voices of Sinn Féin members from being broadcast on television and radio
SFWP	Sinn Féin the Workers' Party. The name adopted in 1977 by Official Sinn Féin, which had earlier split with Provisional Sinn Féin. In 1982, the organisation was rebranded as The Workers' Party
Siege of Drumcree	Attempts by the Orange Order to parade through nationalist-populated sections of Portadown against the wishes of local residents
Six Counties	A term used, particularly in the early decades following partition, to describe Northern Ireland. The Irish Government mostly used this term until the 1960s and occasionally thereafter. It is sometimes referred to as 'the North'
Stormont	The seat of Northern Ireland's Government from the time of the building's completion in 1932, until 1972, when direct rule from Westminster was imposed. More recently, it has housed the Northern Ireland Assembly and its power-sharing executive
TACA	A controversial and short-lived Fianna Fáil fundraising organisation established in 1966 ('taca' means 'support' in the Irish language)
Tánaiste	Deputy Prime Minister

Taoiseach	Prime Minister (singular)
Taoisigh	Prime Ministers (plural)
TD	Teachta Dála (member of parliament)
Tory	A term frequently employed to describe a member of the British Conservative Party or the party itself (plural Tories)
Twenty-six Counties	Since 1937, constituionally referred to as 'Ireland' or in the Irish language Éire. The territory was called the Irish Free State between 1922 and 1937. It is sometimes referred to as 'the Republic of Ireland' or simply 'the Republic'
UDA	Ulster Defence Association (a loyalist paramilitary organisation)
UDP	Ulster Democratic Party
UDR	Ulster Defence Regiment (a unit of the British Army with strong ties to loyalist paramilitary organisations)
UFF	Ulster Freedom Fighters (a loyalist paramilitary organisation)
UKIP	United Kingdom Independence Party
UKUP	United Kingdom Unionist Party
Ulster	One of the four historic provinces of Ireland, comprising nine counties. Until 1920, unionists also used this term when referring to the nine counties but after partition frequently employed it when referring to the six counties of Northern Ireland only
UUP	Ulster Unionist Party
UUUC	United Ulster Unionist Council
UVF	Ulster Volunteer Force (a loyalist paramilitary organisation)
UWC	Ulster Workers Council
West Brit	A derogatory term for an Irish person who is perceived as supportive of British rule in Ireland
Westminster	Seat of the British Parliament in London, including the House of Commons and the House of Lords
Whitehall	A metonym for the British civil service

Preface

Why this book?

It is common for prefaces to explain how the tome in your hand differs from the many others on the same subject that have been written. Such a formula is less necessary for this publication. *From Partition to Brexit* is the first book to chart the political and ideological evolution of Irish government policy towards Northern Ireland from the partition of the country in 1921 to the present day. It assesses the achievements and failures of successive Dublin administrations, evaluating the obstacles they faced and the strategies used to overcome them. Challenging the idea that Irish Governments have pursued a consistent set of objectives and policies towards Northern Ireland, this study reveals a dynamic story of changing priorities. The picture that emerges is one of complex and sometimes contradictory processes underpinning the Irish Government's approach to the conflict.

This is not another book about Northern Ireland, arguably the most researched piece of territory per capita in the world. Books dealing with various phases of the Troubles have generally confined their analysis to the conflict within Northern Ireland and make only cursory reference to the Irish Government. This omission is all the more curious considering that, since the early 1970s, Dublin has been recognised as a key actor vital to any conflict resolution process. In terms of books that have some focus on Irish government policy towards Northern Ireland, Catherine O'Donnell's *Fianna Fáil, Irish Republicanism and Northern Ireland, 1968–2005* is relevant. As the title suggests, however, it is limited to consideration of one party, irrespective of whether or not it was in government, and to a much shorter period (the majority of the book is devoted to the period 1992–2005, which coincides with the early stages of the peace process). Similarly, John Bowman's groundbreaking *De Valera and the Ulster Question, 1917–1973*, first published almost four decades ago, deals solely with the views of one politician and for a limited time frame (much of which was spent out of office). My own *Destiny of the Soldiers*, published in 2010, surveyed Fianna Fáil's policies towards Northern Ireland from its foundation in 1926 until the beginning of the Troubles over four decades later. This has since been complemented by Stephen Kelly's *Fianna Fáil, Partition and Northern Ireland, 1926–1971*, though both books cover but one party and conclude almost half a century ago. Kelly has also produced a significant assessment of Charles Haughey's relationship with Northern Ireland.[1] Gareth Ivory's articles have produced some important insights but, again, these have been primarily devoted to Fianna Fáil and confined to a portion of the Troubles.[2] *From Partition to Brexit* is also influenced by research on Irish foreign policy, which until Patrick Keatinge's works published in the 1970s had been virgin territory in academia.[3] Since then our appreciation of this topic has been informed by several individuals, such as Michael Kennedy,[4] John Doyle,[5] Ben Tonra[6] and Noel Dorr,[7] who have individually and collectively[8] helped create a greater understanding of the dynamics of Irish foreign policy.[9] Finally, the increasing literature on Anglo-Irish relations has also illuminated how Dublin and London interact on a variety of issues, including Northern Ireland.[10]

This book explores the gap between the rhetorical objective of Irish unity and actual priorities, such as stability within Northern Ireland and the security of the Irish state. To do this, it has drawn on extensive archival research and interviews, as well as relevant secondary sources. Identifying key evolutionary trends, *From Partition to Brexit* demonstrates how in its relations with the British Government, Dublin has been transformed from spurned supplicant to vital partner in determining Northern Ireland's future, a partnership jeopardised by Britain's decision to leave the European Union.

Some words about words

Conflict in Ireland extends to, and is reflected by, the words we use to describe protagonists, institutions and territories. In the interests of stylistic variation a number of terms are employed to depict 'Ireland'. These include the 'Republic of Ireland', 'the Republic' and, occasionally, 'the South'. 'Éire' and 'Southern Ireland' are not used, and neither is 'the 'Irish Republic', except when referring to the period 1916–1921. When discussing events before 1937, the term 'Free State' is frequently employed, as this was then the official name. 'Dublin' and 'London' are sometimes treated as synonyms for the Irish and British Governments respectively. 'Northern Ireland' is used throughout with occasional reference to 'the North'. Reflecting Irish government policy at the time, earlier chapters frequently describe Northern Ireland as 'the six counties', a practice largely abandoned from the 1960s onwards. Northern Ireland is described as a 'state' before 1972 and occasionally as a 'regime' or 'statelet'. It is also described as a 'region' but never as a 'province', given that the province of Ulster includes three counties in the Republic of Ireland. The Northern Ireland Government is occasionally described as 'Stormont' or 'Belfast', mainly to avoid repetition.

The terms 'north'/'northern' and 'south'/'southern' are capitalised when describing a regime, polity or party, or when an integral part of a proper name (e.g. Northern Ireland, the North) but not when they are used primarily in the geographical sense or to refer to a body of opinion (e.g. southern unionists, northern trade unionists). When 'Unionist', 'Nationalist', 'Loyalist', 'Republican', 'Conservative', begin with capital letters, it is to denote a political organisation or association; the use of these terms without capitals refers to the wider community or supporters of these movements. The British Government's Secretary of State for Northern Ireland is frequently referred to as the Northern Secretary. Also, for simplicity's sake, 'Foreign Minister' is often used to describe the Minister for Foreign Affairs and Trade, a position that until 1969 was officially titled 'Minister for External Affairs'. Representatives of the British Conservative Party are sometimes referred to as Tories, again for the sake of variation. The term 'republicans' is in general used interchangeably with those militants or their supporters seeking to use force to secure a British withdrawal from Northern Ireland. Although the author does not subscribe to the view that the conflict is theologically inspired, the terms 'Protestant' and 'Catholic' are frequently used when referring to the two main political communities in Northern Ireland.

Notes

1 Kelly, *Failed Political Entity*.
2 Ivory, 'Fianna Fáil, constitutional republicanism'; Ivory, 'Revisions in nationalist discourse'; Ivory, 'Fianna Fáil, Northern Ireland'.
3 Keatinge, *The Formulation of Irish Foreign Policy*; Keatinge, *A Place among the Nations*.
4 Kennedy is longtime executive editor of the multi-volume *Documents on Irish Foreign Policy*, which is produced periodically by the Royal Irish Academy, and has helped disseminate seminal archival documents to a wider public. For the purposes of this research, his most relevant work is the highly informative *Division and Consensus*, which examines cross-border relations in Ireland before the outbreak of the Troubles.
5 In addition to his numerous publications relating to Northern Ireland, John Doyle has, since 2004, been editor of *Irish Studies in Interntional Affairs*, the only journal devoted to Ireland's foreign relations.

6   See, for example, Tonra and Ward (eds), *Ireland in International Affairs*; Tonra, *Global Citizen and European Republic*.

7   Given that Irish diplomats are notoriously discreet and loath to publish memoirs, Noel Dorr has performed a great service in producing two useful books based on his time working in the United Nations. Dorr, *Ireland at the United Nations*; Dorr, *A Small State at the Top Table*. Unfortunately, an additional memoir, tantalisingly entitled *The Road to Sunningdale: Irish Government Policy on Northern Ireland 1969–1974* had not been published before this book was completed.

8   The four have co-edited *Irish Foreign Policy*, the only textbook devoted to the subject.

9   Other notable contributions include Joseph Morrison Skelly's research on Ireland's relationship with the United Nations (*Irish Diplomacy at the United Nations*) and Gerard Keown's book on Irish diplomacy from 1919 to 1932 (*First of the Small Nations*).

10 Significant examples include the works of Thomas Hennessey, Ronan Fanning, Eamonn O'Kane, Tony Craig and Daniel C. Williamson. Earlier monographs based on PhD research such as Deirdre McMahon's 1984 work on Anglo-Irish relations during the 1930s (*Republicans and Imperialists*) and Robert Fisk's major study of Ireland during the Second World War (*In Time of War*) have stood the test of time.

Acknowledgements

In putting together a work like this some debts inevitably accumulate. I would like to acknowledge the assistance I received from many institutions and individuals, including the staff of the following archives and record offices: the National Archives of Ireland, Dublin; the National Archives, London; the Public Records Office of Northern Ireland, Belfast; the Military Archives at Cathal Brugha Barracks, Dublin; the Linen Hall Library, Belfast; the Queen's University of Belfast, Main Library; the National Archives, Maryland; the John F. Kennedy Archives, Boston; the National Library of Ireland, Dublin and, finally, our excellent library at Dublin City University. I am also very grateful to those who agreed to be interviewed for my research.

This book received financial support from the Faculty of Humanities and Social Sciences Book Publication Scheme at Dublin City University. I have greatly appreciated the support of my colleagues in the School of Law and Government, and the wider community at DCU, especially our Head of School, Professor Gary Murphy, Faculty Dean, Professor John Doyle, and university President, Professor Brian MacCraith. DCU's Institute for International Conflict Resolution and Reconstruction (IICRR) has also been a major resource for facilitating and disseminating research.

I appreciate very much my friends and colleagues Dr Brian Murphy, Dr Rob Kevlihan, Professor John Doyle and Professor Eileen Connolly who took the time to read parts of the manuscript and provide expert comment. While standard formulae dictate that I should relieve them of responsibility for any errors that remain and claim these slip-ups as my own, I will privately hold them to account should a blunder have escaped their scrutiny. I am also indebted to my old friend, Paul McGuill, for the endless hours discussing topics connected with the focus of this book. Special thanks are due to Dr David McCullagh who took the time to read the entire manuscript in advance of publication and to offer constructive feedback.

My wife Karolina devoted much time (and even more patience) reading earlier drafts of the book and debating the issues with me. Had she read the small print of our marriage contract she would have seen it included an obligation to read all major written works in advance of publication.

I would like to express my appreciation to the anonymous reviewers for their constructive comments and to the production staff at Manchester University Press that ushered the manuscript through the publication process. These include Diane Wardle, Danielle Shepherd, Alun Richards, Chris Hart and Robert Byron. I also wish to thank Tony Mason, senior commissioning editor, for his assistance, not least for his forbearance in waiting for me to complete the manuscript.

I shall always be grateful to my mother, Deirdre, and my sister, Caoilfhionn. Alas, my father, Brendan, my grandmother, Kathleen, and my aunt, Medb are no longer around to celebrate this book. I know they would have derived immense satisfaction and happiness from seeing it in print. They encouraged my love of learning and are present in everything I do.

Finally, and most importantly, I would like to pay tribute to my wife Karolina and to our daughter, Gaia, without whom life is unimaginable. As with all my other endeavours, this book is dedicated to them.

Donnacha Ó Beacháin
Chişinău, July 2018

Introduction: Parties and policy making in Ireland

Continuity

One of the most remarkable aspects of post-Treaty Ireland was how well the political institutions established by the British colonial administration survived. This is not altogether surprising when one considers that the Irish struggle for independence ended in 'a compromise with the former coloniser which denied true emancipation'.[1] Many members of the new elite 'found nothing better to do with their freedom than to duplicate the British system' while 'a new use was found for the Irish language as a kind of green spray-paint to be coated over the remaining British pillar boxes, systems and titles, in order to conceal the ever-growing similarity with the British way of life'.[2] Kevin O'Higgins's conviction that they 'were probably the most conservative-minded revolutionaries that ever put through a successful revolution'[3] gives some idea of the limitations and parameters within which the Free State would take shape.

The survival of the British civil service, based in Dublin Castle, provides a striking example of the basic continuity that followed the Treaty. 'Independence', Basil Chubb notes, 'did not much affect the well-established and powerful departments' and for the former British civil service 'life went on much as before'.[4] Under the Treaty, the position of former colonial administration employees was protected and most managed to exchange political masters with equanimity. A small number (about one hundred) voluntarily transferred to Belfast to serve the Northern Ireland administration. The transition from colonial power to a native administration did not, therefore, impinge greatly on the civil service. The incoming Free State Government inherited 21,000 civil servants and to this number it added a mere 131 of its own and reinstated 88 others. Chubb notes that

> The administrative machinery of the new state did not have to be created: what existed was taken over by nationalist rebels, most of whom were by no means revolutionaries looking to effect great social and political reforms ... Their senior civil service advisers, steeped in the British tradition, saw no need for changes in administrative structures or practices. They looked for and got much friendly cooperation and avuncular advice from the Treasury, the very centre of British bureaucratic traditions ... The very smoothness of the operation and the overwhelming sense of continuity led to the central administrations being carried over into the new regime to a great extent unaltered and in working order.[5]

Centralisation

Since independence, government in Ireland has been centralised to an extent almost unrivalled in a democracy. At the apex of the decision-making hierarchy is the cabinet, which is constitutionally limited to fifteen ministers including the Taoiseach (prime minister). This supremacy is ring-fenced by a weak legislature and feeble local government system. Though drawn from the legislature (Dáil), the cabinet's primacy over Parliament is rarely challenged when a Government enjoys a majority. The executive dictates the content and schedule of the legislative agenda.

The Dáil is not 'an active participant in the process of making laws, let alone broader policy'.[6] The ordinary parliamentarian (Teachta Dála; TD), if not aligned with a party or technical group (seven TDs) can make little contribution on the floor of the house. Moreover, for most of the period covered in this book, TDs enjoyed few resources to challenge government dominance. On the eve of the 1970s, for example, an age before mobile phones, faxes and the internet, deputies laboured in collective offices without Oireachtas secretarial assistance and with one direct telephone line per party whip.[7] As most deputies represented non-Dublin constituencies they spent three days in the capital before returning to their constituency duties for the remainder of the week. The average lifespan of a government has been little more than three years, meaning that most TDs find themselves on an election treadmill involving permanent campaigning. Even ministers are vulnerable to losing their seats, often to a party rival, if deemed to have lost touch with constituents. The realities conspire to provide little space or encouragement to the average politician to think of national issues, let alone foreign affairs. Executive supremacy is, arguably, most pronounced in foreign policy, which generally excites few parliamentarians given the parochialism and clientelism fostered by Ireland's PR-STV electoral system, leaving many a

TD with little to do but harass civil servants with minor requests.[8] These trends have also encouraged TDs to see parliament as a forum for raising constituency issues rather than debating the virtues of competing foreign policies.

Parliamentary committees, frequently an outlet for robust scrutiny in many European legislatures, are comparatively weak in Ireland, with legislative proposals typically discussed only after the plenary stage of a bill. The Joint Committee on Foreign Affairs and Trade, a relatively recent innovation established in 2011, has provided little scrutiny of Northern Ireland policy. This is partly due to its wide brief and competing demands on members' time. Committee delegates are not afforded the resources or staff necessary to challenge government policy, making them vulnerable to over-reliance on Department of Foreign Affairs officials who generally see their role as explaining and defending government policy. This lack of a strong parliamentary committee system has reduced opportunities for parliamentarians and opposition parties to play a meaningful role in policy formulation and provided little incentive for constructive debate.

The upper house of parliament, the Seanad, duplicates rather than challenges the lower house and enjoys far fewer powers. Elected mainly by public representatives and with the Taoiseach nominating eleven of the sixty senators, the Government's Dáil majority is reproduced in the upper house. In any case, the Seanad can only delay Dáil legislation and during the eight decades following the enactment of the Irish Constitution it has only twice (1957 and 1964) rejected a Dáil bill. While narrowly surviving a 2013 referendum designed to abolish it, the Seanad remains unreformed, despite occasional recommendations to alter its electorate, composition and powers.

The president, whose powers are largely ceremonial, can offer little resistance to government initiatives and is constitutionally required to have his or her speeches and engagements cleared by government. It is worth noting, however, that the only presidential resignation stemmed from the Northern Ireland crisis when, in 1976, Cearbhall Ó Dálaigh utilised one of his few powers by referring the Emergency Powers Bill to the Supreme Court.[9] It says much of presidential impotence that his successor, Patrick Hillery, served for fourteen years without ever being subjected to an election.[10]

The Taoiseach and Minister for Foreign Affairs

The Taoiseach and Minister for Foreign Affairs, along with their respective departments, have been to the forefront in devising Northern Ireland policy. While the Taoiseach has traditionally been the formal authority for all major initiatives on Northern Ireland, the Department of Foreign Affairs, which has a specialised Anglo-Irish Division, is responsible for day-to-day policy implementation. In recent years, the Minister for Foreign Affairs has been assisted by two ministers of state (sometimes called junior ministers), one for European Affairs (introduced in 1987) and a second responsible for overseas aid and, recently, North–South Cooperation.

For much of its time in office, Fianna Fáil governed as a single-party administration whereas Fine Gael had to contend with between one and four junior coalition partners. Since 1989, all administrations have been coalitions and consequently the main restraint on a Taoiseach has been his or her government partners. During the first decades following independence Taoiseach and Foreign Minister were drawn from the same party; in de Valera's case they were one and the same person for sixteen years, as the Fianna Fáil leader proved unwilling to delegate Anglo-Irish relations. The brief break from this practice during the novel inter-party Government (1948–1951), when Clann na Poblachta leader Seán MacBride held the Foreign Affairs portfolio in a Fine Gael-led administration, would not be repeated until the 1990s when Labour leader Dick Spring served as Foreign Minister in successive Fianna Fáil- and Fine Gael-led coalitions. Eamon Gilmore repeated the feat for Labour in 2011 but as holding the Foreign Affairs portfolio exposed him to accusations of losing touch with his party's support base, he was forced to resign, only three years after leading Labour to its best ever electoral performance.

Traditionally, Foreign Affairs has been a prestige portfolio given to a figure drawn from the leader's inner circle and demonstrating clear potential to succeed as Taoiseach or the leader of the junior coalition partner. Several Taoisigh, such as Liam Cosgrave, Garret FitzGerald and Brian Cowen, had previously served as Minister for Foreign Affairs. Leaders such as Seán MacBride, Dick Spring and Eamon Gilmore sought the portfolio as the price of coalition. Given the calibre and profile of many of the office-holders it is perhaps surprising that there has not been greater tension between the Taoiseach and his Minister for Foreign Affairs. In practice there has been a division of labour rather than of policy. In situations where the party of the Taoiseach and Minister for Foreign Affairs has been different (as in 1948–1951, 1992–1997 and 2011–2014) the fundamentals have been negotiated before entering government to minimise acrimony and ensure the harmonious implementation of an agreed approach.

Political parties and the Irish party system

The Irish party system bears little resemblance to its European counterparts. The classic cleavages around which democratic politics have generally been conducted (centre–periphery, church–state, urban–rural, class) are not reflected in Ireland.[11] Rather, Ireland's party system remains a product of the civil war of 1922–1923. As a result of the 2016 election, for example, the three main 'civil war parties', Fianna Fáil, Fine Gael and Sinn Féin, garnered over two-thirds of the vote, demonstrating the remarkable longevity of this cleavage.[12] The electorate has proven less forgiving of smaller coalition parties, and when Labour has coalesced with larger right-of-centre partners it has always been punished in subsequent elections.

Fianna Fáil

Fianna Fáil's traditional dominance has been another major feature of Irish politics. Originating in the losing side of the civil war, the party maintained a decades-long winning streak. Initially strongest in the non-Dublin periphery, particularly amongst small farmers, the petite bourgeoisie and urban working class, Fianna Fáil's rise to power laid the basis for a 'periphery-dominated centre'[13] before transforming itself into a classic catch-all party claiming to encompass all strands of society.[14] Until 2011, Fianna Fáil was one of a select few democratic parties that had established themselves as the dominant force in national politics, on a par with organisations such as Sweden's Social Democrats and Japan's Liberal Democrats. In the half century following the Second World War, no other European party surpassed Fianna Fáil's electoral performance. Indeed, in 2002 Fianna Fáil was identified as Europe's 'most consistently successful vote-getter'.[15] Subjected to a gradual erosion of support, reflected in an inability to form a single-party majority administration after 1981, the party endured a sudden collapse in 2011, when its parliamentary representation plunged from seventy-seven seats to twenty. This debacle did not prove fatal as had been the case with Italy's Christian Democrats and within five years the party had more than doubled its number of Dáil deputies.

Fianna Fáil governed Ireland for fifty-four of the seventy-nine years between 1932 and 2011. Consequently, it played a major role in framing how Northern Ireland was viewed in the Republic. Party supporters argued that being in power for such prolonged periods – most of them without the nuisance of a coalition partner – afforded Fianna Fáil the opportunity to take the long view.[16] Fianna Fáil also believed that its republican credentials gave it a unique ability to appreciate the importance of the 'national question'. Its narrative of post-independence history depicted Fine Gael as national quislings, the heirs of those that had compromised Ireland's independence during the Treaty negotiations and acquiesced in the partition of Ireland by virtue of the tripartite agreement of 1925 arising from the Boundary Commission report.

Few opportunities were lost to stress the revolutionary credentials of Fianna Fáil's leaders and to present the party as the custodians of the 1916 tradition. All but two of the party's first seven-member executive had fought in the Easter Rising, and every member of that executive had fought in the War of Independence and on the republican side in the civil war. Such national records, integral to party morale and self-image, helped Fianna Fáil to frame its political lineage in terms of a much longer resistance to imperial rule. It enabled the leadership to dampen criticisms of its anti-republican legislation and lack of progress in ending partition. However, the incomplete nature of the nationalist project, with partition institutionalised in the 1921 and 1925 agreements, also made the example of 1916 a problematic one for a governing party committed to constitutional politics.

Following long periods in office, Fianna Fáil made inroads with voters traditionally associated with its main rival, Fine Gael. By the 1960s, the party had secured substantial backing amongst the wealthier professional classes, a trend institutionalised by the establishment of TACA, an organisation that, amongst other things, facilitated businessmen meeting ministers over dinner for a fee. Over time, policies converged and the divide between Fianna Fáil and Fine Gael became increasingly superficial. Party realignment did not occur, however. Following the 2016 general election, Fianna Fáil turned down an historic offer from Fine Gael leader Enda Kenny to join forces when parliamentary arithmetic suggested that only such a combination could offer stable majority government. Fear of being absorbed or overshadowed, and of leaving a vacuum on the opposition benches, inhibited a new departure through uniting the two major 'civil war' parties.

Fine Gael

For much of the period under consideration in this book, Fine Gael's time in office constituted relatively brief interludes between prolonged spells of Fianna Fáil governance. In 2016, the party for the first time took office for a second consecutive term – though this was with little more than a third of the parliamentary seats – in coalition with a motley crew of independents, and reliant on the sufferance of old rivals Fianna Fáil from the opposition benches.

Though some members trace the party's origins to Michael Collins, implying that he was its first leader, Collins was killed a full decade before the establishment of Fine Gael and eight months before its predecessor, Cumann na nGaedheal.[17] The pro-Treaty Sinn Féin from which many Fine Gael leaders emerged rapidly transformed into a conservative party that favoured membership of the British Commonwealth.[18] The two splinters in Cumann na nGaedheal during the 1920s both stemmed from disillusionment with the party's level of republicanism and with its Northern Ireland policy. These defections, combined with an influx of ex-unionists and former Home Rulers, significantly altered the character of the party.[19] Far from being the stepping-stone that Collins had envisaged, the Treaty rapidly developed into an end in itself, with security becoming the major plank of policy. By 1948 support for Fine Gael had dipped below 20 per cent and its parliamentarians, increasingly part-time amateurs who treated politics as a hobby, were as likely to reside in the law library as in Leinster House. The party's second foundational name – the United Ireland Party – was quietly dropped in later years.

During its first couple of decades, Cumann na nGaedheal and its successor Fine Gael were considered the party of the large farmer, successful businessmen, the Protestant minority and the upper middle classes. The brief spell at the helm of a five-party coalition Government from 1948–1951 reinvigorated Fine Gael and, by declaring a republic, facilitated a rebranding of the party so that it no longer orientated itself on articulating the Commonwealth cause. Subsequent attempts during the 1960s and 1980s to rebrand Fine Gael as a social democratic party never succeeded in replacing its support base, which remained primarily conservative and relatively well-off financially.

Labour

Traditional wisdom has suggested that Labour's decision not to contest the seminal 1918 general election condemned it to the political periphery thereafter. As a newly enfranchised nation affirmed its political allegiances through the ballot box for the first time, Labour stood aloof. When it re-emerged as a choice on the ballot paper, most of the electorate had already committed themselves to either pro- or anti-Treaty wings of Sinn Féin. Fianna Fáil's expansion during the 1920s and 1930s, based on a dynamic socio-economic programme couched in radical republican language, succeeded in making the Labour Party's programme appear incomplete and insufficiently national. Labour offered mild-mannered opposition within the Dáil, prompting taunts from Seán Lemass in 1929 that 'so long as they cannot be accused of being even pale pink in politics they seem to think they have fulfilled their function towards the Irish people'.[20] Despite – or perhaps because of – the party's moderation it proved remarkably sensitive to red-baiting, so that when, during the 1940s, Seán MacEntee accused the Labour Party of harbouring communists, the party obligingly split in two. A brief flirtation with radical slogans during the late 1960s – all the more peculiar coming from the socially conservative party leader Brendan Corish – proved ill-fated. Under the banner of 'the seventies will be socialist', Labour briefly tried to cast off its conservative image before reverting to its default position when it failed to result in significant electoral gains.

During the 1950s and 1960s, the party reorganised within Northern Ireland, garnering modest electoral success before being eclipsed by the Northern Ireland Labour Party. Within the Dáil, Labour deputies articulated some of the most radical republican positions on Northern Ireland, though these were eclipsed during the 1970s by the influence of the party's iconoclastic spokesperson, Conor Cruise O'Brien. Condemned to be the mudguard of its senior coalition partner, the electorate have never rewarded Labour for participation in government. During the 1990s and again in the 2000s an engorged Labour Party demanded and received the Foreign Affairs portfolio but on both occasions the party suffered huge losses. The 'Spring Tide' of 1992 went out five years later when the party lost half its parliamentary seats while in 2016 its Dáil representation collapsed from thirty-seven seats to just seven following another five-year coalition with Fine Gael. During the later coalition, party leaders Eamon Gilmore and Joan Burton fell on their swords in response to a haemorrhaging of support for Labour.

Minor parties

Most other parties, like meteors in the sky, shone briefly and brightly before breaking up in the inhospitable political atmosphere. Noteworthy amongst these are the agrarian Clann na Talmhan and republican Clann na Poblachta, both of which participated in the inter-party Government of 1948–1951. In more recent times, the Progressive Democrats (PDs) and Democratic Left (DL) wielded disproportionate influence in their respective coalitions before being absorbed into Labour (DL) or disappearing altogether (PDs). While only once in government (2007–2011), and with no relevant ministerial portfolio, the Green Party has played little role in the devising of Northern Ireland policy but, significantly, is organised on an all-Ireland basis. On the rare occasions that parties, such as Aontacht Éireann, were formed to emphasise the Northern Ireland problem they failed to thrive. Independent Fianna Fáil, however, endured for three decades due to the personality and organisational mastery of its founder, Neil Blaney, and its bailiwick of Donegal, the most northerly county in the Republic.

Sinn Féin

Sinn Féin is an unusual party that has flitted in and out of electoral politics but is key to any appreciation of Irish government policy towards Northern Ireland. Until relatively recent times the party vacillated between dormancy and occasional electoral intervention on an abstentionist basis. It was only in 1997 that Sinn Féin managed to elect a representative willing to take their seat in Leinster House. Moreover, while in many ways a new force in parliamentary politics, the party claims the oldest political lineage. Sinn Féin has endured many splits, factions and transformations. Eclipsed by its early progeny, Fianna Fáil and Fine Gael, the party has now become a major force in both parts of Ireland, as near-permanent members of the Northern Ireland executive and as a major opposition party in the Republic. Despite being a legal political party, Sinn Féin had the distinction of being banned from radio and television in Ireland for virtually all of the Troubles and for the last half-dozen years of the conflict in the United Kingdom. The Irish Government's ban extended not only to party representatives and spokespeople but also to ordinary members irrespective of the topic they discussed.[21]

Conclusion

Devising the Irish Government's Northern Ireland policy has been the purview of remarkably few parties. Only four parties participated in government during the Troubles and these administrations have been very much dominated by Fianna Fáil and Fine Gael. While for the purposes of this book, Northern Ireland policy is defined in terms of the actions of successive Taoisigh and their cabinets, it is important to note that such policies are not devised or implemented in a vacuum but rather react to, and interact with, a whole range of factors and actors. These include the views of domestic public opinion, opposition parties and senior civil servants, while external restraints include the position of the British Government and international actors such as the European Union and United Nations, not to mention economic considerations. While bi-partisanship on Northern Ireland has frequently been the order of the day, this should not be interpreted as meaning that there has been a consensus. This, as we shall see, could not always be achieved at the cabinet table, let alone within political parties or society at large.

Notes

1   Coulter, *Ireland*, p. 4.
2   Kiberd, 'Inventing Ireland', p. 21.
3   *Dail Debates*, 2/11 (6 December 1923).
4   Chubb, *The Government and Politics of Ireland*, pp. 236, 249.

5　Chubb, *The Government and Politics of Ireland*, pp. 240, 250.

6　Gallagher, 'The Oireachtas'.

7　See Desmond, 'A Larkinite in power'.

8　Chubb, '"Going about persecuting civil servants"'.

9　See chapter 5.

10　Hillery's candidature for the seven-year presidency was unopposed in 1976 and 1983 due to a consensus between the major parties.

11　See Mair, *The Changing Irish Party System*.

12　Independents of various hues constituted the next biggest grouping following the 2016 election while the largest parliamentary party not rooted in the civil war (Labour) won only seven seats.

13　Garvin, 'Political cleavages'.

14　Kirchheimer, 'The transformation of the Western European party systems'.

15　Coakley, 'The election and the party system', p. 240.

16　Hannon, *Taking the Long View*.

17　Fine Gael was formed in 1933 as a merger between Cumann na nGaedheal, the Centre Party and the National Guard, a militant organisation with fascist overtones popularly known as the Blueshirts. Eoin O'Duffy, the mercurial leader of the Blueshirts, was selected as Fine Gael's first leader. After a year at the helm, he stepped down as Fine Gael leader and founded the fascist National Corporate Party, before organising a brigade to fight for Francisco Franco in the Spanish civil war. It is clear that O'Duffy's foundational leadership of Fine Gael embarrasses the contemporary party. On the Fine Gael website, reference is made and pictures provided of all party leaders, with the solitary exception of O'Duffy. See 'History of Fine Gael'. Available at www.finegael.ie/the-party/history-of-fine-gael. Accessed 11 December 2017.

18　See Regan, *The Irish Counter Revolution*.

19　Ó Beacháin, 'The dog that didn't bark', pp. 46–47.

20　*The Nation*, 19 October 1929.

21　See Corcoran and O'Brien, *Political Censorship and the Democratic State*.

1

The politics of partition, 1920–1932

Westminster's passing of the Government of Ireland Act in March 1920, which partitioned the country, resulted from the inability, or unwillingness, of the British political elite to reconcile the conflicting demands of their loyal supporters, who constituted 18 per cent of the Irish population, and the majority wish for complete separation from the United Kingdom. The exclusion from Dublin's jurisdiction and the size of the new six-county 'Northern Ireland' very much catered for the demands of Ulster Unionists and their supporters at Westminster. Partition's major victims were that section of the nationalist majority that found themselves a minority, constituting just over a third of Northern Ireland's population. The nationalist majorities in counties Fermanagh and Tyrone were greater than the unionist majorities in Derry and Armagh, and Northern Ireland would contain cities like Derry and Newry that had large nationalist majorities. In fact, in not one of the six counties was the unionist majority greater than the nationalist majority in Ireland as a whole. Rather than separating two peoples that could not live peaceably together, partition brought them closer together. Its aim was clearly to produce Protestant rule in perpetuity even in areas with Catholic majorities.

Having placated six-county unionists with their own administration, opened by King George V on 22 June 1921, the British Government set about seeing what could be done to mollify 'disloyal' nationalist Ireland. Emboldened by the landslide victory for Sinn Féin at the 1918 general election and embittered by the British military's suppression of the independence movement, Irish republicanism had moved from the periphery to the mainstream. Hunger strikes, executions and atrocities such as those committed on Bloody Sunday punctuated what was in retrospect a mercifully short war for independence. Almost 2,000 people were killed between January 1919 and July 1921, of whom about a quarter resided in the six counties of what became Northern Ireland. In Belfast, where most of the northern fatalities occurred, British state forces combined with loyalist irregulars to target the Irish Republican Army (IRA) and minority Catholic community.

A truce between British forces and the IRA, operative from midnight, 11 July 1921, was generally observed but failed to take hold in Belfast. Eamon de Valera, the Sinn Féin leader and President of the unrecognised Irish Republic, met with British Prime Minister David Lloyd George shortly after the suspension of military hostilities. Controversially, de Valera chose to stay in Dublin while his hand-picked team of plenipotentiaries led by Arthur Griffith, a moderate within the Sinn Féin party, and IRA leader Michael Collins negotiated with Lloyd George and his cabinet colleagues between October and December.

The two issues central to the talks were the status of Ireland and the position of Ulster. Both teams believed that if negotiations broke down on Ulster, the British would be blamed for violating Ireland's territorial integrity, against the wishes of the vast majority of Irish people. The fact that the republicans were willing to concede a local parliament for Belfast with wide-ranging powers but subject to Dublin's jurisdiction reinforced the apparent reasonableness of the nationalist position. Conversely, all sides realised that if it could be demonstrated that the breakdown had occurred solely because the Irish refused the offer of dominion status, similar to that enjoyed by Canada and Australia, and stuck rigidly to complex constitutional formulae, then the British Government would have few qualms in renewing war to protect its vital interests. Taking cognisance of these realities, the two opposing strategies emerged. Which would prevail depended largely on the competence and diplomatic skill of the respective negotiating teams.

Lloyd George's administration had entered negotiations under considerable international pressure. They would not tolerate an independent republic off their shores and were confident they could carry world opinion on this. On Ulster, however, the British negotiating team had shown a significant degree of manoeuvrability and were vulnerable to pressure. Lloyd George admitted to his cabinet that in Ulster they had 'a very weak case'. The strong sentiments that the Conservatives had been able to exploit between 1912 and 1914 had been replaced by a feeling that the unionists were 'unreasonable' and 'narrow'.[1] Queries on Ulster evoked an embarrassed and evasive response from London's negotiators. When Michael Collins enquired why the British would not concede local plebiscites, Austen Chamberlain, a veteran cabinet member who had ardently resisted Irish home rule, could only reply meekly that 'you could not put a more difficult question to us in the light of the history of recent years'.[2] Despite the fragility of the British case on Ulster, however, the Irish delegation came away from London with a Treaty that failed to secure London's recognition of an

Irish republic and entrusted the destiny of the six counties of Northern Ireland to a nebulous Boundary Commission. Prime Minister Lloyd George had threatened 'immediate and terrible war' should the Sinn Féin plenipotentiaries refuse to agree to this final offer, which included the creation of a twenty-six-county Irish Free State with circumscribed powers, enforced membership of the British Commonwealth and a compulsory oath of fidelity to the British King to be taken by all Irish parliamentarians.

Partition was not emphasised during the subsequent Treaty debates in Dáil Éireann as many accepted Collins's argument that the new north-eastern state would be unable to survive mutilation by the proposed Boundary Commission outlined in Article 12 of the accord. The narrow passing of the Treaty – by 64 votes to 57 – paralysed Ireland's political elite. Division on this issue would constitute the fault-line on which the brief but bloody civil war of 1922–1923 was fought. It would also form the basis of the Irish party system. A majority of the Irish electorate today still vote for parties whose formation and identity are tied to the Treaty divisions and subsequent civil war.

The Northern policy of Michael Collins

Collins viewed the Treaty as providing a breathing space during which a national army could be trained and equipped ready to renew a war with Britain should the new agreement prove unsatisfactory. Within a month of the Treaty being signed, Seán Hales was telling doubters that Collins 'says the British broke the Treaty of Limerick, and we'll break this Treaty when it suits us, when we have our own army'. Similarly, General Eoin O'Duffy informed a gathering of senior IRA officers in Clones that the Treaty 'was only a trick' in order to procure arms with a view to continuing the fight. IRA members were further impressed when O'Duffy repeated that he would never take an oath to the British Crown, or ask anyone else to take it.[3] Collins, moreover, told the IRA's 2nd Northern Division that 'although the Treaty might have [seemed] an outward expression of Partition, the Government plans [to] make it impossible ... Partition would never be recognised even though it might mean the smashing of the Treaty.'[4] Collins would be ably assisted in implementing this policy by fellow IRB man and cabinet member, Richard Mulcahy, who informed the North-Eastern Advisory Committee – established to keep Collins informed of developments in the North – that they had accepted the Treaty in order to destroy it.[5]

To understand the reasons why Collins adopted the Northern policy he did, it is important to understand the conditions that prevailed for the nationalist community in the six counties at this time. Between July 1920 and July 1922 (which closely corresponds with the period from the imposition of the Government of Ireland Act to the beginning of the civil war), 453 people were killed in Belfast alone. Catholics constituted the vast majority of deaths, despite the fact that they constituted only a quarter of the city's population. Of Belfast's 93,000 Catholics, nearly 11,000 had been ejected from their place of employment and 23,000 had been driven from their homes. In addition, over 500 Catholic-owned shops and businesses had been destroyed.[6] Streams of Catholic refugees fled south to the dubious safety of Dublin.

One of the first steps taken by the six-county Government was the mobilisation of a large section of the Protestant community to police their Catholic neighbours.[7] The Special Constabulary was drawn from the Ulster Volunteer Force (UVF) militias formed to block home rule by force of arms 'and where there weren't enough UVF men they were recruited from the Orange Lodges'.[8] By 1922, there were 50,000 members of the police and Special Constabulary – constituting about one-sixth of the adult male Protestant population – and these were complemented by sixteen battalions of the British Army.[9] As these forces were directed exclusively against the Catholic population, one is left with the remarkable statistic that for every two able-bodied adult Catholic males there was an armed member of the state forces to patrol them. The problems of financing an entirely Protestant force drawn from the ranks of loyalist militants were highlighted by General Ricardo, a founder member of the UVF, who later became disenchanted with the force: 'It will never be possible to recover the arms from the "B" specials … To allow the specials to become mixed [with Catholics] was to destroy the security, in loyalist minds, of their state.'[10]

The state's military might was supplemented by various wide-ranging pieces of legislation, the most notorious of which was the Special Powers Act, enacted in March 1922, which provided for the death penalty, flogging, arrest without warrant and the prohibition of inquests. It also permitted Northern Ireland's Minister for Home Affairs to make further regulations – each with the force of a new law – without consulting Parliament, and to delegate his powers to any policeman. In case there was any provision the Act had overlooked, it was further stated that

> If any person does any act of such a nature as to be calculated to be prejudicial to the preservation of the peace or maintenance of order in Northern Ireland and not specifically provided for in the regulations, he shall be deemed guilty of an offence against the regulations.[11]

Within a short time the Special Powers Act had been used to impose curfews, to imprison indefinitely without charge or trial, to destroy houses, to outlaw organisations and to put individuals under house arrest. All these measures were implemented exclusively against the nationalist population. Their predicament was succinctly described by Nationalist MP Joe Devlin, in the aftermath of the killing of a Catholic family on 23 March by uniformed members of the Special Constabulary: 'If Catholics have no revolvers they are murdered. If they have revolvers they are flogged and sentenced to death.'[12]

The plight facing the nationalist community[13] moved Michael Collins greatly. Of particular interest to him were the activities of the 'Cromwell Club', a notorious unit of the Special Constabulary established at Unionist Party headquarters involved in random sectarian attacks to instil terror amongst the Catholic populace. Through his North-Eastern Advisory Committee, Collins ensured that he was kept fully informed of the activities of individuals such as the Royal Ulster Constabulary (RUC) District Inspector of the Shankill area and the head of the Belfast Detective Division.[14] Convinced that these officers were acting in 'collusion with their superiors who were acting on even higher instructions', Collins formulated plans for their assassination.[15]

Collins attempted to mobilise public opinion against partition and framed the responsibilities of the nascent Irish Government in terms of protecting the nationalist minority within Northern Ireland. At a public meeting, in Wexford, on 9 April, he informed his audience that

> The acceleration of cowardly and murderous violence in North-East Ulster allays an inexorable and unquestionable duty of every Irish patriot – a duty which is as definite and immediate as if the British were again violently threatening our nation ... If the so-called Government in Belfast has not the power nor the will to protect its citizens, then the Irish Government must find means to protect them.[16]

Regarding the six counties, Collins's political strategy (as opposed to his military one) involved close cooperation with northern nationalists and non-recognition of, and non-cooperation with, the Stormont regime. Thus he introduced a scheme whereby the Provisional Government assumed liability for the payment of primary and secondary school teachers in the six counties who refused to recognise the Unionist Government. Indeed, for the secondary schools resisting unionist authority the Intermediate examinations in June 1922 were held under the auspices of the Provisional Government, which established centres in the six counties for that purpose.[17] In addition, Collins made it government policy to financially support the local councils that had pledged their allegiance to Dáil Éireann. The powers of the Belfast Government were rigorously monitored to ensure they did not exceed the functions conferred by the 1920 Act, and all requests from the Northern civil service for the transfer of files were blocked.[18]

Collins's strategy to protect six-county nationalists and destabilise the Northern regime included a number of military initiatives that flagrantly violated the Treaty. Within days of the Treaty's ratification, Collins had approved a northern IRA policy – agreed to by both wings of the republican movement – and established an Ulster council command with Frank Aiken at its head and Seán MacEoin as his deputy.[19] The immediate catalyst for the formation of this body was the arrest of Monaghan Gaelic football players travelling to Derry to play in the Ulster final. They included the IRA Officer Commanding (O/C) of the 5th Northern Division, Major-General Dan Hogan, whom the Northern authorities rightly believed was planning to release three IRA prisoners due for execution in Derry jail.[20] Collins responded by approving – with fellow cabinet member Richard Mulcahy and pro-Treaty IRA leader Eoin O'Duffy – the kidnapping of forty-two prominent loyalists from Fermanagh and Tyrone. Churchill complained to Griffith, but Collins succeeded in securing the release of the Monaghan football team and the Derry prisoners they were endeavouring to rescue. During the subsequent months, Collins released the loyalist hostages – the pace being dictated by his attitude to developments in the North.

As head of the pro-Treaty Provisional Government and Commander-in-Chief of its army, Collins endeavoured to undermine the new regime in Belfast and cooperated with the anti-Treaty IRA to that end. He continued to meet anti-Treaty IRA leader Liam Lynch after the split, and with his cooperation Collins organised the dispatch of large consignments of arms to the IRA in the six counties. To avoid implication in the plan, arms and equipment supplied by the British Government were given to the anti-Treaty IRA in exchange for a similar amount of weapons that were sent to the North.[21] In February, Collins planned an attack on the Belfast City Guard, while in March the IRA attacked barracks in Belcoo, Maghera and Pomeroy. The Belcoo offensive was executed by the pro-Treaty 1st Midland Division led by Seán MacEoin, who publicly appealed for volunteers in Mullingar for border action.[22] IRA leaders of the 1st Southern Division were sent to take charge of the Northern Divisions, and volunteers from Cork and Kerry travelled north to strengthen the IRA there.[23] Frank Aiken, soon to be Chief of Staff of the anti-Treaty IRA, coordinated attacks with the cooperation of MacEoin's pro-Treaty Midland Division. The majority of the southern recruits appear to have come from anti-Treaty units while pro-Treaty General Headquarters (GHQ) under the supervision of Michael Collins provided the financial resources.[24] Much of the arms were transported by South Derry IRA leader, Seán Haughey, whose son, Charles, would some decades later find himself charged with illegally importing arms destined for northern republicans.[25]

In furtherance of Collins's objective to destabilise the six-county Government, a massive IRA offensive was planned for 19 May 1922. However, poor communication and advance British knowledge condemned the assault to failure. Despite the odds, the offensive went ahead. Belfast was engulfed in dozens of serious fires, railway stations and mills were destroyed and a Stormont MP assassinated. The Belfast Government responded with reprisals against Catholic families and the introduction of internment. By the end of the month the campaign was already on the wane but it was at this time that the IRA planned its most audacious attack. A triangular area of Co. Fermanagh, bounded by the villages of Beleek and Letter, was completely separated from the rest of the new 'Northern Ireland' by Lough Erne and all roads to the area led through the twenty-six counties under the control of the Provisional Government. Fifty members of the paramilitary Special Constabulary (already referred to as 'Specials') that had been hastily dispatched to the area were ambushed on 27 May, as were their reinforcements, with the result that all Northern security forces were evacuated from the triangle. By 1 June the entire area, comprising eighty to one hundred square kilometres, was under IRA control. Churchill acted swiftly and sent two companies of British troops into the twenty-six counties with the intent of re-taking Pettigo. After a five-hour gun-battle, on 4 June, the British Army captured Pettigo, and Beleek barracks, killing a number of pro-Treaty troops and taking fifteen prisoners.[26]

Churchill made plans for further attacks but his increased belligerency earned him a rebuke from Lloyd George. These events came shortly after the Collins–de Valera pact and coincided with deliberations over the content of the proposed Free State Constitution. Lloyd George perceptively sensed a re-run of the Treaty negotiations, with Collins attempting to achieve a republic by stealth while orchestrating a rupture on Ulster. 'We are not merely being rushed into a conflict', the Prime Minister told Churchill, 'but we are gradually being manoeuvred into giving battle on the very worst grounds which could possibly be chosen for the struggle.'

> I am not convinced that a break is inevitable. On the contrary, with patience, with the adroitness of which you have such command, I believe we can get through in the end. But even if I am wrong in entertaining these hopes, we should do our best to avoid a conflict except for the reasons which would be acknowledged, not merely by our public at home but by the Empire and the whole world as inevitable. Ulster divides British opinion at home and throughout the Empire. It consolidates American opinion against us. The same thing applies to French, Italian and Belgian opinion. But if the Free-Staters insisted on a constitution which repudiated Crown and Empire and practically set up a Republic we would carry the whole world with us in any action we took. That is why the Anti-Treatyites are forcing the issue on Ulster.

Moreover, Lloyd George stressed, 'our Ulster case is not a good one'. He pointed out that the British Government was financing 50,000 Specials and had thousands of its own troops in the six counties. Though the region was only one-sixth the territory of the Free State, over 400 Catholics had been killed and 1,200 wounded without a single person being brought to justice.

> Quite frankly, if we force an issue with these facts we shall be hopelessly beaten. There will be a great [unionist] Die-Hard shout which will last for a very short time but we shall have no opinion behind us that will enable us to carry through a costly strangling campaign. Let us keep on the high ground of the Treaty – the Crown, the Empire. There we are unassailable. But if you come down from that height and fight in the swamps of Lough Erne [in Co. Fermanagh] you will be overwhelmed.[27]

The London cabinet feared a *rapprochement* between the two republican factions, which had divided on the Treaty. Moreover, they dreaded the prospect of the Irish manoeuvring a conflict on partition. Such an eventuality would unite republicanism and preclude the British Government from securing the support of international opinion necessary to resume an all-out war in Ireland. In an effort to prevent the materialisation of such an unsavoury situation the British had endeavoured to encourage a conflict within republicanism, an outcome that would have the added advantages of creating a 'reliable' administration in Dublin and securing a viable future for Northern Ireland by diverting attention elsewhere. This plan had become unstuck as a result of the hostilities in Northern Ireland, and Churchill bemoaned that 'there is really none too much difference between the Free State and the Republican parties and there is general reluctance to kill one another'.[28] In order to reverse this perceived deficiency in the Irish character, the British retained a few options. Foremost among these was the Free State Constitution that Collins had drawn up to conform to his own republican instincts and to secure the widest possible acceptance. By insisting on an imperial Constitution, the British succeeded in engineering a break in the republican camp on the issue of Empire. The result of their efforts was civil war.

Collins was to survive the outbreak of civil war by seven weeks. Throughout the previous six months he had embarked on a high-risk policy with the aim of forcibly bringing down the Belfast Government and protecting the northern nationalist population. His aggressive, pro-active approach towards events in the North brought him into deadly battle with the British Government whose leader feared that Collins had allowed himself to 'become obsessed with the Ulster situation'.[29] His government colleagues – with the important exception of the other major military figure in the cabinet, Richard Mulcahy – were largely oblivious to the details of Collins's Northern policy.[30] The civil war had forced Collins to direct his attentions to an internecine republican feud that would have a deleterious impact on his hopes for a unified republican movement and a united Ireland. However, on 23 July Collins sent a message to William Cosgrave, who in a month would replace him as head of the Provisional Government:

> I am forced to the conclusion that we have yet to fight the British in the North-East. We must by forceful action make them understand that we will not tolerate this carelessness with the lives of our people … It is not individuals who are in charge of shooting parties or 'Hold-up' parties that are the guilty ones. The guilt lies with the high authorities, and we must face that.[31]

With this in mind, Collins sent a memo to Army GHQ on 7 August requesting the development of an extensive Intelligence system in the North-East. Five days earlier, Collins had arranged a meeting in Dublin with the officers of the IRA's Northern Divisions to explain the state of his Northern policy in the wake of the outbreak of civil war. From a military point of view, Collins recommended that they avoid direct confrontations with the British forces, as he would be unable to render effective assistance. Instead, they were to continue a policy of 'non-recognition of the Northern Government and positive resistance to its function'. Their role was also to protect the nationalist community from assault. While the civil war was in progress, he told the officers, 'I cannot give you men the help I wish to give and mean to give'. He would 'use the political arm against Craig so long as it is of use' but 'if that fails the Treaty can go to hell and we will all start again'.[32] Three weeks later Collins was dead, and with him the last vestige of a Northern policy based on non-recognition of the Stormont regime.

How events might have developed if not for Collins's death, aged just thirty-one, remains 'a subject of fascinating but useless speculation',[33] though few historians can resist the temptation to indulge in counterfactuals. The Northern IRA immediately noticed a change in government policy following Collins's death.[34] That such a shift had occurred is not surprising. Michael Hopkinson has noted that individuals like Collins, Mulcahy and O'Duffy had attached 'a much greater importance to the North than that which generally applied in Southern Sinn Féin circles',[35] while Tim Pat Coogan has argued that

> The bulk of the people in the twenty-six counties wanted a return to peace, not adventures across the border. This wish was amply reflected in the composition of [the] cabinet, particularly in the views of figures like Griffith, MacNeill, O'Higgins, Hogan, Blythe and Cosgrave. Their priority was bringing the crisis in the South to a head so as to crush the 'Irregulars' as they both termed and thought of their opponents, before they grew too powerful. They were fully prepared to settle down to building what they could within twenty-six county confines, leaving the solution of partition to the future.[36]

The new leader of the Provisional Government, William Cosgrave, differed markedly in temperament and outlook from his predecessor. The stark division between Collins the guerrilla fighter and Cosgrave the administrative leader was no clearer than in their respective approaches to the North. When Cosgrave met James Craig for the first time he protested to the Northern Premier that 'I've been pushed into this. I'm not a "leader of men".'[37] Craig, for his part, confided that he and Cosgrave had 'got on very well together', and that Cosgrave was more moderate than many of his contemporaries.[38]

As Collins became immersed in the conduct of the civil war, his government colleagues had initiated moves for the development of a radical shift in Northern policy. On 1 August, while Collins was absent from the cabinet, Blythe drew up an eight-page memorandum every line of which constituted 'a stinging indictment of Collins's [Northern] policy'.[39] The day after Collins's burial the memorandum was circulated to all members of the cabinet. The key departures centred on whether the Belfast Parliament should be given official recognition, and what attitude should be adopted by nationalists who found themselves on the 'wrong' side of the border.

> As soon as possible all military operations on the part of our supporters in or against the North-East should be brought to an end ... The ... one logical and defensible line is full acceptance of the treaty. This undoubtedly means recognition of the Northern government and implies that we shall influence all those within the Six Counties who look to us for guidance to acknowledge its authority and refrain from any attempt to prevent it working. Pending the boundary arbitration the Northern government is entitled to claim obedience in the whole of the Six Counties and we are bound by the treaty not to encourage unconstitutional attacks upon it.[40]

In line with this new post-Collins policy, the payment of northern teachers was abruptly terminated, leaving nationalist schools in a vulnerable position. All relations with local bodies that refused to recognise the Belfast Parliament were similarly halted. This weakened nationalists' effective bargaining power with the forthcoming Boundary Commission which, as chronicled below, cynically weighed up the potential ability to retaliate of those who might be disaffected by any agreed report. Full precautions would be taken to prevent a resumption of border raids and 'any offenders caught by us should be definitely handed over to the Northern authorities'.[41] Moreover, northern nationalists, who had been the victims of a concerted murderous assault by the newly established and British-financed Special Constabulary, were urged to disarm and, thus, place their trust in the unionist security forces. Parliamentary representatives were advised to take their seats in the Belfast legislature and those brought before the six-county courts should recognise the authority of those courts. Finally, the unionist Government should be relieved of the pressure (or 'minor nagging' as Blythe preferred to describe it[42]) that had hitherto been exerted upon it by the Provisional Government.

On hearing the news that Cosgrave had made it clear that his Government did not object to northern nationalists taking a declaration of loyalty to the British King and to the Northern Government, Seamus Woods – with whom Collins had maintained close contact and who was the IRA leader in the six-county area – complained to Mulcahy that 'a new situation ha[d] now arisen'. Woods wrote that Collins had made it clear

> that the government in Dublin intended to deal with the Ulster situation in a very definite way, and as far as this Division was concerned, every officer present felt greatly encouraged to carry on the work when we had a definite policy to pursue and an assurance that the government here would stand by us … Recognition of the Northern government, of course, will mean the breaking up of our Division … The breaking up of this organisation is the first step to making partition permanent.[43]

The government memorandum was, in effect, a lengthy farewell note to the northern nationalist community, who were now urged to fend for themselves. Faced with a non-interventionist Dublin administration and an impotent and demoralised six-county nationalist population, the unionist Government drew a collective sigh of relief and embarked on a series of measures designed to cement the gains already made and to institutionalise their position of unbridled supremacy. As Nationalist MP, Cahir Healy, commented ruefully a month after Collins's death: 'We have been abandoned to Craig's mercy.'[44]

The Boundary Commission: process, results, consequences

The civil war had deflected government attention from partition, and the establishment of the Boundary Commission as provided for in Article 12 of the Treaty was postponed. The longer the issue was deferred the more stable and permanent the new six-county state would become. However, the Government's position was weakened while the civil war was in progress for, as Kevin O'Shiel noted, it could hardly seek to attain more territory until its jurisdiction was effectively under control and at peace.[45] The majority of northern nationalists had supported the Treaty, and placed all their hopes in the Free State's successful handling of the Boundary Commission.[46] For its part, the Free State cabinet feared that a judgement which fell short of what had been promised could cause the ensuing nationalist indignation in the North to spill over into the Free State and bring down the Government.[47]

The crux of the matter lay in the apparent ambiguity of Article 12. While there is little doubt that the Irish signatories to the Treaty believed 'that they were putting their names to an agreement which would ensure reunion with two counties and parts of three others',[48] Lloyd George had succeeded in devising a formula that represented a subtle break from the established practice of the time when settling disputed territories. A comparison with the provisions contained in the 1919 Treaty of Versailles for the future of Upper Silesia illustrates this point. In determining the future of the region, regard would be taken 'to the wishes of the inhabitants as shown by the vote, and to the geographical and economic conditions of the locality'.[49] While the terms at Versailles suggested equal consideration of democratic and geographic/economic factors, the same could not be said for Article 12 of the Treaty, which declared that the matter would be resolved 'in accordance with the wishes of the inhabitants, *so far as may be compatible* with economic and geographic conditions'. The possible subordination of the wishes of the inhabitants to other considerations was reinforced by the omission of provision for a plebiscite to determine local preferences.

All hinged on the interpretation that the proposed Commission would take on Article 12. The British Government wisely calculated that the analysis would depend on the Commission's composition and acted accordingly. But first there was the matter of preparing public opinion in Ireland for a judgement which, though some years off, had been decided long before the Commission's formal establishment. No sooner had the ink dried on the Treaty signatures but a steady stream of speeches had emanated from Westminster claiming that the purpose of the Commission was 'to settle boundaries, not to settle territories'.[50]

Lloyd George confided to his cabinet that the Commission 'could possibly give Ulster more than it would lose'.[51] Indeed, such was the regularity and conviction of these minimalist interpretations of the Commission's terms of reference that Cosgrave was moved to exclaim that 'had such pronouncements been made at that time there would not have been Irish signatories to the Treaty'.[52] In October 1922, Lloyd George's shaky coalition had collapsed, a victim of its own contradictions, and had been replaced by a Conservative administration led briefly by Andrew Bonar Law and then by Stanley Baldwin.[53] Baldwin's great fear was that with another election pending, the House of Lords, under James Craig's influence, would reject the Commission's findings. Not only would this block implementation of the Commission's report for two years but, more importantly for Baldwin, it would damage his prospects at the subsequent election.

The choice facing any British administration had been outlined by Unionist Westminster MP, Charles Craig, brother of the six-county premier, who declared that 'the Government have got themselves into the position that either they must break faith with the people of Ulster or with the Sinn Féiners'.[54] 'The people of Ulster', in Craig's vocabulary, did not include Sinn Féiners – or nationalists for that matter. Nevertheless, when confronted by such a political choice – between nationalist and unionist claims – there was little doubt which side Baldwin would take. On 17 August 1923, Prime Minister Baldwin travelled to Belfast to meet the Unionist leader, James Craig. Summarising the conclusions reached at their meeting, Baldwin wrote:

> If the Commission should give away counties, then of course Ulster couldn't accept it and we should back her. But the Government will nominate a proper representative [for Northern Ireland] and we hope that he and Feetham will do what is right.[55]

The British Government found such a 'proper representative' in J.R. Fisher, a 'staunch Ulster Unionist'[56] who had privately advocated the inclusion of Donegal into the Northern statelet.[57] Craig had refused to appoint a Commissioner but Fisher's appointment allowed the Unionist leader to enjoy the best of both worlds – having a staunch ally on the Commission who remained in constant contact during the deliberations while being able to disavow any responsibility for his actions. Craig's abdication of responsibility also created a situation whereby the British Government chose two of the Commission's three members. The other 'neutral' member selected was Richard Feetham – an Englishman and a Supreme Court judge in South Africa, where he had also been a member of the Unionist Party. As a majority report could be binding, the British Government had indeed produced a Commission that would draw the 'right' conclusions.

The Free State representative nominated to participate in this packed jury was Eoin MacNeill. On face value there was much to recommend the 'scholar revolutionary'. A man of substantial intellect, he was also an Antrim Catholic and could thus be expected to appreciate the predicament facing northern nationalists should the Commission report fail to meet their expectations. These advantages, however, were more than out-weighed by other considerations. While participating on the Commission, MacNeill was also executing his duties as Minister for Education in the seven-man cabinet, making it difficult 'to afford all the time for the Commission that might have been desirable and [this] may explain the somewhat passive role he played'.[58] It is bizarre that the Free State Government did not consider it appropriate or necessary to appoint a full-time representative to participate in a Commission convened to decide so important an issue as the borders and size of the state over which it was to govern.

There is also the question of MacNeill's qualifications to adequately fulfil his designated function. The Minister for Education was, indeed, a former university professor but his area of academic pursuit was Early Irish History. Armed with a specialist knowledge of Celtic Studies he was sent to participate on a part-time basis in a quasi-judicial Commission with a Supreme Court judge and a barrister, both authors of legal textbooks and participating full time in the work of the Commission. The British Government may have created a lob-sided Commission but the Free State did little to improve matters by appointing MacNeill. The question inevitably arises – why did the Dublin cabinet act so amateurly? J.J. Lee argues that Cosgrave and his cabinet colleagues were aware of the forthcoming disaster and sought in MacNeill 'not so much an effective negotiator as a suitable scapegoat'.[59]

Shortly after the establishment of the Boundary Commission, the Free State Government submitted a memorandum to the Commission Secretary making it clear that it considered itself 'in the position of a trustee' for nationalists excluded from its jurisdiction. Furthermore, it was claimed that the Treaty had not envisaged 'that any area within "Northern Ireland" should have the right to withdraw permanently from the jurisdiction of the Irish Free State' unless the majority of the inhabitants in a given area favoured such a course.[60] Basing its claims on the results of successive elections, the Free State's minimum demands would diminish the territory of Northern Ireland by a third, its population by a fifth.[61] Dublin's maximum claim involved shrinking the six-county state to half its size and reducing its population by a third.[62]

Feetham, however, refused to consider the political circumstances that had led to the inclusion of Article 12 in the Treaty and insisted on adopting a minimalist interpretation. He noted the absence of provision for a plebiscite[63] and concluded that they 'must treat the existing boundary as holding good' and 'the onus is … on those who desire a change to prove that the facts justify a change'.[64] That a nationalist majority existed in a given area, he argued, did not in itself guarantee an alteration of the border. Hence, the report declared that

> no wholesale reconstruction of the map is contemplated by the proviso – the Commission is not to reconstitute the two territories, but to settle the boundary between them. Northern Ireland must, when the boundaries have been determined, still be recognisable as the same provincial entity; the changes made must not be so drastic as to destroy its identity or make it impossible for it to continue as a separate province of the United Kingdom with its own parliament and government for provincial affairs under the Government of Ireland Act.[65]

This interpretation was completely at variance with what the Treaty signatories had been encouraged to believe by Lloyd George. Nationalists, to their dismay, immediately formed the impression during the Commission's formal hearings that Feetham was unsympathetic to their claims.[66] Unionists, to their obvious delight, drew similar conclusions. During the Omagh hearings in July, Fisher was able to confide to the wife of a prominent Unionist MP, Florence Reid, that 'it will now be a matter of border townlands for the most part ... the result will, I think, be a stronger and more compact territory, with not inconsiderable bits added'.[67]

Fisher's actions – he regularly informed several Unionist leaders and private individuals of proceedings – contrasted with those of MacNeill, who kept Dublin in the dark regarding the impending disaster. Hand comments sympathetically that 'inconveniently for themselves, the rulers of the Free State had appointed a man of honour to the commission and so July [1925] found them ... less well informed than Mrs. Reid (and others?) as to the way things were shaping'.[68] As the deliberations approached conclusion, Fisher's elastic concept of secrecy permitted him to write another letter to Edward Carson, dated 18 October 1925 and marked 'Very Private', in which he displayed great satisfaction with the outcome of the Commission's deliberations:

> I am well satisfied with the result which will not shift a stone or a tile of your enduring work for Ulster ... No centre of even secondary importance goes over, and with Derry, Strabane, Enniskillen, Newtownbutler, Keady and Newry in safe keeping your handiwork will survive. If anybody had suggested twelve months ago that we could have kept so much I would have laughed at them.[69]

On 7 November, the *Morning Post*, an English daily of a conservative-unionist hue, published a detailed and largely accurate account of the Commission's report, which was almost certainly leaked by Fisher.[70] The accompanying map published in the paper caused extreme panic within the Dublin cabinet, which had never anticipated losing territory to Northern Ireland. The Irish Government further abdicated resposibility by deciding that the crucial decision of whether to sign the Boundary Commission report or not would be left to MacNeill's sole discretion and that he did not need to inform the Executive Council of his intention beforehand.[71] Under mounting pressure from representative opinion throughout Ireland, MacNeill resigned from the Commission on 20 November and from his cabinet post four days later.[72]

The transfers or territory envisaged by the Commission report were:[73]

	Sq. Km	Population	Catholics	Others
To the Irish Free State:	741	31,319	27,834	3,476
To Northern Ireland:	199	7,594	2,764	4,830

Cosgrave was careful to distance himself from the deliberations:

> For many months the Boundary Commission have been sitting, shrouded in an
> atmosphere of secrecy; all their sittings have been held in private; all their deliberations
> have been conducted behind closed doors ... As a consequence neither I nor any
> other Minister, with the exception of course of Dr MacNeill, had any knowledge of
> what was taking place.[74]

Bizarrely, the President went on to say that even at this stage he did not possess
much inside information about how the Boundary Commission operated, save
what he had learned from Justice Feetham during their recent meeting at Stanley
Baldwin's office in the House of Commons.[75]

On 24 November, MacNeill faced the Dáil having just announced his resignation
from the Government.[76] The task of explaining his actions was made more
difficult by a statement issued the previous day by the two remaining Commissioners, who stressed that MacNeill had agreed to the proposed award in October.[77]
During the Dáil debate, MacNeill freely admitted that he might not have been
the most suitable candidate for Commissioner: 'It is probably true that a better
politician and a better diplomatist, if you like, a better strategist, than I am
would not have allowed himself to be brought into that position of difficulty.'[78]
It was not the first time MacNeill had expressed self-doubt. On 10 October, as
the Commission report was being finalised, he wrote to Cosgrave bemoaning
the fact that 'I am the only one of the three who is not a lawyer.'[79] But, as in
his resignation speech, it was a little late to confess such glaring deficiencies.

As the Treaty stipulated that the report would become binding should a
majority of Commissioners concur, MacNeill's resignation was but a futile gesture
of defiance. Determined that the report be 'banned or buried',[80] the Free State
Government embarked on a campaign of damage limitation. With the spectre
looming of a virtually unchanged boundary and of conceding existing Free State
territory, Cosgrave rushed to London to meet British ministers. After a few
days he returned, reported the substance of those meetings to the cabinet, and
hastily dispatched a Government delegation to London.[81]

In London, the Derry-born Minister for Industry and Commerce, Patrick
McGilligan, pointed out to British ministers that if his Government were to
stand before the Dáil with the package presented to Cosgrave, it would 'disappear
politically'.[82] A possible life-line suggested by O'Higgins to the British cabinet
Secretary, Tom Jones, was the introduction of far-reaching concessions and
safeguards for northern nationalists, who had endured the brunt of unionist
coercion in the run-up to the boundary report. According to the Free State
Vice-President, such safeguards would also help to dissipate nationalist rancour

by dividing the border nationalists, who had expected inclusion in the Free State, from those in east Ulster who had never seriously entertained such hopes, at least in the short term.[83] This strategy came to nothing when the Free State delegation had their long-awaited meeting with a determined James Craig, who rejected proposals to disband the Special Constabulary, reinstate proportional representation and end discrimination.[84]

Eventually, a deal was struck. The border would remain the same as before, and the British Government would waive whatever monies they were likely to have received under Article 5 of the Treaty, which stipulated that the Free State would have to contribute to the payment of Britain's national debt.[85] One of the most embarrassing aspects of the deal, however, was the stipulation that the Free State Government would assume the cost of the 1919–1921 war in Ireland.[86] In addition, compensation to unionists for damage to property was to be increased by 10 per cent.[87] The contrast with the lack of provision for the plight of northern nationalists attracted considerable critical comment.

O'Higgins expressed the hope that the trade-off between Article 12 and Article 5 would 'deaden in the twenty-six counties the echo of the outcry of the Catholics in North East Ulster'.[88] The Free State Vice-President was very alive to the dangers his Government faced should the Commission report be enforced, and his prediction that the Free State would collapse and republicans assume power[89] influenced the British.

The Chancellor of the Exchequer, Winston Churchill, advised his cabinet colleagues that a settlement was of paramount importance as 'a complete collapse into the hands of the republicans would mean much more than the loss of Article 5', including £1.75 million which was being received annually for pre-independence Royal Irish Constabulary pensions and £3.5 million that was being collected from Free State farmers in payment of land purchase annuities.[90] Even without Article 5, the amount that the Free State was still liable to pay Britain annually was proportionally greater than the reparations that Germany had to pay under the Treaty of Versailles.[91]

Under such circumstances it was never likely (and this was the consistent argument of the Free State Government prior to the boundary settlement) that the British would have sought a large sum from the provisions of Article 5. The Treaty had stipulated that the amount involved would be a matter for negotiation, and it is improbable that London could have obtained much from a state that already had an enormous national debt and had just fought an expensive civil war. Indeed, as Baldwin pointed out, if any more money was squeezed out of the Irish exchequer, 'a continuous flow of immigration of a poor class of people into Great Britain' was the likely result.[92] Thus, the achievement in deleting Article 5 was, to a great extent, a Pyrrhic one, though that did not prevent the

Free State Government from heralding it as a monumental triumph that had saved Ireland from bankruptcy.

Oblivious to irony, Cosgrave told the Dáil that he had got what he sought from the British – 'a huge zero'.[93] In another memorable phrase, the President described the trade-off of Article 12 for Article 5 as 'a damn good bargain'.[94] Government deputies made similar claims, variously describing the boundary settlement as 'a great diplomatic triumph', 'a laudable achievement of Statecraft' and 'a very excellent bargain'. Another encapsulated the position by commending the agreement as 'we now know exactly where we stand – know it in the clearest terms of pounds, shillings and pence'.[95] A contemporary journal adopted a less laudatory tone when commenting on this aspect of the transaction:

> The brave men and women that held so steadfastly with the South and West of Ireland during the Anglo-Irish War, have been most heartlessly thrown over, and their exchange value is not even of the substance of the proverbial mess of pottage … the loss of this territory and of these people could never be estimated in the terms of this huxter's cash bargain.[96]

The Labour Party was equally scathing in its attacks and claimed that the six-county nationalists had been 'sold – and sold for less than nothing'.[97] On the charge that northern nationalists had been bartered, it is interesting to note that, during the London talks, O'Higgins had admitted that 'the Free State government would be open to the taunt of having sold the Roman Catholics in Northern Ireland' but claimed that such an argument would 'only be a half-truth'.[98] 'Even in a private discussion', Michael Laffan notes, 'one might have expected a more forceful and hypocritical denial.'[99]

While the negotiations in London were taking place, northern nationalists had attempted to convey their fears to the Free State Government.[100] A joint protest to Cosgrave from the Nationalist MPs for South Armagh and South Down and the Chairman of Newry Urban Council declared that nationalists in the disputed area were not 'sheep or cattle to be given from one government to another against their wishes. They insist on self-determination … Irish nationality is not to be bartered or sold. It is not for the marketplace.'[101]

During the debates on the Boundary Agreement, a revealing incident occurred that provided an 'example of moderate nationalists' haste to divest themselves of the embarrassing burden of the northern minority'.[102] A deputation of six-county MPs arrived at the Dáil and requested permission to address the legislature. Unsure of how to proceed, the ceann comhairle left it to the House to decide, adding that in 'this very exceptional case' he would be prepared to agree to a motion being heard on the subject.[103] Pádraig Baxter of the Farmers Party claimed that the question was unique and that they were 'deciding the destinies of people not represented here, whose views cannot be heard and who, beyond question, are entitled to be heard in this matter'. He asked if it would be possible for the Dáil to adjourn for an hour so that the northern deputation could be heard in the reading room, thus giving them the opportunity to air their views and for deputies to hear them, given the importance of the issue they were being asked to decide.[104] At this point, President Cosgrave intervened by saying that he was 'certainly not in favour of allowing the deputation to address the Dáil' and that

> An occasion might arise in the future in which some of our own citizens, for whom we have a direct responsibility, may have a case if a precedent has been made in respect of those for whom we only act as trustees.[105]

Cosgrave's intervention killed the initiative.

Even at this early stage, there was evidence of a psychological detachment between the Free State ministers of the ruling Cumann na nGaedheal party, formed from the pro-Treaty section of Sinn Féin, and the northern nationalist community. Individuals resident in the twenty-six counties were 'our citizens' and these were to be clearly distinguished from the northern nationalist community, with whom until very recently they had waged a common struggle. The argument about setting a precedent is unconvincing and reflects the legalistic pedantry that laced much of Cosgrave's contribution to the discussion. Reference was made, for example, to a similar recently rejected petition from representatives of Dublin Corporation.[106] It had been stressed at the time that Dublin had twelve representatives in the Dáil who could decide on the merits of any information proffered by the Corporation. In the case of the Boundary Commission, however, it was pointed out that the delegation represented a community that had no Dáil representation and, given the profound importance of the matters under consideration, deserved a hearing.[107]

Nevertheless, the Government remained adamant that they would not countenance a meeting with the six-county representatives. The delegation was sent home with nothing but the unpromising suggestion that they should direct their concerns to the Unionist administration in Belfast. With partition affirmed and entrenched, no safeguards for the minority secured and the Council of Ireland jettisoned, northern nationalists, or at least those who had entertained reasonable expectations of being transferred to the Free State's jurisdiction, were despondent. As Cahir Healy, a leading nationalist politician, put it: 'The Free State leaders told us that our anchor was article 12; when the time came, they cut our cable and launched us, rudderless, into the hurricane, without guarantee of security, even for our ordinary civic rights.'[108]

An almost forgotten casualty of the 1925 Agreement was the Council of Ireland provided for in the Government of Ireland Act 'with a view to the reunification of the whole island of Ireland',[109] and which was to be composed of forty parliamentary representatives drawn in equal numbers from the two Irish jurisdictions.[110] In the latter months of 1924, the Labour Party leader, Tom Johnson, had protested against the postponement of the Council, and Kevin O'Higgins had responded on the Government's behalf in the following terms:

> I could never understand the Deputy's apparently very great belief in the usefulness of that Council. In my opinion the powers, from our point of view, said to exist in that Council were of a very nugatory character. As a link, or a bond of union, it might, to people given to that kind of thing, have a certain sentimental value, but it had little more. It had, I suggest, very little practical value. Now I understand that I am trampling, in a very hob-nailed way, on one of the Deputy's most cherished illusions … But I have felt for some time back the necessity of relieving my feelings about all this, which seems to me very fatuous enthusiasm on this subject of a Council of Ireland.[111]

While O'Higgins and some of his colleagues viewed the Council of Ireland contemptuously, representatives of the northern nationalist community did not share their scepticism. The provision contained in the Government of Ireland Act for the Council's establishment was formally abandoned as part of the tripartite agreement[112] and, as Cahir Healy put it, 'with it disappears the last hope of unity in our time'.[113] It was, in retrospect, an ill-judged decision on the part of the Free State Government. Indeed, almost fifty years would pass before a similar institution was temporarily established. When the Council of Ireland was included as an integral part of the 1973 Sunningdale Agreement, few commented on the fact that what had been attained through exhaustive negotiations was in substance the same as had been voluntarily abandoned a half-century earlier.

If the Irish Government were disappointed with the outcome, they did their best to conceal it. Cosgrave privately thanked Churchill for his efforts,[114] and MacNeill, whom he told 'did what was possible in most difficult circumstances'.[115] In a statement to the editors of the two major newspapers of the day, the *Irish Times* and the *Irish Independent*, Cosgrave and O'Higgins declared that

> To-day we have sown the seeds of peace. The problem with which we were confronted is not new. It has baffled two generations. We faced it in circumstances fraught with the gravest possibilities. We bring back an instrument solemnly executed by the representatives of three Governments – an instrument which provides a sane and constructive solution. Born of a generous desire for peace and friendship, this agreement, accepted in the spirit in which it was negotiated and signed provides the basis of a sure and lasting peace. We confidently recommend it to the Irish people.[116]

The Boundary Commission fiasco triggered a minor split within Cumann na nGaedheal. In protest against the abandonment of northern nationalists and the apparent jettisoning of the Treaty promise of a united Ireland, three government deputies, William Magennis, Christopher Byrne and Padraic Ó Máille, resigned their seats and founded a new party, Clann Éireann. Clann Éireann described itself as a 'constitutional republican party' that sought the abolition of the oath of allegiance, repudiation of the boundary agreement and a protectionist economic policy. The formation of Fianna Fáil three months later killed off any slim chance Clann Éireann might have had of making an electoral impact. Its seven candidates secured a derisory vote in the June 1927 election, and it quietly disbanded, with Magennis, Byrne and Ó Máille all subsequently joining Fianna Fáil.

This defection came just over a year after nine TDs left Cumann na nGaedheal *en masse*. Impatient with the progress made towards the attainment of an all-Ireland republic, and unhappy with the Government's handling of army demobilisation following the end of the civil war, the dissident TDs, led by Minister Joe McGrath, resigned their seats and established the National Party.[117] Their resignations necessitated a mini-general election but only one of the nine dissident TDs consented to contest (unsuccessfully) the resultant by-elections.[118] Quite simply the party 'opted out of political life',[119] registering their disenchantment with the erosion of republican ideals within Cumann na nGaedheal.

Between the National Party and Clann Éireann defections, Cumann na nGaedheal lost almost 20 per cent of its deputies elected in 1923 and their replacements were not always of the same republican outlook. Combined with the influx of former unionists and Home Rulers, the defections significantly altered the character of the party, the nucleus of which had already consisted largely of the more moderate elements within the broad Sinn Féin coalition.[120] Security became the major policy that united government supporters, and the party became virulently anti-republican. In words similar to those employed by Winston Churchill in his more prosaic moments, Kevin O'Higgins explained to an Oxford University audience the basis of republican resistance to the state he governed as

> a situation precipitated by men who had not cleared the blood from their eyes, and reinforced by all the backwardness of a people with whom, by dint of historical circumstances, a negative attitude had tended to become traditional. With many it was the reaction from a great fear. With others it was fanaticism pure and simple. With others still it was something that was neither pure nor simple, an ebullition of the savage, primitive passion to wreak and loot and level when an opportunity seemed to offer to do so with impunity.[121]

By 1926, Kevin O'Higgins was promoting the idea of a dual monarchy at Imperial Conferences, implausibly telling one English statesman: 'Try and get the King crowned in Ireland as King of Ireland; that would pacify the Irish.'[122] Reflecting on this forty years later, Richard Mulcahy claimed that O'Higgins 'had a wooden, rigid function of mind in terms of the king, lords and commons of Ireland' which, though possessing some kind of an organic quality when Griffith first espoused it, by the 1920s was 'narrow and rigid and bloodless'.[123] Far from being the stepping-stone that Collins had envisaged, the Treaty was rapidly becoming an end itself, a reality indicated by Ernest Blythe's defiant declaration, in 1927, that 'if we could get a republic for the Free State by holding up a finger, I would not hold up that finger'.[124]

The Boundary Commission shelved the partition issue for the remainder of Cumann na nGaedheal's tenure in office. Until losing office to Fianna Fáil in 1932, the Free State Government did not develop any new anti-partition policy. Instead, it focussed its attention on combating a challenge from a resurgent republicanism spearheaded by de Valera's new party, Fianna Fáil, which, under protest, had decided to take its seats in the Free State legislature.[125] The Boundary Commission influenced the attitudes of many nationalists in the six counties towards the main party alternatives in the Free State. Northern nationalists had adopted a more moderate stance than many of their southern counterparts during the revolutionary period. In 1918, Sinn Féin had eclipsed the nationalists in what would become Northern Ireland and had taken their seats in the first Dáil. However, to prevent a split vote, eight seats had been divided between Sinn Féin and the Irish Parliamentary Party, which saved the blushes of the Home Rulers somewhat. In 1921, the two parties obtained six seats each in the new Belfast Parliament, though Sinn Féin's vote was significantly higher.[126] The majority of northern nationalists had accepted Collins's optimistic interpretation of Article 12 of the Treaty and this was reflected in the renewed ascendancy of the Nationalist Party after the 1924 election.[127] The Boundary Commission fiasco, however, fatally weakened nationalist confidence in the Cosgrave Government and they 'switched their hopes to de Valera'.[128] The expectations of nationalists rose further in 1932 when Fianna Fáil came to power.[129]

Notes

1   Jones, *Whitehall Diary III*, pp. 110–111.
2   Laffan, *The Partition of Ireland*, p. 82.
3   Quotations from Coogan, *Michael Collins*, p. 339.
4   Quoted in Hopkinson, *Green Against Green*, p. 79.
5   Hopkinson, *Green Against Green*, p. 79.
6   See Farrell, *Northern Ireland*, pp. 21–65.

7　See Farrell, *Arming the Protestants*.

8　Farrell, *Northern Ireland*, p. 35.

9　Farrell, *Northern Ireland*, p. 61.

10　Quoted in Hopkinson, 'The Craig–Collins pacts of 1922', p. 153.

11　Section 2 (4).

12　Macardle, *The Irish Republic*, p. 683.

13　See Baker, *The McMahon Family Murders*; Liggett, *A District Called the Bone*, pp. 13–18.

14　See Baker, *The McMahon Family Murders*, pp. 21–28.

15　See Coogan, *Michael Collins*, pp. 352, 355–356; Baker, *The McMahon Family Murders*, pp. 22, 25–26.

16　Coogan, *Michael Collins*, p. 341.

17　See Phoenix, *Northern Nationalism*, pp. 188–191.

18　Coogan, *Michael Collins*, p. 347.

19　Hopkinson, 'The Craig–Collins pacts of 1922', p. 150.

20　See Short, *The Ulster GAA Story*, pp. 79–80.

21　Neeson, *The Civil War*, pp. 23, 106; Coogan, *Michael Collins*, pp. 350–351.

22　Hopkinson, *Green Against Green*, p. 81. See also Neeson, *The Civil War*, p. 106.

23　Hopkinson, *Green Against Green*, p. 84.

24　Hopkinson, *Green Against Green*, p. 84.

25　See statement of Joseph Sweeney quoted in Griffith and O'Grady, *Curious Journey*, p. 275. See also Coogan, *Michael Collins*, p. 351.

26　Gilbert, *World in Torment*, p. 726; Farrell, *Northern Ireland*, p. 59; Forester, *Michael Collins*, pp. 309–310.

27　Lloyd George to Churchill, 8 June 1922. Full text quoted in Gilbert, *World in Torment*, pp. 729–730. A copy of the letter was sent to King George.

28　Cabinet meeting, 16 May 1922. Quoted in Neeson, *The Civil War*, p. 22.

29　Quoted in Coogan, *Michael Collins*, p. 366.

30　Hopkinson, *Green Against Green*, p. 85. See also Cosgrave's speech during the opening day of the Third Dáil. *Dáil Debates*, 1/86 (9 September 1922).

31　Quoted in Coogan, *Michael Collins*, p. 383.

32　Quoted in Coogan, *Michael Collins*, pp. 382–383.

33　Laffan, *The Partition of Ireland*, p. 98. Fanning describes the question as 'one of the great imponderables of Irish history'. Fanning, *Independent Ireland*, p. 17. J.J. Lee has claimed that 'Collins was irreplaceable. Only Collins might, just possibly, have significantly influenced the course of history. Lee, *Ireland 1912–1985*, p. 64.

34　See Phoenix, *Northern Nationalism*, pp. 252–255.

35　Hopkinson, *Green Against Green*, p. 88.

36　Quoted in Coogan, *Michael Collins*, p. 340.

37　Quoted in Curran, *The Birth of the Irish Free State*, p. 251.

38　Fanning, *Independent Ireland*, p. 37.

39　Fanning, *Independent Ireland*, p. 34.

40　Memorandum by Ernest Blythe on policy relating to Northern Ireland and covering letter, Dublin, 9 August 1922. UCDA P24/70.

41   Memorandum by Ernest Blythe on policy relating to Northern Ireland and covering letter, Dublin, 9 August 1922. UCDA P24/70.

42   Memorandum by Ernest Blythe on policy relating to Northern Ireland and covering letter, Dublin, 9 August 1922. UCDA P24/70.

43   Seamus Woods to Richard Mulcahy, 29 September 1922. NAI DT S1801A.

44   Hopkinson, 'The Craig–Collins pacts of 1922', p. 157.

45   Laffan, *The Partition of Ireland*, p. 99. The pro-Treaty paper edited by Seán Milroy, the *United Irishman*, also argued that 'the restoration of law in the Twenty Six Counties must first be accomplished before Dáil Éireann can concentrate on the solution of our N.E. frontier'. *United Irishman*, 19 May 1923.

46   See reproduction of *Ulster Herald* editorial entitled 'The boundary question' in the *United Irishman*, 26 May 1923. The editorial also alluded to the divisions between the Belfast nationalists led by Joe Devlin, and those nationalists who could reasonably be expected to be included in the Free State.

47   Laffan, *The Partition of Ireland*, p. 99.

48   Hand, 'MacNeill and the Boundary Commission', p. 203.

49   Treaty of Versailles, Article 88, annex 5.

50   Speech by British Secretary of State for War, Sir Laming Worthington Evans, in House of Commons, 17 February 1922. Quoted in Hand, 'MacNeill and the Boundary Commission', p. 207.

51   Younger, *Ireland's Civil War*, p. 202. Ryle Dwyer, *Michael Collins and the Treaty*, p. 153.

52   *Dáil Debates*, 8/2502 (15 October 1924).

53   See Gilbert, *World in Torment*, pp. 863–870.

54   Quoted in Hand, 'MacNeill and the Boundary Commission', p. 207.

55   Quoted in Hand, 'MacNeill and the Boundary Commission', p. 228.

56   Hand, 'Introduction', p. xi.

57   Ervine, *Craigavon*, pp. 481–482. Fisher believed that the exclusion of Donegal would leave a hostile 'Afghanistan' on Northern Ireland's flank.

58   Hand, 'Introduction', p. xi. This point was also alluded to by Labour leader Thomas Johnson during the debate following MacNeill's resignation. *Dáil Debates*, 13/805 (24 November 1925).

59   Lee, *Ireland 1912–1985*, p. 147.

60   *Report of the Irish Boundary Commission*, p. 8. The memorandum accompanied a letter dated 20 November 1924 that was submitted to the Commission. The purpose of the memorandum was to give an account of the historical circumstances that preceded the signing of the Treaty.

61   Laffan, *The Partition of Ireland*, p. 99.

62   See O'Sheil, 'The problem of partitioned Ireland'.

63   *Report of the Irish Boundary Commission*, pp. 27–28.

64   *Report of the Irish Boundary Commission*, p. 52.

65   *Report of the Irish Boundary Commission*, p. 29.

66 Hand, 'MacNeill and the Boundary Commission', pp. 236–239. Fisher and MacNeill rarely volunteered contributions during the formal hearings.

67 Phoenix, *Northern Nationalism*, p. 323. See also Ervine, *Craigavon*, pp. 499–500.

68 Hand, 'MacNeill and the Boundary Commission', p. 239.

69 Hand, 'MacNeill and the Boundary Commission', pp. 274–275.

70 Hand, 'MacNeill and the Boundary Commission', pp. 250–252.

71 Extract from minutes of a meeting of the Executive Council (C.2/224), 10 November 1925. NAI DT S1801O.

72 Letter from MacNeill to Cosgrave, 21 November 1925. NAI DT S1801O. 'Resumé of a statement by Eoin MacNeill at a meeting of the Executive Council', 21 November 1925. NAI DT S1801O.

73 See *Report of the Irish Boundary Commission*, pp. 70–139 for detailed treatment of areas considered by the Commission.

74 Speech by William T. Cosgrave at Emyvale, Co. Monaghan, 22 November 1925. NAI DT S1801C.

75 Letter from Cosgrave to MacNeill dated 22 December 1925. UCDA LAI/H/126.

76 Minutes of meeting of the Executive Council (C.2/227), 21 November 1925. NAI DT S1801O.

77 Hand, 'MacNeill and the Boundary Commission', p. 258.

78 *Dáil Debates*, 13/802 (24 November 1925).

79 Hand, 'MacNeill and the Boundary Commission', p. 248.

80 British cabinet minutes published in the *Irish Times*, 23 January 1968.

81 Minutes of meeting of the Executive Council (C.2/226), 18 November 1925, NAI DT S1801O.

82 Minutes of a meeting between Stanley Baldwin, Kevin O'Higgins, Patrick McGilligan and John O'Byrne (Secret) (I.A. (25) 6) Chequers, 2.45 pm, 28 November 1925 NAI DT S4720A

83 Jones, *Whitehall Diary III*, pp. 241–242.

84 Staunton, 'The Boundary Commission debacle 1925', p. 43.

85 Draft notes of a conference held in the Board Room, Treasury Chambers, Whitehall, London 7.45 pm, 2 December 1925 (Secret) (C.A./H./48 – 7th Minutes), NAI DT S4720A. See also Fanning, *The Irish Department of Finance*, pp. 164–168.

86 Section 3 of Agreement. NAI DT S4720A.

87 Section 4 of Agreement. NAI DT S4720A.

88 Quoted in Staunton, 'The Boundary Commission debacle', p. 44.

89 Farrell, 'How Cumann na nGael [sic]', p. 20.

90 Jones, *Whitehall Diary III*, p. 245. According to the Bank of England's inflation calculator, these figures would be approximately £100m and £200m annually in 2018.

91 Daly, *Industrial Development*, p. 17.

92 Quoted in Fanning, *The Irish Department of Finance*, p. 167.

93 Quoted in Kee, *Ourselves Alone*, p. 173.

94 Staunton, 'The Boundary Commission debacle', p. 44.

95   Quotations from the *Irish Independent*, reprinted in *An Phoblacht*, 11 December 1925. The government representatives were, in order, Mr. Sears TD, Senator Gogarty, Mr. P.J. Egan TD, and Mr. F. Lynch TD.

96   *Honesty*, 12 December 1925.

97   *Voice of Labour*, 12 December 1925.

98   Quoted in Farrell, 'How Cumann na nGael [sic]', p. 20.

99   Laffan, *The Partition of Ireland*, p. 104.

100   See Phoenix, *Northern Nationalism*, p. 331.

101   Quoted in Farrell, 'Cumann na nGael [sic]', p. 20.

102   O'Halloran, *Partition and the Limits of Irish Nationalism*, p. 72.

103   *Dáil Debates*, 13/1541 (9 December 1925).

104   *Dáil Debates*, 13/1541–2 (9 December 1925).

105   *Dáil Debates*, 13/1543 (9 December 1925).

106   Dublin Corporation had not sent a delegation, merely a petition requesting a meeting. The matter had been sent to the Committee on Procedure and Privileges, which reported on 18 February and urged that the House establish no machinery for the receiving of petitions. *Dáil Debates*, 13/1540 (9 December 1925).

107   See contribution of Alfred Byrne. *Dáil Debates*, 13/1543–44 (9 December 1925).

108   Quoted in Phoenix, *Northern Nationalism*, p. 334.

109   Article II of the Treaty. Its abolition is contained in Section 5 of the 1925 Agreement.

110   Seven members each from the Northern and Southern Senates, thirteen members from the Dáil and thirteen from Northern Ireland's House of Commons.

111   *Dáil Debates*, 8/2516 (15 October 1924). Similar sentiments were expressed during the debate on the Boundary Commission. See *Dáil Debates*, 13/1365–66 (7 December 1925).

112   Clause 5 and Clause 6.

113   Quoted in Phoenix, *Northern Nationalism*, p. 333.

114   See letter from Cosgrave to Churchill dated 21 December 1925. NAI DT S4730A.

115   Letter from Cosgrave to MacNeill dated 22 December 1925. UCDA LAI/H/126.

116   Statement by William T. Cosgrave and Kevin O'Higgins to the editors of the *Irish Times* and the *Irish Independent*, 3 December 1925, NAI DT S4720A.

117   For more on the crisis within the Free State Army at this time see Valiulis, 'The "army mutiny"of 1924'. The episode also receives extensive treatment in Regan, *The Irish Counter Revolution*.

118   Cumann na nGaedheal regained seven of the seats in the by-elections while two were lost to Sinn Féin.

119   Coakley, 'Minor parties in Irish political life' p. 279.

120   See Ó Beacháin, 'The dog that didn't bark'.

121   Quoted in White, *Kevin O'Higgins*, p. 84.

122   White, *Kevin O'Higgins*, p. 216.

123   Quoted in MacMillan, *State, Society and Authority in Ireland*, p. 209.

124   Quoted in Rumpf and Hepburn, *Nationalism and Socialism*, p. 71.

125 For the debate within Fianna Fáil on whether to take their seats in the Dáil see Ó Beacháin, '"Slightly constitutional" politics'. Contrary to some retrospective claims from within the party, Fianna Fáil was not established as a response to the Boundary Commission. See Ó Beacháin, *Destiny of the Soldiers*, pp. 31–32.

126 Farrell, *Northern Ireland*, p. 67.

127 Bowman, *De Valera*, p. 132; Farrell, *Northern Ireland*, pp. 99–100.

128 Bowman, *De Valera*, p. 132.

129 Buckland, *The Factory of Grievances*, pp. 72–73.

2

De Valera's Northern Ireland policy, 1932–1948

By 1932 northern nationalist representatives, under instructions from Dublin, had participated in the six-county Parliament for almost seven years. During this time, proportional representation for Northern Ireland elections had been abolished and an array of ancillary anti-nationalist measures had been adopted. In May 1932, some four months after Fianna Fáil's election victory, Joe Devlin led the Nationalist Party out of the six-county Parliament. In his final accusatory speech he declared to the unionist representatives present:

> You had opponents willing to cooperate. We did not seek office. We sought service. We were willing to help. But you rejected all friendly offers. You refused to accept cooperation ... You went on the old political lines, fostering hatreds, keeping one third of the population as if they were pariahs ... and relying on those religious differences and difficulties so that you would remain in office for ever.[1]

The reasons for northern nationalist displeasure were manifold. Though the architects of the Northern Ireland state had demanded the inclusion of large swathes of land populated by Catholic nationalists, it was clear their interest was in the territory and not the citizenry. The unionist slogan of 'not an inch' demonstrated that it was land they feared losing rather than the affections of its inhabitants. The Catholics that constituted a majority population in over half the territory of Northern Ireland were not citizens with equal rights but a threat to be eliminated. In 1934, for example, the Minister for Home Affairs, Dawson Bates, wrote to the Prime Minister, James Craig, and informed him that

> The Derry Unionists find increased difficulty, as is felt in other areas, in getting suitable people returned to the corporation and therefore they are promoting a scheme for the alteration of the wards and reducing the number of members ... I need hardly point out to you that unless something is done now, it is only a matter

of time until Derry passes into the hands of the Nationalist and Sinn Féin parties for all time. On the other hand, if proper steps are taken now, I believe Derry can be saved for years to come.[2]

Such 'proper steps' were duly taken, and in 1936 Derry's electoral wards were revised again. As unionists controlled the corporation, they ensured that if houses were built for Catholics they were located in the electoral wards where their co-religionists already constituted an impregnable majority. By depriving Catholics of state employment, unionists hoped that nationalists would emigrate and cease to present a demographic 'problem'. In 1948, Unionist MP E.C. Ferguson outlined the persistent challenge that nationalist majorities represented for his co-religionists in Fermanagh and had identified the most appropriate remedy. Speaking in the (nationalist majority, unionist controlled) town of Enniskillen he said:

> The Nationalist majority in the county, notwithstanding a reduction of 336 in the year, stands at 3,684. We must ultimately reduce and liquidate that majority. This county, I think it can be safely said, is a Unionist county. The atmosphere is Unionist. The Boards and properties are nearly all controlled by Unionists. But there is still this millstone around our necks.[3]

Despite their numerical inferiority, unionists enjoyed a 33–17 majority on Fermanagh county council during this time.

Stormont's attitudes and policies towards the Catholic minority resembled those of an Orange lodge rather than a democratic government, a fact not altogether surprising considering the overlap in membership between the ruling Ulster Unionist Party (UUP) and the Orange Order. Basil Brooke, who would later govern Northern Ireland as Prime Minister for two decades, publicly declared at a meeting held on the outskirts of the overwhelmingly nationalist village of Newtownbutler that

> There was a great number of Protestants and Orangemen who employed Roman Catholics. He felt he could speak freely on this subject as he had not a Roman Catholic about his own place (Cheers). He appreciated the great difficulty experienced by some of them in procuring suitable Protestant labour, but he would point out that the Roman Catholics were endeavouring to get in everywhere and were out with all their force and might to destroy the power and constitution of Ulster ... He would appeal to loyalists, therefore, wherever possible to employ good Protestant lads and lassies.[4]

When asked by the MP for South Fermanagh, Cahir Healy, whether Brooke's speech represented government policy, Prime Minister Craig told Parliament that Brooke had spoken 'as a Member of His Majesty's Government' and that 'there is not one of my colleagues who does not entirely agree with him'.[5] As it was clear that it was government policy to guarantee that only those deemed loyal prospered in Northern Ireland, Patrick O'Neill asked Craig how the loyalty of an individual could be tested, to which the Prime Minister replied:

> There are ways of finding that out. The honourable Member knows just as well as I do there are ways of discovering whether a man is heart and soul in carrying out the intention of the Act of 1920, which was given to the Ulster people in order to save them from being swallowed up in a Dublin Parliament. Therefore, it is undoubtedly our duty and our privilege, and always will be, to see that those appointed by us possess the most unimpeachable loyalty to the King and Constitution. That is my whole object in carrying on a Protestant Government for a Protestant people. I repeat it in this House.[6]

Anti-minority discrimination was based on the syllogism that all disloyal citizens should fear the Government and be deprived of civil and political rights, and, as all nationalists were by definition disloyal, no nationalist would be afforded full citizenship rights. Moreover, these statements emanated from the very highest echelons of government, bolstering anti-Catholic bigotry amongst unionist employers and workers. Despite British subventions, unemployment in Northern Ireland remained significantly higher than other parts of the United Kingdom and sectarian rhetoric distracted criticism away from the Government and onto the 'other'. The unionist political elite, large landowners and factory owners in the main, rarely found it difficult to garner support from the Protestant proletariat, which believed they had little in common with their Catholic fellow-workers. Though they might not entertain hopes of upward mobility in terms of class, Protestant workers knew that when it came to vacancies in state or (predominantly Protestant-owned) private industry their chances of employment were immeasurably superior to those of their Catholic counterparts.

By sustaining a 'labour aristocracy', the unionist regime provided a strong economic basis for Protestant workers favouring the maintenance of apartheid. Sectarianism, sparked by Orange marches, led to riots in 1935, which left eleven dead, hundreds wounded, over 500 mostly Catholic families expelled from their homes and a couple of thousand Catholic workers banished from their work. The Belfast coroner's verdict at the subsequent inquest was that 'the poor people who commit these riots ... are influenced almost entirely by the speeches of men in high and respected positions'[7]. Northern nationalists were disappointed when de Valera declined to meet them during the 1935 crisis, the Fianna Fáil leader perhaps accurately predicting that such consultations might further inflame passions.[8]

Though the riots had necessitated the deployment of British troops and cast a rare spotlight on Northern Ireland's sectarian structures, London's political elite took refuge in the erroneous claim that it was beyond their power to ameliorate the situation, as these matters were within the jurisdiction of Stormont rather than Westminster. On the rare occasions during this period that Stormont received a query regarding its anti-Catholic policies from across the water, the standard response was that all citizens were treated equally. When, for example, the Catholic peer Lord Rankeillour wrote to Prime Minister Craig in 1932 seeking explanations, *inter alia*, as to why there had been no Catholic judges in Northern Ireland, Craig denied discrimination but rather maintained that it had 'not been possible to find a Catholic lawyer fully-qualified to hold a judgeship'.[9] Why there wasn't a single suitably qualified Catholic in the whole of Northern Ireland was an obvious follow-up question that was never asked.

Fianna Fáil and partition

Despite its anti-partitionist rhetoric, Fianna Fáil was from the beginning a twenty-six-county party with the avowed aim of taking power in the Free State. While in opposition, the party had sought to capitalise on Cumann na nGaedheal's failure to make progress on tackling the partition issue, and repeatedly charged the Free State Government with capitulation to the British Government and its unionist satellite regime in the six counties. The Fianna Fáil leadership's decision to enter the Free State legislature, Dáil Éireann, meant that the civil war was fought anew in parliament. De Valera's imprisonment in Belfast for a month during 1929 bolstered his reputation as a militant anti-partitionist.[10]

De Valera's rise to power in the Free State following his party's election victory in February 1932 boosted nationalist confidence within Northern Ireland. Many northerners, some of whom had openly forsaken de Valera in favour of his Free State rivals during the early 1920s, rallied behind the Fianna Fáil leader and looked to him for guidance. De Valera, however, prioritised maximising the sovereignty and independence of the Free State rather than embarking on a determined initiative to undermine partition. Indeed, the Fianna Fáil leadership often implied that full sovereignty for the twenty-six counties would facilitate reunification and therefore should be achieved first, before approaching the Northern Ireland question.

It is impossible to consider Irish government policy from 1932–1948 without focussing on Eamon de Valera, the Fianna Fáil leader who dominated the political landscape, first as President of the Executive Council and, from 1937, as Taoiseach (both positions approximating to that of prime minister). According to his own political narrative, it had been Edward Carson's defiance of the British Government and the unhindered arming of northern loyalists against the measure of Irish freedom afforded by the Home Rule Bill in 1912 that had pushed him from his teaching vocation into the political arena.[11] Shortly after the conclusion of the 1938 Anglo-Irish negotiations, de Valera declared that until the day he died the partition of Ireland would be 'the first thing in my mind'.[12]

De Valera exercised control over party and state in a manner unparalleled in modern Ireland. Burnt by his experience in 1921, when his plenipotentiaries signed the Treaty without first referring it back to him, de Valera communicated with the British Government directly and not through intermediaries within his cabinet. During Fianna Fáil's first sixteen years in office, de Valera held the Foreign Affairs portfolio in addition to his duties as Prime Minister. Only when the Treaty had been dismantled, and partition left as the one outstanding Anglo-Irish matter of fundamental dispute, did de Valera, in 1951, appoint his staunch ally, Frank Aiken, as Minister for External Affairs. Originally from County Armagh, in what was now Northern Ireland, Aiken would hold the portfolio for most of the 1950s and 1960s.

While in opposition, Fianna Fáil had countered grassroots pressure and invitations from across the border to extend the organisation to Northern Ireland and to contest seats there. These requests had not been turned down as a matter of principle. Rather it was argued that Fianna Fáil could best assist northern nationalists and end partition by attaining power in the Free State.[13] But having successfully fought a general election and moved into government buildings, the party leadership displayed no enthusiasm for either extending the Fianna Fáil party north of the border or contesting seats there.

Fianna Fáil refused to involve itself in six-county politics ostensibly on the grounds that such involvement would either divide northern nationalists or be seen to take sides amongst different anti-partitionist groups within Northern Ireland. However, these same six-county politicians argued that Fianna Fáil's intervention would not only unite northern nationalists but also provide a bridge between north and south that would be of immense value, politically and symbolically. In consistently rejecting such overtures, despite the idea having considerable traction amongst Fianna Fáil grassroots, de Valera was most likely trying to save Fianna Fáil from damaging divisions, rather than northern nationalists. A Fianna Fáil party that included Northern Ireland might be ideologically attractive but would be organisationally untidy. Faced with a membership that straddled two different jurisdictions, one over which they wielded complete control, the other over which they exerted none, northern nationalists, frustrated with their impotency within the six counties, might try to involve themselves to an ever-greater extent in Free State politics. Unable to fulfil the duties of citizenship (taxation), they would focus on their position as separated brethren, perhaps becoming an embarrassing reminder or, worse, irritating critics, of the leadership's failure to end partition.

A complimentary policy of advocating the inclusion of elected representatives from Northern Ireland in Dáil Éireann also attracted substantial support amongst Fianna Fáil members. Nationalists in the six counties had participated in the first Dáil, and de Valera had condemned their exclusion following the Treaty. In February 1933, Cahir Healy and Joe Devlin privately approached de Valera and Seán T. O'Kelly in Dublin and requested that they be permitted to take their seats in the Dáil as elected representatives of Ireland. De Valera not only shot down the idea but also refused to advise the MPs on the most appropriate strategy for northern representatives.[14] While the Fianna Fáil leader supported abstention from Stormont, he offered his visitors no plan of action. De Valera's decision to contest the South Down seat in the November 1933 election revived hopes that he intended to make the removal of partition a central policy of his Government. It was also hoped that his overwhelming victory in the Northern Ireland constituency, securing 92.3 per cent of the vote, would provide him with additional leverage when negotiating with the British.

By 1936 Fianna Fáil had been four years in power and, much to the disappointment of northern nationalists and the party's most fervent anti-partitionists, no major reunification initiative had been undertaken. While the Treaty had been systematically dismantled and the Economic War had affirmed Fianna Fáil's commitment to self-sufficiency, there had been no erosion of the border. Northern nationalists expressed increased frustration at the lack of progress. In October 1936, Donnelly wrote to Healy, declaring in exasperation that 'partition is now in operation for fifteen years and we are worse today than when we began', and that the time for resolutions and delegations to Dublin had gone. His solution was simple: Nationalist MPs should leave Stormont and demand admission to the Dáil. Donnelly believed that such a strategy would unite northern nationalists, accelerate the pace of anti-partition agitation and make the question of reunification of Ireland 'practical politics again'.[15]

Although de Valera had championed the proposal during much of the 1920s,[16] once Fianna Fáil was established he refused to be bound to such a strategy.[17] When ard fheis delegates regularly raised the issue it was argued that the matter would be pertinent only in the context of a new constitution. Consequently, when preparations for Bunreacht na hÉireann were in progress, the issue became a live one, with proposals put down at the 1936 and 1937 ard fheiseanna and at the National Executive.[18]

The Constitution as an expression of Northern Ireland policy

The new Constitution of 1937, Bunreacht na hÉireann, made no provision for Northern Ireland MPs to take seats in the Oireachtas. In response, a strong motion was put down at the 1938 Fianna Fáil ard fheis demanding a constitutional clause enabling 'the elected representatives of North East Ulster to sit, act and vote in Dáil Éireann'.[19] The topic continued to be discussed at Fianna Fáil's National Executive,[20] only to be put on hold during the Second World War, and Clann na Poblachta made it a central plank of its electoral platform in 1948.

Despite this omission, the 1937 Constitution was used in part as a vehicle for the expression of the state's Northern Ireland policy. Indeed, as this document constituted the state's fundamental law, the new Constitution in effect defined the position, or at least the parameters, of the state with respect to Northern Ireland, regardless of future changes of administration. The new Constitution distinguished between the concept of the *state*, which referred to the twenty-six counties under Dáil Éireann's *de facto* control, and that of the *nation*, which encompassed all those living on the island of Ireland. The primacy of the nation was established at the beginning of the document. The preamble remembered with gratitude the 'heroic and unremitting struggle to regain the rightful independence of *our Nation*' and stressed the need to promote national reunification.[21] The first two sections of the Constitution reinforced the distinction between nation (Articles 1–3) and state (Articles 4–11). Article 1 affirmed the 'inalienable, indefeasible and sovereign' right of the Irish *nation* to govern itself. Article 2 then defined the territorial limits of the Irish nation and Article 3 sought to reconcile the claim that Ireland constituted the entire island with the reality of partition:

Article 2.
The national territory consists of the whole island of Ireland, its islands and the territorial seas.

Article 3.
Pending the re-integration of the national territory, and without prejudice to the right of the Parliament and Government established by this Constitution to exercise jurisdiction over the whole of that territory, the laws enacted by that Parliament shall have the like area and extent of application as the laws of Saorstat Éireann [Irish Free State] and the like extra-territorial effect.

The prospect of Stormont retaining its legislative independence but transferring ultimate authority from London to Dublin was provided for in Article 15.2.2, which determined that provision could be made for 'the creation or recognition of subordinate legislatures'. Articles 1, 5 and 6 emphasised the republican ethos of the Constitution,[22] but to the disappointment of some supporters Article 4 did not proclaim the state to be a republic. Instead the name of the State was declared to be *Éire*, 'or in the English language, Ireland'. Though neither was otherwise well disposed to the Irish language, London and Stormont quickly adopted Éire as the name of the twenty-six-county state (for unionists it had the advantage of highlighting the foreign character of their neighbour).

Some in Fianna Fáil sought the retention of Article 2 without the *de facto* acknowledgement of partition as a temporary phenomenon in Article 3, and wanted seats in the Dáil for Northern MPs.[23] At the end of 1937 Éamon Donnelly tried to introduce a motion to the party's National Executive that advocated the formation of an all-Ireland national party under de Valera's leadership with its headquarters in Dublin.[24] Fianna Fáil would contest all parliamentary seats in Northern Ireland at the next general election and hold a general election in the twenty-six counties on the same date. The National Executive, however, never considered the motion.[25]

International pressure and anti-partition propaganda campaigns

Successive Irish Governments between 1922 and 1948 decided not to raise Northern Ireland at the League of Nations, the major international organisation to which Dublin was a party. Initially it had been thought that the League might be able to apply leverage on the British Government and the Ulster Unionists should they persist in dragging their heels in establishing the Boundary Commission stipulated by Article 12 of the Treaty. Indeed, it was for this possible eventuality, as well as demonstrating the international character of the agreement, that the Government decided to register the Treaty at the League of Nations, despite British objections.[26] The fact that Northern Ireland could not, as a sub-state actor, join the League of Nations, made Dublin's membership all the more significant, emphasising as it did the superior status it enjoyed relative to the unionist administration in Belfast. In the words of Kevin O'Sheil, a Free State civil servant originally from the North, Dublin's admission to the League made it known to all powers that what was at stake was 'a border dispute between a state internationally recognised and a province subordinate to another state'.[27] O'Sheil's enthusiasm for raising the boundary issue should the British and/or unionists prove truculent was not shared by the long-time Secretary of the Department of External Affairs, J.J. Walshe. Claiming to be merely expressing the views of his Minister, Walshe wrote that the League was not the appropriate forum to raise the boundary quarrel and that such a course of action should be considered only if 'all other means of settling this dispute with Great Britain have failed'.[28] This was despite the fact that a precedent had been set by the League's successful handling of the Silesian border referendum in 1921.[29]

Once the Boundary Commission failed to dismember Northern Ireland, Dublin demurred from raising partition at the League of Nations, a policy that predictably attracted the displeasure of northern nationalist politicians who believed it provided a unique forum to publicise their cause. De Valera initially placed great stead in the League's potential in international affairs, but also doubted the wisdom of using the League as an arena in which to take the anti-partition fight to the British. When the idea of bringing partition before an international tribunal was informally raised close to the end of the Second World War, de Valera, in the words of one British memorandum, 'evidently did not like the idea, but did not rule it out. He suggested that it would be hard to find a tribunal to examine such a case.'[30]

At times, de Valera hoped for American intervention to pressurise the British. As President of the unrecognised Irish Republic, he had campaigned for a year in the United States during the War of Independence, and nine months of his five years in opposition as Fianna Fáil leader had been spent there, primarily on fundraising tours. After taking office, however, de Valera did comparatively little to mobilise Irish-American opinion or to involve the US political elite, focussing instead on bilateral relations with Britain. In 1938, he was disappointed that the incoming US ambassador to the UK, Joseph Kennedy, would not take up his appointment until after the Anglo-Irish negotiations were likely to have been concluded, though this was based on an over-estimation of American interest in applying pressure on the British to reach an agreement.[31] De Valera no doubt also hoped that Kennedy, with his Irish heritage, would have been inclined to support the Irish government position.

The conflicting positions of the two Irelands during the Second World War reduced sympathy for Dublin's stance on Northern Ireland in the very political centres the Government might hope to target as part of any international anti-partition efforts. In David Gray, the US ambassador to Ireland, the Government had found an implacable opponent who made it his mission to discredit de Valera personally and stymy any attempt to get a sympathetic hearing in Washington, particularly on the issue of partition. Described by Keith Jeffreys as an 'ineffably ill-informed Hibernophobe',[32] it was Gray's connection to the Roosevelts through marriage (his wife was the aunt of Eleonor Roosevelt) rather than any diplomatic experience that recommended him for the post in Dublin, where he harried the Government from 1940 to 1947. Befitting his amateur diplomatic status, Gray was convinced that he had the panacea to cure the Irish condition. De Valera would abandon neutrality in return for a British guarantee to end partition, which they would deliver by coercing the unionists into submission. As Maurice Hayes notes, when de Valera failed to embrace the plan 'Gray behave[d] like a spurned lover. No stick [was] too small to beat de Valera with, no charge too outlandish to sustain, no rumour too incredible to report to Washington'.[33] Moreover, the British were quite confident that though the Irish Government might consider mobilising influential sections of the US political elite and population, it should not underestimate the sympathy and resources that Ulster unionists could arouse from a US administration that had benefited from bases in Northern Ireland during the war. The war, according to one British diplomat, had 'altered the whole picture', and he recorded de Valera's agreement with this assessment.[34]

Non-use of force

During their early years of opposition within the Dáil, prominent Fianna Fáil leaders, including de Valera, had offered support for armed republicanism.[35] The relationship between Fianna Fáil and the IRA changed fundamentally when the former came to power. After a short-lived honeymoon, during which the IRA supported Fianna Fáil's 1932 and 1933 election campaigns, the governing party and its erstwhile militant allies diverged.[36] Emergency and anti-subversive legislation enacted by the Cumann na nGaedheal Government and repealed by Fianna Fáil was reintroduced and complemented by new wide-ranging measures, most notably the 1939 Offences Against the State Act.[37] During the 1940s, the Irish Government would intern over 1,500 republicans and execute several IRA leaders while allowing others to die on hunger strike. Some of these, like the 1916 veteran Patrick McGrath, executed in 1940, were well known to the Fianna Fáil leadership.[38]

Despite these repressive acts against militant republicans, de Valera frequently told foreign representatives that he understood the motives of the rebels and that were he of a different age and position he could see himself joining their ranks. Such confessions were likely made with a view to impressing on his audience that partition had to be tackled urgently and that so long as the status quo persisted, violence was inevitable. In 1938, for example, three days before the opening of negotiations with the British, de Valera confided in the US ambassador, John Cudahy,[39] that despite having suppressed the IRA, de Valera still understood what drove them. He confided that were he a younger man 'he would get back the "six lost counties" even if he had to do by force'.[40]

Some of de Valera's most candid discussions on Northern Ireland took place with Sir John Maffey, whom Chamberlain had appointed in 1939 as the UK's first representative to Ireland (but not as an ambassador, due to Ireland's Commonwealth membership) and who held that position for a decade. Speaking in 1946, and in what Maffey described as his customary 'very friendly' and 'very frank' style, the Taoiseach opined that his Government, which 'detested' the border, disliked having to take firm action against 'men who are moved to violence and martyrdom by their strong resentment against partition'. Shortly after IRA leader Seán McCaughey's death on hunger and thirst strike in May 1946, de Valera told the British envoy that state censorship during the war had kept 'would-be martyrs' in check, but 'there would undoubtedly be successors to McCaughey' and the 'only reason' his Government, comprised mostly of 1916 veterans, were able to act firmly against the IRA was because of their national record as former IRA leaders.[41] De Valera told Maffey that 'if he were to-day a young man in Northern Ireland, he felt that he would be giving his life to fight the existing order of things'. Maffey asked whether now, as an older man, he felt that such a course would be wise, before proceeding to argue that partition could only be ended by consensus, and not coercion, which would be counterproductive. Partition, he maintained, 'did not rest on British bayonets and British subsidies as was incorrectly believed in many quarters here' and it was futile to hope that any British Government would take action to influence the majority in the North to go against its own wishes. Maffey warned that coercion of the North by the British would only lead to 'a violent political outbreak'.[42] According to Maffey's report, de Valera accepted this reasoning. However, while the Taoiseach maintained that force was not a realistic policy option, he ruled it out not as a matter of principle but, rather, because it would not work.

De Valera's offer that the North could continue to have its own legislature, with the powers reserved for Westminster transferred to Dublin, was by now standard government policy. Frustrated with the lack of progress towards ending partition, however, de Valera privately entertained more radical policy options as the Second World War neared its end. These included repartition as an interim measure so that nationalist-majority territories would come under Dublin's jurisdiction on the basis that, as Maffey summarised it, 'half a loaf is better than no bread'.[43] De Valera also toyed with the idea of population swaps, with unionists in Northern Ireland being exchanged for nationalists living in Britain. When asked directly and in confidence by the British representative in Ireland what he could offer northern unionists (habitually referred to as 'northerners'), de Valera replied that the national majority could offer no further concession on the issue of the King, beyond the current symbolic form engineered with unionist sensitivities in mind. If this concession was unacceptable, the Taoiseach said he would urge 'that such people should be physically transferred to the country to which they wished to adhere'. Earlier in the conversation, the Taoiseach had argued plainly that 'if the difficulties of amalgamating the North with the South were insuperable then there should be a transfer of population out of the North so that nothing insuperable remained'.[44]

Direct negotiations with the British

During the first decades of independence, a central tenet of government policy, irrespective of party, was that the solution to partition ultimately lay in London. Britain had imposed partition and so, the argument went, only Britain had the power to reverse it. In 1938, for example, de Valera told John Cudahy that 'Northern Ireland should never have been created … it was conceived and initiated in bitterness and vindictive spirit as a punishment to the South for its antagonism to England … The British were responsible for this anomalous, intolerable situation; they had done it, now let them undo it.'[45] Policies and tactics flowed from this basic assumption. Thus anti-partition tours or campaigns that might generate external pressure on the British Government were considered potentially fruitful, as was raising the partition issue during Anglo-Irish meetings irrespective of how tangential it might be to the issues at hand. All this was done with a view to encouraging London to sit down with their counterparts in Dublin to devise plans for a British disengagement from Northern Ireland and the consequent reunification of the national territory.

Direct high-level talks between the Irish and British Governments that focussed on partition were always going to be unlikely so long as the economic war persisted.[46] Two long informal conversations between de Valera and the Secretary of State for Dominion Affairs, Malcolm MacDonald in Geneva, where both were attending meetings of the League of Nations, were significant exceptions.[47] The meetings helped clarify Dublin and London's key differences on Northern Ireland. Though the British had imposed partition, their approach now implied that they had inherited it. London professed an indifference to the ultimate fate of Northern Ireland while simultaneously declaring their intention to defend against all comers the preference of the unionist majority they had artificially created. The Northern Irish were both 'us', in that they had been a part of the United Kingdom for generations, and 'them' in that they were Irish and might one day leave. The British acknowledged unionist loyalty without ever quite understanding it. They accepted this allegiance dutifully rather than enthusiastically, a latter-day variation of the 'white man's burden'. London maintained that they supported partition only because it was the will of the people of Northern Ireland and would be happy to disengage in the unlikely event that that sentiment ever changed.

Though inter-communal differences might trigger the occasional security crisis, such as the 1935 riots that had necessitated the deployment of British troops, there was little sense that London understood that the Northern Ireland it funded was a bitterly divided society with endemic political and socio-economic ills. An appreciation of the northern nationalist community was completely absent not only from their public statements but also from their private discourse. For the British, the division between nationalist and unionist neatly coincided with the Irish border and there was therefore a natural justice in the fact that each persuasion had a legislature that reflected its ethos, a view that chimed with that of the UUP. It explains the incomprehension the British regularly articulated as to why the Irish appeared stuck in the past, obsessed with nursing old grudges as if the contemporary reality of partition and the consequent ill-treatment of the six-county minority bore no relation to the larger field of Anglo-Irish relations.

Many strands of the Irish government position on partition had been articulated and would be refined over the years through repetition. The island of Ireland constituted the historic home of the Irish nation and the partition of Ireland had been unnatural and undemocratic. As partition had been created by a unilateral act of Westminster so too could it be reversed by British legislation. London's contention that they would only legislate for unity when a majority in Northern Ireland petitioned for it was a recipe for inertia. Bolstered by British support, the unionists would only moderate their intransigence when Westminster used its leverage for the cause of reunification. This assumption explains de Valera's attempts to see if the British could be persuaded to declare publicly for Irish unity or, at a minimum, to express their disinterest in maintaining partition. As a compromise the Irish Government was willing to guarantee the retention of a legislature in the six counties enjoying the same powers as Stormont, with the prerogatives reserved for London transferred to Dublin, and with the North's Westminster MPs taking their seats in Dáil Éireann. If the British could not be persuaded to act, the Irish Government would attempt to exert pressure via international propaganda campaigns that highlighted the inequity of partition and the plight of the northern nationalist population. In sum, Dublin's anti-partition crusade was to be fought on the international diplomatic and Anglo-Irish fronts but no provision was made at this time for engagement with northern unionists or their political institutions.

Many voters believed that the 1938 Anglo-Irish talks – the first of their kind since Fianna Fáil had assumed office and the first face-to-face discussions on

fundamentals between de Valera and a British prime minister since July 1921
– constituted a rare opportunity to end partition. De Valera was also subjected
to pressure from northern nationalists, who had criticised the Taoiseach's decision
not to defend the South Down seat he had won in 1933. James Craig had initiated
a pre-emptive strike by calling an election for 9 February 1938 to be fought on
the traditional 'Ulster in Danger' slogan. By returning a predictable unionist
majority, the vote was calculated to highlight the strength of loyalist opposition
to a united Ireland as London embarked on negotiations with de Valera's
Government.

The composition of the Irish negotiating team was noteworthy. De Valera
was the key representative at the talks, assisted by Seán Lemass (Minister for
Industry and Commerce), Seán MacEntee (Minister for Finance) and James
Ryan (Minister for Agriculture). However, other senior figures such as Frank
Aiken, Seán T. O'Kelly and Patrick Ruttledge – all of whom might have been
expected to be more hardline – were absent. Aiken's omission is particularly
significant given that defence issues were at the heart of the negotiations. However,
all negotiating documents were relayed back to Dublin for examination. The
cabinet decided on 7 January that any basis for a settlement agreed to by the
negotiators would have to be approved by the Government as whole before it
could be signed. There would, in short, be no repeat of 1921. The high-profile
British delegation consisted of Prime Minister Neville Chamberlain, Sir John
Simon (Chancellor of the Exchequer), Sir Samuel Hoare (Home Secretary),
Malcolm McDonald (Secretary of State for the Colonies), W.S. Morrison (Minister
for Agriculture), Sir Thomas Inskip (Minister for Coordination of Defence) and
Oliver Stanley (President of the Board of Trade).

De Valera finally concluded an agreement with the British Government on
25 April 1938. The land annuities issue that had helped bring Fianna Fáil to
power six years earlier was finally put to rest with a payment of £10 million to
the British exchequer, a small fraction of what was 'owed'. Not only did the
amount represent only two years of payments but de Valera managed to normalise
trade relations with Britain and, most importantly, secure the return of the
three naval bases retained by the British since 1921 at Cóbh, Castletown Bearhaven
and Lough Swilly.[48] Though in later years the agreement would be presented as
one of de Valera's greatest achievements, a tribute to his opportunism and
diplomacy, the Fianna Fáil leader did not articulate this sense of accomplishment
at the time. De Valera said that the sum to be paid to Britain could be described
as 'ransom money' and that if justice had prevailed reparations would be paid
'in the opposite direction'.[49] Partition remained unresolved; indeed there had
been no movement at all on the issue. 'No fires would burn on the hills', he
told the American representative in Dublin, John Cudahy.[50] However, Fianna

Fáil quickly exploited the deal's popularity by calling a snap general election for 17 June 1938. The party not only reversed losses sustained in the 1937 contest but obtained the largest share of the vote in Irish electoral history (52 per cent).

Northern nationalists were less pleased. They had told de Valera directly that any deal with the British should be concluded only on terms that would bring about Irish unity[51] and they bitterly resented his failure to wrangle concessions on partition during the negotiations. 'De Valera made a civil war about the difference between Documents 1 and 2, but he is not prepared to say "boo" to Chamberlain over the loss of the six counties', Cahir Healy later complained to Éamon Donnelly; 'after all, he concluded another good bargain for the twenty-six counties'. The implicit reference to the 1925 agreement was not coincidental and Healy prophesised that the Fianna Fáil leader would go the way of his predecessor, William Cosgrave, 'unless he got on top of the issue'.[52]

During a meeting in London on 25 March 1939, de Valera pushed Chamberlain on the issue of discrimination against northern nationalists but the British premier's mild entreaty to Craig for a gesture was met with a call from the Ulster Unionist leader to impose conscription on Northern Ireland.[53] Chamberlain's subsequent announcement, on 26 April 1939, of the reintroduction of national service (i.e. conscription) and the Compulsory Military Training Bill, which allowed its extension to Northern Ireland, facilitated a united mobilisation of nationalist forces north and south. De Valera cancelled a trip to New York during which he had planned a mini anti-partition tour and warned Chamberlain that were conscription imposed the political temperature would reach that of a 'white heat'.[54] It quickly became apparent to London that the conscription crisis might have international repercussions, alienating friends and providing ammunition for enemies. In the course of a two-hour speech, for example, Hitler asked why Roosevelt had requested guarantees from Germany when the Taoiseach himself was accusing the British of continuous aggression.[55] The British media, already unsympathetic to Craig's demands, took note of Hitler's statement and editorialised that it would be unwise[56] for the Government to repeat the mistakes of 1918 when they had tried to extend conscription to Ireland and in so doing had obtained little beyond boosting support for Sinn Féin.

The Catholic Church weighed in and proclaimed that its followers had a moral right to resist conscription. Criticisms from influential figures in Irish America risked alienating US opinion as world war approached and there was an additional danger of an IRA-led militant backlash in Northern Ireland. As in 1918, the British Government ultimately weighed up the options and estimated that imposing conscription would most likely attract more trouble than the advantages it might yield. Those who wished to join the British Army – in the main from the unionist political community – would do so anyway and a recalcitrant body of Irish nationalists within the armed forces might be a destabilising force. Chamberlain backed down and a hasty visit by Craig to London failed to persuade the cabinet to reverse the decision.[57]

The Second World War and the prospect of a 'grand bargain'

The cause of a united Ireland was further postponed by the Second World War, or 'the Emergency', as the Irish Government dubbed it. De Valera was quick to proclaim Ireland's non-belligerent status and adopted a consistent policy throughout the war that was neutral in form if collaborative with the allies in practice. The Taoiseach was determined to save the territory under his jurisdiction from involvement in a European war for which it was thoroughly unprepared. If all Irish soldiers were taken from barracks and from the cities and sent to defend the shores there would have been three soldiers for every kilometre of coastline. The Irish Air Force, such as it was, contained just four fighter planes of any consequence. The Government had no anti-aircraft facilities and its Navy was miniscule. The Irish forces would be completely unable to contribute to the direction of the conflict on the continent and powerless to repel an attack.

Most of Ireland's political elite in 1939 owed their positions to the stance they had taken during the 1916 rebellion and subsequent War for Independence, which had dislodged the hegemonic Irish Parliamentary Party that had enjoyed unrivalled dominance for almost half a century. The Government was keenly aware that if a world war could radically transform politics, they, as the beneficiaries of the status quo, had much to lose. De Valera, in particular, was determined to avoid the fate of his erstwhile rival John Redmond, whose party of Home Rulers had been dramatically eclipsed by a resurgent Sinn Féin, which had had many of the current Irish Government at the helm.

Some nationalists, north and south, believed that, as during the previous world war, a major European conflagration involving Britain might provide an opportunity to advance their cause. Many of these looked to the Irish Government to provide guidance on how best the nationalist cause might profit from international political uncertainty. In early 1940, de Valera met in Dublin with a representative delegation of northern nationalists, which included Cahir Healy, Eugene Coyle and Peadar Murney.[58] The Fianna Fáil leader made it clear that he had abandoned his guiding principle of two decades earlier, that England's difficulty was Ireland's opportunity. Accordingly, he said there was a 'definite danger' of a German invasion and he warned the northern delegation against cooperating with any external forces.

De Valera left the delegation in no doubt that his priority was 'to maintain the status of the 26 counties' against any invader and that 'the retention of the 26 county status was considered to be of such value that the loss of it could not be risked in any effort to reintegrate the country'. De Valera showed 'definite signs of impatience' when asked what sacrifices the south might be willing to make to facilitate reunification. He had 'done all that was possible', he said, and cited his initiation of an anti-partition campaign in Britain, which he felt had been thwarted by the IRA's bombing campaign, and his planned anti-partition trip to the US. Nationalists charged de Valera with his responsibility for devising policies to end partition and to unite the nationalist forces. Without guidance from Dublin, northern nationalists had dissolved into factions and they demanded that the Taoiseach should 'at least share our responsibility for guiding north-eastern nationalists'. The delegation said that de Valera's oft-repeated 'moral right to speak for all Ireland ... carried with it the obligation for formulating a policy for the 32 counties'. In the event of a German invasion of the North, nationalists there, de Valera realised, would be in a 'difficult position' but said it would be up to them to determine what course of action to take. The Taoiseach refused to provide any guidance beyond stating his 'definite opinion' that they should not cooperate with Stormont's defensive measures 'or do anything ... to maintain the present regime'. On the night that war was declared, the Northern Ireland Government introduced internment and rounded up suspected members of the IRA. So great did the numbers become that the British Government sent a prison ship to accommodate the surplus republican internees. The most visible northern nationalist leader, veteran MP Cahir Healy, was arrested by the RUC and shipped to Britain for internment at Brixton prison.[59]

Immediately after the invasion of the Low Countries Sir John Maffey, apparently without direct instructions from London, approached de Valera and urged him to join the British war effort. According to Maffey's account, de Valera immediately invoked 'the old bogey of Partition. If things had worked out according to his plan, the nation would have been in a United Ireland and his freedom of action and the spirit of the people would be totally different.' As things were, the Irish people would not be persuaded to fight on behalf of liberty 'when freedom was denied in a portion of Ireland owing to the influence of an uncompromising minority ... I cannot understand why Mr Chamberlain does not tell Craigavon [James Craig] to fix up his difficulties with us and come in. That would solve the trouble.'[60]

During the war the British twice made approaches with what seemed to be offers of Irish unity in return for Dublin's agreement to join forces. In June 1940, Chamberlain offered a solemn undertaking that Britain would support Irish reunification after the war in return for an immediate alignment with the British war effort. The proposal evolved over several meetings during the latter part of June 1940. However, it quickly became apparent that while the reality of unity was to be postponed until after the war, and seemed conditional on securing the agreement of the Northern Ireland Government, the price of entry into the war was to be paid upfront. The fundamental ambiguity remained when Chamberlain wrote to de Valera on 28 June with the revised formula, agreed to by Churchill's war cabinet. The message promised that the declaration in favour of the principle of a united Ireland 'would take the form of a solemn undertaking that the Union is to become at an early date an accomplished fact from which there shall be no turning back' and the functions of the joint North–South governmental body would be directed towards establishing 'at as early a date as possible the whole machinery of Government of the Union'. In this plan, Ireland would no longer be required to abandon its neutrality – or 'non-belligerency' as the British preferred to call it – but rather British military forces would enter Ireland to protect it from external attack. Despite all of this, however, Chamberlain still retained the vital qualification that London 'cannot, of course, give a guarantee that Northern Ireland will assent'.[61]

Responding to a message informing the Northern premier that there was 'little likelihood of progress', James Craig sent a bizarre response to Chamberlain in which he claimed that he possessed 'confidential information' that the Taoiseach was 'under German dictation and far past reasoning with' and that 'he may purposely protract the negotiations till [the] enemy has landed'. Craig's remarkable telegram ended with a suggestion that the British Navy immediately occupy the harbours and advance southwards by force.[62] On the same day, Craig publicly declared to his supporters that de Valera was 'once again blackmailing the British Government to end Partition, and this, at the very moment when the enemy is at our gates. It is sinister evidence that something serious is afoot. I wish, therefore, to declare that I will be no party, directly, or indirectly, to any change in the constitution conferred upon Northern Ireland.'[63]

In a memorandum sent to Churchill a few days later, Craig outlined the terms under which he would commit Northern Ireland to an 'All-Ireland Defence Force'. In what has been described as the work of a 'truly eccentric mind',[64] the British would impose martial law over the whole island and establish a military headquarters in Dublin with a British military governor at the helm with a deputy in Belfast. Both civilian administrations in Dublin and Belfast would be subservient to this British military rule. It's hard to imagine how Craig thought it possible for an Irish Government, now enjoying the first fruits of independence, and led by men that had cast off English rule less than two decades earlier would now invite the British military back again.

On 5 July, Chamberlain received de Valera's response composed the previous day on behalf of the Irish cabinet. The Taoiseach said his Government could not accept the proposal, which, they noted, was 'purely tentative' and had not been submitted to Craig and his colleagues. The plan foresaw Ireland's entry to the war, something for which the Government could not take responsibility and which Dáil Éireann would surely reject. While neutrality had its dangers, departure from it would only bring even greater risks. Moreover, while the British scheme involved an immediate jettisoning of neutrality it gave 'no guarantee that in the end we would have a united Ireland, unless indeed concessions were made to Lord Craigavon opposed to the sentiments and aspirations of the great majority of the Irish people'.[65] In essence, de Valera was making clear that the north-eastern tail would not wag the national dog, and that coming together based on moving back towards the empire was not an acceptable form of unity; rather, only a united sovereign Ireland, free to decide its destiny even if it diverged from Britain, would be satisfactory.

The ghost of John Redmond and his home rule party hovered continuously over the negotiations. During the First World War, the British had promised a parliament in Dublin with jurisdiction over the whole of Ireland, only to renege. Moreover, key to the British case in 1940 was that the common experience of fighting side by side in a major war would magically weld together the two political traditions despite their centuries of animosity. But Irish unionists and nationalists had fought together during the First World War and the end result had been partition, not a unified Ireland.

Indeed, the British completely underestimated the legacy of the First World War when their political elite, including the current premier, Winston Churchill, had encouraged Irish politicians to send a generation of their compatriots to early graves for a cause of no direct relevance to them and for a chimerical promise of a united Ireland under domestic home rule. The fact that these British politicians subsequently chose to partition Ireland while offering the mirage of the Boundary Commission conjured up during the final tense days of the Treaty negotiations led many in Dublin to believe that British promises made rashly when desperate times arose were quickly dishonoured when the crisis had subsided.

De Valera's position, shared it seems by his cabinet, was that to invite the British military to re-enter the twenty-six counties to defend the territory would be not only to abandon any credible façade of neutrality, but would also provoke Germany into an attack on Ireland for which it would be wholly unprepared. In particular, de Valera feared an aerial bombardment of Dublin and other urban centres against which the Government had no anti-aircraft weaponry, aircraft or bomb shelters. Moreover, the Irish cabinet were convinced that the British were on the verge of military defeat and that to align themselves with the losing side would amount to political, if not national, suicide.

After the Japanese attack on Pearl Harbor it briefly appeared that Churchill was repeating Chamberlain's offer when, in the early hours of 8 December 1941, Maffey personally delivered a brief enigmatic telegram from Churchill, which read: 'Now is your chance. Now or never. "A nation once again". Am very ready to meet you at any time.'[66] When told by the departmental secretary, J.J. Walshe, of the purpose of Maffey's impending visit, de Valera had assumed it was to communicate an ultimatum from the British war cabinet and had accordingly instructed the Irish army leadership to take up their defensive positions.[67] The cryptic message therefore was something of an anti-climax and de Valera turned down the request to travel to London for elaboration on the grounds that such a journey would be 'misunderstood by our people and regarded to have a significance beyond anything which it would really have'.[68] Maffey too magnified the importance of the telegram – the first direct communication between Churchill and de Valera since the outbreak of the war. With its ambiguous reference to an old Irish nationalist song, de Valera initially assumed that Churchill was reviving the Chamberlain initiative and advocating a unity for neutrality swap, which he immediately ruled out.[69] De Valera was understandably wary. Just eighteen months earlier, Churchill had made a passionate speech in the House of Commons vehemently rejecting the idea of sacrificing 'the loyal province of Ulster' in return for Ireland's entry into the war when Chamberlain had first suggested the linkage.[70]

As it turned out, Churchill had not been offering unity at all. When the misapprehension over the phrase 'A Nation once again' emerged, the Dominions Secretary, Lord Cranborne, who had approved the original telegram, wrote to Churchill explaining that he had interpreted the quotation to mean that

> by coming into the war, Ireland would regain her soul. Mr. de Valera seems to have read it quite differently to mean that Northern Ireland and Southern Ireland should be reunited … Ought we to leave him under this misapprehension? His Cabinet, on reconsideration, might accept your invitation on this basis, and then feel we have led them up the garden path.[71]

Churchill confirmed Cranborne's interpretation by adding to the note that he had 'certainly contemplated no deal over partition' and that Irish unity could 'only come by consent arising out of war comradeship between north and south', a message then conveyed to the Taoiseach.[72]

The subsequent meeting between de Valera and Cranborne in Dublin was predictably futile, with each side restating their well-rehearsed positions. De

Valera, who, according to Cranborne, was 'extremely friendly' throughout, revived his proposal of Stormont retaining its existing powers and within its current jurisdiction but with Westminster's authority transferred to an all-Ireland legislature. Cranborne responded by warning that if Dublin stayed out of the war a solution to partition would be 'postponed indefinitely'.[73] Considering the power imbalance between the two Governments when it came to determining the future constitutional status of Northern Ireland, this was less a casual prophecy than a threat that London might be expected to carry out.

Throughout the war the Irish Government protested against any suggestions – which peaked in 1941 – that conscription might be extended to Northern Ireland. In a personal appeal to Churchill – approved by the cabinet – de Valera forcefully maintained that 'the conscription of the people of one nation by another revolts the human conscience' and that 'no fair-minded man can fail to recognise it as an act of oppression upon a weaker people'.[74] Churchill was confronted with the same pressures as Chamberlain two years earlier and abandoned the plan. The US entry into the war following the attack on their forces at Pearl Harbor exacerbated de Valera's position, as he now had to withstand pressure to abandon neutrality not only from his traditional adversary, Britain, but also from the United States. Henceforth, the US ambassador, David Gray, already noted by the Irish political elite for his aggressive behaviour, would find his Anglophilic instincts bolstered by a conviction that they coincided with America's national interests.

The arrival of US troops in Northern Ireland during 1942 elicited protests from de Valera and further alienated him and his cause from the White House and the State Department. While contextualising the Irish–US relationship as one absent of hostility, de Valera proclaimed on 27 January 1942 that 'it is our duty to make it clearly understood that no matter what troops occupy the Six Counties, the Irish people's claim for the union of the whole national territory and for supreme jurisdiction over it, will remain unabated'.[75] Throughout the war and after, Ireland would be criticised by the US and Soviet Governments for maintaining its non-belligerent status, with both regimes conveniently forgetting that they had enjoyed long periods of profitable neutrality, which had been abandoned not as a matter of principle, as Ireland was invited to do, but only when they themselves had come under attack from the Axis powers.

The infamous American note of 1944, which prompted de Valera to call a general election, signified how the Allies continually underestimated the Irish Government's attachment to neutrality. The demand to close down the German and Japanese legations, ostensibly on security grounds, could have allowed de Valera to partially redeem himself in the eyes of the British and US leaders who sought the gesture. Moreover, the direction of the war was now clear, with German defeat simply a matter of time. Thus Gray's and Churchill's threats of making Ireland a pariah, and the risk of missing out on aid, and participation in post-war institutions, could be presented as rational reasons why Dublin could now symbolically join the Allied war effort without fear of German retaliation. Even on 30 April 1945, the day that Hitler committed suicide, de Valera refused to compromise Irish neutrality, though political expediency might have counselled otherwise. When Gray requested that the archives of the German embassy be handed over to him and expressed 'hope that he [de Valera] would take advantage of this opportunity to show some mark of friendliness to us', the Taoiseach responded by reiterating that Ireland was neutral and 'would continue to behave entirely correctly as neutrals'.[76]

The official position of absolute neutrality, rigorously projected for public consumption, camouflaged the substantial covert assistance afforded by the Irish Government to the Allied war effort. Despite this, Anglo-Irish relations, or at least those between Churchill and de Valera, remained chilly, exemplified by the British premier's victory broadcast of 13 May 1945, in which he indicated that the contrasting actions of the Dublin and Belfast Governments would have repercussions for how London interacted with both. Britain might have 'perish[ed] for ever from the earth' had it not been for 'the loyalty and friendship of Northern Ireland' while Churchill congratulated himself for having 'never laid a violent hand' on the 'Southern Irish', whose leader (repeatedly pronounced as 'Devil Eire') had jeopardised British security. De Valera's restrained reply, in which he requested understanding for the Irish nation that had withstood aggression not just for a few years but for several centuries and chastised Churchill for implying that Britain's necessity might be considered a moral code, was domestically popular but did little to improve Anglo-Irish relations.

Post-war prospects for ending partition remained bleak despite the election for the first time of a British Government composed exclusively of Labour Party MPs. De Valera believed, as he had confided to US ambassador Cudahy, that partition was ultimately a party affair and, as James Craig was a Conservative, a British administration of the same party was unlikely to risk antagonising him. For the Fianna Fáil leader, Governments in London 'did not think enough benefit to England would be gained by conciliating Ireland bringing about the solution of partition to offset this displeasure'.[77] However, the main planks of British policy – support for Stormont and non-interference in Northern Ireland's internal affairs – did not change under Labour. From the moment Labour took power in Britain until Fianna Fáil's defeat almost three years later, de Valera made no formal approach to London on the partition issue.[78]

Notes

1　Quoted in Phoenix, *Northern Nationalism*, p. 369.

2　Hepburn, *Conflict of Nationality*, pp. 159–160.

3　Livingstone, *The Fermanagh Story*, pp. 364–365. Ferguson was appointed Crown Solicitor for Co. Fermanagh in October 1949.

4　*Fermanagh Times*, 13 July 1933.

5　*Parliamentary Debates, Northern Ireland House of Commons*, 16/617–18 (20 March 1934).

6　*Parliamentary Debates, Northern Ireland House of Commons*, 17/72–73 (21 November 1934).

7　Phoenix, *Northern Nationalism*, p. 378.

8　Phoenix, *Northern Nationalism*, p. 380.

9　Rankeillour to Craigavon, 16 October 1932, Craigavon to Rankeillour, 20 October 1932. PRONI CAB 9B/205/1.

10　Ó Beacháin, *Destiny of the Soldiers*, pp. 92–93.

11　Memorandum of interview with Mr. de Valera on Saturday, 18 May 1946 (21 May 1946). NAUK DO 35/2094.

12　Quoted in Bowman, *De Valera*, p. 299.

13　Ó Beacháin, *Destiny of the Soldiers*, pp. 95–96.

14　Phoenix, *Northern Nationalism*, p. 370.

15　Letter from Donnelly to Healy, 30 October 1936. Cahir Healy Papers, PRONI D2991/B/10.

16　Minutes, Committee of Ten, 19 May 1922. Mulcahy Papers, UCDA P7/A/145. Minutes, Comhairle na dTeachtaí, 7 August 1924. MacSwiney Papers, UCDA P48/C/8.

17　See letter from Mary MacSwiney to J.J. O' Kelly (8 June 1926). MacSwiney Papers, UCDA P48/D/25.

18　Cláracha, 1936 and 1937 ard fheiseanna. National Executive Minutes, 21 December 1936, 4 January 1937, 1 February 1937, 8 November 1937, 14 February 1938. UCDA FF/342.

19　Clár, Section A, resolution four. UCDA FF/709.

20　Minutes of Fianna Fáil National Executive, 8 November 1937, 14 February 1938, 12 July 1938. UCDA FF/342.

21　Quotations from Bunracht na hÉireann unless otherwise stated. Italic added.

22　Articles 1 and 6 declare that all powers of government, executive, legislative and judicial, are derived from the Irish people who possess an inalienable right to choose their own form of government. Article 5 states that 'Ireland is a sovereign, independent, democratic state'.

23　Bowman, *De Valera*, p. 149.

24　Fianna Fáil National Executive Minutes, 8 November 1937. UCDA FF/342.

25　Fianna Fáil National Executive Minutes UCDA FF/342.

26　See Kennedy, *League of Nations*, pp. 253–271.

27　Kennedy, *League of Nations*, p. 29.

28　Walshe to McGann, 1 August 1923. Quoted in Kennedy, *League of Nations*, p. 57.

29 See Wilson, 'Ghost provinces, mislaid minorities'.

30 Conversation between Maffey and de Valera, 10 November 1944. NAUK DO/35/281.

31 McMahon, *Republicans and Imperialists*, p. 238.

32 Quoted on the back flap of Bew (ed.), *David Gray*.

33 In a review of *David Gray* published in the *Sunday Independent*, 19 August 2012.

34 Memorandum of interview with Mr. de Valera on Saturday, 18 May 1946 (dated 21 May 1946). NAUK DO 35/2094.

35 See Ó Beacháin, *Destiny of the Soldiers*, pp. 71–129 passim.

36 See Ó Beacháin, *Destiny of the Soldiers*, pp. 130–139.

37 See Ó Beacháin, *Destiny of the Soldiers*, pp. 152–157.

38 See Ó Beacháin, *Destiny of the Soldiers*, pp. 152–199.

39 Officially called Envoy Extraordinary and Minister Plenipotentiary during this time.

40 McMahon, *Republicans and Imperialists*, p. 241.

41 Memorandum of interview with de Valera on 18 May 1946 (21 May 1946). NAUK DO 35/2094.

42 Memorandum of interview with de Valera on 18 May 1946 (21 May 1946). NAUK DO 35/2094.

43 Conversation between Maffey and de Valera, 10 November 1944. NAUK DO/35/281.

44 Conversation between Maffey and de Valera, 10 November 1944. NAUK DO/35/281.

45 McMahon, *Republicans and Imperialists*, pp. 217–218.

46 For a background to the Anglo-Irish trade war see Ó Drisceoil, 'When Dev defaulted'.

47 Memo circulated to cabinet entitled 'Relations with the Irish Free State' (6 October 1937). NAUK CAB/24/271.

48 *Dáil Debates*, 71/32–60 and 71/164–304 (28 April 1938).

49 *Dáil Debates*, 71/41–2 (27 April 1938).

50 Raymond, 'John Cudahy', p. 256.

51 Meeting on 17 June 1936 between de Valera and Northern nationalist deputation led by Cahir Healy and Anthony Mulvey. See Mulvey to de Valera, 1 June 1936. PRONI D2991.

52 Healy to Donnelly, 18 February 1939. Éamon Donnelly Collection. NMM 2011/29/1.35.

53 Phoenix, *Northern Nationalism*, pp. 388–389.

54 Canning, *British Policy*, pp. 237–238.

55 Fisk, *In Time of War*, p. 94.

56 Fisk, *In Time of War*, p. 94 provides examples from the *Manchester Guardian*, *The Times*, *Daily Mirror* and *Evening Standard*.

57 Fisk, *In Time of War*, p. 97.

58 Phoenix, *Northern Nationalism*, pp. 389–390. Subsequent quotations from the same source.

59 See Norton, 'Internment of Cahir Healy'.

60 Fisk, *In Time of War*, pp. 171–172.

61 See de Valera to Chamberlain, 4 July 1940, UCDA P150/2548; Cabinet Minutes (G.C.8/182), 27 June 1940 NAI CAB 2/3; Maurice Moynihan, Memorandum of Government meeting (27 June 1940) NAI DT 2001/6/500; Joseph P. Walshe,

Memorandum of talks between de Valera and Malcolm MacDonald (28 June 1940) NAI DFA Secretary's Files P13; confidential report from John W. Dulanty to Joseph P. Walshe, No. 41 (5 July 1940) NAI DFA Secretary's Files P13.

62   Chamberlain to de Valera, 29 June 1940. NAUK PRO PREM 3/131/2.

63   Quoted in Fisk, *In Time of War*, p. 212.

64   Fisk, *In Time of War*, p. 211.

65   Letter from de Valera to Neville Chamberlain, 4 July 1940. UCDA P150/2548.

66   Telegram from Churchill to de Valera, 8 December 1941. Churchill Archives Centre; CHAR 20/46/41.

67   Fisk, *In Time of War*, p. 323.

68   Memorandum by Eamon de Valera of a meeting with Sir John Maffey (undated). UCDA P150/2632.

69   Bowman, *De Valera*, p. 247.

70   Bowman, *De Valera*, p. 196.

71   Cranborne, note on conversation with de Valera, 17 December 1941. NAUK DO 130/17.

72   Cranborne to Maffey, 9 December 1941. NAUK DO 130/17.

73   Cranborne to Churchill, 19 December 1941. NAUK PRO PREM 3/131/6.

74   Confidential report from John W. Dulanty to Joseph P. Walshe, No. 15 (26 May 1941). NAI DFA Secretary's Files P12/14/1.

75   Telegram from Department of External Affairs to Irish Legations at Washington (No. 24) and the Holy See (No. 10) and to the High Commission in London (No. 11), 27 January 1942. NAI DFA Secretary's Files P43.

76   Fisk, *In Time of War*, p. 534.

77   McMahon, *Republicans and Imperialists*, p. 260.

78   *Irish Times*, 23 October 1947. See also *Irish Times*, 19 June 1947.

3
Failed campaigns, 1948–1969

The inter-party Government

John A. Costello, a compromise candidate for Taoiseach, made no secret of the fact that he had never sought the prime ministerial position but that, rather, it had been 'imposed' upon him.[1] Even had he been so inclined, the new Taoiseach, a barrister by profession, was never going to be able to adopt a presidential style of governance, given the structural limitations. In contrast to de Valera, who enjoyed supremacy in a one-party Government, Costello was not even leader of his own party and presided over a five-party coalition, which resulted in a general relaxation of procedural norms, most notably the principle of collective responsibility.[2] For sixteen years, Taoiseach and External Affairs Minister had been the one person, de Valera; now they were not only different people but from different parties, with Seán MacBride, who little more than a decade earlier had been the IRA's Chief of Staff, directing much of the Government's anti-partition policies.

To step into de Valera's shoes and to satisfy the expectations of his coalition partners, Clann na Poblachta, Costello realised he would have to talk and think big on partition. On 23 July 1948, the new Taoiseach told the Dáil that 'for the first time since 1922, this cabinet will, by its policy and its actions, give some hope of bringing back to this country the north-eastern counties of Ulster'.[3] To further this objective, the Government established an all-party, anti-partition body, which quickly became known as the Mansion House Committee. Lavishly produced anti-partition pamphlets were distributed and a news agency was established to present an Irish perspective on current affairs so that international audiences would not have to rely on British sources for keeping abreast of events in Ireland. Though de Valera participated in the work of the Committee, he was half-hearted at best about the venture 'given [his] lack of enthusiasm for involvement in any anti-Partition strategy which he was not controlling'.[4]

Costello's unilateral declaration of intent to repeal the External Relations Act (ERA) and, consequently, to declare a Republic of Ireland outside of the Commonwealth not only shocked the British Government but also caught the Irish electorate and his cabinet colleagues by surprise. The timing seemed designed to outflank de Valera and MacBride and to establish the new Taoiseach's reputation as an ardent republican. While some have argued that the repeal of the ERA meant that the Government had prioritised sovereignty over unity,[5] the Act had done nothing to attract unionists, who made it clear that any efforts to change the constitutional position of Northern Ireland, even if initiated in London, would be resisted by force. And if unionists were unwilling to contemplate unity when Britain's very survival was at stake in June 1940, it was highly unlikely that their position would change simply because the twenty-six-county state retained a tenuous link with the Commonwealth.

The manner in which Costello declared the Republic damaged relations in Britain, not least amongst MPs in the normally sympathetic Labour Party. Ireland's ambassador in London, Freddie Boland, privately rued that Costello had 'as much notion of diplomacy as I have of astrology'.[6] The British Government responded by enacting the Ireland Bill, which reinforced the guarantee to Ulster unionists by proclaiming that 'in no event will Northern Ireland or any part thereof cease to be part of His Majesty's dominions and of the United Kingdom without the consent of the parliament of Northern Ireland'.[7] The inclusion of the phrase 'or any part thereof' was widely considered an attempt to prevent the possibility of nationalist-majority regions in Northern Ireland seceding.

After meeting to discuss the Ireland Bill for eleven hours over 6–7 May, the cabinet decided to send an *aide memoire* to the British Government and to move a condemnatory motion in the Dáil. All major parties gathered in the Mansion House on 9 May to protest, and to announce a mass rally in O'Connell Street. The official parliamentary response came the following day with Dáil Éireann's support for a resolution jointly proposed by Costello and de Valera, which went as follows:

Dáil Éireann,

SOLEMNLY RE-ASSERTING the indefeasible right of the Irish Nation to the unity and integrity of the national territory,

RE-AFFIRMING the sovereign right of the people of Ireland to choose its own form of Government and, through its democratic institutions, to decide all questions of national policy, free from outside interference.

REPUDIATING the claim of the British Parliament to enact legislation affecting Ireland's territorial integrity in violation of those rights, and

PLEDGING the determination of the Irish people to continue the struggle against the unjust and unnatural partition of our country until it is brought to a successful conclusion;

PLACES ON RECORD its indignant protest against the introduction in the British Parliament of legislation purporting to endorse and continue the existing Partition of Ireland, and

CALLS UPON the British Government and people to end the present occupation of our Six North Eastern Counties, and thereby enable the unity of Ireland to be restored and the age-long differences between the two nations brought to an end.

The resolution represented the first declaration of policy regarding partition unanimously adopted by Dáil Éireann since 1922 and was transmitted to the governments and parliaments of all countries with which Ireland had diplomatic relations. Reflecting an emotional surge in popular sentiment that rival parties wished to harness, Costello launched a rhetorical offensive against the British Government. To applause, he told the Dáil that 'we can hit the British government in their prestige and in their pride and in their pocket'.[8] At a monster rally in Dublin on 13 May, reported as one of the largest ever held in the city, Costello told those assembled that 'we are here to enter a solemn but dignified protest against an affront to our national dignity, an insult to our national aspirations and to take up and answer a challenge to the indefeasible right of the Irish people to the unity of their country and the territorial integrity of this ancient nation'.[9]

The international diplomatic offensive

The inter-party Government's term in office witnessed Dublin's most concerted attempt to internationalise partition since the foundation of the state. In some respects, it echoed the attempts by the Irish revolutionary Government of 1919–1921 to raise consciousness and support for the Irish independence struggle. Freed from the responsibilities of high office, de Valera embarked on a party-funded world tour to put 'an anti-partition girth around the world', attracting large crowds in America, Britain, Australia, New Zealand and India. Launching the campaign, he declared that 'the phrase "Partition must go" must henceforth be on every Irishman's lips, to be used on every appropriate occasion, that is, in season and out of season, until the continuing crime against our country shall have ceased'.[10]

By 1948, however, concern for Irish affairs in most of these countries had diminished.[11] De Valera was politely received but secured no concrete promises of support on partition, let alone intervention. The Second World War had resulted in the redrawing of several national boundaries and attempts to arouse Europe's indignation towards the 'crime of partition' fell flat. That the world was largely indifferent to Ireland, and that de Valera was often merely preaching to the converted, mattered little for the expedition was, in the words of Lee and Ó Tuathaigh, 'essentially an Irish election tour, not a world tour except in a purely geographical sense'.[12] Moreover, de Valera's international initiative increased pressure on the new inter-party Government to be seen to be doing something about partition.

The high-publicity campaign produced no obvious benefits, despite raising expectations amongst nationalists in both parts of Ireland that the Government was on the verge of a breakthrough. When the surge of argument and agitation brought paltry dividends, an inevitable disillusionment set in. For some younger people, particularly those already inclined towards militant republicanism, it confirmed the futility of constitutional action in bringing partition to an end. Moreover, the campaign did nothing to enhance the lives of northern nationalists, many of whom lost faith in the Nationalist Party's moderate petitioning.

The Irish Government's campaign had also strengthened the Ulster Unionist Party's position by placing the constitutional status of Northern Ireland – the only issue uniting the Protestant majority – at the forefront of electoral politics. This played into the UUP's hands and helped them avoid close scrutiny of their socio-economic policies, as voters were encouraged to vote for or against the border. The fact that the Irish Government now funded anti-partition candidates and that these funds were being raised outside Catholic churches (a normal fundraising mechanism for political parties in the Mass-going twenty-six counties) allowed the Stormont Government to present itself as being under siege from hostile external forces. The focus on partition combined with the method of collecting funds prompted the 1949 contest to be dubbed 'the chapel gate election'.

By polarising politics in Northern Ireland, and allowing the Stormont regime to play the Orange card to masterly effect, the 1949 election did not advance Irish Government objectives. Instead, it highlighted one of the recurring dilemmas for successive Irish Governments tackling partition. If they did nothing, or at least nothing publicly, they risked arousing public disfavour, opposition taunts and charges that they had abandoned the ideal of a united Ireland and, with it, their northern nationalist brethren. However, if they tried to highlight partition and the plight of the six-county minority, they risked further alienating Northern Ireland's unionists whose insecurities and prejudices would be played out on the nationalist community by means of state-supported discrimination.

In many respects the international diplomatic offensive, despite its assertive rhetoric, was the product of frustration and impotence. Deep down, the Government realised that only through direct talks with the administrations in London and Belfast could an advance towards unification be negotiated. In this sense, a propaganda campaign should ideally be aimed in their direction but traditional unionist truculence, combined with Westminster's passing of the Ireland Act, had encouraged the belief that a receptive ear could not be found in either Westminster or Stormont. However, the idea that either the British or Northern Irish might be encouraged to adopt a fundamental reappraisal of policy based on the (at best) polite conveying of Dublin's grievances by disinterested third parties was never going to bear fruit.

The timing of the initiative was not coincidental. With full sovereignty attained within the twenty-six counties under Dublin's jurisdiction, it was natural that attention would now focus, however briefly, on the last remaining constitutional issue for Irish nationalism. During the late 1940s, all parties vied to adopt the most robust anti-partition stance. Highlighting the inequity of partition was one thing; providing clear, cogent and realistic strategies to combat it quite another. As the Irish ambassador to Britain reflected in 1951: 'Partition was so wrong morally that it was hard for people in Ireland to think of it as a political problem which had to be approached tactically.'[13] The Government's diplomatic resources were always going to be substantially inferior to the long-established networks of power and influence enjoyed by the British. The UK Government was also not above mobilising its own pro-partition Irish constituency. For example, when Ireland raised partition at the Council of Europe's Consultative Assembly, the British Government attached to their delegation a unionist representative from Belfast who had, in the words of Frank Aiken, the 'sole function [to] reply to every intervention from our side'.[14]

Perhaps the campaign's most enduring result was the Government's refusal to join the North Atlantic Treaty Organization (NATO) in 1949. On receiving an *aide memoire* from George Garrett, the US ambassador in Dublin, inviting Ireland to join the new organisation, Seán MacBride replied that 'any military alliance with, or commitment involving military action jointly with, the state that is responsible for the unnatural division of Ireland, which occupies a portion of our country with its armed forces, and which supports undemocratic institutions in the north-eastern corner of Ireland, would be entirely repugnant and unacceptable to the Irish people'.[15] Ted Achilles, a senior State Department official involved in establishing the alliance, perhaps best encapsulated the American reaction to Ireland's linkage of partition to NATO membership:

> We did invite Ireland to join the pact ... We doubted that they would accept. They replied that they would be delighted to join provided we could get the British to give back the six Northern counties. We simply replied, in effect, that 'it's been nice knowing you', and that was that.[16]

Ireland's ability to exert diplomatic leverage was clearly very limited and the US would not even countenance a bilateral defence agreement with Dublin, which was offered as a substitute for NATO membership. Indeed, the Cold War and NATO reinforced partition. Northern Ireland had proven its worth during the recent continental conflagration and through UK membership its territory was guaranteed to the alliance. Indeed, so great was Northern Ireland's obvious strategic value to the Allies during the war that it revived the view in Irish political circles that the British would hold on to the six counties irrespective of whether a majority there favoured remaining in the UK. Consequently, it was clear that if London were to be persuaded of the virtues of Irish unity some kind of undertaking to cooperate in defensive affairs would be necessary. By the mid-1940s, de Valera was sending signals that in the event of Irish unity the British could legitimately expect a private understanding in advance on strategic issues.[17] The western powers had little interest in supporting a united Ireland outside of their defence structures. Indeed, only two days before the formal offer to join NATO, the Americans had already decided in consultation with the British to seize Ireland in the event of an international crisis involving the Soviet Union.[18]

De Valera was keenly aware from his direct experience of attempting to internationalise the partition issue that the 'sore thumb' policy had absorbed great energy and resources with precious little to show for it. Former Cumann na nGaedheal Minister for Finance, Ernest Blythe, was cruel but perhaps not entirely inaccurate when he mused that 'our speeches and articles about the injustice of partition ... must be likened to the shooting off of good ammunition at the smoke-trail of a ship which has passed by and is long out of range'.[19] Not until the onset of the Troubles two decades later would the Irish Government feel compelled to embark on another diplomatic offensive of this kind.

The Fianna Fáil leader lost little time in re-centralising Northern Ireland policy upon his election in June 1951. He ordered an end to Irish government funding for the Anti-Partition Leagues in Northern Ireland and Great Britain and allowed the All-Party Anti-Partition Committee to wither away. Despite monopolising policy decisions, de Valera did not demonstrate clarity of purpose.

When an outline was sought in the Dáil of what policy on partition his Government intended to pursue, de Valera displayed little of the confidence evident during his international tour:

> If I am asked, 'Have you got a solution for it?' in the sense 'Is there a line of policy which you propose to pursue, which you think can, within a reasonable time, be effective?' I have to say that I have not, and neither has anybody else. All I can do is choose the methods which seem most likely to produce the best results.[20]

The independent deputy who posed the question, Jack McQuillan, characterised de Valera's policy as one of 'hoping for a miracle'.[21]

Military neutrality, which emerged as an unintended by-product of anti-partitionism, and enjoyed all-party support, became a cornerstone of Irish foreign policy.[22] De Valera's formal relinquishing of the party's Foreign Affairs portfolio in 1951 to his loyal lieutenant, Frank Aiken, marked the end of an era. Serving three Taoisigh, Aiken would become a key player in Anglo-Irish relations during the next twenty-one years, right up until the outbreak of the Troubles in August 1969.

Contact with people in Northern Ireland

In the wake of this downgrading in official efforts to draw attention to partition, the Government very occasionally sent officials to Northern Ireland to gauge opinion. One such visit in 1955 was typical; the 'unionists' consulted were marginal, unrepresentative and well disposed, while the nationalists – political notables in the main – were reported to be 'fed up'.[23] Despite the recent election to Westminster of IRA prisoners Philip Clarke and Tom Mitchell, the Government made no effort to meet anyone from the republican movement. Five years passed before the Government dispatched another fact-finding delegation, and the Department's rationale illustrated well the perfunctory nature of these trips: 'Another visit seems to be called for', the officials concluded, 'if only to show the Six-County people that we are still with them.'[24]

While ad hoc and sporadic meetings with northern opinion were one thing, some institutionalised form of contact, such as a 'right of audience' was another matter entirely. Nationalist representatives who met Costello and de Valera emphasised the importance of gaining access to the Oireachtas to demonstrate the efficacy of constitutional agitation to an electorate increasingly attracted to militant republicanism.[25] However, the policy of not admitting northern nationalist representatives to Dáil Éireann – even to address the House – was pursued consistently throughout the 1950s. In January 1952, for example, de Valera vehemently rejected a suggestion made by two Westminster MPs from Fermanagh and Tyrone that they should be permitted to take seats in Ireland's toothless upper House, the Seanad. The Fianna Fáil leader could offer little advice regarding what alternative he wished them to pursue, having recommended they abstain from Westminster. Even though abstentionism meant the two MPs would receive no remuneration, de Valera rejected suggestions that the Dáil should defray their salaries so they could devote themselves to constituency work. De Valera then lectured the MPs on how much he 'resented statements' that he had done nothing to end partition. A 'steady policy in the direction of re-unification had been, and would continue to be, pursued', he said, though he did not elaborate on the details of this policy.[26]

As with the question of Dáil representation for six-county MPs, the Fianna Fáil leadership during its formative years had actively considered establishing the party in Northern Ireland.[27] In power, however, de Valera consistently discouraged discussion on the matter at successive ard fheiseanna and at the National Executive.[28] The matter did not resurface until 1970, when the party's National Executive turned down a request to extend the party organisation to Northern Ireland by recognising the Wolfe Tone cumann in Belfast as a branch of Fianna Fáil.[29]

Partition and the United Nations

Ireland's entry to the United Nations in 1955 opened up another potential forum to highlight partition. The UN was, after all, considered to be the floor of international opinion. That a Soviet veto had delayed Ireland's UN membership for a decade only heightened the sense of occasion accompanying the country's long overdue entry, a deprivation all the more acute given Ireland's stellar role in the League of Nations. While affirming Ireland's non-aligned status, Liam Cosgrave's maiden speech at the UN as Minister for External Affairs left the audience in no doubt where Ireland stood on the Cold War. Ireland would, he said, 'maintain a position of independence, judging questions … strictly on their merits' but was nonetheless part of 'Christian civilization' and thus supportive of the 'powers responsible for the defence of the free world'.[30] There was obvious potential for tension between the principles of independence and affinity with the West.

When the question of UN membership first arose, de Valera told the Dáil: 'I do not think myself, looking through the Charter, that one could reasonably hope that through the organisation itself we would be able to bring about the unity of our nation', though he also speculated that 'circumstances might develop in the future which would lead in that direction'.[31] Any hope that the UN might provide a platform to further an anti-partition agenda had to be counterbalanced with the reality that, institutionally, the UN was weighted in favour of a small club of states that had emerged victorious from the Second World War. Consequently, Britain was afforded a permanent seat on the UN Security Council and could thus stymie any Irish initiative to seek UN action on partition. Moreover, the British Government could always seek to prevent discussion on Northern Ireland by citing Article 2.7 of the UN Charter, which forbade interference in the internal affairs of member states.

The Government made occasional and fleeting references to partition at the UN.[32] There were also allusions to the inequities of territorial divisions in other countries, some of which might suggest indirect references to Ireland, but these probably went over the heads of most delegates.[33] These frequently oblique references were made largely with a view to impressing domestic opinion in Ireland rather than the international community at large, who knew little of Ireland's historical woes and probably cared even less.

During the late 1950s a debate took place within the Department of External Affairs regarding the virtues of formally placing an anti-partition resolution on the UN agenda.[34] A question emphasising the unity of Ireland and couched in terms of self-determination was considered preferable to one that focussed on human rights abuses in Northern Ireland, which would only generate the same levels of international support and unionist/British hostility while jettisoning the essential aspiration towards reunification. In terms of tactics, a simple majority within the UN was required to get a question on the agenda, and while the British would protest, citing Article 2.7, the assembly had recently overridden a similar objection from France on the question of Algeria. As both Northern Ireland and Algeria were considered integral parts of the UK and France respectively, it was thought that the precedent would assist Ireland's attempt to get partition inscribed on the agenda.

As European empires dissolved and decolonisation took root, successive UN resolutions outlawed the practice of partition by departing imperial powers,[35] and although these decrees came some decades too late to be applied to Ireland, they established a principle to which the Irish Government could refer. However, those in Irish political and diplomatic circles who argued that the primary forum to discuss partition was between Dublin, London and Belfast believed that the UN could play no useful role and opposed the tabling of a formal resolution. The advent of *rapprochement* and functional cooperation with Terence O'Neill's administration during the mid-1960s would provide an additional reason not to antagonise the British or Northern Ireland Governments. Privately, the Minister for External Affairs, Frank Aiken, conceded that UN General Assembly resolutions were of 'little or no value' as they were not binding. To support his claim, the Tánaiste cited the number of resolutions adopted by the UN criticising apartheid, which had had no visible effect on the South African dictatorship.[36]

A further rationale for inertia was the likely outcome should the partition issue be put to a vote at the UN. Ireland did not enjoy an extensive network of embassies and was certainly no match for the British in this respect. While ordinary diplomatic channels in western states would be utilised, one Government report estimated that the most that could be hoped for was 'an occasional abstention', with the remainder voting against Ireland.[37] Members of the Commonwealth would also be reluctant to offend British sensitivities. By contrast, no campaigning at all was deemed necessary in communist countries, as 'we can safely assume [they] will vote for us in any case'.[38] As for the Middle and Near East, it was thought that all Arab states (with the exception of British-influenced Iraq and Jordan) would certainly back the Irish position. In sum, while the Irish might generate sympathy, they could not expect sufficient support at the UN for a resolution on partition that challenged the United Kingdom's territorial integrity.

The Government believed that anything other than a successful motion, securing the required two-thirds majority, would be considered a negative verdict on Ireland's claims. There were, however, significant domestic political pressures to contend with, and care had to be exercised to challenge the perception that the Government was not sufficiently exploiting all avenues to highlight the injustice of Ireland's territorial division. The policy of not raising partition at the United Nations was contested in the Dáil on many occasions. When the IRA border campaign began in earnest during 1957, several county councils and other local bodies passed resolutions calling on the Government to demand the introduction of a UN peacekeeping force in the North. When this strategy was not adopted, it prompted bitter responses from some TDs. Deputy Jack McQuillan, for example, complained that 'we can be a sore thumb at UNO [the United Nations] on every other subject except Partition'.[39] Indeed, silence on the issue was such that one journal commented sarcastically that Ireland's UN delegation 'might as well have emanated from Lapland'.[40]

In these years before joint membership of the European Economic Community (EEC) and an institutionalised Anglo-Irish relationship, the UN was the major focus of Irish foreign policy, with Aiken spending several months every year encamped in New York. The Irish Government sought to be a global good citizen and, through a judicious foreign policy and extensive contributions to peacekeeping, build up capital and credibility with fellow UN member states with the mild hope that these chips could be cashed in at some future date.

However, as Aiken explained to the Dáil in 1969, 'none of our Governments was convinced that during its period of office the adoption of a United Nations resolution would contribute to the restoration of Irish unity'.[41]

Home rule and Rome rule

The 1950s was a bleak decade marked by political instability. Unlike the sixteen years of uninterrupted Fianna Fáil rule, the country witnessed changes of government in each of the four elections between 1948 and 1957. The revolutionary generation that had been in power since the 1920s demonstrated extraordinary political longevity, with parliamentary careers spanning four decades. The economy stagnated, epitomised by the remarkably high levels of emigration. About 500,000 (mostly young) people left the Republic during the 1950s and by the end of the decade the population hovered just above the 2.8 million mark, leading to talk of 'the vanishing Irish'. For several decades emigration had been the traditional channel for releasing the young, energetic, ambitious and disenchanted from Ireland, acting as a safety valve. Had these young emigrants stayed, it is likely that some would have joined the ranks of militant republicans.

Many emigrants were drawn to a new life in Britain, where Harold Macmillan confidently proclaimed in July 1957 that his electorate had 'never had it so good'. The contrast between a booming Britain and an Ireland struggling to survive was not lost on debates regarding reunification. How could Dublin seek additional citizens and territory when it had proved unable to manage that already under its jurisdiction?

Ireland retreated into itself. Those who didn't emigrate frequently took refuge in religion; vocations flourished and there was a proliferation of novenas and grotto construction. No faction within the Irish political elite was willing or eager to embark on a *kulturkampf* to assert state supremacy over formidable religious institutions. Instead, the informal power wielded by the Catholic Church supported unionist contentions that home rule had indeed turned out to be Rome rule. The ill-fated Mother and Child Scheme demonstrated the ease with which the Catholic Archbishop of Dublin could block government legislation.[42] To combat the alarmingly high rates of child mortality in Ireland, the plan would have provided for free maternity care and free health care for all children up to the age of sixteen. When the Catholic Church objected, on the grounds that the proposals smacked of communism and might lead to greater access to birth control, the Government embarked on an obsequious climbdown. Taoiseach John A. Costello defended his stance by reference to the Catholic Church's 'special position' in the Constitution and the uniformly Catholic composition of his Government, which in turn represented an overwhelmingly Catholic people:

> I have no hesitation in saying that we, as a Government ... when we are given advice or warnings by the authoritative people in the Catholic Church, on matters strictly confined to faith and morals ... [we] will give to their directions ... our complete obedience and allegiance.[43]

The Taoiseach regretted that the episode might somehow be 'misrepresented in the North' and to counter such calumnies, Costello repeatedly claimed that the Catholic Church hierarchy confined themselves to faith and morals and did not seek to interfere in politics or government.[44] However, as the Catholic Church claimed a celestial mandate to involve itself in all matter of human behaviour, the point where 'faith and morals' ended and politics began was not clearly defined.

Those hoping that the Labour Party, occasionally depicted as crypto-Marxists by Fianna Fáil at election time, might offer a more secular alternative, would have been disappointed when, two years later, future party leader Brendan Corish, while speaking on an attempt to introduce a revised health care scheme, told the Dáil:

> I am an Irishman second; I am a Catholic first ... If the Hierarchy gives me any direction with regard to Catholic social teaching or Catholic moral teaching, I accept without qualification in all respects the teaching of the Hierarchy and the Church to which I belong.[45]

The Mother and Child Scheme fiasco undermined the efforts of Dublin's allies in Britain and provided ample ammunition for unionist propaganda, facts readily conceded by one of Ireland's top diplomats who reported back to the Department of External Affairs:

> In view of the fact that the Left Wing of the [British] Labour Party have for months been using the religious discrimination [within Northern Ireland] argument as the main lever for their effort to pull the Partition issue back into the British political arena, Dr Browne's action in publishing the correspondence with the [Catholic Church] Hierarchy hit them a grievous blow. As mentioned above, the Six County Information Office spared no effort to bring the correspondence to the notice of Members of the House [of Commons] and [debate sponsor] Geoffrey Bing and others are satisfied that it prejudiced a substantial volume of opinion against them.[46]

Arguably, the debacle arising from the failure to introduce the Mother and Child Scheme had a far greater influence in reinforcing northern unionists' attitudes to the Republic than the international anti-partition tour the Government sponsored during this time. Similarly, a domestic dispute within a mixed marriage in Wexford's Fethard on Sea in 1957 escalated into a brief but highly publicised saga closely observed in the North.[47] Put simply, after refusing the local priest's demands that she raise her offspring as Catholics, a Protestant mother absconded with the children to Belfast, leading the parish priest to organise a boycott of the local Protestant population, endorsed by his diocesan bishop. While the couple eventually reconciled without any sacrifice of principle on the mother's part, the boycott highlighted the infamous *Ne Temere* decree, which obliged Catholics to bring up their children as Catholics, irrespective of their spouse's preference. In rural neighbourhoods, where citizens of minority or no faith were few and marriage to Catholics more likely, many viewed this as an attempt to liquidate Ireland's non-Catholic population.

There were other issues during the 1950s and 1960s, such as literary censorship, that were frequently cited to illustrate the incompatibility of the Republic's overt Catholicism with the necessity of creating a society in which northern Protestants might feel comfortable. By the time of the 1967 Censorship of Publications Act, which relaxed standards and facilitated the immediate sale of over 5,000 previously banned books, Ireland had become a major outlier in the western world, with the censor preventing widely acknowledged literary greats from being read.

The prohibition on contraception and divorce (both legally available, if not necessarily widely utilised, in Northern Ireland) also provided material to those who sought to paint a picture of a priest-ridden South unable to attract the civil libertarians of the North. In truth, the significance of these differences can be, and has been, frequently exaggerated. On most social issues, Catholics and Protestants in Ireland shared a conservative outlook that differentiated them from Britain and many western European countries. It is frequently overlooked, for example, that the main Protestant denomination, the Church of Ireland, agreed with the Catholic Church position on the Mother and Child Scheme, with its *Gazette* describing the Government initiative as a 'communist interference in the family'.[48] However, since unionists had declared resistance to living in a Catholic state as a fundamental reason for supporting partition, manifestations of how Catholicism influenced government policy sustained that resolve.

The use of force and the sovereignty of Dáil Éireann

John A. Costello had claimed that his chief motivation in accepting the position of Taoiseach for the first time, and a primary object of his Government, was, as he put it, 'to take the gun out of Irish politics'.[49] It was, therefore, a source of some embarrassment that it was during his second term as Taoiseach (1954–1957) that the gun re-entered the Irish political scene more forcefully than at any point since the 1920s, with IRA units commencing a campaign of cross-border raids in late 1956. These military efforts were complemented by electoral breakthroughs; in the 1955 Westminster election Sinn Féin enjoyed its best electoral performance since 1921, taking 150,000 votes and the vital seats of Fermanagh-South Tyrone and Mid-Ulster. There was, however, no fundamental reappraisal of Irish government policy.[50]

In January 1956, the coalition received an aide memoire from the British Government that alleged 'a total unwillingness' of the Gardaí to collaborate with the RUC in identifying and apprehending suspected IRA members. In response, the Department of External Affairs delivered a candid rebuff, which left London in no doubt that they could expect little cooperation on the matter.[51] Costello had already responded to British and unionist demands for extradition by arguing that armed republicanism was a product of partition and British/ Unionist misrule.[52] In relation to republican attacks on the Northern Ireland state, the Fine Gael leader went on to spell out future government policy on extradition:

> I must … emphasise, in order to prevent any future controversy or discussion on this point, that there can be no question of our handing over, either to the British or to the Six-County authorities, persons whom they may accuse of armed political activities in Britain or in the Six-Counties.[53]

The IRA's attacks on British border military installations quickly produced two martyrs – Seán Sabhat and Fergal O'Hanlon – killed at the beginning of 1957 in an unsuccessful raid on Brookeborough RUC barracks.[54] Sabhat's funeral, the biggest in Limerick since 1921, was transformed into a national procession as it travelled through the country. Among the fifty thousand mourners who watched as the city's republican plot was opened for the first time in thirty-four years were several high-profile public representatives including the city's mayor and TDs.[55]

The international political environment influenced popular attitudes. Those who viewed Northern Ireland through the prism of British imperialism referred to the EOKA struggle against British rule in Cyprus, murderous air attacks against civilians in Aden (Yemen) and/or British coercion against Egypt following the nationalisation of the Suez Canal. Within days of the deaths of Seán Sabhat and Fergal O'Hanlon, for example, Dáil deputies Jack McQuillan and Patrick

Finucane requested the Taoiseach to immediately recall the legislature to discuss 'two motions of grave national importance'.[56] The motions read:

> That Dáil Éireann is of the opinion that, as the situation in the Six Counties is on a parallel with that obtaining in Hungary, Egypt and Cyprus, our permanent delegate to the United Nations should be instructed to demand of the Secretary-General the immediate dispatch of UN observers to the occupied part of the national territory.

> That Dáil Éireann is of the opinion that the Government should discontinue immediately the use of the Irish Army and the Gardaí Síochána as instruments of British policy in helping to maintain partition; and that the men recently taken into custody as a result of such use should be released forthwith.

The Taoiseach declined the request and sought instead to clarify his position through a national radio broadcast, which focussed not on growing tension in the North but rather emphasised the potential spillover effects for the Republic and the need to discourage the IRA.[57] Costello's trenchant opposition to the IRA campaign prompted a motion of no confidence from Clann na Poblachta, in part because of the Government's failure 'to formulate and pursue any positive policy calculated to bring about the re-unification of Ireland'.[58] Rather than face parliamentary defeat, Costello dissolved the Dáil and called a general election.

Fianna Fáil returned to power with a large overall majority and quickly reintroduced internment.[59] In its first foray into twenty-six-county electoral politics since 1927, Sinn Féin took four seats and over 10 per cent of the vote in the nineteen constituencies it contested. Its impact on deliberations within the Dáil was, however, limited by its policy of absentionism. Emboldened by Sinn Féin's election successes and hopeful of the Dublin Government's non-interference, the IRA was more optimistic of success than objective circumstances permitted. Motions of sympathy to the relatives and friends of the slain IRA men passed by dozens of local government bodies must also have heartened them.[60] Some of these called for intervention at the United Nations and for a UN force to be sent to the North while others were more militant in content, such as that of Sligo Corporation, which offered 'congratulations to the resistance forces in the Six Counties in their struggle against British Imperialism and extending best wishes for success'.[61]

Although the border campaign officially halted in 1962 it had substantially concluded by the time de Valera retired as Taoiseach to take up the presidency in June 1959. Enjoying few resources, little active support and with internment on both sides of the border, the combined security measures of the Dublin, Belfast and London Governments overwhelmed the IRA. The five-year campaign, officially called Operation Harvest, had resulted in the deaths of six RUC men and twelve republicans, all bar two of whom had died accidentally as a result of their own devices.

Economic policy as a basis for ending partition

Throughout the 1950s, de Valera found it difficult to articulate a cogent Northern Ireland policy. Fianna Fáil's initial dynamism had been sustained by the struggle for full sovereignty in the jurisdiction over which it governed but this had been fully achieved by 1948. The party had run out of steam when it came to addressing the larger constitutional issues associated with Northern Ireland. During the 1957 election, de Valera claimed that 'politically we have been successful as far as five-sixths of the national territory is concerned' before asserting unimaginatively that 'time will settle the other thing'.[62]

Seán Lemass is frequently credited with radical shifts in Ireland's economic policies and in his approach to Northern Ireland. In truth, however, these policy changes were agreed to before he took over as Taoiseach in June 1959. Détente with the Northern Ireland Government, which had de Valera's blessing, would have to wait until Terence O'Neill replaced Lord Brookeborough as Prime Minister in Belfast but attempts to rescue the Irish economy by a move away from import substitution and towards free trade were also in place during the premiership of Fianna Fáil's founding father. When the cabinet officially endorsed the new economic policy on 17 December 1958, de Valera characteristically presented the 'Whitaker Plan' as being 'merely a continuation of long established policy'.[63] Naming the new plan after a civil servant reflected a desire to depoliticise the move towards free trade, enabling the Government to distance itself from what was a major policy reversal, in effect rejecting the traditional dogma of self-sufficiency that had guided the economy for over a quarter century.

Lemass adroitly linked the jettisoning of the old Sinn Féin policy of economic nationalism with the patriotic struggle. The relationship between the new programme and the ending of partition took two forms. The first strand sought to counter arguments that Northern Ireland's superior economic conditions justified unionist reticence about involving themselves in a unitary Irish state:

> There are people today in the north-east of the country who say that we here are paying an uneconomic price for our freedom. We have got to prove them wrong. We have got to demonstrate that we can bring about a higher level of achievement and greater progress with freedom than without it. And when we have demonstrated that – demonstrated it beyond question and doubt and dispute, as we can do – we

will have cleared away the one continuing argument that is being used to justify the partitioning of our country.[64]

Thus, by supporting the new programme, people would promote the struggle for a united Ireland. This disingenuous argument relied on the dubious premise that unionist objections to a united Ireland were solely based on economic considerations. In this way it conformed with the republican belief that unionist recalcitrance was because they were 'loyal to the half crown rather than the Crown'.

Political and religious differences mattered more to northern unionists than economic differentials. However, to confront unionists' substantive criticisms would have entailed opening up a Pandora's box of political and constitutional challenges. Matters such as the place of the Irish language in education and the civil service, the constitutional prohibition of divorce and the unavailability of contraception might have to be assessed anew. It was easier to concentrate on the economy and to portray economic divergences between North and South as 'the *one* continuing argument' that unionists employed to rationalise their distaste for a united Ireland. This argument conveniently allowed the Irish Government to pursue a drive for prosperity under the guise of anti-partitionism when in fact the primary motive was to mollify an electorate increasingly dissatisfied with economic atrophy. There was nothing new in this approach. In 1929, for example, Cumann na nGaedheal had argued that

> In the state of affairs that now exists the thing that would be more helpful towards a solution of the Boundary problem would be five years of complete neglect. If we were to apply to the Saorstat [Free State] during that period the Sinn Féin policy of unremitting economic reconstruction and concentration on our affairs, we should do a hundred times more towards winning the North than could be done in any other way ... The building up in the Saorstat of a notably progressive and efficient scheme of public administration and of a sound flourishing system of industry would provide the people of the North with an inducement to join us which they had not had in the past.[65]

Others had followed suit. The Labour Party advocated the provision of better social services which, it argued, would help those in Northern Ireland 'realise the advantage of joining with their fellow-countrymen in an all-Ireland assembly'[66] while farming interests argued that the prosperity of Free State farmers would entice Ulster farmers to see that their future lay in a united Ireland.[67] In each case sectional groups were seeking to extract support for their preferred domestic policies by exploiting the widespread desire for Irish unity. In moments of extreme pessimism de Valera also took refuge in this argument. When asked in 1933 whether he possessed a policy to abolish partition the Fianna Fáil leader replied that

> The only policy for abolishing partition that I can see is for us, in this part of Ireland, to use such freedom as we can secure to get for the people in this part of Ireland such conditions as will make the people in the other part of Ireland wish to belong to this part.[68]

De Valera's downbeat assessment did not, however, inhibit raising false optimism during successive ard fheiseanna and election campaigns.

Lemass's arguments indicated that the Irish Government had to prove the advantages of independence not only to northern unionists but also to their own electorate:

> I have emphasised on other occasions the close relation which we see to exist between our economic development effort and the national hope that the unity of the Irish people can be restored, and the whole Irish nation, organised in a political entity, able to unitedly promote the welfare of all its people and take its full and proper place in the world. We have to confound these northern defenders of partition who contend that joining us in freedom would be an economic disadvantage to the north-eastern counties by showing, in the scale of our achievements here that we, under equal conditions and in the exercise of our freedom, can move faster and go further in economic progress than they can hope for, handicapped as they are.[69]

The phrase 'handicapped as they are' illuminated the Government's underlying assumptions. As a political concept, Irish nationalism had assumed that political independence, like marriage in a fairy tale, was the panacea for all social and economic ills. Consequently it was considered axiomatic that Ireland would be better off as an independent state than if it remained part of the United Kingdom. The economic malaise of the 1950s represented a direct challenge to this sacred maxim of the nationalist credo. 'After thirty five years of native government', T.K. Whitaker said at the time, 'people are asking themselves whether we can achieve an acceptable degree of economic progress.'[70] Whitaker later recalled that the Irish people were experiencing 'a dark night of the soul in which doubts were prevalent as to whether the achievement of political independence had not been futile'.[71]

Terence O'Neill and his rivals

Despite the formal end of the IRA's border campaign, violence was never far beneath the surface of Northern Irish politics and on occasion aggressive sectarianism bubbled over. It was apathy rather than ignorance that prevented the British Government from rectifying the excesses of the Stormont regime. Jim Callaghan, British Home Secretary during the late 1960s, made clear in his memoirs that while injustices were known to exist in Northern Ireland they were thought not to be sufficiently pressing to warrant intervention.[72] The Government in London considered Terence O'Neill, who became Northern Ireland's fourth Prime Minister in 1963, a safe pair of hands who might introduce long-delayed reforms. As one British cabinet member reflected: 'We had been relying on O'Neill to do our job of dragging Northern Ireland out of its 18th century Catholic–Protestant conflict.'[73] British government policy during this period has been accurately described as one of 'leaving it to O'Neill'.[74]

O'Neill inherited from the old guard a position for life but realised that his party's monopoly of power had led to complacency, inefficiency and stagnation. It had also eliminated the need to humour Northern Ireland's large nationalist minority. As O'Neill later pointed out, his predecessor, Lord Brookeborough, had 'never crossed the border, never visited a Catholic school and never received or sought a civic reception from a Catholic town'.[75] Shortly after assuming the UUP leadership, O'Neill announced a reform programme advocating inclusive, accountable and open politics to encourage societal harmony and economic restructuring. O'Neill's rhetoric quickly developed a dynamic of its own. It simultaneously raised expectations amongst those who had most to gain (Catholic nationalists) and enraged those content with the status quo (Protestant unionists).

While in terms of age O'Neill represented a new generation of leaders, he did not enjoy unrivalled support within the party and there were some, most notably Brian Faulkner and Bill Craig, who entertained ambitions to replace him sooner rather than later. O'Neill's position was further weakened by the economic strategy he chose to pursue and the political policies that such a strategy necessitated. Many unionists feared that his focus on centralisation, which involved dismantling Northern Ireland's archaic, multi-layered and inefficient political system, would disrupt traditional patronage networks.

Allied to the concept of centralisation was the modernisation of the North's industrial base. Unemployment stood at 11.2 per cent when O'Neill became Prime Minister, a direct result of the decline and contraction of the North's traditional manufacturers. The linen industry was decimated after the advent of synthetic fibre, and employment in agriculture fell by 33 per cent between 1950 and 1961. The major decline, however, was in the shipbuilding industry, a bastion of militant loyalism. O'Neill's solution was to accept the contraction of traditional industries as irreversible and to entice foreign multinationals to locate in Northern Ireland through the provision of lucrative grants underwritten by the British exchequer. His promise to 'transform the face of Ulster' proved successful in reclaiming Protestant working-class votes from a revitalising Northern Ireland Labour Party, but modernisation also weakened Unionist control over the distribution of employment and thus threatened their long-standing hegemony.

O'Neill's new economic philosophy necessitated a reversal of ideological orthodoxies, including recognition of the Dublin-based Irish Congress of Trade Unions and the development of stronger economic ties with the North's nearest trading partner, the Republic of Ireland. However, O'Neill's cordial relations with the traditional enemy and the secretive manner in which his first meeting with Lemass took place fuelled extremist fears and deepened cabinet divisions. Though his motivation for initiating contact with the Republic was purely economic, he was never able to convince party *ultras* that the policy was without political and constitutional ramifications.

More complex but equally divisive were O'Neill's policies towards the Catholic community in Northern Ireland. Devoid of substance, they were charged with a symbolism that simultaneously raised nationalist expectations and loyalist fury. When Pope John XXIII died in June 1963, O'Neill made the unprecedented gesture of sending condolences to Cardinal Conway at Armagh and flying the Union Jack at half-mast over Belfast city hall. O'Neill's attempts to invite the 'Irish Catholic' John F. Kennedy to Belfast and his condolences following the US President's assassination also aroused loyalist ire. Furthermore, on 24 April 1964 O'Neill made his much-publicised visit to a Catholic school in Ballymoney, Co. Antrim.

O'Neill's initiatives were entirely superficial in nature, symbolic rather than substantive, but as the author of a major sociological study of Ulster loyalism has suggested, 'people respond to symbols and perceptions, and O'Neill broke new symbolic ground'.[76] His gestural bridge-building policies gave him the worst of both worlds. Catholics were left with the erroneous impression that a major reform programme was in gestation and became increasingly frustrated when it failed to materialise. Meanwhile, O'Neill's rhetoric of conciliation alienated members of the unionist community, leading to a counter-mobilisation effort inspired by fears of a challenge to their identity and by the apparent weakness of the Unionist elite. Linking the growing mobilisation of marginalised Catholics within Northern Ireland to the irredentist threat of the Republic that threatened the fundamental character of the Stormont regime, unionist counter-elites emerged to challenge the O'Neillite establishment, which they feared was pursuing a policy of appeasement.

Foremost amongst these dissidents was the Reverend Ian Paisley, who had first come to prominence during the 1950s in opposition to the emerging ecumenical movement working for reconciliation between Catholicism and Protestantism. Paisley's synthesis of religious evangelicalism and political fundamentalism reinforced the traditional link between Protestantism and unionism that O'Neill seemed intent on dismantling.[77] The key to Paisley's success was the influence he was able to exert on the Unionist Party from the loyalist periphery. Indeed, though not a member of the Unionist Party, the Presbyterian Church or the Orange Order, Paisley arguably wielded more influence within these three organisations than any of their respective leaders. As the political temperature rose in Ulster, O'Neill found that many influential party members, even ministers, were openly endorsing Paisley.

Functional cooperation: Lemass and O'Neill

The logic of Lemass's new economic philosophy suggested that stronger economic ties should be developed between the Republic and its nearest trading partner, the United Kingdom, and, more controversially, Northern Ireland. All efforts to engage the Northern Ireland Prime Minister Lord Brookeborough had been rebuffed and tariff walls had reduced cross-border trade to a trickle.[78] In a broader context, Lemass sought a comprehensive trade agreement with the British Government, and a *rapprochement* with Stormont was a logical step in that direction.

Shortly after becoming Taoiseach, Lemass defined the problem of restoring national unity as one of 'breaking down the barriers of suspicion, antagonism, prejudice and misunderstanding' that divided 'a minority in the north east from their fellow countrymen'. Policy and actions would be determined by the simple maxim that 'anything which tends to break or lower these barriers is good; anything which tends to raise or strengthen them is bad'.[79] The contradiction that neither Lemass nor his successor could reconcile was that to highlight the grievances of the northern nationalist community antagonised the Unionist regime. Hence in an effort to progress relations with the Stormont Government, civil rights abuses in Northern Ireland were de-emphasised during these vital years when ameliorative action might have defused the Troubles before they ignited in 1969.

Lemass's most important articulation of Northern Ireland policy was arguably his 1963 Tralee speech in which he argued that 'a new situation would develop' from 'the extension of useful contacts at every level of activity', and that, in essence, 'the solution of the problem of partition is one to be found in Ireland by Irishmen'.[80] That Brookeborough rejected Lemass's overtures did not surprise the Taoiseach but he displayed ill-concealed impatience when O'Neill adopted a similar stance.[81] Shortly after O'Neill's selection as Prime Minister, Lemass had repeated his 'willingness to meet at any level without preconditions'.[82] O'Neill, however, called for an end to 'public statements either in Ireland or abroad about the "ultimate reunification of our country", the "evil of partition", the "Six County area" and similar subjects'. 'Talk will not of itself change things', he remonstrated; 'there is more to the winds of change than hot air.'[83] O'Neill also rejected Lemass's argument that joint membership of the EEC would render partition an anachronism[84] by claiming that Northern Ireland would 'no more become part of the Irish Republic if Eire joins the Common Market than Yorkshire will become a German province'.[85]

Behind the scenes, Department of Finance Secretary, T.K. Whitaker, and Terence O'Neill's Private Secretary, Jim Malley, worked diligently to secure a common basis for a meeting agreeable to their respective Prime Ministers. Lemass accepted an invitation from O'Neill to visit Stormont on 14 January 1965 to participate in an historic summit. Given that the official meeting took less than an hour and covered almost a dozen issues, it is not surprising that it was devoted to a purely cursory exploration of possibilities. Indeed, O'Neill's cabinet Secretary, Cecil Bateman, noted that 'no final conclusion' was reached on any of the matters raised and the discussion was purely a 'preliminary *tour d'horizon*'.[86] After the talks, the Prime Ministers issued a terse two-line statement declaring that they had 'discussed matters in which there may prove to be a degree of common interest' and that the talks, which 'did not touch on consti-tutional issues', had been conducted 'in a most amicable way'.[87] In keeping with the ecumenical spirit of the meeting, O'Neill had welcomed Lemass 'to the North', thus avoiding any embarrassment that might arise from reference to 'Northern Ireland'. In reality, and unlike many of his party supporters and cabinet colleagues, Lemass had no reservations about employing terminology that recognised Stormont and its leader, whom he addressed in correspondence as 'Dear Prime Minister'.[88]

Lemass's public response to the event was initially cautious. The meeting was 'significant', he said, though 'its significance should not be exaggerated'.[89] However, in response to overwhelming public acclamation, the summit was upgraded the very next day to one of 'tremendous significance', because of which 'things can never be the same again'.[90] Lemass became ever more audacious as the weeks elapsed. In a speech to a Fianna Fáil cumann in Dún Laoghaire, he reaffirmed that 'our aim is to re-unite the Irish people in one nation and one state' and that 'our method is to remove the barriers of misunderstanding and prejudice which have divided the Irish people in the past'.[91] In an interview with the *Irish Times*, O'Neill countered suggestions that some people consid-ered the meeting a step on the road to reunification. When asked whether

North–South relations would be improved if censorship regulations in the Republic were eased and the prohibitions on birth control and divorce lifted, O'Neill replied that

> Moves such as those would be welcomed here as indications of a liberalisation of attitude, but I would not like anyone to think that they would make Northern Ireland leave the United Kingdom. I seem to keep on stressing this point, but you see the inference in questions like this is that if the South makes certain changes, we will be encouraged to unite with it. Well, it is complete and utter rubbish to think that the border is going to fall suddenly like the Walls of Jericho … I found Mr. Lemass most realistic about this.[92]

O'Neill was equally unimpressed by suggestions that the North might enter a federal relationship with the Republic should the latter rejoin the Commonwealth. The Stormont premier stressed the importance of the British welfare state and said that he could see 'no economic advantage in joining with Éire',[93] though this only reinforced the Taoiseach's argument that prosperity in the Republic would cause unionist antipathy to wither away.

Functional cooperation had been contemplated in 1925 when the three Governments in London, Dublin and Belfast had signed a tripartite agreement following the ill-fated Boundary Commission report. Since then, there had been sporadic contact between the Dublin and Stormont administrations, though the Foyle Fisheries authority, established in 1952, stood as a solitary example of what such cooperation could achieve. Other proposals in the field of tourism and transport had met with political rather than economic objections from the Unionist Government.[94] A proposal to make both parts of Ireland a free trade area was discussed by the Stormont cabinet throughout 1959 but also came up against hardline resistance.[95]

Terence O'Neill's premiership provided the vital catalyst for dialogue as, unlike his predecessor, he did not insist on a public declaration from the Irish Government that it recognised Northern Ireland as a part of the United Kingdom. O'Neill told Stormont's House of Commons that he attached less importance to pieces of paper than to action: 'if Mr. Lemass was prepared to drive through the gates of Stormont and to meet me here as Prime Minister of Northern Ireland he was accepting the plain fact of our existence and our jurisdiction here'.[96] Furthermore, O'Neill said that 'the benefits for which I look are not entirely, or even mainly, practical'; rather he hoped that the exchanges would alter 'many of the myths about Northern Ireland current in the South' which were 'misconceptions based on ignorance'.[97]

The Irish Government Information Bureau's official statement referred to Captain O'Neill as the 'Prime Minister of Northern Ireland' but within the cabinet only Neil Blaney argued that the visit had legitimised the six-county government,[98] a concern echoed by Sinn Féin.[99] The *Irish Times* diplomatic correspondent wrote that 'whatever the feeling in Dublin, it will certainly be accepted in Belfast that some form of recognition has been granted'.[100] While little of economic benefit came from the North–South summits, the meetings did produce one important political result. Lemass succeeded in persuading the Nationalist Party in Northern Ireland to abandon its abstentionist policy and to assume the role of official opposition in Stormont, a development that O'Neill saw as furthering his bridge-building policies and legitimising the Unionist regime.[101] Nationalist Party leader Eddie McAteer later recounted that throughout his many trips to Dublin he received 'hospitality but little real support'. During his first meeting with Lemass following the historic summit with Terence O'Neill, the Taoiseach surprised McAteer when he said that 'it appeared to him that Catholics in the North were just as intractable as the Protestants'. McAteer was also disinclined to share the Taoiseach's optimism that industrial progress in the twenty-six counties would bring the unionists towards a united Ireland. The Nationalist Party leader 'came away with the conviction that as far as Seán Lemass was concerned, the Northern Irish were very much on their own'.[102]

Nationalist discontent and disillusionment with Dublin's performance was never publicised given the need to present a united front, maintain morale and deter unionist aggression.[103] As a former editor of the *Derry Journal* recalled, northern nationalists

> scrupulously projected, for Unionist consumption, the view that Dublin automatically sided and sympathised with them. The assumption that Dublin identified with the Northern minority was a telling factor in bolstering Catholic morale, while ensuring Unionist caution about what would happen if their extremists ever launched an all-out assault on the Catholic community. In fact, this Dublin 'guarantee' of Northern minority rights was no guarantee at all. It was a myth, pure and simple.[104]

Détente between the Prime Ministers in Dublin and Belfast created additional difficulties for Northern Ireland's Nationalist Party. Moderate nationalists had traditionally fended off challenges from more radical elements. As pervasive anti-Catholic prejudice and unionism's inbuilt permanent majority had rendered parliamentary agitation ineffective, cooperation with Dublin constituted the only high-level forum at which the party could hope to get a hearing. Confronted now with an administration that increasingly viewed northern nationalists as a liability in their efforts to enhance relationships with the Stormont and British Governments, the Nationalist Party's impotence made them increasingly vulnerable to being outflanked by an emergent civil rights movement that used more direct and radical means to promote their objectives.

The rise of Jack Lynch

There was a brief but intense flurry of inter-governmental meetings following the historic summit at Stormont. Basking in popular acclamation and already thinking of retirement, Lemass called a general election and Fianna Fáil stayed at the helm. Despite the 1965 election campaign slogan of 'Let Lemass Lead On', Lemass stepped down in November 1966 after engineering a successful leadership transition to Jack Lynch, the first party leader of the post-revolutionary generation. Not only had the new Taoiseach been born into a family with no background in party politics, but it was also one that had not participated in the 1916–1921 independence struggle, during which the fathers of most of Lynch's government colleagues had played prominent roles. Lynch's cabinet rivals did not overlook this revolutionary manqué, and many believed that when approached by both Fianna Fáil and Fine Gael to stand as a candidate in the 1948 general election Lynch, as befitted a hurling captain, had tossed a coin to decide the issue.

Lynch's prowess as a hurler and Gaelic footballer (he won six All-Ireland medals between 1941 and 1946) might have compensated for deficiencies in his republican lineage, but his leadership qualities as evidenced in sport were conspicuously absent during much of his early political career. While he brought intelligence and competence to every position he held, the summation offered by his Secretary at the Department of Education – that he was a 'superb administrator' but not an 'ideas man' – seems appropriate.[105] Another observer who served under Lynch at the Department of Industry and Commerce also noted his administrative skills but added that 'he was very low-key, and went out of his way to avoid confrontation rather than to invite it'.[106] In sum, Lynch had been considered a competent mild-mannered figure devoid of ambition for high office.

Why then did this unassuming Corkman, with no republican background, a minister who was neither radical nor spectacular, and who alone amongst the possible contenders did not want the top job, come to be the successor of de Valera and Lemass? Ultimately Jack Lynch became Taoiseach not in spite of his disinterest, but because of it. That he could not be readily identified with a party faction made him a popular choice. Lynch's selection as Taoiseach also proved the most acceptable option to his more ambitious cabinet colleagues who preferred a neutral compromise leader to a rival. The new Taoiseach's tenure witnessed the gradual loosening of the bonds of collective responsibility, which would ultimately lead to open warfare and anarchy within the cabinet.

Apart from his passive style and lack of republican antecedents, Lynch's relative youth also diminished his authority within the cabinet, for, in his own words, he was 'never viewed as a father figure within the party as previous leaders had been'.[107] To compound this vulnerability, he had yet to face the electorate as Taoiseach. Lynch was acutely aware that 'electoral defeat might cost him the leadership' and 'the prospects for the next election did not appear too promising'.[108] It would not be until 1969 that Lynch would prove himself to be an electoral asset, but by then his authority within the cabinet and his confidence as leader had been eroded. Lemass had appointed Lynch's cabinet colleagues, most of whom were young and felt they had bright ministerial futures ahead of them. Many years later Lynch candidly explained how this affected his authority:

> Seán Lemass had already effected the transition from one generation to another and I had merely to endorse the changes he had made. While superficially this made life easier for me, it did cause problems for I was thereby deprived of one major strength every Prime Minister usually enjoys: the power of cabinet appointment. Of course I had that power formally but in effect most ministers knew that they owed their position to Seán Lemass, not to me.[109]

The new Taoiseach's inability to hire and fire ministers curtailed his manoeuvrability and circumscribed his powers in a manner unknown to his predecessors. Hence, on becoming leader, Lynch made only cosmetic changes in the cabinet: no minister was dropped from the Government and no new ministers were appointed. In reality the changes in ministerial portfolios constituted a minor cabinet reshuffle necessitated by Lemass's departure and the need to fill Lynch's previous portfolio of Finance. Finally, it is necessary to acknowledge the perception, deeply ingrained in the minds of many, that Lynch had assumed the leadership of the party in a caretaker capacity. John Healy reflected this sentiment in his influential *Irish Times* 'Backbencher' column when he wrote that 'George Colley is well aware and does not need me to tell him that Thursday's decision was merely decision postponed. It was a compromise by a party which opted to save itself from a public eating of its entrails by electing a "safe" man.'[110]

To many of his cabinet colleagues, Lynch's reign was merely a temporary phenomenon to be endured until a more powerful aspirant consolidated his position sufficiently to assume the leadership. Lynch later acknowledged the prevalence of this view within Fianna Fáil, which further undermined his credibility:

> One of the irritations I encountered at the time was that people, knowing of my reluctance to stand for the leadership, assumed that my first wish would be to get

out of the job. They used to say things like 'don't worry you won't be there long – there is always the Park [i.e. the largely symbolic presidency]'.[111]

Although Lynch wished to demonstrate that he had 'no intention of being a caretaker Taoiseach', he gave credence to this view by claiming shortly after his election that he was a compromise candidate. It was an expression that would haunt him politically and one he 'bitterly regretted'.[112]

During the crucial years leading up to the outbreak of armed conflict in Northern Ireland, the new Taoiseach 'failed to establish his authority over the cabinet at any stage'.[113] Many of the more charismatic figures within the cabinet were like 'powerful medieval barons when faced by a rather weak monarch'.[114] Lynch faced potential threats to his authority from several cabinet colleagues, particularly Charles Haughey, George Colley and Neil Blaney, each of whom had been a contender for the party leadership and could be said to represent a particular 'wing' of the party. Whereas Colley would eventually accept the position of heir apparent, Haughey and Blaney would ultimately be dismissed from cabinet in May 1970 as a result of the Arms Crisis. Given the centrality of Northern Ireland and 'republicanism' to Lynch's leadership woes it is worthwhile to briefly assess his main rivals within the Government and determine on what basis they posed a threat to the new Taoiseach.

The opportunistic challenger: Charles Haughey

Flamboyant, debonair, sardonic, Charles Haughey cultivated a lifestyle that launched a thousand rumours. Like Donagh O'Malley and Brian Lenihan, the new Finance Minister was an urban realist who came to represent the 'Young Turks' within Fianna Fáil. Haughey's affluence, displayed ostentatiously, his apparent political atheism and the myriad of influential connections he enjoyed with the business community made him at once an object of admiration and envy. He was a man who could inspire unquestioning loyalty but could also enkindle intense enmity and hostility. Thus Haughey was, and could only aspire to be, the leader of a faction, securing the blind faith of his adherents, the eternal odium of his opponents. His subsequent tenure as Taoiseach was to be a predictable testament to these divisive personal qualities.

Having withdrawn from the leadership race in favour of Lynch, Haughey was rewarded with the prestigious Finance portfolio, which he would hold until his dismissal from office in 1970. Haughey was to be a pivotal figure in the Lynch cabinet between 1966 and 1970 without ever endearing himself to a sizeable portion of the Fianna Fáil party. Though he would be increasingly identified with the cabinet's republican faction from August 1969 onwards, few suspected him of republican sympathies before then. While his family was of Northern stock, it had split on the Treaty. Haughey's tenure as Minister for Justice, when he introduced special criminal courts to combat militant republicans, did not suggest that he had any difficulty in vigorously confronting the IRA.

While admirers saw him as 'the modern man, essentially pragmatic and business-minded',[115] opposition to Haughey stemmed from several influential groups within Fianna Fáil. Senior party figures viewed his opulent lifestyle with suspicion and were critical of his ability to become a millionaire while serving the state for a relatively modest ministerial salary. Oscar Traynor, Gerald Boland and Frank Aiken were amongst these critics and according to the Secretary of the Department of Justice, Peter Berry, they were representative of a much larger section of the party hierarchy.[116] In addition, Haughey's alienation of farmers while holding the Agriculture portfolio made him an unattractive leader for the party's substantial rural support base. According to Dick Walsh, Haughey's withdrawal from the leadership contest was 'a tactical retreat on the assumption that Lynch would accept his role as interim leader and that his reign would be short'.[117] By holding the key portfolio of Finance, Haughey was ideally placed to assume the leadership when Lynch completed his period as 'caretaker' Taoiseach.

The traditionalist challenger: George Colley

While in later years George Colley would be perceived by his supporters as the moderate alternative to Haughey's extreme nationalism, during the 1960s it was Colley, more than any other of Fianna Fáil's new generation of politicians, that was seen as 'the champion of the original pristine values, Gaelic and republican, of the party'.[118] Unlike Lynch and Haughey, Colley possessed an impeccable republican background. His father, Harry Colley, a veteran of the 1916 Rising, had been Adjutant to the IRA's Dublin Brigade during the 1920s. Though based in the capital, Colley espoused de Valera's rural values and was a devout Irish-language enthusiast. He viewed with distaste the effects of the Lemassian economic revolution on the party, advocating 'the reconstruction and recovery of Fianna Fáil' and the renewal of its 'adherence to the principles of the Republican, Democratic Programme of 1919'.[119]

In marked contrast to Haughey, Colley enjoyed favour amongst many of the Fianna Fáil hierarchy. Foreign Minister Frank Aiken was his most prominent sponsor and promoted his candidature for the party leadership. However, the Irish Times noted that while Colley had 'much support among the older and republican wing of the party, the de Valera wing … his support among the greater number of younger members [was] not so wide'.[120] Haughey had unseated

Colley's father in 1957 and, though disillusioned with party politics, Colley Junior stood for election four years later to regain the family's foothold in Dublin North-East. Contesting the same parliamentary constituency, an intense rivalry would develop between the two deputies, ending only with Colley's untimely death in 1983.

Colley's ambition was exemplified by his decision to contest the 1966 leadership after only five years' service in the Dáil and barely a year within the cabinet. Despite this relative inexperience, Lemass had allowed Colley to entertain leadership ambitions and summoned him from government business in New York to facilitate his nomination. Colley's motivation in contesting the election, even after Haughey's and Blaney's withdrawal, was 'to demonstrate the seriousness of his intentions and to ensure that there would be a vote next time round when his *real* opponent was in the field'.[121] For Colley, the leadership issue had not been resolved but merely postponed.

The republican challenger: Neil Blaney

Neil Blaney was arguably the one who did most to undermine Lynch's authority as Taoiseach. Like George Colley, his family possessed a flawless revolutionary pedigree. At the time of Blaney's birth in 1922, his father was under sentence of death and was only saved from execution by the republican ceasefire in 1923 announced by Frank Aiken, with whom Blaney now sat in cabinet. Blaney's republican outlook was also influenced by his geographical proximity to the border. Partition had rendered Donegal a political island, with only a narrow six-kilometre stretch connecting the county to the rest of the Republic. Economically, politically and socially, Donegal, more than any other county, was adversely affected by partition, which had severed the area from its natural hinterland. As a TD, Blaney travelled through Derry, Tyrone and Fermanagh several times every week, a routine in marked contrast to that of Corkman Jack Lynch. Blaney built an extensive line of contacts with northern nationalists and arguably had a 'more acute awareness and a fuller understanding of the Six-County situation than any other member of Dáil Éireann'.[122] Throughout his ministerial career, Blaney would repeatedly assert his right as a 'border representative' to espouse his own interpretation of political events and on partition generally.

When Lemass announced his retirement and the party was confronted with a choice between Colley and Haughey, Blaney along with his chief ally in the cabinet on Northern Ireland matters, Kevin Boland, were determined that neither would become Taoiseach. Haughey had already approached Blaney for support, only to be told that he hadn't the necessary background.[123] Seán Haughey's position in the Free State Army that had raided Blaney's home and sentenced his father to death had not been overlooked. Moreover, unlike the Blaneys and the Bolands, Haughey's family had played no active role in the founding and development of Fianna Fáil. As for Colley, he had the background but didn't share the same sense of urgency on partition.

Blaney successfully created his own local fiefdom in Donegal and applied his organisational skills at national level.[124] He personally directed all five by-election campaigns forced on the Government before Lynch's first general election in 1969. Fianna Fáil emerged victorious in all five by-elections, a remarkable feat for a party that had been in power for over a decade. Blaney's pre-eminence in the party network was a double-edged sword for both him and his party leader, Jack Lynch. His organisational success afforded him a degree of autonomy bordering on immunity, allowing him a disproportionate influence within cabinet. However, by securing by-election victories for the party, Blaney also bolstered Lynch's position and risked transforming the avuncular Taoiseach from a pliant leader to a political animal able to withstand pressure. In effect, both Lynch and Blaney relied on the other to exercise power and achieve their designs. Political and organisational power was divided and neither could function effectively without the cooperation or acquiescence of the other.

Blaney's entry into the succession stakes at the eleventh hour had been a tactical move. He made it clear at the outset that he would agree to withdraw from the contest only if Lynch consented to go forward.[125] Lemass, he accurately predicted, would be appalled by the prospect of a three-way faction fight and would apply renewed pressure on Lynch to stand as a unity candidate. If this proved impossible then Blaney would remain a challenger and fight to win. Both Haughey and Colley were urban based, and with Blaney's intervention rural deputies who had previously aligned themselves with one or other of the Dublin candidates now switched to Blaney. Many believed he could have defeated the other contenders[126] but within hours of Blaney's announcement Lemass persuaded Lynch to stand and Blaney promptly withdrew from the contest. This left only Colley in the field, who Lynch comprehensively defeated by fifty-two votes to nineteen.

Blaney's primary motivation throughout was to insure that neither Colley nor Haughey was installed as Taoiseach and that the eventual incumbent would be a malleable individual responsive to pressure exerted by the party's organisational master. From this perspective, Lynch's only attraction was that, unlike Colley or Haughey, he could be controlled. Blaney had settled for the role of 'kingmaker'. His organisational strength within the party and his promotion to Agriculture Minister would allow him to undermine the Taoiseach's authority with relative impunity. As the North began to unravel, Blaney would represent Lynch's most formidable and audacious rival.

The civil rights movement

The rhetoric of modernisation, so central to the declared mission of Northern Ireland's Prime Minister, Terence O'Neill, did little to improve the lives of six-county Catholics. In September 1967, after four and a half years in power and when nationalists believed O'Neill had had ample time to consolidate his position, the Government reappointed members of three public boards, but of seventy-nine appointments made to the Youth Employment Board, Hospitals Authority and General Health Services Board only seven were Catholics. As Michael Farrell pointed out, 'the functions of these boards affected Catholics as much as Protestants ... and there was no shortage of middle-class Catholics eager to serve on them'.[127] Even the *Belfast Telegraph*, a liberal unionist newspaper, claimed that the appointments 'made a nonsense of the prime minister and all that is said about a bridge-building policy'.[128]

The gap between O'Neill's rhetoric and performance infuriated Catholics and contributed to the establishment, in January 1967, of the Northern Ireland Civil Rights Association (NICRA). The NICRA had relatively modest objectives, including the introduction of a points system for housing allocation, repeal of the Special Powers Act, the appointment of an impartial ombudsman and (most controversially) 'one man, one vote', a reference to inequalities in electoral rights which deprived non-ratepayers (disproportionately Catholic due to unfair housing and job allocations) of the vote, while endowing businessmen (disproportionately Protestant) with up to six ballots. Combined with an extensive system of gerrymandering, the absence of 'one man, one vote' ensured that Catholics remained an electoral minority in many towns and cities where they constituted a substantial majority of the adult population.

The violent dispersal of a civil rights march through Derry city on 5 October 1968, which included the beating up of prominent nationalist public representatives in the presence of visiting British Labour MPs and television cameras, raised the political temperature further. Two weeks after the clash, Eddie McAteer announced that the Nationalist Party would no longer act as official opposition within the Northern Ireland Parliament, thus ending the brief experiment promoted by Seán Lemass three years earlier.

Cabinet divisions on Northern Ireland

The violence in Derry prompted an inconsistent response from the Irish Government that reflected cabinet divisions on the root cause of the disturbances and on the best policy for ameliorating the situation. There were those, including

Jack Lynch, who believed the issue to be one of civil rights and who saw cooperation with Stormont as the most effective way of remedying the political ills that
had brought the NICRA to the fore. However, an influential minority within
the cabinet attributed the trouble to partition and favoured bilateral talks with
the British Government to confront it with its responsibility for dividing Ireland
and to seek a declaration of its intention to withdraw from the North. Lynch's
initial response to the violence reflected his own inclinations and preferred
strategy. Addressing an audience in Kilkenny on 6 October, the Taoiseach had
reiterated his belief that the lack of civil rights for Catholics in Northern Ireland
constituted the fundamental problem when he expressed the hope that

> the root cause of such disturbances would soon be eliminated, so that people of
> different religious beliefs and political convictions would be treated as equals in every
> respect, and would be permitted to live with each other in peace and harmony, free
> to enjoy their lawful democratic rights.[129]

When addressing a referendum meeting at Clonmel two days later, however,
Lynch put forward an entirely different argument, in the guise of a 'clarification':

> In commenting briefly at Kilkenny on Sunday on the incidents in Derry city I expressed
> the hope that the root causes of such demonstrations would soon be eliminated so
> that people of different religious and political persuasions and convictions would be
> able to live together in peace and harmony free to exercise and enjoy their lawful
> democratic rights. The people of Ireland know what the root causes are. I know
> them. The Northern Ireland Prime Minister, Captain O'Neill, knows them and the
> British Prime Minister Mr Wilson knows them also. Partition is the first and foremost
> root cause. And Partition arose out of British policy. The methods necessary to
> maintain Partition against the wishes of the vast majority of the Irish people and
> local majorities in areas like Derry City, that is: gerrymandering, discrimination in
> jobs and housing, suppression of free speech and the right of peaceful protest could
> not be continued without the political and the huge financial support received from
> Britain.[130]

To assuage those dissatisfied with his comments in Kilkenny, the Taoiseach had
been forced to quickly 'refine' and 'expand' with a classic restatement of his
party's traditional position on partition.

As the civil rights protests and the state security response locked both sides
into a cycle of escalating violence, the embryonic efforts made to achieve some
level of cooperation between Dublin and Belfast stalled. The traditionalist wing's
ascendancy within the cabinet was in evidence when the Taoiseach was dispatched
to London on 30 October 1968 to inform the British Prime Minister of 'the

views of the Irish Government in relation to the recent civil rights protest in Derry and to indicate to him that we regarded the partition of our country as its root cause'.[131] The initiative was a predictable failure, with Lynch, by his own admission, receiving 'no positive comment' from Wilson on partition.[132] Indeed, Wilson advised Lynch to desist from 'banging the drum'.[133] Going into the meeting the Government had hoped to persuade Wilson to use Westminster's financial leverage to push O'Neill in the direction of reform.[134] The Prime Minister, however, fell back on the long-established tradition of maintaining that the matters raised by the Taoiseach fell within Stormont's jurisdiction.[135]

Lynch realised that the policies of functional cooperation and pressurising the British Government were mutually exclusive; the success of *rapprochement* with Stormont had depended, and continued to depend, on confining discussion to economic and social matters to the exclusion of the constitutional issue. Unionists had to be convinced that there was no hidden agenda in pursuing a policy of neighbourly cooperation. It was not surprising, therefore, that Lynch's actions precipitated a return to the megaphone diplomacy of the pre-Lemass era.[136] On 30 April O'Neill resigned and was replaced by his cousin, Major James Chichester Clark, who, offering O'Neillism without O'Neill, had seen off Brian Faulkner's challenge by a single vote.

While O'Neill had broken with his predecessors by publicly dedicating himself to improving relations between the two communities in Northern Ireland his motivations were 'pragmatic rather than liberal' and merely represented 'a rhetorical alternative to sectarianism'.[137] Indeed, it was the loyalist reaction to his rhetoric that allowed O'Neill to present himself as a progressive force when in fact 'no actual strategy of reforming sectarian relations existed'.[138] Unionism had institutionalised political inequality through a myriad of exclusionary practices which O'Neill could not have removed even if – and there is little to suggest it – he was sincerely intent on dismantling the discriminatory edifice. The politics of domination could only survive in the absence of large-scale mobilisation of the marginalised nationalist minority.

During his last year in office, O'Neill had come under relentless attack from civil rights activists and the right wing of his own party. The demands of these two groups – equality versus supremacy – were mutually exclusive and O'Neill ultimately found himself unable to satisfy the claims of either section. Ultimately, O'Neill's reluctance to antagonise his own supporters exposed the limitations and contradictions of his policies and mobilised an active and radicalised Catholic intelligentsia determined to achieve real change. This in turn increasingly undermined his position within Ulster Unionism as hardliners pushed for ever more repressive measures producing a cycle of events that diminished O'Neill's standing in both communities.

O'Neill's departure provided further evidence that the policy of functional cooperation in place since 1965 had come unstuck and the Irish Government feared it also signified a victory for those within unionism opposed to reform.[139] As late as April 1969, Frank Aiken had confidently told the British ambassador that O'Neill's policies to end discrimination had 95 per cent of 'the Northern people' behind him and that he had already succeeded in defeating and isolating the 'Orange extremists'.[140] By May, Lynch had placed the focus back on reform within Northern Ireland and away from partition, although he emphasised that 'my concentration at this juncture on fundamental political and social rights in no way derogates from the right of the Irish people as a whole to the unity of Ireland'.[141]

The confused signals emanating from Dublin continued when Aiken emphasised to the British ambassador in January 1969 that he was 'not suggesting that Stormont should be coerced militarily or financially by Britain but that the British should point out to O'Neill that they carried the responsibility for the Northern denial of democratic and human rights, and that under the 1920 Act they bore the ultimate responsibility for guaranteeing non-discrimination in the Six Counties'.[142] This negated the emphasis Lynch had placed on partition when he had met Wilson in London two months earlier, but then the Taoiseach had on that occasion also contradicted previous statements of his own.

The republican (or interventionist) faction within the Government led by Kevin Boland and Neil Blaney scored two important, if ultimately Pyrrhic, victories during the day-long emergency cabinet session, convened in response to the Derry riots of 19–20 April 1969. The first was a decision that Lynch would immediately seek another meeting with his British counterpart, Harold Wilson. The previous dispatch of the Taoiseach to London in October, also at Boland and Blaney's goading, had jeopardised, if not fatally weakened, the functional cooperation policy at the heart of the Lemassian approach to Northern Ireland which Lynch had followed, but not deepened or expanded.

The second cabinet decision that day was to send a clearly reluctant Frank Aiken to meet with UN Secretary-General, U Thant, in New York to 'advise him of the situation'.[143] The UN initiative was unprecedented, being a clear break from established government policy, and the Minister for External Affairs expressed serious reservations during the cabinet deliberations.[144] However, considering the options open to the Government at the United Nations, the initiative was of a very limited nature. Moreover, the cabinet decided to raise Northern Ireland with the weakest UN institution, the Secretary-General, rather than the more powerful General Assembly or the Security Council.

In the course of the meeting on 23 April 1969, Aiken provided the UN Secretary-General with a brief background of the origins of partition before outlining the Government's aim of a united Ireland in which Stormont would retain its powers. Recalling the policy of all parties in the Dáil to resolve the problem peacefully despite periodic difficulties with those who favoured the use of force, Aiken summarised the positive changes that had occurred following Captain O'Neill's selection as Prime Minister. According to the report of the meeting prepared by Ireland's UN representative, Con Cremin, Aiken 'described Captain O'Neill's departure from the 19th century narrow outlook',[145] citing as an example his response to the death of Pope John XXIII, before outlining unionist opposition to 'O'Neill's liberalising policies' and the grievances of the nationalist minority in the realm of civil rights. Aiken's account of events made clear that the Government had not quite managed to separate the gloss of O'Neill's liberalising rhetoric from his unwillingness to address pervasive state-sponsored anti-Catholic discrimination. He did, however, remain faithful to one aspect of the Blaney–Boland line, by putting the onus of responsibility on the British Government. Aiken told U Thant that by virtue of the Government of Ireland Act of 1920, and Britain's financial support for the Stormont regime, which he estimated to be half of public expenditure, responsibility for the status quo lay with Westminster.[146] The Tánaiste said that at recent government meetings there had been interest in having a UN observer or special representative of the Secretary-General and there was also the possibility that the Irish peacekeeping contingent might have to be withdrawn from Cyprus 'should developments necessitate close surveillance along the border'.[147]

If Cremin's report is to be credited, U Thant said little throughout the meeting. Though he thanked Aiken for such a detailed briefing and had shown 'great interest in the Tánaiste's exposé', the Secretary-General was non-committal, simply describing the matter as 'important but delicate'. U Thant said he would reflect on what he had been told and be in touch with Cremin. In the meantime it was agreed that no details of the meeting would be conveyed at the subsequent press conference and that, if pressed, the Tánaiste should simply say (accurately) that he had made no request of the Secretary-General. In his public statements Aiken also did little to disguise the purely cosmetic nature of the exercise, making clear that neither the decision to meet Wilson nor the Secretary-General had come from the Taoiseach but rather had been at the behest of the cabinet.[148]

The dual strategy of confronting Britain with its responsibility for partition and raising the issue at international fora neatly conformed to the preferences of the Blaney–Boland wing of the cabinet, given its potential to mobilise world opinion against the British Government. This strategy was, however, totally incompatible with functional cooperation and would also make a meeting with Wilson less likely to yield results. Neither the Taoiseach nor the Minister for External Affairs believed that a meeting with U Thant would make a difference

within Northern Ireland; rather they hoped that the exercise would silence
critics who believed that the Government was insufficiently responsive to the
deteriorating situation in the North. The UN initiative was not well received
in London. The Government had known it risked alienating Wilson who, despite
many imperfections, was preferable to his only alternative, Tory party leader,
Edward (Ted) Heath. The Conservative and Unionist Party, as it was officially
called, was considered less sympathetic to Dublin's position and, indeed, the
Ulster Unionist Party took the Tory party whip at Westminster. Two weeks
after Aiken's meeting with U Thant, Heath sought out cabinet minister Erskine
Childers at a gathering in London and in a 'somewhat hectoring tone' pointed
out that the Tory party which, in Heath's words, 'would be the next government',
was extremely anxious about 'Eire's' interference into the affairs of the United
Kingdom. Northern Ireland was, according to Heath, as British as Yorkshire
and bringing the subject to the UN was 'the very last thing the Irish Government
should have done'. The Tory leader went so far as to threaten to review the
terms of the Anglo-Irish Free Trade Area Agreement, which, according to the
Fianna Fáil Minister, 'amounted to a threat of economic sanctions unless "Eire"
ceased to intervene'.[149] Childers's reminder that Ireland had never formally
raised partition at the UN did little to mollify Heath.

When Fianna Fáil returned to office in June 1969 it would be the last election
for three decades in which the Troubles in Northern Ireland would not be part
of the political backdrop. Lynch received his first electoral mandate, but his
confidence had already been dented. Party veteran Frank Aiken, the IRA Chief
of Staff that in 1923 ordered republicans to dump arms and who had served in
every de Valera Government since 1932, stepped down from the Foreign Affairs
portfolio and was replaced by forty-six-year-old Patrick Hillery, a popular figure
within the party closely identified with Jack Lynch and considered a likely
successor. When the North erupted on 12–13 August 1969, Hillery would be
enjoying a painting holiday on Achill Island. The days of quiet summer holidays
for Irish cabinets were now well and truly over.

Notes

1   'I repeat again in this House that I joined this Government, that I accepted the
     position of trust that was given to me—that was imposed on me'. Dáil Debates,
     114/819 (2 March 1949).
2   See Chubb, The Government and Politics of Ireland, p. 194.
3   Dáil Debates, 112/1520 (23 July 1948).
4   Bowman, De Valera, p. 273.

5   Foster, *Modern Ireland*, p. 567. In his memoirs, Brian Faulkner described the move
     as 'an action which drove even further wedges between Irishmen, North and South'.
     Faulkner, *Memoirs of a Statesman*, p. 17.

6   Quoted in McCullagh, *John A. Costello*, p. 197.

7   Section 1 (2).

8   *Dáil Debates*, 115/807 (10 May 1949).

9   *Irish Press*, 14 May 1949.

10   Moynihan, *Speeches and Statements*, p. 522.

11   See for example Mannix, *The Belligerent Prelate*, p. 8.

12   Lee and Ó Tuathaigh, *Age of De Valera*, p. 109.

13   [Secret] Memorandum composed by Ambassador F.H. Boland, 7 December 1951.
     NAI DFA P203.

14   Con Cremin, 'Expansion of provisional resume of 25 April' (20 May 1969). NAI
     DFA P203.

15   Quoted in Keane, *An Irish Statesman and Revolutionary*, p. 121.

16   Quoted in Fanning, 'The United States and Irish participation in NATO',
     p. 38.

17   Conversation between Maffey and de Valera, 10 November 1944. NAUK DO/35/281.

18   McNay, *Acheson and Empire*, p. 85.

19   Quoted in Kelly, 'A policy of futility', p. 9.

20   *Dáil Debates*, 126/2024 (19 July 1951).

21   *Dáil Debates*, 128/2024 (19 July 1951).

22   See also speech by Brendan Corish, *Dáil Debates*, 138/842–43 (29 April 1953).

23   [Secret and Confidential] Report on Visit to Six Counties by Mr Belton and Dr
     MacWhite, 20–23 September, 1955. NAI DFA P 273/1. Two other meetings in July
     and August 1955 also took place between Irish government officials and northern
     representatives.

24   See unsigned memos dated 1 January 1960 and 20 February 1960. DFA P 273/1.
     Eventually, in August 1960 (eight months after the suggestion), a meeting was arranged
     with three nationalist public representatives.

25   'Deputation from South Armagh Constituency Committee of the Irish Anti-Partition
     League', 19 May 1955. NAI DT S6390C.

26   'Deputation from Fermanagh-Tyrone', 9 January 1952. NAI DT S6390C.

27   See report of the first ard fheis in the *Irish Independent*, 25 November 1926 and the
     Irish Times, 26 November 1926. Report of the Honorary Secretaries (1 October
     1928) presented to the Fianna Fáil ard fheis, 25–26 October 1928. UCDA FF/702.
     See also *The Nation*, 3 November 1928 and the Report of the Honorary Secretaries,
     1929 ard fheis. UCDA FF/703.

28   See, for, example, National Executive Minutes, 8 and 22 November 1937. UCDA
     FF/342.

29   Fianna Fáil, Minutes of National Executive, 27 July 1970. Another request from the
     same cumann was turned down by the National Executive on 14 September 1970.
     UCDA P176/350.

30   O'Brien, *The United Nations*, p. 128.

31   *Dáil Debates*, 102/1323 (24 July 1946).

32   See for example Aiken's contributions to General Assembly Debates on 20 September 1957 and 6 October 1960. *Irish Press*, 21 September 1957, *Irish Press*, 7 October 1960.

33   Examples include Aiken's reference to the partition of Germany (General Assembly, 23 September 1959) and to the debate on 'Question of Algeria' (General Assembly, 15 December 1960). *Irish Press*, 24 September 1959, *Irish Press*, 15 December 1960.

34   There is extensive interdepartmental correspondence on the subject in NAI DFA 2006/44/432.

35   See Kattan, 'Self-determination during the Cold War'.

36   Meeting between James C. Heaney, Chair of the American Congress for Irish Freedom, and Frank Aiken, 2 August 1968 (letter with transcript dated 27 March 1969). NAI DFA 2006/44/432.

37   Memorandum 'Question of raising the Partition issue formally in the United Nations', 23 January 1958. NAI 2006/44/432.

38   Memorandum 'Question of raising the Partition issue formally in the United Nations', 23 January 1958. NAI 2006/44/432.

39   *Dáil Debates*, 192/841 (23 November 1961).

40   *Hibernia*, June 1968.

41   *Dáil Debates*, 240/6 (29 April 1969).

42   See Cooney, *John Charles McQuaid*, chapter 17.

43   *Dáil Debates*, 125/783 (12 April 1951).

44   *Dáil Debates*, 125/784 (12 April 1951).

45   *Dáil Debates*, 138/840 (29 April 1953). This quotation is frequently misattributed to Costello.

46   Confidential report from Ambassador F.H. Boland to the Secretary of the Department of External Affairs, 6 June 1951. NAI DFA P203.

47   See Fanning, *The Fethard-on-Sea Boycott*.

48   *Irish Times*, 18 November 2014.

49   He reiterated this when explaining his decision to repeal the External Relations Act. *Dáil Debates*, 114/817–818 (2 March 1949).

50   See Bowyer Bell, *The Secret Army*, p. 269.

51   Farrell, *Sheltering the Fugitive*, p. 42. *Irish Independent*, 1–2 January 1990.

52   *Dáil Debates*, 153/1336–50 (30 November 1955).

53   *Dáil Debates*, 153/1345 (30 November 1955).

54   *Irish Times*, 1 January 1957 and 4 January 1957.

55   *Cork Examiner*, 5 January 1957 and 7 January 1957. See also the *Limerick Leader*, 12 January 1957.

56   *Irish Times*, 4 January 1957.

57   *Cork Examiner*, 7 January 1957.

58   *Irish Press*, 29 January 1957.

59   See Aide Memoire, 'Offences Against the State activities'. NAI DT S11564G.

60   'Members sympathise with relatives of men who lost their lives', *Clonmel Nationalist*, 12 January 1957; 'Give Republicans support of Army', *Tipperary Star*, 12 January 1957. See also *Cork Examiner*, 8 January 1957; *Irish Times*, 8 January 1957.

61   *Western People*, 12 January 1957. See also *Cork Examiner*, 9 January 1957; *Irish Times*, 9 February 1957.

62   *Irish Times*, 4 March 1957.

63   Quoted in McCarthy, 'Ireland's turnaround', p. 51.

64   *Irish Press*, 20 June 1960.

65   *The Star*, 30 March 1929.

66   *Dáil Debates*, 64/720 (19 November 1936).

67   *Dáil Debates*, 64/728–9 (19 November 1936). In this case the relevant deputy, Alexander Hazlett, advocated the abandonment of the Economic War, which he felt was injurious to the interests of Free State farmers. 'Let us do away with this so-called economic dispute', he declared, 'and it will go a long way towards settling and easing the Partition problem'.

68   *Dáil Debates*, 46/192 (1 March 1933).

69   *Irish Press*, 9 November 1960.

70   Department of Finance, *Economic Development*, p. 5.

71   Whitaker, 'Economic development 1958–1985', p. 11.

72   See Callaghan, *A House Divided*, pp. 2, 4.

73   Crossman, *Diaries of a Cabinet Minister, p.* 381.

74   Rose, 'Labour, Northern Ireland', p. 97.

75   Quoted in Crawford, *Loyal to King Billy*, p. 69.

76   Bruce, *The Red Hand*, p. 21.

77   Nelson, *Ulster's Uncertain Defenders*, p. 42.

78   In 1963, the South exported £34.6m of goods by land to the North while importing £21.8m. *Northern Ireland Progress* (Journal of the Belfast and Northern Ireland Chambers of Commerce), 15/8 (August 1965), p. 6.

79   *Dáil Debates*, 176/140 (23 June 1959).

80   *Irish Times*, 30 July 1963.

81   *Dáil Debates*, 201/736 (4 April 1963).

82   *Dáil Debates*, 201/113 (2 April 1963).

83   *Irish Times*, 19 October 1963.

84   *Irish Times*, 17 January 1962.

85   *Irish Times*, 24 February 1962.

86   'Meeting with the Prime Minister of the Irish Republic' (undated memorandum), PRONI CAB/9U/5/1.

87   Communiqué, 14 January 1965, NAI DT 98/6/429.

88   See for example letter from Lemass to O'Neill dated 3 February 1965, NAI DT 98/6/429.

89   Statement by Lemass (14 January 1965), NAI DT 98/6/429. See also *Irish Times*, 15 January 1965.
90   *Irish Times*, 16 January 1965.
91   Speech by An Taoiseach, 26 January 1965. NAI DT 98/6/495.
92   *Irish Times*, 25 January 1965.
93   *Irish Times*, 25 January 1965.
94   *Irish Times*, 4 January 1982, p. 7; *Irish Times*, 1–2 January 1991.
95   *Irish Times*, 1–2 January 1990.
96   Speech delivered on 3 February 1965. O'Neill, *Ulster at the Crossroads*, p. 158.
97   O'Neill, *Ulster at the Crossroads*, p. 159.
98   Kevin Boland, interview with the author.
99   *Irish Times*, 10 February 1965.
100   *Irish Times*, 15 January 1965.
101   O'Neill, *Autobiography*, p. 73.
102   Quoted in Curran, *Derry*, pp. 37–38.
103   Brian Feeney, interview with the author. O'Connor, *In Search of a State*, pp. 231–232.
104   Curran, *Derry*, p. 37.
105   Jim Dukes quoted in O'Mahony, *Jack Lynch*, p. 75.
106   Quoted in O'Mahony, *Jack Lynch*, p. 75.
107   Lynch, 'My life and times', *Magill*, November 1979, p. 43.
108   Lee, *Ireland, 1912–1985*, p. 409.
109   *Magill*, November 1979, p. 43.
110   *Irish Times*, 5 November 1966.
111   *Magill*, November 1979, p. 43.
112   Walsh, *The Party*, p. 91.
113   *Magill*, May 1980, p. 38.
114   Chubb, *Cabinet Government*, p. 37.
115   *Irish Times*, 4 November 1966.
116   'Peter Berry diaries', *Magill*, June 1980.
117   Walsh, *The Party*, p. 91.
118   Bew et al., *The Dynamics of Irish Politics*, p. 90.
119   Speech delivered by Colley. *Irish Times*, 6 December 1968.
120   *Irish Times*, 5 November 1966.
121   Walsh, *The Party*, p. 91. Emphasis added.
122   Brady, *Arms and the Men*, pp. 29–30.
123   Quoted in Rafter, *Neil Blaney*, p. 36.
124   Sacks, *The Donegal Mafia*.
125   *Irish Times*, 4 November 1966.
126   John Healy reported that 'By five [o' clock] yesterday evening there was "a flood of votes" going to Neil Blaney and the "solid-for-Colley" bloc had melted. And Charlie? He was still smiling at least'. *Irish Times*, 4 November 1966.
127   Farrell, *Northern Ireland*, p. 242.
128   Harkness, *Northern Ireland*, p. 149.

129   *Irish Times*, 7 October 1968.

130   'Taoiseach's remarks on Derry incidents – extract from speech made at Clonmel, 8 October 1968'. NAI DFA 2000/5/12.

131   *Dáil Debates*, 236/2015 (5 November 1968). See also 'Taoiseach's remarks on Derry incidents – extract from speech made at Clonmel, 8 October 1968'. NAI DFA 2000/5/12.

132   'Transcript of press conference given by An Taoiseach at the Irish embassy, London, on Wednesday, 30 October' (30 October 1968), NAI DT 2000/6/657. See also *Irish Times*, 31 October 1968.

133   'Note of a meeting between Jack Lynch and Harold Wilson in London on 30 October 1968' (1 November 1968), NAI DT 2000/6/657.

134   'Brief for Taoiseach for his discussion with Mr Wilson on the subject of the Six Counties on Wednesday, 30 October 1968', NAI DFA 2000/5/38.

135   'Note of a meeting between Jack Lynch and Harold Wilson in London on 30 October 1968' (1 November 1968), NAI DT 2000/6/657. Wilson did, however, try to exert this kind of leverage when he met O'Neill and other ministers from the Northern Ireland Government a few days later. See 'Meeting at 10 Downing Street on 4th November, 1968', (4 November 1968) PRONI CAB/4/141.

136   *Irish Times*, 1 November 1968.

137   O'Leary and McGarry, *The Politics of Antagonism*, pp. 163–164.

138   Bew and Patterson, *The British State and the Ulster Crisis*, p. 12.

139   'Comments by Jack Lynch on the resignation of Terence O'Neill (28 April 1969)', NAI DT 2000/6/144.

140   'Notes prepared by Frank Aiken relating to a meeting with the British Ambassador to Dublin, 8 January 1969', NAI DT 2000/6/144.

141   Jack Lynch, speech at Annual Dinner of Cavan Comhairle Cheantair, Fianna Fáil, at Kingscourt, 1 May 1969, NAI DT 2000/6/657.

142   'Notes relating to a conversation between Frank Aiken and the British Ambassador to Ireland, 8 January 1969', NAI DT 2000/6/144.

143   Draft note by Frank Aiken, 21 April 1969. NAI DT 2000/9/1 G.C.12/175; 2000/6/557. See also *Irish Times*, 22 April 1969. Kevin Boland, interview with the author.

144   Kevin Boland, interview with the author. Boland attributed some of this reluctance to the influence of Conor Cruise O'Brien, who had been a significant figure in the Department of External Affairs during Aiken's tenure as minister.

145   Meeting between Tánaiste and UN Secretary-General on 23 April 1969. Provisional Resume prepared by Con Cremin, dated 25 April 1969 and Con Cremin, 'Expansion of provisional resume of 25 April' (20 May 1969). NAI DT 2000/6/657.

146   Meeting between Tánaiste and UN Secretary-General on 23 April 1969. Provisional Resume prepared by Con Cremin, dated 25 April 1969 and Con Cremin, 'Expansion of provisional resume of 25 April' (20 May 1969). NAI DT 2000/6/657.

147   Meeting between Tánaiste and UN Secretary-General on 23 April 1969. Provisional
      Resume prepared by Con Cremin, dated 25 April 1969 and Con Cremin, 'Expansion
      of provisional resume of 25 April' (20 May 1969). NAI DT 2000/6/657.
148   Press conference given by Tánaiste, Frank Aiken, New York, 23 April 1969 (24
      April 1969). *Dáil Debates*, 240/7–8 (29 April 1969).
149   Notes of a meeting between Erskine Childers and Edward Heath in London on 5
      May 1969, NAI DT 2000/6/657.

4

War, 1969–1974

The Government was caught off-guard when Northern Ireland finally imploded in August 1969, and it faced a calamity that could potentially overwhelm the state. Previous experience suggested that crises in Northern Ireland were of relatively short intensity; few realised that the region was only at the beginning of a conflict that would endure for decades. Almost 1,600 would be killed during the peak of the 'Troubles' between 1972 and 1976, including 400 members of the British military forces and 235 paramilitaries (mainly IRA). To put this in perspective, the death toll would be the equivalent of about 60,000 people being killed in Britain during the same period as a result of political upheaval. Civilians constituted a majority of the death toll, with 60 per cent of these being Catholic, despite making up just one-third of the population. In the absence of uniformed opponents, loyalist paramilitaries usually settled for random Catholics. Moreover, as the focus of the British military campaign was in nationalist areas, Catholics also bore the brunt of its excesses.

The conflict in Derry triggered the reintroduction of British troops on the streets of Northern Ireland. Aided by state security forces (the RUC and B-Specials), unionist civilians attacked nationalist neighbourhoods, leading to defensive barricades being thrown up during what became known as the Battle of the Bogside. The Irish Government's profound interest in the conflagration was counterbalanced by its apparent inability to influence the course of events. During a meeting two weeks before the Battle of the Bogside, the British had made it clear to Patrick Hillery that 'responsibility for this area rests with the Stormont and London governments and not with your government' and there was 'a limit to the extent to which we can discuss with outsiders—even our nearest neighbours, this internal matter'.[1]

But just as the British were instructing Dublin to back off, the Government was besieged with requests to support the northern nationalist community. The cabinet meeting of 13 August exposed deep divisions on how best to respond. Kevin Boland, Neil Blaney and Charles Haughey advocated some kind of military action. This might take the form of a limited intervention by the Irish Army into Northern Ireland or requesting the dispatch of a UN peacekeeping force. According to Blaney's advisor, 'the entry of a mere company of soldiers ... would have brought Britain to the conference table for the first time in half a century on the basic question of the partition of Ireland'.[2] For Boland, who fretted that the party had lost its mission, this was 'the moment of truth for [Fianna Fáil], the time for the solution to the final problem'.[3] Neil Blaney, emotionally invested given his family history and border home, argued that 'we had the same right to protect any citizen of the Six Counties as we would have had if it had happened in Cork', deliberately referring to the Taoiseach's home county.[4] Lynch, supported by Childers and Colley, maintained that an Irish Army incursion into Northern Ireland would expose beleaguered nationalists in Belfast to pogroms.[5]

The prepared statement Lynch had brought to the meeting – largely composed by the Department of External Affairs Secretary, Hugh McCann, and dismissed by Boland as 'civil service gobbledegook' – was dissected and amended beyond recognition.[6] Haughey, who had emerged as an unexpected ally of Blaney and Boland, was entrusted with rewriting the document, which was subjected to further discussion and amendment before being unanimously approved.[7] When Lynch arrived at the RTÉ studios, the Deputy Head of News, Des Fisher, looked at Lynch's almost indecipherable notes and insisted they be typed up and made legible before the Taoiseach went on air.[8] Such was the Taoiseach's condition that Fisher brought him whiskey to 'steady his nerves'. Lynch took the unusual step of asking Fisher what he thought he should do and, in particular, whether he should send the Irish Army into Northern Ireland as some of his advisors counselled. When Fisher answered that he thought they would get about twenty miles into Down or Derry before being massacred by the British, Lynch confirmed that he had reached the same conclusion.

While stating that 'the reunification of the national territory can provide the only permanent solution to the problem', Lynch told the nation that

> It is evident also that the Stormont Government is no longer in control of the situation. Indeed the present situation is the inevitable outcome of the policies pursued for decades by successive Stormont Governments. It is clear also, that the Irish Government can no longer stand by and see innocent people injured and perhaps worse.[9]

The phrase 'can no longer stand by' led many to believe that the Government had a plan of action but the speech was essentially a holding operation. Some interpreted the broadcast as meaning the Government was actively considering military intervention if matters did not improve. Unsure of Lynch's intentions the British Government advised Home Secretary Jim Callaghan to return from holidays.[10] In terms of action, Lynch could do little, however. The British simply ignored his requests to apply to the UN for the dispatch of a peacekeeping force and to enter into early negotiations to review Northern Ireland's 'present constitutional position'. His announcement that the Irish Army would establish field hospitals adjacent to Derry and at other points along the border reinforced the perception that military intervention was a possibility. According to Blaney, the term 'field hospital' was used merely as a sop to international opinion and to avoid raising the political temperature:

> It was the view of myself and others that we had to send our troops to protect the people and it was agreed to send the army to the border, under the cover of field hospitals. But as it turned out, the deviousness of certain minds thereafter utilised the 'good cover' as just that. But the field hospitals idea we went along with: I didn't give a goddam how they went up as long as the army went up and were there to go in. And that is what was on the minds of, I'd say, the majority of the cabinet that day.[11]

Lynch's speech, according to one of Haughey's biographers, had been 'calculated to offer the illusion that the Fianna Fáil government was doing all it could to defend Northern Ireland Catholics',[12] but it also raised expectations. The front page of the *Evening Press* on 14 August maintained that

> The people are hopeful that aid in some form will arrive from somewhere. Their eyes are turned chiefly to the Border only five miles away where they have heard Irish troops are building up. The news spread through the Bogside this morning like wildfire. It is one of the things that keeps men at the barricades, gives them the courage and strength to hurl stones and bombs at the police and the bravado to stand while tear gas bombs are bursting all around them. But, why don't they come? Why didn't they come last night?

Talk of a role for the Irish Army in Northern Ireland had to be tempered by the fact that the Government had neglected the defence forces during the previous twenty-five years. Equipment was in poor condition and old. Not only was the army's full-time strength a mere 8,000 men but a 400-member unit was in Cyprus on peacekeeping duty. About two-thirds of the 30,000-strong An Fórsa Cosanta Áitiúil (FCÁ), a second-line reserve of indifferent quality, could have been mobilised in an emergency.

Cognisant of these deficiencies, those in government that favoured military intervention never envisaged armed combat with the British Army but rather contemplated either the seizure of a symbolic piece of unpopulated territory ('even a football field', according to one ministerial emissary[13]) or to send the troops in to take up position in the west bank of the Foyle in Derry, where they could easily defend their position behind the barricades. Such actions would, it was hoped, internationalise the crisis and attract UN intervention at a time when the British Government was presenting the conflict as a purely internal affair. Thus the argument for an invasion at this early stage was a political rather than a military one in that Dublin's right to negotiate an exit from the crisis would have to be acknowledged. As Boland recalled, 'our opponents in the Cabinet kept on talking irrelevant nonsense about the inadequacy of our Army as opposed to the British Army. We would be wiped out in the first few hours, we were told ... [however] no one contemplated war with the British Army.'[14] There were also fears for the fate of nationalists in areas the Irish Army was unlikely to reach. As veteran minister Seán McEntee wrote to Kevin Boland, these people were 'hostages for our good behaviour'.[15]

As the lines of communication between Dublin and London were effectively closed, the Government postponed a decision on what to do next in order to dispatch the Foreign Minister, Patrick Hillery, for an unannounced meeting with his British counterpart. The mission simply confirmed the British Government's reluctance to discuss the matter. As Hillery recalled, Lord Chalfont and Lord Stoneham (junior ministers in the Foreign and Commonwealth Office and Home Office respectively) claimed that 'it wasn't any of our business'. Throughout the meeting the British looked for a guarantee that Irish soldiers would not cross into Northern Ireland, but Hillery refused to give one, saying, 'I did not come here to give assurances but to seek them.' Chief amongst these was protection of the six-county minority from the RUC ('at best, not an impartial force') and the B-Specials (a 'partisan, armed mob, such as is found only in dictatorships'). While Hillery declared that 'Northern Ireland is part of Ireland' and that 'our people do not accept that it is part of the United Kingdom',[16] he left London empty-handed with his proposal of a meeting with Harold Wilson rejected. The introduction of British soldiers on the streets of Derry on 14 August and Belfast a day later brought a new dimension to the problem, not least because Lynch had claimed in his television address that their deployment would be 'unacceptable' and not conducive to restoring peace, 'certainly not in the long term'.[17]

There were further desperate requests for assistance as fears increased that a bloodbath was at hand in which the northern minority would be the primary victims. A delegation of three Stormont MPs[18] that visited government buildings late on the night of 16 August begged for Irish army intervention and, failing that, weapons. Aware of the potential diplomatic implications of their request, they claimed that 'nothing need be done openly or politically – a few hundred rifles could easily be "lost" and would not be missed'.[19] Shortly afterwards, a first-hand account from a government operative within Northern Ireland reported that

> The feeling inside the barricades with those with whom I spoke … is that they are awaiting help from the South. By this I mean military help. They can see no going back to what was before. [As in] Derry the Taoiseach's address on radio and television had a tremendous effect here [Belfast]. I did find some of the clergy who are against any intervention from the South and who accused the Government in Dublin of 'playing politics', but the bulk of the people inside the barricades who are running the refugee centres and are manning barricades are completely committed to an end of the Stormont regime and return to jurisdiction of an Irish Government.[20]

On 16 August the cabinet decided that a sum of money, the amount and distribution of which would be determined by Haughey, would be made available 'for the victims of the current unrest in the Six Counties'.[21] This was the money that would be used for the procurement of arms, leading ultimately to the Arms Crisis of May 1970. Boland argued that any UN initiative would necessitate the Government demonstrating its willingness and ability to take effective action. Consequently, he demanded that the Irish peacekeeping unit in Cyprus be immediately withdrawn and the first-line reserve, composed of former members of the regular army, be called up. Boland announced his resignation from the cabinet when this was not acceded to and only President de Valera's intervention convinced him to reverse his decision and not go public with his misgivings.[22] After the cabinet meeting Hillery flew to New York and addressed the UN Security Council, where he aired Irish grievances but achieved little else.[23]

While London complained that the Taoiseach 'as usual conducts his political campaign not by diplomacy but by public statements',[24] it overlooked that, in ruling out direct talks with Dublin, it had left the Government with little choice. The British were also aware that while for public consumption Lynch needed to project an image of a Government actively working for a united Ireland, this was very much a long-term objective. In one particularly illuminating communication, the British ambassador to Ireland and former intelligence officer, Andrew Gilchrist, tried to piece together the Government's policy towards Northern Ireland from Lynch's frank off-the-record exchanges. Gilchrist reported that the belief in the inevitability of a united Ireland was unquestioned in Dublin but when he asked Lynch directly what he would do were Northern Ireland immediately handed to him 'on a plate', the Taoiseach replied, 'I would faint'.[25] Dublin could not afford to match London's annual subvention to Northern Ireland and despite pointed criticisms, which Gilchrist attributed to pressure from 'the youth' and members of his cabinet, Lynch believed Anglo-Irish relations to be 'excellent'. The Taoiseach's preference for a federal solution stemmed it seemed from a desire – similar to that which motivated the British – not to exert direct control over Ulster's problematic affairs for, as Lynch confided, 'we don't want the problem of Paisley'.[26]

Plans for Irish army intervention in Northern Ireland

During August 1969 the Government decided to bring the military to a state of maximum preparedness and, to this end, army reserves were to be called up, an extensive recruitment campaign launched and a rearmament process undertaken. Although the initial explosion of violence in the North had subsided, the situation remained very tense, and the emphasis shifted from an invasion of Northern Ireland (though this remained an option) to obtaining weapons for six-county nationalists. In line with this policy, the army moved five hundred rifles from Cathal Brugha Barracks in Dublin to a warehouse in Dundalk on 2 April 1970 during widespread rioting in the Ballymurphy district of Belfast. Minister for Defence Jim Gibbons was entirely at a loss at the subsequent arms trial to explain why these arms were moved to Dundalk if they were not being prepared for distribution amongst Northern civilians. Moreover, at Fort Dunree in Donegal, the army briefly trained Derry republicans in the use of weapons. To fulfil their potential missions, the military sought large quantities of ammunition for offensive armaments sufficient for prolonged combat as well as anti-tank and anti-aircraft weapons, along with high-powered machine guns. Proposals for secret war games were devised 'to study, plan for and rehearse in detail the intervention of the Defence Forces in Northern Ireland in order to secure the safety of the minority population'.[27] The army's Quartermaster-General informed Minister Gibbons of the need to diversify sources of weaponry and to build stockpiles, as in the event of hostilities normal channels of supply (mainly from Britain) would be disrupted.[28]

By 27 September, the army had produced an interim report based on government directives outlining four different scenarios in which Northern nationalists might be threatened and how best they could be assisted. These envisaged the army undertaking a wide range of unconventional diversionary operations in different parts of Northern Ireland to 'draw forces off the area of direct conflict', and supplying arms, ammunition, equipment and medicine to the northern minority. While armed confrontation with the British military was foreseen in a situation whereby the Catholic population found itself in conflict with British forces, the emphasis throughout was on guerrilla warfare rather than conventional set-pieces.[29] Other scenarios contemplated the infiltration of 'elements armed and equipped to [organise], train and advise Catholic and nationalist groups' in vulnerable areas, such as Belfast, with troops being sent across the border to keep routes open for refugees fleeing south. In view of their proximity to the border and political significance, Derry, Strabane, Enniskillen and Newry were considered the most suitable targets for military operations, but given the modern surveillance equipment at the British Army's disposal 'guerrilla operations in Northern Ireland would be difficult to conduct over a protracted period'. The report also noted that as most of the North's vital installations, such as the international airport, television studios and docks were in the greater Belfast area, military operations against these would preferably be of the unconventional type.[30] Later, on 6 February 1970, the Government issued a directive to the army instructing it 'to (1) prepare to train the forces for incursions into Northern Ireland (2) make weapons and ammunition available and (3) make gas masks available'.[31] Accordingly, truckloads of these items were put at readiness to be available in a matter of hours.

The IRA's inability to protect nationalist enclaves in Belfast combined with long-simmering ideological differences led to a split within the republican movement, into 'provisional' and 'official' IRA (and Sinn Féin) factions within months of the conflagration. In general terms, the Provisional IRA attracted a more militant and less Marxist membership than its 'official' counterpart. Moreover, the Official IRA favoured contesting elections and taking seats in the Dublin, London and Belfast legislatures, which the Provisionals strongly opposed. The split made it easier for Irish-Americans and government ministers that favoured arming northern nationalists but had been alienated by the Official IRA's Marxist rhetoric. Neil Blaney later said that had the weapons been transported to Belfast in April 1970 'they'd have gone into Ballymurphy and to whoever was capable of handling, using and directing their organisation'. By this he meant that they would 'very probably' have gone to the newly formed Provisionals, and there was 'no way' that they were going to be distributed to the Officials.[32]

Arms Crisis

During the spring of 1970, Irish army captain James Kelly and John Kelly of the Belfast IRA and Citizens Defence Committee made several trips to the Continent to negotiate an arms deal with the knowledge and approval of the Minister for Defence, Jim Gibbons, and the Director of Military Intelligence, Col. Michael Hefferon.[33] Albert Luykx, introduced to them by Neil Blaney, accompanied the Kellys, and Charles Haughey, from whose Department of Finance budget the arms would be paid, had arranged the necessary customs clearance. The plans were by necessity top secret and neither the Department of Justice nor the Gardaí was informed. After learning of the arms importation, the Secretary of the Department of Justice, Peter Berry, approached Jack Lynch at the end of April and expected prompt action, only to be told by the Taoiseach that the matter was closed.

All changed when during the night of 5 May, Liam Cosgrave approached the Taoiseach and told him that he had information suggesting that Captain Kelly, Colonel Hefferon and Ministers Gibbons, Haughey and Blaney were involved in a plot to bring in $80,000-worth of arms destined for Northern Ireland.[34] The information came in the form of an anonymous message simply signed 'A Garda', though the source is more likely to have been British intelligence. Lynch's hand was forced and he had to devise a strategy. One option, consistent with the facts, would have been to summon Gibbons to confirm that the operation was official and designed to provide nationalists with the means of defence should the situation in the North deteriorate further. Instead he chose to take the line, which would be trenchantly defended in the coming months and years, that the arms importation had no authority and, consequently, a government purge was necessary. Lynch sacked Blaney and Haughey, while Kevin Boland resigned in protest.[35] Mícheál Ó Móráin, known for his anti-Lynch views, had been forced to resign two days earlier, ostensibly on health grounds. With these four men, constituting more than a quarter of the Government, replaced by Lynch loyalists, the Taoiseach emerged from the crisis immeasurably stronger.

The subsequent arms trial, a remarkable spectacle convened to adjudicate whether government ministers, an Irish army officer and the IRA had together conspired to illegally import arms, exonerated the defendants of any wrongdoing in October 1970. In essence, the court determined that an arms importation had been attempted but had not been illegal given the Government's involvement.[36] Blaney, Boland and Haughey all called on Lynch to resign but any putative challenge wilted in the face of Fianna Fáil's legendary discipline aided by some targeted arm-twisting.[37] Liberated from his militant cabinet colleagues, Lynch adopted a remarkably conciliatory tone towards the British and Stormont administrations. Addressing the twenty-fifth commemorative session of the UN General Assembly on 22 October, the Taoiseach said he did not 'question the honesty of purpose of the [Northern Ireland] Prime Minister, nor of his predecessor'.[38] As before, the essential divergence within the governing party centred on those who pinned responsibility for the Northern crisis on Britain and those who advocated a *rapprochement* with Stormont.

A general election on 18 June 1970 produced a new British Government headed by Edward Heath. With a slim majority of only twenty-two, the new Conservative administration, already inclined towards a military solution to the problem, was vulnerable to pressure from the eight Ulster Unionist Party Westminster MPs. Initially, many nationalist residents had welcomed the British Army as they had expelled the RUC and B-Specials from their neighbourhoods. However, the primary function of British troops was to support the exclusively unionist civil administration, a reality starkly illustrated when, on 3 July, Lieutenant-General Ian Freeland declared a curfew on the entire Falls Road area in Belfast. During thirty-six hours of mayhem the British Army killed five people and injured dozens more before giving two unionist MPs a tour of the subjugated area in a tank. Sixteen hundred canisters of CS gas had been fired into the densely populated streets, a situation exacerbated by brutal house-to-house searches. The curfew proved to be a seminal blunder. By treating the citizenry of the entire Falls area of Belfast as an enemy population, the British Army pushed much of that community into supporting the emerging Provisional IRA.

The SDLP

On 21 August 1970, an important new actor was introduced to the Northern political stage with the establishment of the Social Democratic and Labour Party (SDLP). It brought together a disparate collection of rural nationalists, urban socialists and veterans of the civil rights campaigns. The SDLP also halted the fragmentation of the Catholic vote that had followed the eclipse of the Nationalist Party and the Northern Ireland Labour Party's adoption of pro-Union policies. The haphazard formation of this unlikely coalition was, to some extent, dictated by the squeezing of the moderate Catholic position from two radically different sources. Increasing nationalist alienation had resulted in a surge of support for armed republicanism. At the same time the policies of the newly formed bi-confessional Alliance Party had enticed some Catholics who sought progress through participation and reform within Northern Ireland.

The SDLP was the natural outcome of the gradual embourgeoisement of a section of the Catholic community. With the emergence of an articulate well-educated Catholic middle class that demanded a higher level of political participation came the need for a professional party organisation capable of achieving this goal. In contrast to its predecessors, the SDLP produced numerous policy documents on a wide range of socio-economic issues and it was rather naively hoped, initially at least, that the party would attract a considerable number of

Protestant voters disenchanted with the sterility of Northern politics. However, while Garret FitzGerald welcomed the movement as a belated trend towards a more left/right orientation in politics, the SDLP became *de facto* a nationalist organisation with the bond between party representatives being 'less ideological than that all their constituencies [had] Catholic majorities'.[39] Most unionists considered the SDLP as merely an old wolf dressed in new sheep's clothing, an officially pluralist but essentially republican party.

Reformist in outlook, the SDLP did not, initially, seek Stormont's abolition. It adopted a gradualist and consensual approach to the concept of a united Ireland which, it recognised, could only be a long-term objective, irrespective of its own preferences. At its first press conference, the SDLP announced its aim to 'promote cooperation, friendship and understanding between North and South with a view to the eventual reunification of Ireland through the consent of a majority of the people in the North and in the South'.[40] It was not the dedication to a united Ireland that was remarkable but, rather, the argument that a majority in the North would be necessary to establish and legitimise a unitary state. The party's acceptance that a majority in the island as a whole did not in itself create the conditions necessary to sustain a united Ireland represented a crucial break with the traditional orthodoxies of earlier northern nationalist parties.

The emergence of a moderate representative nationalist party in the North held obvious attractions for the Irish Government. Communications with nationalist opinion would become more effective with a well-organised, disciplined party rather than the previous necessity of consulting with a vast array of individual personalities. Despite the fact that the SDLP was an untried electoral force, and would remain so until the 1973 local elections (when it gained only 13 per cent of the vote), the Irish Government established immediate and intimate bonds with the party. Not surprisingly, the Republic proved to be the SDLP's most lucrative source of finance.[41] Indeed, the SDLP achieved a degree of parity with other parties in the Republic by being permitted to hold annual Church-gate collections to raise funds, unnerving some who remembered the divisive 'Chapel-gate election' of 1949.[42]

As the prospects for reform within Stormont became increasingly remote, the SDLP's dependence on the Irish Government increased and they became natural allies, finally dispelling unionist doubts, if any had existed, of Dublin's gravitational pull on the SDLP. The Irish Government needed the SDLP but the SDLP also depended on Dublin; both sought a moderate interim solution through constitutional means and both needed the other to lend credibility to their policies.

Internment and direct rule

On 9 August 1971, the Northern Ireland Government, having received the necessary approval and resources from London, reintroduced internment to Northern Ireland. It was supposed to be a short-term expedient – 'strictly temporary', in Heath's words – delivering a sharp decisive blow against 'the terrorists'.[43] As it turned out, internment would formally be in place for four years and more than any other policy decision transformed the Troubles from a low-intensity conflict to all-out war. The numbers speak for themselves; sixteen people had died in 1969 as a result of politically inspired violence and twenty-six in 1970. Before the introduction of internment thirty-four people had been killed in 1971, spiking to 174 fatalities by the end of the year. In 1972, almost five hundred people would lose their lives as a result of the Troubles.

Although the Irish Government consistently opposed imprisonment without trial in the North, it had unwittingly given some legitimacy to the idea the previous December when the Taoiseach notified the Council of Europe of Ireland's intention to derogate from the European Convention on Human Rights with a view to introducing internment in the Republic should a threat to national security persist.[44] By openly embracing internment as a possible strategy, Lynch played into the hands of those in Stormont who favoured employing arbitrary arrest and imprisonment to meet a more imminent threat. In March 1971, Brian Faulkner had replaced Major Chichester Clark as Northern Ireland's Prime Minister, signalling a further drift to the militant right within the governing UUP. Faulkner would earn the dubious distinction of being Northern Ireland's last and shortest-reigning Prime Minister.

On the night internment was introduced, as British soldiers descended on hundreds of homes throughout Northern Ireland, Lynch received a letter from Heath. The Taoiseach is recorded as having read the letter on 9 August and, as the first doors were kicked in at three in the morning, there was very little time, if any, between this notification of impending internment and its implementation. In what seemed an effort to pre-empt criticism, Heath said he was already 'well aware' of the implications and dangers internment would pose for the Irish Government, though he immediately added that its chances of success would increase were Lynch to follow suit and introduce a parallel policy of detention without trial. The Prime Minister noted, however, that the British ambassador's report of his recent talk with the Taoiseach had held out no possibility of this. Heath said that he had made clear to the Northern Ireland Government that 'the measures taken should not discriminate between the different sections of the community', though he added the caveat 'except as the facts of the situation makes inevitable'.[45] This proved to be an idle assurance given that of the more than five hundred people on the initial swoop list, all were drawn from the Catholic nationalist community, with the first loyalist being interned only in 1973.

Heath then came to the real purpose of his letter, which was less to inform than to seek Lynch's cooperation. He hoped the Taoiseach could respond to the measures 'with understanding' and then tried to explain what he had in mind. 'There will be many who will call for violent action in response to these measures: a reminder from you that violence serves no purpose, and that internment is aimed at particular individuals who are avowedly working for a breakdown of law and order, would be invaluable.' Heath saw no contradiction in introducing such a violent measure aimed exclusively at the nationalist community with a suggestion that Lynch should make a supportive statement eschewing the use of force. The Prime Minister also hoped that 'whatever you might feel *obliged* to say in public, you will in practice be able to keep up the pressure of harassment of the IRA south of the border'. Heath then proceeded to dangle the carrot of potential (though ill-defined) reform once the current unpleasant medicine had been administered, and concluded with a series of honeyed words. 'Above all', Heath hoped that these measures would not spoil 'the good relationship which you and I have established and the close relations between our two countries' before referring to their shared intent of joining the EEC.[46]

The letter encapsulated many strands of Anglo-Irish affairs on the eve of internment. The asymmetrical character of the relationship was compounded by Heath's tactic of trying to hide behind the Belfast Government, obscuring Stormont's absolute dependence on Westminster for its survival. Heath maintained that Dublin should understand and support British interests and needs while assuming that there were no measures his Conservative administration could undertake that might jeopardise this support even if, as was the case with internment, the decision was made against the express wishes and interests of the Irish Government. The decision to send Lynch advance notice of internment, even if by minutes, may have been designed to implicate the Taoiseach; if he could not deny he had been forewarned, opponents might accuse him of collaboration with a deeply unpopular policy.

The shallowness of Heath's approach was quickly exposed when Lynch did not follow the script prepared for him in Downing Street. Internment triggered an explosion of violence in the North, the most notorious massacre occurring in Ballymurphy where British soldiers killed eleven civilians. As had been the case following the outbreak of the Troubles in August 1969, thousands of refugees fled south. While Heath and Faulkner met in London from 18–19 August to review events, Lynch sought to air Dublin's position by sending a telegram to the Prime Minister, which was simultaneously released to the press. At just 172 words, the Taoiseach's statement, while measured, calm and inviting dialogue, was terse. Claiming that events since 9 August had clearly indicated the failure of current military operations as a remedy to Northern Ireland's problems, Lynch emphasised the need to identify solutions through political means based on the principle of immediate and full equality of treatment for everyone in Northern Ireland irrespective of political views or religion. Brian Faulkner was no longer referred to as 'Prime Minister of Northern Ireland', a title first conferred on Terence O'Neill, but rather the 'Head of the Stormont Administration'.[47] In the event that the 'policies of attempting military solutions' continued, the Taoiseach declared his intent to 'support the policy of passive resistance now being pursued by the non-Unionist population'. He concluded by expressing a willingness to participate in a meeting with all interested parties to find ways and means to promote progress throughout Ireland 'without prejudice to the aspiration of the great majority of the Irish people to the re-unification of Ireland'.[48]

Heath's swift response, which was also disseminated to the press, displayed undisguised fury. It began by describing the Taoiseach's telegram as 'unjustifiable in its contents, unacceptable in its attempt to interfere in the affairs of the United Kingdom and can in no way contribute to the solution of the problems of Northern Ireland'.[49] The Prime Minister claimed that Lynch 'should know' that equality of treatment for everyone in Northern Ireland irrespective of political views or religion was already being 'fully implemented'. Heath stuck to the line that the military operations implemented by the Belfast and London Governments in the North were simply to protect all the people from armed terrorists, 'many of which originate in or are supported from the Republic', and were a necessary prelude to the 'restoration of greater harmony between the communities in Northern Ireland'. The Prime Minister also dismissed Lynch's offer to participate in talks with a reiteration that he '[could not] accept that anyone outside the United Kingdom can participate in meetings designed to promote the political development of any part of the United Kingdom'.[50]

Not surprisingly perhaps, given the audience and context, Heath's message lacked any self-analysis or concession that internment, widely considered a disaster, was not working. Instead he attempted to blame the Taoiseach, maintaining that it was not the slaughter and dislocation stemming from British military excesses but rather Lynch's brief reference to supporting passive resistance that had been 'calculated to do maximum damage to the cooperation between the communities in Northern Ireland which it is our purpose, and I would hope would be your purpose, to achieve'. Indeed, Heath went so far as to publicly accuse the Taoiseach of adopting a position 'calculated not only to increase the tension in Northern Ireland but also to impair our effort to maintain good relations between the United Kingdom and the Irish Republic'.[51]

The enormity of what Heath had unleashed on Northern Ireland forced a swift reversal of approach. In September, he invited both Faulkner and Lynch to Chequers for inconclusive talks after which the Taoiseach said he would not consider another trip to London given how little had been achieved so far. Lynch's position had quickly changed from that of a spurned petitioner to one where he was now deciding whether or not to accept invitations to talks.[52] Realising that Heath had entered a political cul-de-sac, and under pressure from domestic opinion, Lynch had little to gain in following the Prime Minister's lead. Moreover, reports soon emerged that internees were being tortured by their captors, who employed 'deep interrogation' techniques refined in earlier colonial emergencies such as in Kenya. Despite intense pressure from London to desist, Dublin took a case to the European Court of Human Rights, which eventually found the British Government to have been guilty of 'inhuman and degrading treatment' of internees.[53]

Following a meeting with Faulkner on 8 October, Heath informed Lynch that the British military would be unilaterally eliminating access to eighty-four roads connecting north and south by blowing them up.[54] The intention was to have a small number of 'approved' roads traversing the Irish border, facilitating in-depth searches of vehicles and people. Expressing 'grave disappointment' with the decision, the Taoiseach claimed it merely diverted attention from 'the fundamental fact that their [Stormont's] capacity to govern fairly and honestly is itself the only cause of the breakdown of Northern society. No solution can be found to this by increasing, military pressure on the dispossessed.'[55] The Taoiseach took particular offence at the suggestion that violence in Belfast and throughout the North originated in the Republic: 'I regret that you should feel obliged, through the measures now proposed, to lend your authority and prestige to such propaganda [from Stormont] against a Government which has consistently sought to reduce tensions in the North and to urge political solutions by peaceful means.'[56]

After the introduction of internment, Lynch returned to the line expressed in his seminal TV address of 13 August 1969 that Stormont was thoroughly discredited and incapable of reform, a position he had largely abandoned following the Arms Crisis of May 1970. The Taoiseach again argued that military repression could not substitute a political solution and would enhance the position of 'men of violence' at the expense of 'men of moderation'. 'Violence in the North', he now stressed, was 'a direct product of the determination of Unionism to govern as it pleases', and measures such as blowing up the roads connecting both parts of Ireland were not alone 'directed at the wrong problem in the wrong place ... they will aggravate a deteriorating situation'.[57] Heath in turn responded that he could not wait for political progress, that military action was essential, and blamed 'the minority' for the lack of political progress given the refusal of their political representatives to engage in talks while internment continued.[58]

Internment reactivated the civil rights movement and triggered numerous large protests, which in turn put pressure on Faulkner to prove that imprisoning opponents without trial was delivering results. When, on 30 January 1972, the British Army's Parachute Regiment fatally wounded fourteen people at a civil rights march in Derry and injured dozens more, Dublin came under immense pressure to respond. In both private and public communications, Heath refused to accept any responsibility for what quickly became known as 'Bloody Sunday' but rather blamed the protesters, and the Irish Government for not doing more to combat republicans.[59] With large spontaneous demonstrations throughout Ireland – one in Dublin, described by the *Irish Times* as the largest in a generation, ended with the destruction of the British embassy[60] – Lynch feared for his own position and for the stability of the state.

The Minister for Foreign Affairs, Paddy Hillery, was dispatched on an international tour to explain the government position but never managed to address the UN General Assembly, as it was not in session, or the Security Council, which was meeting in Addis Ababa. Hillery couldn't secure a meeting even with the UN Secretary-General, Kurt Waldheim and so had to settle for meeting his deputy in New York. During his tour of European capitals the Foreign Minister was politely received but obtained no promises of support. Those states that offered encouragement, such as the Soviet Union, were the kind of allies that Dublin was not eager to cultivate.[61]

Heath suspended Stormont on 30 March 1972 and imposed direct rule on Northern Ireland. Consequently, the British Government assumed direct responsibility for managing the North's day-to-day affairs for the first time since partitioning Ireland.[62] As London had approved, and funded, all aspects of the military campaign, unionists felt they had been scapegoated for shared failures and it would take them a long time to acclimatise to this new reality.[63] Lynch believed the suspension of Stormont provided an opportunity for a fresh start. The Irish ambassador, Dónal O'Sullivan returned to London despite the fact that the issue that had triggered his withdrawal – Bloody Sunday – remained unresolved, and soon afterwards a British Government inquiry conducted by Lord Widgery exonerated the paratroopers and their political masters.

To the surprise and consternation of many in Lynch's cabinet, the British Government flew IRA leaders to London for talks with the Secretary of State for Northern Ireland and other ministers on 7 July 1972. There was no meeting of minds and the short-lived IRA truce collapsed soon afterwards with 200 separate incidents during which shootings occurred reported that weekend.[64] The British appeared not to comprehend how their actions had undermined one of the main threads of Irish government policy – no official talks or negotiations with the IRA. When the Irish ambassador met William Whitelaw, the first Secretary of State for Northern Ireland, a new office created after the imposition of direct rule, Whitelaw merely expressed his hope that his Government's meeting with the IRA had not caused Dublin any embarrassment.[65] Less than a year earlier the Labour leader and former Prime Minister, Harold Wilson, had flown to Dublin for secret talks with the IRA. On that occasion, Wilson had travelled on the pretext of conferring with the Taoiseach but this had in fact been a cover for his real objective of meeting the IRA leadership, which afterwards dismissed the initiative as a fishing expedition on Wilson's part.[66] As the *Irish Times* reported, the British establishment had by-passed the Irish Government by negotiating directly with the IRA. In the process they had not only, in effect, recognised the republican movement, but had also given the impression that the IRA 'represented Ireland'.[67]

Confirming the collapse of the talks, the British Government announced its intention 'to carry on the war with the IRA with the utmost vigour'.[68] On 30 July, it launched 'Operation Motorman' during which 22,000 British soldiers, including twenty-seven infantry and two armoured battalions, advanced on the 'no-go' areas of Derry and Belfast, which had been controlled by the IRA for three years. The breakdown of talks between the British and the IRA came as a relief to Dublin and the Irish Army arrested some of those who managed to escape over the border to Co. Donegal fleeing Operation Motorman. At this point, the Irish Government had begun to pick up positive signals from Heath, who appeared to have reappraised some of his earlier positions. During a private meeting with the Irish ambassador immediately after the Operation Motorman offensive, the Prime Minister 'talked freely about reunification, which he said must come about' and described Jack Lynch as 'a good friend'.[69] But Heath also proved unpredictable and accusatory. During their meeting in Munich on 4 September, he told Lynch of the widespread view in Britain that the IRA could have been quickly suppressed had Dublin taken more decisive action to counter it, forgetting that only two months earlier his Government had undertaken face-to-face negotiations with the republican leadership. The Prime Minister also continued to apply pressure on the Irish Government to drop its case against

Britain at the European Court of Human Rights arising from the torture of internees in British custody.[70]

As the North had been engulfed in widespread violence following the imposition of internment, Fianna Fáil's Minister for Communications, Gerry Collins had invoked, on 8 October 1971, Section 31 of the 1960 Broadcasting Act. This prevented the transmission on radio or television of 'any matter that could be calculated to promote the aims and activities of any organisation which engages in, promotes, encourages or advocates the attaining of any political objective by violent means', a directive so broad and ambiguous as to potentially prohibit, for example, US or British government representatives from defending their actions in Vietnam and Northern Ireland respectively. It soon became clear, however, that the directive's sole intention was to prevent the reporting of republican spokespersons or views considered by the Government to converge with those of the IRA. When, in November 1972, Kevin O'Kelly presented a scripted report of an interview he had conducted with the then IRA Chief of Staff, Seán Mac Stíofáin, the RTÉ journalist was arrested and briefly imprisoned while the Government sacked every member of the state broadcaster's governing authority. From London, where Lynch had just arrived for a meeting with Heath, the Taoiseach explained that the dismissals were an 'exercise in democracy ... to protect our community' and that the RTÉ Authority had breached a directive 'not to project people who put forward violent means for achieving their purpose'.[71] The Government's purge had a profound effect on RTÉ, as one of its senior producers later recalled:

> The shock waves in RTÉ were enormous and are still felt. In the atmosphere of daily controversy in RTÉ, managers learn that most conflicts blow over. Only on the most sensitive subject of Northern Ireland have heads rolled and these were the most important heads in the organisation, those of the RTÉ authority itself. Such cases act as examples and become part of the folk memory in broadcasting organisations. It only takes one such case every decade or so to remind everybody to be cautious.[72]

The Government had planned for a snap election in December 1972 on the issue of law and order and the opposition's failure – with the notable exception of Fine Gael leader Liam Cosgrave – to support the Offences Against the State (Amendment) Bill. Explosions in Dublin city centre on the night of the crucial parliamentary vote, which killed two CIÉ bus drivers and were erroneously blamed on the IRA,[73] helped swing Fine Gael behind Liam Cosgrave, saving his leadership in the process and averting an election. By the time the election was called in February 1973, Fine Gael and Labour had mended fences sufficiently to present a common platform. The electoral pact meant that although

Fianna Fáil's vote increased, it obtained six fewer seats than in 1969, and while the combined vote of Fine Gael and the Labour Party fell, they gained five seats. The result brought Fianna Fáil's second sixteen-year spell in office to an abrupt end.

Sunningdale

The new Government – the first non-Fianna Fáil administration since the mid-1950s – was headed by Fine Gael leader Liam Cosgrave as Taoiseach and Labour Party leader, Brendan Corish, as Tánaiste. Ministers holding portfolios relevant to Northern Ireland policy included Garret FitzGerald (Foreign Affairs), Paddy Donegan (Defence) and Paddy Cooney (Justice). Conor Cruise O'Brien, although Minister for Posts and Telegraphs, retained his position as Labour's spokesman on Northern Ireland, enabling him to continue speaking publicly on the issue, and he demonstrated a remarkable ability to shoehorn discussions on the North and nationalism into many of his Dáil contributions. The main strands of government policy towards Northern Ireland remained intact. As an interim solution to the immediate problem of upheaval in the North, the Government sought a devolved power-sharing administration, an end to discrimination against the Catholic/Nationalist minority, and some form of institutionalised link to the Republic without prejudicing unionist insistence that the six counties remain within the United Kingdom or, indeed, the longer-term objective of a united Ireland.

The British Government's position on Northern Ireland had substantially converged with Dublin's and, while still operating a controversial military campaign, Heath realised that the problem had a political complexion and could not be solved by force alone. In its Green Paper (October 1972) and White Paper (March 1973), the British Government recognised a so-called 'Irish Dimension', meaning any settlement 'must also recognise Northern Ireland's position within Ireland as a whole' and 'be so far as possible acceptable to and accepted by the Republic of Ireland'.[74] The paper also acknowledged that there were 'strong arguments' for minority participation in the exercise of executive power within Northern Ireland.[75]

From 6–9 December 1973, the two Governments along with representatives from the UUP, the SDLP and the Alliance Party met at Sunningdale, England, for historic and unprecedented talks. For the first time since the imposition of partition, representatives from unionism and nationalism in the North along with the Prime Ministers of Britain and Ireland sat down to negotiate a political settlement.[76] The participants agreed to a power-sharing administration for

Northern Ireland, which would be jointly led by Unionist leader Brian Faulkner as Chief Executive and SDLP leader Gerry Fitt as Deputy Chief Executive. The remaining nine ministers were composed of five unionists, three SDLP and the leader of the Alliance Party, Oliver Napier. There were four other ministers (two SDLP, one Alliance, one Unionist) that were part of the administration but not in the executive itself. The Council of Ireland would embody the 'Irish Dimension', contain representatives from Northern Ireland and the Republic, and consist of a Council of Ministers and a Consultative Assembly. A permanent secretariat would 'supervise the carrying out of the executive and harmonising functions and the consultative role of the council'. The two Governments addressed the thorny issue of Northern Ireland's constitutional position in Paragraph 5 of the agreement. Dublin 'fully accepted and solemnly declared' that there could be no change in the status of Northern Ireland until a majority of its people desired such a change. For its part, London declared its policy was to support the preference of the majority of the people of Northern Ireland, which currently was to remain in the United Kingdom but that if in the future the majority should indicate a wish to become part of a united Ireland, the British Government would support that wish.

On New Year's Day 1974, the power-sharing executive became Northern Ireland's new Government. In retrospect, the experiment's ultimate demise seems inevitable, as if it was always travelling inexorably down a predestined path to extinction. While the participant parties had reservations about certain aspects of the Sunningdale package, and were acutely aware of opposition to the agreement, they argued that with power sharing firmly established and seen to be working effectively, the executive would, in due course, refute its critics and win over the doubters. However, the executive would be denied the time to prove its value.[77]

A full meeting of the Ulster Unionist Council, the UUP's governing body, convened on 4 January and attended by over 800 constituency delegates, supported by 428 votes to 374 a motion proposed by former Stormont minister John Taylor that rejected 'the proposed all-Ireland Council settlement' after five hours of acrimonious debate.[78] Faulkner resigned, though he hinted at the possibility of establishing a new party to pursue his policies.[79] Coming only four days after the inauguration of the power-sharing initiative, this early setback gave the loyalists an important victory, both practical and psychological at a time when the executive needed to consolidate its position. Those dedicated to undermining the agreement were now in control of the well-oiled unionist party machine complete with headquarters and resources. The defeat also left Faulkner in the anomalous position of being Chief Executive of the administration and leader of the pro-assembly Unionists while not being a member, let alone a leader, of any political party. The split formalised a division within unionism between moderates and *ultras* that had existed from the time of O'Neill's premiership and had been magnified by the loss of power following Stormont's abolition.

For several weeks the issue of whether Dublin had recognised Northern Ireland's right to self-determination overshadowed relations between unionists in the power-sharing executive and the Irish Government. On 17 December, Kevin Boland, the former Fianna Fáil minister now leading the small Aontacht Éireann party, submitted a case to the High Court seeking an interlocutory injunction on the Government and the Attorney-General to restrain them from implementing certain parts of the Sunningdale Agreement. Boland's senior counsel, Seán MacBride, sought to establish that the Sunningdale communiqué was repugnant to the Constitution. The kernel of the case involved consideration of whether Paragraph 5 of the communiqué was in conflict with Articles 1–6 of the Constitution, which related to Ireland's sovereignty and territorial integrity.

The Government's defence, submitted on 11 January 1974, proved to be the most damaging aspect of the Boland case. It was obvious that the sentiments expressed in Paragraph 5 were incompatible with, in particular, Articles 1–3 of the Constitution which, because they stated that sovereignty resided in the people of Ireland as a whole, precluded the possibility of a minority within the national territory limiting the exercise of that sovereignty. The Articles represented a clear rejection of partition while Paragraph 5 of the Sunningdale communiqué appeared to commit the Government to conceding that the unionist majority in the six counties had a *de jure* right to remain outside Dublin's jurisdiction.

In an attempt to reconcile these anomalies the Government adopted a legalistic approach that sought to downplay the status of the commitment given in the Sunningdale communiqué.[80] This entailed a denial that the declarations contained in Paragraph 5 were part of an inter-governmental *agreement*. It was also denied that the Government had acknowledged that Northern Ireland was part of the United Kingdom or that the declaration purported to limit the national territory to a portion of Ireland. Furthermore, the Government had to refute the notion that Paragraph 5 prejudiced the right of the Irish Government and parliament to exercise jurisdiction over the whole of the national territory, or precluded the courts established under the Constitution from exercising jurisdiction over the whole island of Ireland. Accordingly, the Government's defence team claimed that the declaration was merely a statement of policy and did not acknowledge the right of any national minority to opt out of the nation. Legally, the Government presented a convincing case. Politically, it was a disaster.

The legal subtleties of this abstruse, albeit necessary, line of argument eluded many unionists, and further weakened Faulkner's credibility. To his opponents, it confirmed their belief that the Chief Executive had been outmanoeuvred and outwitted at Sunningdale.[81] Faulkner reacted swiftly by stating that unionists had been assured that the declaration constituted a clear recognition that Northern Ireland was part of the United Kingdom and that there could be no alteration of that status without the consent of a majority within the North.

To address the impasse, Cosgrave ignored Neil Blaney's suggestion to recall Parliament for an emergency debate and instead contacted Faulkner by phone. 'It was clear', Faulkner recalled in his memoirs, 'that he in turn had been surprised by the strength of the Unionist reaction to the affair. He agreed that he should have talked to me about it before, but argued that our alarm was based on a misapprehension and that he and I should meet quickly to thrash out an understanding.' Faulkner flew to Dublin on 16 January for a five-hour meeting with Cosgrave. The Unionist leader maintained that unless the status question was resolved and 'firm action' taken against the IRA it would be impossible for the power-sharing administration to survive. Cosgrave challenged Faulkner's contention that the Government's security policies were inadequate and produced statistics on the number of convictions obtained by the Special Criminal Court in addition to citing the recent expansion of the Gardaí. The Taoiseach also explained the rationale behind the Government's High Court defence. It was imperative, he argued, that they successfully demolished Boland's case and the approach adopted had been necessary to achieve that objective. Cosgrave told Faulkner that so long as the constitutional claim remained intact, 'any form of recognition that he and his colleagues could agree to would have to be capable of a technical defence that it did not infringe the letter of the law, even if – as was inevitable and even desirable – it infringed the spirit'. Faulkner inquired whether it would be possible to delete Articles 2 and 3 of the Constitution by referendum. While the Taoiseach did not rule out such a course in principle he stressed that a vote on so sensitive an issue would be defeated and thus counterproductive. 'Look', he said, 'We accept Northern Ireland as it is, and we want to co-operate with you, and that's all there is to it.' Faulkner accepted the Taoiseach's judgement and good intentions.[82]

Both leaders considered the meeting a success. Faulkner's fears had been allayed and he declared himself content with the Government's High Court defence, which, he argued, had been misinterpreted by the media. During the court case the Attorney-General had advised Cosgrave that further statements on the issue could affront the court and prejudice the outcome. However, the Taoiseach had assured Faulkner that he would make a clear statement in the Dáil when the case was successfully concluded. On the same day as the Cosgrave–Faulkner meeting the High Court decided in the Government's favour but as

Boland appealed the case to the Supreme Court the matter became *sub judice* again.

Loyalists mobilised throughout the North to demonstrate their implacable opposition to Sunningdale. At a 'Save Ulster' rally in Larne, Ian Paisley preached his own unique brand of sectarian vitriol:

> We will not put our necks under the jackboots of priest-craft at any price ... Protestant liberty is more important than priestly, Popish tyranny. The choice is with the Bible or the Pope. We do not accept the slanderous bachelor on the banks of the Tiber. It is a sorry day when our so-called leader has run to Dublin. The only time we will be running to Dublin is when we will be chasing them. The people of Ulster will not be deceived.[83]

When the newly established Northern Ireland Assembly convened on 23 January for its first meeting since the Sunningdale Agreement, Faulkner was immediately confronted with hostile unionists determined to make the legislature unworkable. After several interruptions a farcical *melee* ensued, with Professor Kennedy Lindsay standing on top of the Speaker's table, microphone in hand, shouting continuously: 'we have driven the money changers from the Temple' before chaining himself to a bench.[84] The Assembly was suspended five times and eighteen loyalist members were forcibly ejected from the chamber. It was difficult to see how any institution could continue indefinitely if such opposition persisted.

Cosgrave and seven senior ministers travelled on 1 February with eight officials by helicopter to Hillsborough for a meeting with Faulkner and seven members of the executive. It was to be, in effect, the first and the final meeting of the Council of Ireland at ministerial level. The historic significance of the gathering was not lost on its participants, with Paddy Devlin later recalling that 'it was an unprecedented meeting between Irish political leaders, North and South, and significant, not least of all, because there was no British participation'.[85] While Faulkner declared that the Council of Ireland would be a valuable institution he also stressed that its development depended on movement on other issues important to unionists. These included an unambiguous public declaration by the Taoiseach of the right of the people of Northern Ireland to self-determination and enhanced security cooperation between the Gardaí and the RUC.[86]

Fianna Fáil and the challenges of bi-partisanship

As an organisation that considered itself the natural party of government, Fianna Fáil's first year in opposition had been a period of agonising readjustment. Fianna

Fáil speeches during this period betrayed ambivalence towards the Sunningdale Agreement.[87] The party leadership desperately wanted to appear supportive, and yet their instincts prevented them from embracing Sunningdale without reservation. Much of this reticence was motivated by simple envy. Under Jack Lynch's guidance, Fianna Fáil had patiently laid the foundations of the Sunningdale Agreement only to see the coalition parties gain all the kudos for completing the process. The party's republicanism, an elastic concept when in power, became more rigid and doctrinaire in opposition. Fianna Fáil now played the green card with renewed vigour, returning to the party's pre-1969 vocabulary on Northern Ireland. Des O'Malley provided a fine example of this vintage republican rhetoric when he stressed the need to be vigilant against compromise by conjuring up the image of the celestial cartographer: 'Ireland is one island, one nation, one country because God made it one. That essential unity cannot be put asunder by the anti-national semantics of Conor Cruise O'Brien or Garret FitzGerald.'[88] While claiming credit for the Sunningdale Agreement's positive aspects, Fianna Fáil reserved the right to criticise 'any part or development of Government policies or actions which we consider to be ill-judged'.[89]

The SDLP realised that a bi-partisan approach to Sunningdale in the Dáil would be crucial in ensuring the agreement's success. On 3 February, John Hume and Paddy Devlin travelled to Dublin for a two-hour meeting with Jack Lynch to brief Fianna Fáil on the Hillsborough summit, the progress achieved to date and the range of functions being considered for the Council of Ireland. The fact that the SDLP had to travel from Belfast to complete a task that could have been adequately accomplished by an informal talk between the Taoiseach and the leader of the opposition did not augur well for bi-partisanship on Northern Ireland policy.

Fianna Fáil believed that the most effective method of galvanising its traditional support was under the banner of republicanism. In furtherance of this objective, constituency conventions were held throughout the state after the party's electoral defeat, a prelude to the party ard fheis held on 17–18 February 1974 and attended by over three thousand delegates. Almost forty party branches submitted critical motions on Sunningdale for discussion.[90] The section of Lynch's presidential address devoted to the North, a fifth of the total script, appealed to the widest spectrum of Fianna Fáil opinion. It declared that 'our first goal is to seek the ending of partition and the reunification of Ireland' and that the 'so-called package' produced at Sunningdale was but one step towards a final settlement.[91] Lynch trenchantly asserted that 'the road to Sunningdale was a course which Fianna Fáil had charted when in Government' and cited in detail his efforts with Heath to achieve the substance of the agreement. Power sharing 'must be given every chance to work' and Lynch reminded his audience that he had consistently advocated a Council of Ireland.[92] Fianna Fáil's 'one major reservation' was Paragraph 5, which related to Northern Ireland's status. The two separate declarations contained in the communiqué were, Lynch argued, in stark contrast to each other. Britain's claim to Northern Ireland was unambiguously asserted while the Irish constitutional position as set out in Articles 2 and 3 of Bunreacht na hÉireann was not referred to at all. The Fianna Fáil leader maintained that the Government had yet to clarify the significance of this anomaly.[93]

Several kites were flown by the party leadership in the hope that supporters would catch the ones they wanted and let the others drift harmlessly by. Thus Fianna Fáil was the republican party *and* the party of reality, the party of compromise but also the party of conviction. What constituted Fianna Fáil's Northern policy was a matter of subjective interpretation. The party's dexterity enabled both critics and supporters of Sunningdale to believe that the leadership was pursuing their own preferred policy.

Many Fianna Fáil criticisms of Sunningdale were dictated by the internal dynamics of party factionalism. Lynch was forced to adopt a delicate balancing act, seeking to placate the republican wing of the party while reassuring the wider electorate that Fianna Fáil was a responsible party that would not undermine Sunningdale. Charles Haughey's election as Joint Honorary Secretary of the party against Lynch's wishes signalled the republican faction's resurgence. Sunningdale had challenged traditional assumptions but while Fianna Fáil's recalcitrance did not impact greatly on the wider political process, the convulsions within Ulster loyalism would soon threaten the very existence of the power-sharing executive.

Sunningdale unravelling

Locked into battle with the British coal miners, Heath called a general election on 7 February, evoking intense dismay in Dublin and amongst the power-sharing executive.[94] Only the recently formed United Ulster Unionist Council (UUUC), a loyalist umbrella group, relished the prospect of an electoral contest. Comprising the Ulster Unionist Party, now headed by Harry West, Bill Craig's Vanguard Unionists and Ian Paisley's Democratic Unionist Party (DUP), the new alliance campaigned on an anti-Sunningdale platform. The election results were even more damaging than the most pessimistic Sunningdale supporters had anticipated. Fighting under the emotive slogan of 'Dublin is just a Sunningdale away' the UUUC took 51 per cent of the vote and eleven of the twelve Westminster seats. The Pro-Assembly Unionist vote plummeted to 13 per cent while the Alliance Party garnered a mere 3.2 per cent of the ballots cast. The SDLP vote was almost static at 22 per cent and Gerry Fitt's victory in West Belfast – the only Sunningdale win – had the slenderest majority of any constituency.

Aside from its implications within Northern Ireland, the UUUC victory had produced eleven anti-Sunningdale unionist seats in the politically volatile British House of Commons. The fact that neither Labour nor the Conservatives had a majority in Parliament allowed the UUUC to exercise considerable political leverage. Rumours that Heath was attempting to negotiate a pact with the UUUC to secure their support in the Commons were met with incredulity in Dublin. Heath, still Prime Minister, sent a telegram to Harry West's home in Fermanagh offering the Conservative whip to the UUUC elected on a mandate to oppose Sunningdale and London's Irish policy. Although the Unionists demurred and Harold Wilson was elected Prime Minister of an unstable minority Labour Government, Heath continued to woo the UUUC MPs. A climate of instability pervaded Westminster and it was clear that the new Labour administration would not endure.

Following a favourable decision by the Supreme Court, Cosgrave made his long-awaited statement on Northern Ireland's 'status' on 13 March. The Taoiseach told the Dáil that he was glad to be afforded the opportunity to 'clarify misunderstandings and correct certain misconceptions'. All parties to the Sunningdale negotiations, he said, had been aware of the divergent political attitudes amongst the participants and had been determined not to indulge in 'essentially arid and potentially divisive arguments as to rights and wrongs of historic events now long past'. Instead they had sought to deal with present realities and the future. Thus, while the Government had been aware of the conflicting claims in Irish and British law, they believed it would have been unhelpful to debate those constitutional differences. The aim of the declaration contained in Paragraph 5 had been to reassure unionists who may have been apprehensive about power sharing or the Council of Ireland. Having outlined the context in which the Government had agreed to commit itself to Paragraph 5, Cosgrave proceeded to make his key statement of 'clarification':

> The declaration was of course referring to the de facto status of Northern Ireland, that is to say the factual position, to which reference is made in recent judgements in the High Court and the Supreme Court. The factual position of Northern Ireland is that it is within the United Kingdom and my Government accept this as a fact. I now therefore solemnly reaffirm that the factual position of Northern Ireland within the United Kingdom cannot be changed except by a decision of a majority of the people of Northern Ireland. This declaration, I believe, is in accordance with and follows from the resolve of all democratic parties in the Republic that the unity of Ireland is to be achieved only by peaceful means and by consent.[95]

On behalf of Fianna Fáil, George Colley welcomed the Taoiseach's clarification, though he criticised the delay and the fact that the declaration had been so 'ambiguously drafted' as to require further elucidation:

> The statement by the Taoiseach that the Government's declaration as set out in Paragraph Five was referring to the de facto status of Northern Ireland is, therefore, welcome, even if belated. The *de jure* positions of the two sovereign Governments concerned remain unchanged. As between the Irish Government and the British Government there are conflicting constitutional claims.[96]

Thus, according to Colley, Cosgrave had done nothing more than acknowledge the reality that Britain governed Northern Ireland. The Fianna Fáil spokesman did not make any reference to the Taoiseach's 'solemn reaffirmation', preferring to emphasise the 'inalienable right of the people of Ireland to a united Ireland'.[97] It was difficult to see what concession to unionists was being made here; Fianna Fáil, after all, had never argued that Northern Ireland did not exist but that it *should* not exist. Anxious to appear supportive, the party had welcomed Cosgrave's 'clarification' but the minimalist interpretation of its significance was designed to preserve doublethink on the issue of consent. Colley's reasoning confused those in Fianna Fáil less acquainted with the demands of sophistry. These included Major Vivion de Valera, son of the party founder, who vociferously condemned Cosgrave's clarification, maintaining that the Taoiseach had come 'perilously near recognising, without qualification, a *de jure* right of a section of the Irish people to maintain the partition of our country'.[98] Faulkner welcomed the Taoiseach's clarification, which he believed to be of historic significance. 'For the first time', he declared, 'a Government of the Republic has made a solemn declaration which accepts our right to remain part of the United Kingdom for as long as that is the wish of the majority of our people.'[99] The UUUC, however, rejected the status clarification, with Ian Paisley describing it as 'a vain attempt to bail out Mr Faulkner'.[100]

The Dublin and Monaghan bombings

Following the defeat, on 14 May, of an anti-Sunningdale motion in the Assembly, the newly formed Ulster Workers Council (UWC), a coalition of loyalist para-militaries, unionist politicians and state employees, declared a 'constitutional stoppage'. Though it initially attracted little support, the strike benefited from British government inertia and loyalist intimidation. Its trump card proved to be the support of unionist workers in the Ballylumford power plant who, by reducing electricity by 60 per cent, forced most employers to send their workers home.

The tumultuous events in the North did not impinge greatly on Dublin's parliamentary life. On 15 May, the day that Northern Ireland ground to a halt, Ulster's slow-motion implosion did not merit a single reference in the Dáil, nor did it the following day.[101] Unionist Vanguard leader Bill Craig warned, however, that the Sunningdale initiative would have to be abandoned or 'there will be further actions taken against the Irish Republic and those who attempt to implement the agreement'.[102] The very next day, on 17 May 1974, three car-bombs, strategically placed in Dublin's city centre, exploded almost simultaneously during Friday evening rush-hour. It was a sophisticated operation designed to inflict maximum civilian casualties. Ninety minutes later, another car-bomb exploded in Monaghan town. In all, thirty-four people died and at least one hundred and fifty were injured, the highest death toll for any one day in Ireland or in Britain during the 'Troubles'. The following day the Ulster Defence Association's (UDA's) press officer, Sammy Smith, declared that he was 'very happy about the bombings in Dublin. There is a war with the Free State and now we are laughing at them.'[103] Similarly, a few days after the bombs, the Ulster Constitutionalist Party's Lindsay Mason, while sporting a National Front badge on his lapel, said 'they should be grateful it was only 31 dead [sic]: next time it will be 331. Let me warn all Republicans: get out of Ulster now if you value your lives, and don't go South for we'll be back.'[104]

Liam Cosgrave called an emergency cabinet meeting in the immediate aftermath of the bombing and in a televised address that night told his electorate that 'everybody who practised violence or preached violence or condoned violence must bear a share of responsibility for today's outrages'.[105] Opposition leader Jack Lynch echoed those sentiments when he stated that 'Every person and every organisation which played any part in the campaign of bombing and violence which killed and maimed people and destroyed property in Belfast, Derry or any other part of our country and indeed in Britain over the past five years, shares the guilt and the shame of the assassins who actually placed these bombs on the streets of Dublin and Monaghan last Friday'.[106] While the outrage was unsurprising, it is remarkable that after loyalists had bombed Dublin and Monaghan the reflex Government response was to blame the IRA and their supporters.

During a televised address on 25 May, Prime Minister Wilson attempted to adopt a defiant posture but in the absence of action his speech appeared unnecessarily offensive by calling the loyalist protesters 'spongers on British democracy'.[107] Wilson's speech was a cruel anti-climax and provoked near-universal feelings of exasperation amongst Sunningdale supporters in Ireland. The executive survived

Wilson's speech, effectively the *coup de grace* for Sunningdale, by a mere sixty-five hours. The British Government made it clear it would not take any substantive action against the strikers but neither would it negotiate with the UWC, whose strike now enjoyed widespread unionist support. On 27 May, in a token gesture to silence criticism, the British Army was directed to commandeer a number of petrol stations in Belfast to provide motorists with fuel. The UWC responded to this feeble initiative by announcing that all essential services would cease to operate within twenty-four hours. The electricity generators in the main turbine hall at Ballylumford were operating at a mere 10 per cent of capacity. The prospect of an automatic shutdown of the station – which would have deprived the North of power for several weeks – was very real.[108]

Faulkner met with civil service departmental heads who painted a very grim picture, conjuring up images of low-lying Belfast being awash with raw sewage within hours. According to Paddy Devlin the civil servants told Faulkner 'that they could conceive a situation where they could no longer support the Executive', eloquently illustrating the sense of mutiny which had permeated all levels of unionism.[109] After an inconclusive meeting of the executive, Faulkner met the Secretary of State for Northern Ireland, Merlyn Rees, and implored him to open negotiations with the UWC. When Rees refused, Faulkner resigned and the British Government announced that the executive no longer enjoyed a statutory basis. The power-sharing experiment had ended. Having endured the trauma of losing the one-party Stormont Government, loyalists and unionists had united to assert themselves and to reject any compromise that involved power sharing or an institutionalised relationship with the rest of Ireland. Almost a quarter century would pass before the negotiation of a similar agreement based on consociationalism and enhanced North–South relations.

Notes

1 Notes of discussion at the Foreign Office at 12.00 on Friday 1 August 1969. NAI DFA 2000/6/557.
2 Notes of discussion at the Foreign Office at 12.00 on Friday 1 August 1969. NAI DFA 2000/6/557.
3 Boland, *The Rise and Decline of Fianna Fáil*, p. 67.
4 Interview with Neil Blaney by Peter Taylor, *Timewatch*, BBC2, 27 January 1993.
5 Boland, *Up Dev!*, p. 11.
6 Covering letter by Hugh McCann, with two draft statements prepared for Jack Lynch, NAI DT 2000/6/657 (13 August 1969); Boland, *Up Dev!*, p. 11. Kevin Boland, interview with the author; Des O'Malley, interview with the author.
7 Kevin Boland, interview with the author.

8   O'Brien, *The Arms Trial*, p. 42. Fisher's parents had lived in Derry and moved to Dublin when he was eleven. *Irish Times*, 25 October 1999.

9   'Statement by the Taoiseach, Mr J. Lynch, Wednesday, 13 August, 1969'. NAI DT 2000/6/657.

10   Taylor, *States of Terror*, p. 213.

11   *Hot Press*, 14 June 1990.

12   Kelly, *Failed Political Entity*, p. 57.

13   Coogan, *IRA*, pp. 465–466.

14   Boland, *Up Dev!*, p. 42.

15   Letter shown to the author by Kevin Boland dated 13 October 1969.

16   'Discussion at Foreign and Commonwealth Office, London, on 15 August 1969 concerning Northern Ireland', minutes circulated to Government at meeting of 18 August 1969. NAUK FCO 2001/6/658.

17   'Statement by An Taoiseach, Mr J Lynch' (13 August 1969). NAI DT 2000/6/557.

18   These were Paddy Devlin (Northern Ireland Labour, Belfast Falls); Paddy O'Hanlon (Independent, South Armagh); and Paddy Kennedy (Republican Labour, Belfast Central).

19   'Visit of Northern Ireland M.P.s to Department', [meeting: 16 August 1969, note composed on 18 August 1969]. NAI DT 2000/6/658.

20   'Eye witness account of the Belfast area', 22 August 1969. NAI DT 2000/6/658 [p. 5].

21   Government cabinet minutes, 16 August 1969, NAI 2000/9/1. See also 'Submission from the Department of Finance to the Public Accounts Committee…', 9 July 1970. NAI DT 2001/6/554.

22   Kevin Boland, interview with the author. See also Boland, *Up Dev!*, pp. 12–14.

23   See Walsh, *Patrick Hillery*, pp. 179–201. For a useful overview see Williamson, 'Taking the Troubles across the Atlantic'; Cremin, 'Northern Ireland at the United Nations August/September 1969'; Schwelb, 'Northern Ireland and the United Nations'.

24   Telegram from Gilchrist to FCO, 29 August 1969. NAUK FCO 33/758/74674.

25   Telegram from Gilchrist to FCO, 1 September 1969. NAUK FCO 33/758/74674.

26   Telegram from Gilchrist to FCO, 1 September 1969. NAUK FCO 33/758/74674.

27   NAI DT S650 P&O file 1, para. 2.

28   Memo from Secretary Ó Cearnaigh to Minister for Defence, 3 September 1969. NAI DT S650.

29   Memo from Secretary Ó Cearnaigh to Minister for Defence, 3 September 1969. NAI DT S650.

30   Memo from Secretary Ó Cearnaigh to Minister for Defence, 3 September 1969. NAI DT S650.

31   Addendum to memo of 10 February 1970, ministerial directive to CF [Chief of Staff]. NAI MDA, copy no. 5, Rn P&O, CCA, 11 February 1970.

32   Interview with Neil Blaney by Peter Taylor, *Timewatch*, BBC2, 27 January 1993. Blaney mentioned Ballymurphy in particular, as he was referring to violent clashes

between the British Army and local civilians which had injected renewed urgency into the quest for arms.

33 John Kelly, interview with the author. A detailed account is available in Ó Beacháin, *Destiny of the Soldiers*, pp. 283–307.

34 Cosgrave had first gone to the press which, given the paucity of corroborating evidence, declined to print the story.

35 The junior minister for local government, Paudge Brennan, though not implicated in the attempts to import arms, resigned in protest against the ministerial sackings.

36 See Ó Beacháin, *Destiny of the Soldiers*, pp. 303–307.

37 After a meeting with the Irish Foreign Minister, Hillery, the British ambassador, Sir John Peck reported back to London: 'Hillery himself was exhausted. He said he had been the hatchet man and had spent the last four days and nights twisting the arms of the dissidents.' Telegram 360 of 31 October 1970. NAUK FCO 33/1201.

38 *Irish Times*, 23 October 1970.

39 FitzGerald, *Towards A New Ireland*; Sunday Times Insight Team, *Ulster*, p. 254.

40 *Irish Times*, 22 August 1972.

41 Paddy Devlin, interview with the author.

42 Devlin, *Straight Left*, pp. 145–146.

43 'Text of a message from Mr Heath to Mr Lynch' (9 August 1971), NAI DFA 2003/17/304.

44 *Irish Times*, 5 December 1970; see *Dáil Debates*, 250/485–513 (9 December 1970); Des O'Malley, interview with the author.

45 'Text of a Message from Mr Heath to Mr Lynch' (9 August 1971), NAI DFA 2003/17/304.

46 'Text of a Message from Mr Heath to Mr Lynch' (9 August 1971), NAI DFA 2003/17/304.

47 'Statement issued by the Government Information Bureau on behalf of the Department of the Taoiseach' (19 August 1971), NAI DT 2002/8/481.

48 'Statement issued by the Government Information Bureau on behalf of the Department of the Taoiseach' (19 August 1971), NAI DT 2002/8/481.

49 Telegram from Heath to Lynch (19 August 1971), NAI DT 2002/8/481. See also NAI DFA 2001/43/1436.

50 Telegram from Heath to Lynch (19 August 1971), NAI DT 2002/8/481. See also NAI DFA 2001/43/1436.

51 Telegram from Heath to Lynch (19 August 1971), NAI DT 2002/8/481. See also NAI DFA 2001/43/1436.

52 Telegram no. 545 of 1 November 1971. NAUK CAB 133/406. Lynch's views were communicated to Peck in conversation with Hugh McCann.

53 Ó Beacháin, *Destiny of the Soldiers*, pp. 351–353. Undated confidential report in advance of Lynch visit of 6–7 September 1971. NAUK FCO 33/1613; brief by Northern Ireland Office and Foreign and Commonwealth Office prepared for Heath–Lynch meeting of 4 September 1972, NAUK FCO 87/27; confidential brief,

16 October 1972, by Foreign and Commonwealth Office prepared for Heath–Lynch Paris meeting, 21 October 1972, NAUK FCO 87/27.

54 Message from Heath to Lynch, 8 October 1971, NAI DT 2002/8/483.

55 Message from Lynch to Heath, 8 October 1971, NAI DT 2002/8/483.

56 Message from Lynch to Heath, 8 October 1971, NAI DT 2002/8/483.

57 Message from Lynch to Heath, 8 October 1971, NAI DT 2002/8/483.

58 Message from Heath to Lynch (12 October 1971), NAI DT 2002/8/483.

59 See Ó Beacháin, *Destiny of the Soldiers*, pp. 331–332.

60 *Irish Times*, 3 February 1972.

61 See Ó Beacháin, *Destiny of the Soldiers*, pp. 334–339.

62 Statement (24 March 1972) by Edward Heath to the House of Commons. PRONI HA/32/2/51.

63 Roy Bradford, interview with the author.

64 'Conclusions of morning meeting' (10 July 1972), PRONI CAB/9/G/27/6/3.

65 Letter from D. O'Sullivan to R. McDonagh (14 July1972), NAI DT 2003/16/465.

66 This was how one of the IRA leaders present, John Kelly, described the meeting in an interview with the author.

67 *Irish Times*, 11 July 1972.

68 'Conclusions of morning meeting' (10 July 1972), PRONI CAB/9/G/27/6/3.

69 Letter from Donal O'Sullivan to Hugh McCann, 2 August 1972. NAI DT 2003/16/466.

70 Report of Heath–Lynch meeting, 4 September 1972. NAUK FCO 87/27; brief by Northern Ireland Office and Foreign and Commonwealth Office prepared for Heath–Lynch meeting of 4 September 1972. NAUK FCO 87/27.

71 *Irish Times*, 25 November 1972.

72 Purcell, 'The silence in Irish broadcasting', p. 61.

73 Another bomb at the same location killed a CIÉ bus conductor the following month. No organisation or individual claimed responsibility for the bomb attacks. The involvement of British Intelligence was widely suspected. See Barron Report (2004), pp. 55–79 passim.

74 Northern Ireland Office, *The Future of Northern Ireland: A Paper*. Para. 78.

75 Para. 79f. 'Statement issued by the Government Information Bureau on behalf of the Taoiseach', following the publication of the British Government's White Paper on Northern Ireland (20 March 1973), NAI DT 2003/16/466.

76 'Note of the conference at Sunningdale on 6–9 December', NAI DT 2005/7/626; 'Memorandum outlining the contrasting positions of the Irish and British Government in the run up to the Sunningdale Conference' (n. d.), NAI DT 2004/21/3.

77 See for example the speeches of Brian Faulkner and Oliver Napier after being sworn in by Secretary of State Pym. *Irish Times*, 1–2 January 1974, p. 8.

78 Most texts, almost without exception, have erroneously cited a 457–374 vote. This was the vote announced at the meeting and reported in the newspapers the following day. However, a counting error was discovered and the figures revised accordingly. This information was publicly disclosed a week after the Council's vote.

79 *Irish Times*, 5 January 1974, 8 January 1974.

80   'Defence statement ... Liam Lysaght, Chief State Solicitor, in the High Court Case ... Kevin Boland v. Irish government' (3 January 1974), PRONI OE/2/3.
81   Oliver Napier, interview with the author.
82   Faulkner, *Memoirs of a Statesman*, p. 154. 'Note of the meeting at Baldonnel Airport ...' (16 January 1974), PRONI OE/1/29.
83   *Irish Times*, 18 January 1974.
84   *Irish Times*, 24 January 1974.
85   Devlin, *Straight Left*, pp. 223–224.
86   'Meeting with Irish ministers, 1 February 1974: brief for Chief Minister' (30 January 1974), PRONI OE/1/28; letter from Brian Faulkner to Liam Cosgrave (6 February 1974), PRONI OE/1/28.
87   *Irish Times*, 24 January 1974, 15 February 1974, 27 February 1974.
88   *Irish Times*, 14 January 1974.
89   *Irish Times*, 4 February 1974.
90   *Hibernia*, 16 February 1974.
91   *Irish Times*, 18 February 1974.
92   *Irish Times*, 18 February 1974.
93   *Irish Times*, 18 February 1974.
94   For the Irish Government reaction see FitzGerald, *All in A Life*, p. 230. For the executive's response see Devlin, *Straight Left*, p. 226.
95   *Dáil Debates*, 271/8 (13 March 1974).
96   *Irish Times*, 14 March 1974.
97   *Irish Times*, 14 March 1974.
98   *Irish Times*, 15 March 1974.
99   *Irish Times*, 14 March 1974.
100 *Irish Times*, 15 March 1974.
101 *Dáil Debates*, 272 (15, 16 May 1974).
102 Quoted in Holland, *Hope Against History*, p. 70.
103 *Irish Times*, 18 May 1974.
104 Quoted in *Hibernia*, 19 July 1974.
105 *Cork Examiner*, 18 May 1974.
106 *Dáil Debates*, 272/1795 (21 May 1974).
107 *Sunday Independent*, 26 May 1974; *Irish Press*, 27 May 1974.
108 See Fisk, *The Point of No Return*, chapter 11.
109 Devlin, *Fall of the Northern Ireland Executive*, p. 28.

5

In fear of Armageddon, 1974–1979

For some six weeks after the Dublin and Monaghan bombings, the Government resisted convening a debate in Dáil Éireann. When it finally occurred, on 26 June, the speeches focussed on condemnation of the IRA and the need to reassure the unionist population. There was little reference to the attacks on Dublin and Monaghan and no interrogation of the motives behind the UWC strike. Like many other ministers, Paddy Cooney aligned himself not with the victims of the recent bombings in his Government's jurisdiction but rather dovetailed with, or even exceeded, traditional British Government conceptions of the 'Irish Question'. His comments on Bloody Sunday and its aftermath were indicative:

> There were public reactions down here of a massive and irrational kind to certain tragic events which led to the burning down of the British Embassy in Dublin a few years ago. This frightened people and led to a questioning of what sort of nation is it? What sort of people are they? Are they all deep down supporters of the philosophy of violence? Again, possibly there has been delay on the part of the people here in coming to a full realisation of the inherent viciousness of the IRA mentality. Indeed, to use the word 'mentality' in regard to IRA people—I have to use the word 'people'; they are human—is to give a dignity to these people they do not deserve because 'mentality' imputes a certain amount of rationality, whereas, by all their actions, they have shown themselves to be mindless, vicious savages.[1]

The murder of fourteen people was therefore referred to opaquely as 'a certain tragic event' with no reference to the fatalities or perpetrators, or a critical analysis of the regime type that would allow such an atrocity to go unpunished. Rather, the Minister for Justice focussed on public empathy with the victims of Bloody Sunday who, in the absence of official justice, had burnt down the symbol of British diplomacy in Ireland. It was this reaction – that caused no injuries, let alone fatalities – that was depicted as 'irrational' and 'frightening'.

Moreover, Cooney did not suggest that nationalists should interrogate the nature of loyalism as a result of the 17 May massacre. Instead he implied that the bombings in Dublin and Monaghan were a natural reaction to republican violence. Such an approach had implications for victims of British state or loyalist violence; relatives of those killed or maimed on Bloody Sunday, for example, complained of harassment by Irish soldiers and the Garda Special Branch when they travelled to Monaghan to offer their condolences and to lay wreaths 'in acknowledgement of the gestures of sympathy they received from the South of Ireland on the occasion of Bloody Sunday'.[2]

The Minister for Justice invoked a stereotype of the garrulous, sentimental Irishman with a romantic facade masking his true, violent, deadly and senseless nature. Cooney stated that the IRA's mindset was 'so irrational that it prohibits us from understanding the mentality of the person who can support or be a member of the IRA. It is an irrational mentality that can go misty-eyed over a song like "The Croppy Boy", "Kevin Barry" or some such sentimental ballad and, at the same time, put a bullet in a neighbour's head.'[3] If republican violence in the North was illogical, there followed no obligation to understand it, but simply to crush it by whatever means necessary, a view that neatly overlapped with the default position of successive British Governments. Equally convergent with London's policy was the contention that the primary two communities in Northern Ireland were not those of the nationalists and unionists, which would emphasise the need for an inclusive political accommodation, but rather the 'people of the North' and the small band of psychopaths who threatened them. This reduced the conflict to a criminal one that defied political negotiations but could only be solved by quashing the trouble-makers. Minister of Justice Cooney is again worth quoting to illustrate this feature:

> We have to reassure the people in the North—and I think it has to go forth from this Parliament—that we are conscious of it as a real evil and that we are determined to stamp it out. We have to reassure the people that this warped mentality, this ambivalence to violence, that they sense is widespread down here is not in fact widespread. This is the task we have to undertake. There is always a worry, I think, on the part of those in the North who have experienced this irrationality to wonder how widespread is it; is there some taint of it in the Irish character as a whole? I think what we have to show is that there is not; that this irrationality is confined to a small minority and that the Establishment— the Government and this Dáil [—] is determined to ensure that it be rooted out of our society.[4]

The Government's acceptance of guilt, on behalf of the Republic's citizenry, by attributing loyalist attacks to Irish society's ambivalence towards the IRA would be a central plank of the coalition Government's Northern Ireland policy. Thus, on 28 May, the Taoiseach, without contradiction from the opposition leader, Jack Lynch, blamed the loyalist strike, the bombs in the Republic and the fall of the power-sharing executive on the IRA: 'As we warned it would, the campaign of the IRA has provoked a massive sectarian backlash.'[5]

It was clear that these assumptions would inevitably inform policy preferences. The Taoiseach warned that violence was working against Irish unity in two ways. First, it was driving apart the two communities within Northern Ireland. Secondly, it had planted in the Republic 'the idea that unity or close association with people so deeply imbued with violence and its effects is not what they want'. 'Violence', he concluded, was 'accentuating the mental partition' and 'killing here the desire for unity'.[6] The notion that people in the Republic would not countenance unity with 'a people so deeply imbued with violence' echoed publicly what Patrick Hillery, then Foreign Minister, had confided privately two years earlier to the British ambassador to Ireland, John Peck, that 'while the Irish were very emotional, the people in the South, on the whole and with exceptions, were not given to violence and murder. It was the men from the North who were cruel and violent and it was noteworthy that many of the recent bank raids and other crimes of violence in the South have been committed by northerners.'[7]

Not only did such statements provide evidence of the psychological detachment between the Irish Government and those in Northern Ireland who wanted to join their jurisdiction, but it also suggested that aggression in the North was one-dimensional and one-sided, occluding rigorous examination of violence perpetrated by unionists and by the British state, which had long traditions in Ireland. Indeed so eager was the Government to distance itself from republicanism of any hue that at times its utterances chimed with those of loyalist paramilitary organisations as, for example, when Minister of Justice Patrick Cooney told the Dáil that he had asked the people for cooperation against the IRA:

> I asked them to refrain from contributing to the collection boxes of front organisations, to refrain from buying the propaganda sheets of the IRA, to be careful not to find themselves patronising a social function with the objective of raising funds for some of these front organisations ... Only by total co-operation between the people and the police will the problem of the IRA be ended in this country. In ending it here we will have done a lot towards re-assuring the people in the North. As I said, when I started, the objective of this debate should be to start on the long road towards re-assuring the people in the North that we have no territorial designs until such time as they are ready to come with us, to reassure them that the old shibboleths and the old stances are no longer apt or proper for this time.[8]

A remarkably similar appeal, or in this case an ultimatum, was made during the previous month by the UVF in its magazine *Combat*:

> Ordinary people in the Republic can prevent a backlash by 1) refuse safehouses and bases, 2) refuse to donate funds, 3) refuse to subscribe to their paper, 4) refuse to join their protests, 5) refuse them admission to pubs. If ordinary rank and file Roman Catholic people are genuinely opposed to the policies and activities of the Provisionals let them make their opposition public by carrying out the aforementioned suggestions.[9]

The UVF had expanded its operations south of the border and its members had been involved in bomb attacks in multiple locations throughout the Republic, including those that had caused such loss of life in Dublin and Monaghan. However, the vast majority of its attacks, along with those of the legal paramilitary organisation, the UDA, targeted Catholics in Northern Ireland.[10] Faced with two sets of mutually exclusive demands in Northern Ireland, both expressed through the use of force, the Irish Government at this time chose to capitulate to one of them. Contrary to how it was presented at the time, such a policy could not be construed as standing up to terrorism but rather choosing by which terrorism to be intimidated.

The Government went so far as to act in a desensitised way towards its own citizens. After just three months, the investigation into the biggest mass murder in independent Ireland was quietly wound down. The Barron Inquiry established almost three decades later to investigate allegations of collusion between Ulster loyalists and the British military and intelligence agencies criticised the inadequacy of the Garda investigation.[11] The report noted that the bombing had dovetailed with unionist opposition to Sunningdale and certainly weakened Dublin's resolve to defend the power-sharing administration.[12] It also concluded that it was unlikely the loyalists acted without assistance, given that in May 1974 they did not have the capabilities to carry out such a sophisticated and large-scale operation.[13] The Secretary of State for Northern Ireland, Merlyn Rees, later confessed that a subversive faction in British Army Intelligence, which in his words was 'out of control', undermined his Government's Northern Ireland policies:

> There's no doubt it [the subversive faction within British Army Intelligence] reflected the views of a number of soldiers, let's go in and fix this lot and so on. But that it went on, and that it went on from [British Army Headquarters in] Lisburn and it went on from the Army Information Service and those associated with it, I have no doubt at all.[14]

Remarkably, considering the loss of life involved, the Barron Report concluded that 'the Government of the day showed little interest in the bombings' and 'when information was given to them suggesting that the British authorities had intelligence naming the bombers, this was not followed up'.[15] This conformed to consistent government practice throughout the 1970s and 1980s of general disinterest in thoroughly investigating cases of collusion between the British Government's military forces and loyalist paramilitaries. As government policy dictated that the British were partners in achieving common objectives and defeating a shared foe, investigating collusion would have complicated the Government's narrative that pitted the forces of law and order on both sides of the Irish Sea against the 'men of violence'.

The other factor that preoccupied the Government at this time was the cost of responding to the Northern conflict, including that associated with the 3,000 members of the Republic's security forces patrolling the border. 'Our whole economy has suffered from the events in Northern Ireland', Cosgrave told the Dáil. The Taoiseach provided figures outlining how the increased funds required to expand the army and police was sufficient to have provided up to 8,000 houses, accommodating up to 40,000 people, or provided industrial grants capable of creating 20,000 new jobs. Children's allowances or non-contributory old age pensions could be increased by 50 per cent or unemployment assistance doubled, and he estimated that tourism would be twice its current level were it not for the Troubles in the North.[16] In his appeal to the electorate to eliminate violence, Cosgrave warned against identifying with those seeking to highlight injustices in Northern Ireland or to accept any parallels with previous crises in Ireland's history. Rather, the Taoiseach declared that 'people must not be tricked into lending credibility to demonstrations which play on natural sympathy for human suffering' and they 'must beware of misleading propaganda which trades on false analogies which have no foundation in events in the past in our history'.[17] This rationale would be used to discredit those who highlighted injustices perpetrated by the British Army or against the nationalist minority in Northern Ireland.

The Government's melancholic fatalism was laid bare when a confidential internal memo written by Labour's spokesman on Northern Ireland, Conor Cruise O'Brien[18] found its way into the public domain. In it, O'Brien framed the conflict in terms of placating unionists or suffering a bloodbath,[19] suggesting that Government policy was now less about embarking on a charm offensive so much as simply staying out of sight lest they provoke loyalist rage. While Sunningdale had been brought down by unionist intransigence and British inertia, O'Brien's memorandum reinforced, if not rewarded, both stances.

An internal US embassy report described the leaked memo as 'the most complete and coherent explanation we have heard of GOI [Government of Ireland] policy toward NI [Northern Ireland]'.[20] That O'Brien had authored the report bolstered the perception that he was pivotal in formulating Government strategy towards the North but the effect of the leak was that 'GOI policy has again been made to look uncoordinated and lacking in leadership from PM Cosgrave'.[21] O'Brien's basic premise that a policy of keeping a low profile might help avert a hardline loyalist majority in Northern Ireland's forthcoming elections appeared, according to the US embassy, 'completely unrealistic' as such a majority seemed inevitable and there was little Dublin could do to forestall it. The embassy found O'Brien's view that the Irish Army would be unable to protect Northern Catholics should the British withdraw even more controversial. While it was 'probably safe' to assume that soldiers under the control of the Irish Government could do little to save Belfast Catholics they might, the report argued, be capable of playing a role in the border regions: 'By entirely excluding this possibility, Cruise O'Brien is supporting the claim of the IRA to be [the] Catholic community's safest line of defence.' Hemmed in between a British Army that viewed them as an enemy to be confronted and an Irish Government that characterised them as a burden that could not be helped, northern nationalists would have to look to themselves. While the collapse of the power-sharing executive had left the Government 'depressed and dispirited', and it was clear that Cosgrave advocated 'a lowering of pressure for Irish unity', the embassy wondered if the 'gloom could cause overreaction'.[22]

The publication of O'Brien's memo ignited a media storm and there was substantial political fallout. SDLP Assembly member for Derry, Michael Canavan, told his party that since the collapse of the Northern executive 'an isolationist trend had been apparent in many of the Dublin Government statements'. Looking through what he described as 'the eyes of the embattled Northern minority', Canavan said 'the policy of many local members of the Dublin Government is disinterest, disengagement and demoralisation. The justification for it seems to be to placate the loyalists.'[23] The US embassy noted that the SDLP felt 'very let down by new GOI line' and their contacts within the Government admitted that 'even SDLP moderates are angry' accusing Dublin of undercutting their negotiating position and removing moral support from Northern Ireland's Catholic community. The embassy report could see how a low-profile policy might appeal to many in the Republic alarmed by violence and eager that it should not spread south, but this sentiment was 'motivated by escapism, rather than by [a] rational desire to placate northern [P]rotestants'.[24] The Irish Government, the report speculated, might end up getting the worst of both worlds – weakening the SDLP, the main bulwark against the IRA, and making no impact on unionists.

While obsessed with how northern Protestants viewed the Republic, the Government failed to link unionist fears with religiously inspired restrictions on civil liberties. In 1974, Cosgrave voted against his own Government's proposals to liberalise the state's draconian contraception laws, ensuring the bill's defeat. As the *Belfast Telegraph* pointed out, while politicians in the Republic were 'ready to ask us to accept revolutionary political change without a quibble, there is no thought of reciprocation in the field of basic human rights'.[25]

Symptomatic of the Government's new line on the North was the consistent threat to hold a referendum to remove Articles 2 and 3 from the Constitution, provisions which Foreign Minister Garret FitzGerald described as 'disastrous' as 'they had no practical effect whatever and were a source of division in this country'.[26] Leading a Fianna Fáil party still finding its feet in opposition, Jack Lynch described the Government's policy that nothing should be said or done that might escalate violence in the North as 'very negative'. One could not, he said, eliminate people's aspirations and they had made clear to unionists that reunification would not be 'push[ed] … down their throats'. He took issue too with the term 'bi-partisan policy', as it implied that both Government and opposition devised policy, and preferred the term 'unified approach', which involved Fianna Fáil supporting the Government when their policies converged.[27] O'Brien countered by claiming that while repeating the 'formulae of the past' might help unite Fianna Fáil, it undermined Government efforts to lower the political temperature in Northern Ireland. He also regretted Lynch's use of the term 'second guarantor' to describe the Irish Government's role as 'it seemed to imply that we had control over events in Northern Ireland, which in fact we had not got. It would be irresponsible to pretend that we had.'[28] As unity was unobtainable in the present circumstances 'it was not a practicable goal of policy' and Minister O'Brien said he was not actively working towards it.[29]

Collusion and the British military campaign in Northern Ireland

As early as July 1972, the British Government had told Dublin that the Ulster Defence Association was a bigger threat than the IRA, not least because of its greater numbers.[30] However, London's indulgence of the UDA transformed that organisation from an amateur motley crew of malcontents into a well-trained and armed sectarian killing machine. This was in large part facilitated by the British Army's locally recruited Ulster Defence Regiment (UDR).

Although the UDR had been established as a replacement of the thoroughly discredited B-Specials, its membership was initially drawn from that very organisation.[31] According to a British Government 1973 report, joint membership of the UDR (i.e. British Army) and UDA (i.e. loyalist paramilitaries) was 'widespread', with soldiers living 'double lives'. Indeed, according to the report many UDR commanders considered such dual membership normal. The UDR was described as the 'best' source of weapons for loyalist terror groups and their 'only significant source' of modern weapons. Moreover, according to the report, many UDR members' primary loyalty was to 'Ulster' rather than to the British Government and they could not be relied upon if London decided on a course of action with which they disagreed.[32]

Rather than being an unintended outcome, the inclusion of loyalist paramilitaries within the British Army resulted from government policy and doctrines. A document from the Ministry of Defence (MoD) to the Prime Minister's Office dated 29 November 1972 outlined official policy in force since July of that year on matters related to UDR members associated with the largest and most lethal of the loyalist paramilitary groups, the UDA. Despite the fact that the UDA would murder seventy-one people during 1972 alone, the document claimed it was official policy that 'an application to join the UDR would not be automatically rejected because of UDA membership'. The document pointed out that the UDA was not an illegal organisation (though that was based on British government policy rather than an objective assessment of the threat it posed) and that one of its 'important functions' was to channel what it described as 'Protestant energies' into 'a constructive and disciplined direction'.[33] Accordingly, the MoD report concluded that 'it was not considered desirable or practical to make membership of the UDA in itself a bar to membership of the UDR'.[34] At this time, the UDR was composed of eleven battalions and fifty-nine companies providing 8,000 troops to the British Army.[35]

Following the breakdown of its talks with the IRA in July 1972 the British Government concluded that 'if the [British] Army did not attack the IRA the probability was that the UDA would' and therefore it advocated that the UDR be 'used more widely than before'.[36] The minutes of this same government meeting reveal that the British Army's General Officer Commanding would be consulting with the UDA later that day to tell them that 'their efforts as vigilantes in their own areas were acceptable'.[37]

The results were predictable. Between 1972 and 1976, loyalist paramilitaries killed 567 people, mainly Catholic civilians, frequently with the support or connivance of Britain's security forces. On 31 July 1975, for example, members of a southern-based music group, 'The Miami Showband', were slaughtered after they stopped at a checkpoint manned by several members of the UDR in uniform who were also members of the (then legal) UVF . Three weeks later two young men returning from the All-Ireland football semi-final at Croke Park halted at a similar checkpoint in Co. Armagh manned by members of the UDR and were promptly murdered. In an attempt to instil terror within the Catholic/ nationalist community and to deter support for the IRA, loyalists carried out retaliatory attacks, frequently on random Catholics, after British Army or police personnel were killed. Indeed, more civilians died at the hands of loyalist para-militaries during the Troubles than any other group operating in Northern Ireland, be they republican or state forces. Civilians constituted 88 per cent of all loyalist killings, with the next biggest group being other loyalist paramilitaries (9.4 per cent) who were more than twice as likely to be killed as militant republicans (4.1 per cent).[38]

British undercover military forces, such as the Special Air Services (SAS), were responsible for multiple extra-judicial killings of unarmed individuals and made several hundred incursions into the Republic. On 13 May 1976, Garret FitzGerald told the Dáil that there had been over three hundred *recorded* cross-border incursions by British soldiers during the previous three years[39] but the number of unrecorded forays during this period is impossible to quantify. That the SAS was an anti-republican force as opposed to one challenging terrorism from whatever quarter it might come was evident from the fact that it was deployed in IRA-dominated South Armagh and not in the loyalist heartland of North Armagh. South Armagh had proved particularly problematic for the British forces: forty-nine British soldiers had been killed there by 1976 in addition to a high number of RUC and UDR casualties while the IRA had yet to suffer a single fatality.[40]

Much of British military thinking towards Ireland was informed by colonial campaigns fought in different parts of their Empire. The chief counterinsurgency strategist for the British Army in Northern Ireland during the early 1970s was Brigadier Frank Kitson, whose previous military operations, for which he had been awarded state honours, were in Kenya and Malaysia, sites of numerous war crimes.[41] The General Officers Commanding in Northern Ireland during this time, Ian Freeland and Harry Tuzo, were veterans of counterinsurgency campaigns in Cyprus and Brunei respectively. A key part of the military doctrine was identifying hostile and friendly forces to be suppressed and incorporated as needs be. In the context of Northern Ireland this involved a one-sided campaign against the IRA and the community from which they sprang, reflected, for example, in the partisan internment campaign, but also involved harnessing loyalist support to buttress the army and minimise the loss of regular soldiers. British ministers have since gone on record maintaining that London had 'no alternative' but to cooperate with loyalists given that they were fighting a common enemy and the undesirability of fighting a war on two fronts.[42]

Responding to British pressure for enhanced security cooperation, the Secretary of State for Northern Ireland, Merlyn Rees, and Minister for Justice, Patrick Cooney, met on 18 September 1974 at Baldonnel military airport along with the RUC Chief Constable and Garda Commissioner.[43] Following the meeting, four specialist panels were set up under the joint chairmanship of senior officers from both police forces who met thereafter on a monthly basis to coordinate cross-border security issues. Remarkably, the Irish side made no reference to the Dublin and Monaghan bombings that had killed thirty-four of their citizens only four months earlier, nor did they seek to coordinate ways to prevent similar atrocities in the future. Instead, the meeting focussed on the IRA, with the Minister of Justice inviting suggestions from the British on how better his Government might combat republicans. This was despite the fact that shortly before and after the Dublin and Monaghan bombings the British Government had had several meetings with the leadership of the UVF, the organisation implicated in the attacks.[44] Indeed, despite the fact that the UVF had already killed twenty-four people during the first four months of 1974, the British Government legalised the organisation in April that year.[45]

Underpinning many of the Irish government positions was an assumption that the interests of the British and Irish states largely converged. Yet, ministers in successive Dublin Governments knew that collusion between the British Government's military forces and loyalist paramilitaries on both sides of the border took place, along with undercover subversion designed to influence or even destabilise the Irish Government. For example, when an MI6 agent was caught red-handed in Dublin receiving classified documents from Detective-Sergeant Patrick Crinnion of the Garda's Special Detective Unit, both men were allowed to leave for Britain without prison sentences.[46] From time to time, concerns were raised about collusion in Northern Ireland but never pursued vigorously and were met with implausible fob-offs.[47]

Preparations for Doomsday

While the withdrawal of British troops from Northern Ireland had been a recurring theme since the outbreak of the Troubles, speculation reached yet higher levels during the summer of 1974. This was in part a reaction to the breakdown of power-sharing institutions, but it also related to Harold Wilson's premiership. After all, in November 1971, when leader of the opposition, Wilson had proposed to the House of Commons steps to achieve a united Ireland over a fifteen-year period. He had outraged the Irish political elite by secretly meeting the IRA in Dublin in March 1972 while his televised address at the peak of the UWC strike suggested a sincere contempt for Ulster loyalism.

The seemingly interminable character of the Northern Ireland conflict, its viciousness, its cost to the British exchequer and the loss of hundreds of British soldiers during the previous three years had all served to encourage a 'troops out' sentiment, consistently reflected in opinion polls. The instability of British politics, reflected in the Labour Government's minority status, was another reason for a Wilson administration to rid itself of an unpopular and expensive war. Ted Heath told John Hume that he believed the Labour Government wanted to withdraw from Ulster, not least because the party had what he called 'a neurosis' about the Northern Ireland seats in the House of Commons, all bar one of which voted with the Tories.[48] However, Dublin took succour from the fact that any British administration would have to consider the damage to trade that would follow the loss of its third largest customer; a likely scenario should a British withdrawal precipitate violence throughout the Republic.

On 10 June, less than two weeks after the collapse of Northern Ireland's power-sharing executive, the Irish Government established a committee to study the implications of a substantial increase in the size of the Irish Army. Despite the Troubles, the numbers employed in the defence forces had dropped well below the established strength of 14,231. Indeed, when one excluded the small naval service and air corps, recruits in training, those engaged in educating the FCÁ command staffs, apprentices, bandsmen and other non-operational elements, the effective fighting force was a mere 5,500 soldiers,[49] substantially smaller than the Ulster Defence Regiment let alone any other armed force in the North. The 16,000-strong FCÁ was insufficiently trained and, even if they could be transformed into combat soldiers, the Government had nowhere near the numbers of troops necessary to respond to a British withdrawal from Northern Ireland. For a successful military intervention to establish complete control of the North, the Government estimated that a force of 60,000 troops would be required costing an additional £220 million.[50] Even this number, however, would be inadequate to maintain essential services such as water and electricity given that, as dramatically illustrated in May, Northern Ireland's power stations were located within loyalist areas and possessed exclusively unionist workforces, making them extremely vulnerable to sabotage. The Government believed that an expansion of the army to 20,000–25,000 soldiers could conceivably be achieved without disrupting the workforce, as the personnel could be drawn mainly from the unemployed or recent school-leavers, but that any force above that number could cause labour shortages. Allied to the costs associated with a massive hike in military spending would be declines in revenue from tourism and foreign investment predicted to be in the region of a quarter of a billion pounds should a conflagration engulf the island.

While the Government might expect the support of the IRA, and the nationalist community generally (78,400 Catholic men of military age lived in the six counties, the report estimated),[51] the army would have to contend with at least twelve loyalist paramilitary groups, which could muster somewhere between 10,000 and 35,000 fighting men. In terms of conventional military capabilities, their resources were considered to be minuscule and they would be 'vulnerable to timely and effective intervention by a disciplined military force'. They might, however, be able to wage 'a protracted war of attrition while wiping out the minority population living in isolated enclaves'. The report concluded that 'the lessons of recent history indicate that it is not possible for an army to impose its will on a society which has the will to resist' and consequently 'an attempt to subdue these groups could result in protracted urban guerrilla warfare which is impossible to eliminate'.[52]

The implications of expanding the army were equally stark and the process of maximising military preparedness might itself trigger an escalation. According to the report, it would be impossible to substantially increase the armed forces without taking measures that would 'clearly indicate our intentions to people in the North, in Britain and in this part of the country'. Any public or unusual methods to substantially increase the armed forces would increase the likelihood of an even greater conflagration and might even 'bring about the contingency for which it was designed to provide but which otherwise might not have become a reality'. It could 'greatly reduce, if not entirely eliminate any degree of impartiality remaining in the RUC and UDR', which would further enhance the capabilities of loyalist paramilitaries. Moreover, an enhanced Irish Army might encourage the nationalist community 'to rely on a degree of protection from our forces which it would not be possible, in practice, to provide' and encourage nationalist representatives to adopt political positions 'contrary to the best interests of their electorate'.[53] Recruitment to the IRA would most likely swell, as they would seek to defend territory believing Irish army assistance would be forthcoming.

Most revealing, perhaps, was the conclusion that were the Irish Government and its army to appear prepared to assume the burden of running Northern Ireland it might encourage the British Government to pull out its forces: 'if we were to appear to be ready to face up to the security and economic burdens of intervention in the North, it might lead the British to hasten their own relinquishment of these burdens'.[54] In other words, the state of economic and military unpreparedness that had characterised the Government's approach to Irish unity for so long might actually induce the British to stay, if only to prevent an even greater catastrophe.

The reality was that the Government would struggle to bring troop levels up to the establishment strength of 14,000 and increase the number of Gardaí. Cosgrave had two days to digest the report before, accompanied by cabinet colleagues Garret FitzGerald and James Tully, he travelled to London for a meeting with his British counterpart, Harold Wilson, Foreign Secretary, James Callaghan, and Secretary of State for Northern Ireland, Merlyn Rees. Without prompting from the Irish side, Wilson said there were two things to which his Government could not agree. The first was any attempt to establish a new Constitution for Northern Ireland other than by an Act of Westminster – an allusion to talk by some unionists of a unilateral declaration of independence – or any arrangement that did not include power sharing and an Irish dimension, as there could be no return to pre-1972 Stormont rule. An independent Northern Ireland would be completely unsustainable, Wilson maintained, and would never gain currency at Westminster, where the eleven loyalist MPs constituted a tiny minority of the 630 parliamentarians. The Prime Minister was in no doubt about London's leverage over recalcitrant unionists and told the Irish delegation that

> The North could not live for a day without Britain. It simply was not a threat to say that the Loyalists could bring the life of the province to a standstill. This was all right as a destructive tactic but you could not run a Government or an administration on this principle. You can do it for a period of weeks but you cannot run a country on the basis of a strike.[55]

In what was perhaps a gesture to persuade the Irish that, Sunningdale debacle aside, they were better with Labour, Wilson expressed anxiety about ongoing talks between Conservative backbenchers and the Unionists in advance of the expected general election. A result that produced a small majority for either of the main parties could produce a difficult situation, Wilson mused, before, realising his audience was composed of a coalition Government, quickly recovering by clarifying that 'it's all right for you but in the Commons there [are] some funny groups of people – oddballs and other types'.[56]

Wilson called the election the following week and though Labour improved its parliamentary representation at the expense of the Tories its majority over all others was only three seats. As time progressed, the Labour Government would, as Wilson had feared, become increasingly reliant on 'oddballs and other types'. In Northern Ireland, the forces of uncompromising unionism that had rejected Sunningdale (the UUP, DUP and Vanguard) won almost 60 per cent of the vote. Faulkner's Unionist Party of Northern Ireland took a mere 2.9 per cent of the vote and quickly disappeared into irrelevance, formalised by Faulkner's premature death in a horse-riding accident two and a half years later. Though it largely escaped the attention of government and media commentators at the time, a substantial section of the nationalist community did not participate in the electoral process.

Deeply discouraged by the election result, the Irish Government now saw a very barren political landscape for the forthcoming constitutional convention with no body of loyalist opinion willing to compromise with nationalists. The temptation to recoil into a ball and hide away was undoubtedly strong. One cabinet minister privately told the US embassy that the Government might be better to simply 'forget about the North' for a few years and focus instead on the economic challenges.[57]

To add to the uncertainty, the British Labour Government, which had opposed membership of the EEC when in opposition, was committed to holding a referendum on whether the UK should stay or leave the trading bloc. Having twice postponed its own application to join the EEC when de Gaulle vetoed British membership, the Irish Government was placed in a dilemma as to whether they should stay in the Common Market without Britain. By July 1974, both Government and opposition had indicated that, irrespective of the outcome of the British referendum, Ireland would stay in the EEC.[58] The issue was put to bed on 5 June 1975 when over 67 per cent of the UK electorate voted in favour of continued EEC membership, though in Northern Ireland the figure was little over half (52 per cent).

The Government was further spooked by communications between Harold Wilson's special assistant, Bernard Donoghue, and assistant cabinet Secretary Dermot Nally, along with a conversation between Liam Cosgrave and Harold Wilson shortly after Labour's return to power in March 1974. On that occasion, Wilson, according to Foreign Minister Garret FitzGerald, had 'placed so much emphasis on British political and public pressure for withdrawal as to suggest that he himself might be thinking along these lines'.[59] Coupled with the policy of combating the IRA, the Government's other objective during the remainder of its time in office would be to ensure that the British did *not* withdraw from the North. These two objectives were, by their nature, defensive and aimed at damage limitation. According to Garret FitzGerald, the SDLP 'wanted to prepare contingency plans for a withdrawal and to discuss them with the British. We refused, however, as this would give the British the excuse they might perhaps want to get out of Northern Ireland, and it was our policy to avoid this at all costs.'[60] In January 1975, FitzGerald had sought and received an assurance from US Secretary of State Henry Kissinger that should the British appear to be on the verge of withdrawing, the US would consider asking London to review its decision.[61] The Americans were not reported to have expressed any surprise that this request contradicted that which had been made just three years earlier by FitzGerald's predecessor, who had toured North America and the world seeking support for a British withdrawal. FitzGerald portrayed Northern Ireland to the US Government as an issue of major international importance that could threaten Western European security, claiming that Cuba's long-distance intervention in

Angola was similar to the role Libya could play in Ireland should the British pull out.[62]

The Foreign Minister developed this line of argument further when he and Jack Lynch met his British counterpart, Jim Callaghan, eight months later at a private informal gathering at FitzGerald's holiday home in west Cork. When Callaghan asked what they thought London should do, FitzGerald complained that it appeared that the British were deliberately creating an air of uncertainty and stressed 'the gravity of the problem that would be created *for us* should the British Government fail to control the situation and to protect the minority'. Such a failure, he argued, could threaten the Republic's very foundations and tempt countries like the Soviet Union, China or Libya to exploit the ensuing political vacuum. To quell Callaghan's scepticism, FitzGerald highlighted the Government's impotence when Dubliners destroyed the British embassy in 1972 and Lynch pointed out the problems he had faced as the Troubles erupted in 1969. When Callaghan sought their opinion on a British declaration of intent to withdraw from the North after a fixed period, Lynch claimed it would be 'highly dangerous' and FitzGerald 'wholeheartedly concurred'.[63] Lynch's depiction of a British declaration of intent as a calamitous act came only two months before he, and the Fianna Fáil party he led, launched their 'Halloween' policy document, the central plank of which was a British declaration of intent to withdraw from Northern Ireland.[64]

Censorship

During the 1973 election, Fine Gael and Labour had presented themselves as the liberal alternative to an authoritarian Fianna Fáil, entrenched after sixteen years in power. When Jack Lynch tried to push through the Offences Against the State (Amendment) Bill in December 1972, Paddy Cooney had asked how the Minister for Justice could 'come into this parliament and ask it to support a bill the like of which can only be found on the statute book of South Africa ... there is a limit to the measures a democracy is entitled to adopt in order to protect itself ... that limit is exceeded in this bill'.[65] Similarly, during the heady days of opposition, when his party defiantly claimed that 'the seventies would be socialist', Conor Cruise O'Brien declared that 'Labour believes that TV and radio should serve the working people and that it should never deceive the people by concealing from them things which the politicians and economic ruling class does not want them to know'.[66] With remarkable ease, both Cooney and O'Brien, along with many of their cabinet colleagues, traded opposition liberalism for government authoritarianism, as the coalition presented itself as Ireland's last remaining defence against anarchy. But, as the influential journal *Hibernia* pointed out,

> Dublin proclaims the virtues of law and order and calls that a policy as if it had thought of coming down on the side of communal violence and decided not to after a hard debate. Law and order is an axiom not a policy, and a government which is reduced to calling it a policy has none. There seems to be no contingency plans, no ability to think of any other solution other than that ill-defined panacea of power-sharing. No wonder the response to the collapse of Sunningdale was no response. Our politicians are prisoners not shapers of events. Without a northern policy the government tends more and more to think in purely 26 county terms, to see the Provos primarily as a threat to the southern state.[67]

Disappointment awaited those who expected that Conor Cruise O'Brien's appointment as Minister for Post and Telegraphs would result in a relaxation of state-imposed media restrictions. On taking office O'Brien had reiterated his 'unequivocal intention to remove Section 31'[68] before quickly becoming the chief champion of state censorship. In March 1974, O'Brien wrote to the Chairman of the RTÉ Authority, Donal Ó Moráin, criticising the station's coverage of 'the civilian front of a political murder-gang' and 'the role of influential elements in the News Room in giving aid and comfort to the Provisional IRA'.[69] After RTÉ's flagship current affairs programme *7 Days* broadcast a programme on internment in October 1974, O'Brien 'exploded' and engaged in a public row with RTÉ's Head of Current Affairs, Des Fisher. A few days later the programme's producer was removed from *7 Days* and sent to the 'Siberia' of light entertainment. As Gene Kerrigan has written, the effect on RTÉ was to 'wipe away from the airwaves for the next decade virtually any view of the Northern conflict or its spin-off in the South which didn't fall within the consensus as defined by government ministers'.[70] Consequently, according to one senior producer, RTÉ 'staggered through the 1970s and 1980s, barely making sense of what was going on in Northern Ireland'.[71] A culture of fear and paranoia developed within RTÉ; journalists and broadcasters became risk-averse in a way that guaranteed non-representation of entire communities in Northern Ireland and sections of opinion in the Republic. As Betty Purcell pointed out while Section 31 was still in force:

> People err on the cautious side where there is doubt. Whole neighbourhoods were silenced because they are too close to a possibility of breaking the ban. The question is not, 'Who is in Sinn Féin?' but 'Who is definitely *not* in Sinn Féin?'[72]

The state broadcaster's implementation of Section 31 was further complicated by the fact that throughout the 1970s and 1980s a small but influential cabal of senior RTÉ figures were members or supporters of the Workers' Party, Sinn Féin's bitterest opponents who had split with the Provisionals some years earlier.[73]

The national broadcaster was emasculated further when, on 14 July 1975, the head of the government information service was appointed to the newly created position of RTÉ's Assistant Director and simultaneously as head of the state's Irish-language radio station, Radio na Gaeltachta. Four members of the RTÉ governing authority were replaced by more amenable substitutes[74] and Section 31 was expanded to prohibit even reports of interviews with either wing of the IRA or 'Provisional Sinn Féin'. Taking no chances, RTÉ further extended the ban to include any member of Sinn Féin, whether speaking in that capacity or not, speaking on any topic irrespective of whether it referred to Northern Ireland or the use of force for political ends. Later, as the Emergency Powers Bill went through parliament in September 1976, *7 Days* was axed altogether, with its editor resigning in protest.[75] Simultaneously, RTÉ's so-called 'Irish Lobby' responsible for Irish-language programming and its flagship current affairs programme *Féach* felt under renewed pressure shortly after Seán Mac Réamoinn, a member of the RTÉ Authority, had publicly disagreed with O'Brien when the Minister described the 1916 Rising as 'anti-democratic and wrong'.[76]

Because Government censorship targeted republicans as opposed to advocates of violence it produced bizarre anomalies. Unionist leader Bill Craig could be reported on RTÉ saying that the kind of action he contemplated might involve killing Catholics, yet a caller to a light-entertainment radio show discussion on the suitability of mushrooms for wine production could not be heard when it was discovered he was a member of Sinn Féin.[77] An RTÉ reporter was fired from her job when she allowed Martin McGuinness's voice to go out on the airwaves as part of a news report[78] while Unionist MP Harold McCusker could be broadcast saying that he would shoot on sight any Garda or Irish soldier he encountered north of the border.[79] The leader of an industrial dispute at a Dublin confectionary plant could not be interviewed due to his membership of Sinn Féin[80] while Ivan Foster, a DUP Assembly member, could be reported at his party conference asking the British Prime Minister to launch nuclear strikes on the Republic.[81] These restrictions applied at all times – including during election campaigns – even though Sinn Féin was a legal political party and even when it outpolled its rivals.

Censorship extended to popular music. Shortly after three senior IRA members escaped by helicopter from Mountjoy jail on 31 October 1973, the Wolfe Tones released *The Helicopter Song*, which enjoyed unprecedented demand despite a complete lack of airplay. The song became the first ever to top the charts in its first week of release and would spend several weeks at number one.[82] When

Dermot Hegarty released a song called *Nineteen Men*, about the escape of republicans from the top-security Portlaoise prison in August 1974, it also topped the charts for a few weeks despite a Government ban.[83] Other noteworthy songs from this period that attracted official ire included Paul McCartney's chart-topper *Give Ireland Back to the Irish* and a John Lennon album containing songs such as *Sunday Bloody Sunday* and *Luck of the Irish*, which accused the British of genocide in Ireland.[84]

Historiography and the commemoration of historical events also proved to be arenas of contentious politics. The Government concluded that positive references to 1916, to earlier IRA exploits, or indeed to pre-independence militancy against British rule in Ireland, benefited the contemporary IRA. This view chimed with that of many vigilante historians who embarked on a crusade to cleanse Irish history of 'myth'. The revisionist project was less about history than contemporary politics, as historian F.S.L. Lyons declared in December 1971 when he issued a rallying call to his fellow-scholars, proclaiming that

> in the present situation, with the dire past still overhanging the dire present, the need to go back to fundamentals and consider once more the meaning of independence, asserts itself with almost intolerable urgency. The theories of revolution, the theories of nationality, the theories of history, *which have brought Ireland to its present pass*, cry out for reexamination and the time is ripe to try to break the great enchantment which for too long has made myth more congenial than reality.[85]

Ostensibly about professionalising history and debunking myths that had fostered animosities between Britain and Ireland, revisionism was frequently tailored for political purposes. Conor Cruise O'Brien warned the Dáil that schoolchildren were in danger of being taught 'the philosophy of bombs' and, referring to an Official IRA attack on a British army base in England, which claimed seven lives, asked rhetorically: 'Were the seeds of Aldershot sown in some Irish schoolroom?'[86] The attack on the headquarters of the British Army's 16th parachute brigade was in direct retaliation for the killing of fourteen civilians by that regiment three weeks earlier in Derry but it suited the Minister's purpose to target primary schoolteachers who had allegedly placed time bombs inside impressionable minds that detonated with deadly effect on reaching adulthood. Similarly, at the inquest into the death of Lord Mountbatten in 1979, the state's coroner said that 'it is necessary to stress again the great responsibility the teachers of any nation have for the way they interpret history and pass it on to the youth of their country'.[87] Such views helped promote the notion that violence in Northern Ireland was a product of poor history teaching in the Republic as opposed to misgovernance in Northern Ireland.[88]

In 1972 the Government had refused to commemorate the 1916 Rising because of 'the Northern situation'[89] and from 1974 the state commemoration of the Irish Republic's proclamation of independence was discontinued indefinitely. Much to the frustration of successive administrations, however, events designed to commemorate patriot heroes of old frequently attracted large turnouts.[90] As the sixtieth anniversary of the Easter Rebellion approached, the Government claimed an official commemoration was impossible given the number of soldiers required for duty along the border with Northern Ireland but forbade others from organising a tribute, in particular a large commemorative parade planned for Dublin's city centre. Over 10,000 defied the ban and those arrested for participating included 1916 veteran Máire Comerford and Nora Connolly-O'Brien, daughter of the executed proclamation signatory, James Connolly. Fiona Plunkett, sister of another executed signatory of the 1916 proclamation, Joseph Plunkett, managed to escape arrest while David Thornley TD was expelled from the Labour Party.

A state of emergency

The coalition Government was beset by a series of security crises, some of which related to the funerals of IRA hunger-strikers who had died in English prisons. Michael Gaughan, a twenty-four-year-old IRA member, had lost half of his already modest body weight during his sixty-four-day hunger strike on the Isle of Wight and was subjected to repeated efforts at forced feeding, the last such attempt precipitating his death. The first IRA member to die on hunger strike since 1946, Gaughan's funeral turned into a major procession as a republican guard of honour brought him to London where thousands lined out to view his casket. From there, his remains were taken to Dublin, where another large turnout awaited, before making their way through Ireland to his homeplace in Mayo. Here, over 10,000 people listened to Daithí Ó Conaill proclaim that Gaughan had been 'tortured in prison by the vampires of a discredited empire, who were joined by decrepit politicians who were a disgrace to the name of Irish men'.[91]

The Government resolved to prevent a recurrence, and so when the thirty-four-year-old Frank Stagg died on 12 February 1976 after sixty-two days without food it went to extraordinary lengths to deny his request of a traditional republican funeral and to be buried beside Michael Gaughan. Sinn Féin, whose national organiser in Britain had been mandated by Stagg's will to oversee funeral arrangements, planned a procession in Dublin, Cork and Galway. In an effort to prevent any displays of support, the Government ordered that the aircraft

taking Stagg's body from London to Dublin be diverted to Shannon, where it
was then hijacked by government security forces and taken by helicopter to
Mayo for a supervised and heavily guarded private burial under metres of concrete.
Almost two years later, and after the twenty-four-hour police guard had been
taken away, Stagg's supporters, including one of his brothers, tunnelled underneath
the concrete, dug up his coffin and reburied him in the nearby Republican plot,
where he has remained ever since.[92]

An IRA ceasefire between February 1975 and January 1976 provided some
respite but this was largely offset by a dramatic increase in murders carried out
by loyalist paramilitaries such as the 'Shankill Butchers'.[93] Collusion between
loyalist paramilitaries and the British Army and police force also facilitated a
spate of attacks against Catholic civilians and republican activists.[94] The assassination of the British ambassador to Ireland, Christopher Ewart-Biggs, on 21
July 1976 triggered a man-hunt involving 4,000 Gardaí and 2,000 soldiers. The
Government recalled the Dáil on 1 September to revoke the state of emergency
that had existed continually since 1939 and to replace it with a new one 'arising
out of the armed conflict taking place in Northern Ireland'.[95] It also introduced
an Emergency Powers Bill and a Criminal Justice Bill. The renewed state of
emergency had all the hallmarks of being seen to do something. The Government
had already an impressive arsenal of legislation with which to tackle subversion
but these laws had been erratically enforced and security was frequently lax.
Days before he was killed, ambassador Ewart-Biggs had confessed to being
unhappy with the level of protection the Gardaí afforded him. In his diary, he
reported that 'they [the Irish security forces] are not very reassuring. They
thought for some reason that an attack on the car was unlikely as "it hasn't
happened yet". It seems to be the department of fingers crossed.'[96]

The Government sought to assure the British and public opinion that they
were on top of security but also identified an opportunity to extend the boundaries
of censorship yet further. Through Section 3 of the Criminal Law Bill, the
Government planned to extend Section 31-type censorship to the print media
by making editors and journalists responsible for any view they reported or
published. When *Washington Post* reporter Bernard Nossiter interviewed Conor
Cruise O'Brien in Dublin, the Minister explained that the threat of ten years'
imprisonment for those who fell foul of the new law combined with the Bill's
deliberate ambiguity would force editors to be hyper-cautious, if only to guarantee
their continued liberty. The Minister informed Nossiter that the Irish had a
cultural problem and the journalist got the 'distinct impression' that he viewed
Section 3 as an 'attempt to change the cultural setting'.[97] O'Brien spoke of 'a
whole framework of [school] teaching, of ballads of popular awe that enabled
the IRA to survive, even to flourish and most of all to recruit young and

impressionable people'.[98] Furthermore, he acknowledged that the Government's proposals could be used to punish music teachers who taught patriotic ballads or history teachers who extolled the virtues of Irish revolutionary heroes.[99]

O'Brien pulled out a file of personally selected reader's letters to the *Irish Press* – all critical of the Government and/or expressing a republican viewpoint – which he maintained represented the 'wrong headed culture' his Government's new legislation would eliminate. Nossiter immediately informed *Irish Press* editor, Tim Pat Coogan, of the Minister's intentions, allowing the paper and the parliamentary opposition to mobilise sufficient resources to force an amendment to the proposed law excluding print media from its purview.[100] However, during the coalition Government's time in office, the editors of all national newspapers were hauled before the courts for coverage related to the Northern Ireland conflict. In the case of *Hibernia*, the publication of a reader's letter, which put the word 'trial' in inverted commas when referring to the no-jury Special Criminal Court, was enough to trigger a legal prosecution.[101]

The Emergency Powers Bill raised sufficient concerns for President Ó Dálaigh, a former Attorney-General and Chief Justice, to refer the legislation to the Supreme Court, much to the Government's annoyance. Within an army barracks, and in the presence of soldiers, the Minister for Defence described President Ó Dálaigh as 'a thundering disgrace' for his 'amazing decision', before declaring that 'the army must support the state'. In essence, the Minister was accusing the army's Commander-in-Chief, and his constitutional superior, of subversion for referring the Bill to the Supreme Court. When Cosgrave refused to sack Donegan, Ó Dálaigh resigned, in what was an unparalleled gesture of defiance from an incumbent president.

The Criminal Justice Bill increased sentences for crimes already punishable under the Offences Against the State Act such as IRA membership. Suspects could now be held without charge for seven days, a period sufficiently long, *Hibernia* maintained, 'to disorientate most prisoners if held incommunicado, and enough time for any bruises that may have been inflicted by over zealous interrogators on the suspect during the initial 48 hour period to have cleared up'.[102] It was around this time that allegations surfaced of a 'Heavy Gang' within Garda Special Branch, already notorious for 'enhanced interrogation techniques' employed against republican suspects.[103] Garda Commissioner Ned Garvey consistently rejected such accusations and proved intolerant of dissent, going so far as to suggest to the Director of Public Prosecutions that the *Garda Review* editor be charged with subversion and incitement to violence for criticising Government policy.[104]

While cases of police brutality had surfaced periodically, given the restrictions of Section 31 and general self-censorship within the media many people first came to know of the 'Heavy Gang' only in February 1977 when the *Irish Times* published the results of a major investigation into the treatment of suspects held in Garda custody. The paper recounted the systematic maltreatment of citizens and the use of oppressive methods for extracting statements, the reliability of which, consequently, had to be doubted. One man known to suffer from claustrophobia related how he had been shut in a locker before Gardaí banged his head repeatedly on the table shouting: 'we'll break you, you fucker, we'll turn you into a vegetable'.[105] A pregnant Northern Irish woman was reported to have been repeatedly beaten by Gardaí in her home in front of her child because they believed she had thrown a milk bottle at their car.[106]

The Garda press office did little to reassure doubters when it declared that 'brutal interrogation methods are not a *routine* practice'.[107] Dismissing calls for an independent investigation, Minister for Justice Paddy Cooney claimed that accusations of Garda brutality 'emanated from people on the subversive side and their fellow travellers and I treat them accordingly and give them the weight they are entitled, and coming from that side they are entitled to very little weight indeed'.[108] In his memoirs, Conor Cruise O'Brien later recounted how a Garda detective had told him of how when one suspect had refused to answer questions 'they beat the shit out of him'. He refrained from telling his ministerial colleagues Garret FitzGerald and Justin Keating 'because I thought it would worry them', before adding 'it didn't worry me'.[109]

The return of Fianna Fáil, 1977–1979

The 1977 election was in many ways a replica of that fought four years earlier, with the North, security and alleged opposition disunity again prominent themes during the campaign. Only the actors had changed places. In 1973, Fianna Fáil had exploited Fine Gael's ambivalence and Labour's outright hostility to the Offences against the State Act. Now, it was Fianna Fáil's criticisms of the Emergency Powers Act and allegations of a Garda 'Heavy Gang' that were seized upon by the Coalition to suggest that Jack Lynch and his party were soft on terrorism. Conor Cruise O'Brien claimed that there was no difference between Fianna Fáil and the IRA and that, while Fianna Fáil might condemn violence, they privately adopted 'the straight Provo line'. The Minister also attributed the failure of a recent Paisley-inspired strike to unionist satisfaction with his Government's Northern policy: 'things would have been very different if there had been a feeling that Dublin was really aiming to take them over'.[110] The Attorney-General, John Kelly, complemented this view, claiming that Fianna Fáil was 'feared and distrusted by the Northern majority, compared at least with the grudging recognition of good intent which most of their leaders make in favour of the Coalition'. He described Haughey as a 'skulking Guy Fawkes' and claimed that 'the empty "Republican" ethos fostered by Fianna Fáil may … have prepared the spiritual ground for the new barbarism'.[111]

Reviewing his administration's performance, the Taoiseach, Liam Cosgrave, said the 'Northern question' had dominated elections and life in Ireland for a decade and he justified the introduction of repressive legislation by linking it with economic progress. Rising crime rates were attributed to the impact of the northern Troubles on southern society. The Government, he said, had made it clear that 'all other progress depends on our ability to eradicate from the country the threat of violence and destruction'.[112] Oliver J. Flanagan, who briefly succeeded Paddy Donegan as Minister for Defence, developed this theme further and claimed that because their government predecessors had been 'involved in the clandestine arming and equipping of an underground army it was no wonder that people from Britain were afraid to spend their holidays here'.[113] The Government's attempted gerrymander of constituencies backfired and exaggerated the swing to Fianna Fáil, which consequently won the largest majority in Irish electoral history. Prominent Government ministers, including Conor Cruise O'Brien and Paddy Cooney, lost their parliamentary seats.

Garret FitzGerald quickly replaced Liam Cosgrave as leader of Fine Gael. In a parting letter to British Prime Minister Jim Callaghan, FitzGerald communicated 'how much I appreciate your deep and genuine concern for the problem of Northern Ireland and, on a personal note, how much I hope that you will continue to be responsible for the affairs of the United Kingdom, and that part of it in particular, in the period ahead'. The outgoing Foreign Minister said he wrote this in the knowledge that under the British constitutional system documents of the previous administration were not shown to the incoming one.[114]

Bolstered by a commanding majority, Jack Lynch returned to office with his party anticipating a full term. The new Foreign Minister, Michael O'Kennedy, would play a key role in implementing Northern Ireland policy. In making George Colley Tánaiste, Lynch had empowered his chosen successor. Haughey, by contrast, was dispatched to the Department of Health where his rivals hoped he would be unlikely to build a power base.[115]

In Britain, Labour had a paper-thin parliamentary majority when Callaghan took the reins of office from Harold Wilson in 1976, but defections and by-election defeats quickly reduced them to a minority administration. Support from the Liberal Party – the so-called 'Lib-Lab pact' – would keep Labour afloat from March 1977 to May 1978 but thereafter they required the support or acquiescence of deputies from Northern Ireland for survival. All this made the Prime Minister risk-averse, particularly with any initiative that might antagonise unionists. On

Northern Ireland, Callaghan spent his brief premiership playing for time. The Irish Government's role in this context was to say as little as possible about a united Ireland, cooperate with crushing the IRA and otherwise acquiesce to British policy, about which they would be neither consulted nor asked for approval. All suggestions of Anglo-Irish summitry on the issue of Northern Ireland were rebuffed.[116]

An opportunity for a get-together short of a summit presented itself in the form of an EEC meeting scheduled for Copenhagen in April 1978, which both Lynch and Callaghan would attend. While Dublin sought a one-to-one consultation between the Prime Ministers on the margins of the meeting, the British countered with a proposal to break out of the EEC summit for fifteen minutes, which the Irish rejected. Apart from being rude to their colleagues from the seven other member states, Lynch insisted that he had much more to say to Callaghan than could be contained in a fifteen-minute talk. In the event, a specially arranged meeting did take place and lasted for an hour and a half. Callaghan made it clear he opposed giving Dublin 'any particular status' on Northern Ireland policy but that 'it was simply common sense that when difficulties arose they could get together and talk privately'. When Lynch disagreed and reminded Callaghan that in the Sunningdale Agreement the Republic had been given 'a very definite and open status', Callaghan said simply that 'things had happened since then' and that he could give 'no encouragement on the prospects for a new Sunningdale'.[117]

At a meeting between Michael O'Kennedy and Northern Secretary Roy Mason later in the year, the British were at pains to emphasise that the summit 'should be treated as one of those occasional series of exchanges between two friendly governments' and nothing more. When it came to Northern Ireland, the British had prepared positions on politics, security and the economy. Regarding the political dimension 'our position is that we are prepared to tell an interested government how we see the situation' while no provision was made for listening to Irish Government perspectives. On security matters, however, 'we would stress that both Governments need to work closely as allies against the common enemy'. Economically the British could envisage cross-border cooperation for mutual benefit but this was considered no different from normal British–Irish relations.[118] Indeed, the British sent Minister of State for the Foreign and Commonwealth Office, Frank Judd, to accompany Mason to demonstrate that the talks were Anglo-Irish in character rather than North–South.

After a disastrous winter marked by widespread industrial action, Callaghan was defeated in the House of Commons on 28 March by a single vote. The subsequent election held on 3 May saw Margaret Thatcher's Conservative Party take almost 44 per cent of the ballots cast to secure a majority of forty-three seats in the House of Commons. Airey Neave had been poised to take over the

Northern Ireland portfolio before his assassination by the Irish National Liberation Army (INLA) at the House of Commons on 30 March. In his stead, Thatcher appointed Humphrey Atkins, who embarked on an ill-fated quest to organise an all-party conference with a view to securing agreement on devolution.

The decline and fall of Jack Lynch

The contrast between the British and Irish premiers could not have been starker. Having spent almost a decade as Taoiseach and thirteen years as party leader, Jack Lynch was weary and clearly in the twilight of his career whereas Thatcher possessed the energy and zeal of the first-time prime minister armed with a handsome majority. As the British embassy in Dublin surmised in a confidential report: 'the Irish are very aware that they are dealing with a strong British Government with a full term office before them'.[119] Fianna Fáil's twenty-seat majority had quickly proved to be a headache. Although the 'Halloween' policy document that called for a British statement of intent to withdraw from the North had been quietly dropped, the Taoiseach occasionally felt obliged to give expression to this aspect of his party's very wide and multi-purpose Northern Ireland policy.[120]

Fianna Fáil performed disastrously in the first direct elections to the European Parliament in June 1979. The party's vote fell from its general election performance of 50.6 per cent to 34.6 per cent, its lowest vote in over fifty years, and it won only five of the fifteen seats available. The election elevated two independent candidates from strongly disaffected bodies of opinion; elected in Munster, T.J. Maher represented farmers, while in Connacht-Ulster, Neil Blaney articulated dissatisfaction with the Taoiseach's Northern Ireland policy. Blaney's comprehensive victory, elected on the first count with over 80,000 votes, was widely interpreted as a direct challenge to Jack Lynch.[121] Moreover, as an internal British report noted, many Fianna Fáil parliamentarians and members, influenced by Blaney's electoral success, 'suggested that it is Mr. Lynch's restrained Northern policy which is putting off voters'.[122] The post-election parliamentary party meeting did little to quell dissent as the leadership neither hinted at a cabinet reshuffle nor promised to redirect policy.

Events in Northern Ireland hastened Lynch's political demise. On the morning of 27 August 1979, Louis Mountbatten, the last colonial Viceroy of India and cousin of Queen Elizabeth II, was assassinated by an IRA bomb planted on his boat off the Sligo coast, which also killed three fellow travellers. Eighteen British soldiers, all members of the Parachute Regiment, were killed on the same day in Warrenpoint, Co. Down, the biggest loss that British military forces had sustained during a single attack in Ireland since 1921 and the Parachute Regiment's worst day since the Second World War.[123] Lynch's subsequent meeting with Thatcher at Mountbatten's funeral 'seemed humiliating from an Irish point of view' with the Taoiseach being 'subjected to a further brow-beating'.[124] On 9 September, Síle de Valera, granddaughter of Fianna Fáil's founding father, publicly expressed the anger and disillusionment within the party in a controversial speech that constituted 'a thinly veiled attack on Lynch's Northern policy'.[125] For a disciplined political party like Fianna Fáil, the time for backbenchers to criticise Northern Ireland policy was usually when out of government but for Síle de Valera and many others there were two Fianna Fáils, one in power, another in opposition, with Charles Haughey the pretender in exile.

During an eight-day visit to the US in his capacity as President of the EEC, Lynch inadvertently drove the final nail into his political coffin. In Washington, journalist Seán Cronin asked the Taoiseach about the then secret border security pact permitting the British Royal Air Force to sweep areas of the Republic for the IRA. In a fatal lapse, Lynch admitted that such a pact existed – something he had denied in the Dáil and to his own party. Its terms, he said, were secret because 'there is no point in telling your enemy [the IRA] what you are going to do to offset or overcome him'.[126] He confirmed that at Mountbatten's funeral Mrs Thatcher had asked him for the right of British troops to cross the border in 'hot pursuit' – something he had also previously denied – but maintained that he had refused. In what was to be the most damaging disclosure, Lynch also divulged that British military aircraft had the right to fly across the border as a result of the pact. Reaction at home was swift, with the Taoiseach's admission making front-page news in all national papers.

Lynch's position was debilitated further when Fianna Fáil lost two by-elections in his native Cork, one in his own constituency. Having personally canvassed during the campaigns and coming a day before the Washington debacle, the Fine Gael victories convinced many in the party that the Taoiseach had become an electoral liability. Fianna Fáil's landslide success in 1977 had created two-dozen new deputies in marginal constituencies and their vulnerability made them seek out a leader who could retain their seats in the next election. George Colley was identified too much with the ailing leadership and many felt that only Haughey could fill the void.

When the Taoiseach returned from the US, Martin O'Donoghue told him that Fianna Fáil was 'in danger of tearing itself apart'.[127] Lynch agreed that it was time to go and soon afterwards – probably 19 November – he told Colley of his intention, but not Haughey. On 5 December, Lynch announced his retirement and said that the election of his successor would take place two days later on 7 December. It was thought that a short campaign would suit Colley, as

Haughey would have little time to organise. Unbeknown to the party hierarchy, however, Haughey and his supporters had been plotting for months.

At the press conference on 5 December, Lynch named four possible contenders for the leadership – George Colley, Charles Haughey, Des O'Malley and Michael O'Kennedy. O'Malley was pledged to Colley and O'Kennedy was a dark horse with little support. This left the contest as it had been in 1966, but now there was no compromise candidate that would satisfy all. The *Irish Press*, the paper most closely identified with Fianna Fáil, did not take sides but argued that whoever became leader would have to keep Northern Ireland policy centre-stage and not simply react to violent events. In what might be considered a criticism of the Taoiseach, the paper editorialised that 'it is plain that there is no use waiting any longer for what crumbs of policy may fall from the not-so-rich-man's table of Whitehall'. It noted too that while economic concerns preoccupied many voters, it was issues relating to Northern Ireland policy that had precipitated Lynch's downfall.[128]

The other two daily national newspapers generally favoured Colley. Writing in the *Irish Independent*, Bruce Arnold claimed that

> There are too many question marks over Charles Haughey. He stalks the corridors of Leinster House, the silken predications of control and power emanating from his person. Yet nobody knows the nature of his republicanism and how it would manifest itself in terms of policy on Northern Ireland or a new attitude towards Britain. It would certainly be more hardline than Jack Lynch's. But how? And to what purpose? And with what results?[129]

On the day of the crucial vote the *Irish Independent* carried an editorial which, while not naming Haughey personally, stressed that

> the need to convince the Northern majority to come down from their battlements and mingle with the rest of us is an absolutely essential task facing any Taoiseach of this country, and he, therefore, must be someone they are not suspicious of ... If they [unionists] do not have confidence in the new Taoiseach they may isolate themselves even more from the rest of us, shutting themselves up in their strongholds and refusing to talk. And the cancer which is Northern violence will continue to spread.[130]

Leaving aside the fact that unionists tended to be suspicious of any Southern politician, the paper betrayed a lack of interest in the views of northern nationalists who, it was assumed, had no stake in the matter. In its election-day editorial, the *Cork Examiner* claimed that Haughey had done himself a disservice 'by not revealing his thoughts on the Northern question in recent times' as 'acquittal or no the spectre of the arms crisis still hangs over him in the public mind'.[131]

With the backing of twenty of the twenty-five members of Government, and thus needing the support of only twenty-two backbenchers, Colley was confident of victory but in what proved to be a contest between cabinet and backbenchers, Haughey defeated the Tánaiste by forty-four votes to thirty-eight. The new backbenchers, many of whom had clinched their seats by less than a thousand votes, were particularly sensitive to talk of the Government haemorrhaging support and, as one of them put it, the ministers voted to save their jobs while they had voted to save their seats.[132] An earlier resignation might have saved Colley but Ireland's hosting of the EEC presidency had precluded Lynch stepping down before December and during the last half of 1979 the Government had stumbled from one crisis to another. It was clear also that some deputies, such as Bill Loughnane and Síle de Valera, who had spearheaded attacks on Jack Lynch during the twilight of his leadership, backed Haughey based on the view that he would more forcefully implement the party's 1975 policy document advocating a British withdrawal from Northern Ireland.[133]

At his post-victory press conference Haughey was surrounded by his largely unknown supporters while cabinet members were conspicuously absent. He claimed that 'two wonderful things' had happened since his election; he had been promised George Colley's 'total and fullest cooperation in my task, and I have been assured by Jack Lynch that all his vast reservoirs of experience as Taoiseach will be totally at my disposal in my new position'.[134] Colley denied any such support while Lynch's offer, if ever made, was never taken up. Haughey's attitude to the IRA also prompted questions given that his silence had sometimes been interpreted as ambivalence. The new Fianna Fáil leader claimed he had not spoken out on the subject before simply because he had had no authority within the party to do so. On this occasion there was no equivocation: 'I condemn the Provisional IRA and all their activities', he told the press conference. Another reporter asked about the Arms Crisis: 'this is very much now a matter for history', he replied. 'I am leaving it to the historians.'[135]

Notes

1   *Dáil Debates*, 273/1598–9 (26 June 1974).

2   Reported in *Irish Times*, 21 May 1974.

3   *Dáil Debates*, 273/1599 (26 June 1974).

4   Northern Ireland situation: motion. 273/1599–1600 (26 June 1974).

5   *Dáil Debates*, 273/100 (28 May 1974).

6   Speech by Liam Cosgrave, 13 June 1974, *Irish Press*, 14 June 1974.

7   Peck to Kelvin White, 2 March 1972, NAUK FCO 87/11.

8   Cooney, *Dáil Debates*, 273/1605 (26 June 1974).

9   *Combat*, vol. 1, no. 9 (May 1974).

10   As a result of decisions made by successive British Governments, the UDA was legal for the vast majority of the Troubles. It was only proscribed in October 1992.

11   *Interim Report on the Report of the Independent Commission of Inquiry into the Dublin and Monaghan Bombings*[The Barron Report] p. 275.

12   The report claims that the Sunningdale Agreement 'constituted the most serious attack on their [unionist] culture, values and traditions for centuries'. Barron Report, p. 237.

13   Barron Report, p. 253.

14   Interview contained in the Channel 4 (UK) documentary *Hidden Hand: The Forgotten Massacre*. Broadcast on 6 July 1993, it played a critical role in leading calls for an inquiry and the text of the documentary is provided as an appendix to the Barron Report.

15   *Barron* Report, p. 276.

16   *Dáil Debates*, 273/1574–6 (26 June 1974).

17   *Dáil Debates*, 273/1577 (26 June 1974).

18   *Irish Press*, 26 September 1974.

19   The doomsday scenario was one that came to obsess O'Brien throughout the remainder of his long life (he died in 2008, aged ninety-one). Liberated from parliamentary politics in 1977 when he lost his seat, O'Brien's unionism became less disguised. In 1996, he joined the UK Unionist Party (UKUP), a small organisation noted for its allergy to compromise, and was part of that UKUP's team to the Northern Ireland Forum. Like his party, he rejected the Good Friday Agreement in 1998 for the reason that it permitted a role for Sinn Féin.

20   'Cruise O'Brien's version of NI policy', 26 September 1974, (Dublin embassy), Wikileaks, 1974DUBLIN01345_b.

21   'Cruise O'Brien's version of NI policy', 26 September 1974, (Dublin embassy), Wikileaks, 1974DUBLIN01345_b.

22   'Cruise O'Brien's version of NI policy', 26 September 1974, 17:03, (Dublin embassy), Wikileaks, 1974DUBLIN01345_b.

23   *Irish Press*, 26 September 1974.

24   'NI policy causing divisions in govt', 9 July 1974, (Dublin embassy), Wikileaks, 1974DUBLIN00891_b.

25   Quoted in 'Cosgrave under fire', 19 July 1974, (Dublin embassy), Wikileaks, 1974DUBLIN00959_b. For a variety of reaction from within Northern Ireland to the bill's rejection see *Irish Press*, 18 July 1974.

26   *Irish Press*, 25 October 1974; *Irish Press*, 16 September 1974.

27   *Irish Press*, 1 July 1974.

28   *Irish Press*, 1 July 1974.

29   *Irish Press*, 1 July 1974.

30   Letter from Donal O'Sullivan to R McDonagh [14 July 1972] reporting discussion with William Whitelaw, Secretary of State for Northern Ireland on his meeting with representatives from the IRA, NAI DT 2003/16/465.

31   Note prepared by B. Ó Moráin on UDR recruitment, 3 November 1970. NAI DFA
     2001/43/1392. The UDR was described as 'a refuge for ex-B-Specials'. In Co.
     Fermanagh, for example, 83 per cent of UDR members were former members of
     the B-Specials, as were the majority in Armagh (64 per cent) Tyrone (61 per cent)
     and Derry city (53 per cent).

32   'Subversion in the UDR', NAUK PRO 21. This was a British army secret report
     written for the Joint Intelligence Committee in London.

33   Letter from R.A. Custis, Ministry of Defence, to the Prime Minister's office (29
     November 1972), PREM 15/1016.

34   Letter from R.A. Custis, Ministry of Defence, to the Prime Minister's office (29
     November 1972), PREM 15/1016.

35   'Conclusions of morning meeting' (10 July 1972), PRONI CAB/9/G/27/6/3.

36   'Conclusions of morning meeting' (10 July 1972), PRONI CAB/9/G/27/6/3.

37   'Conclusions of morning meeting' (10 July 1972), PRONI CAB/9/G/27/6/3.

38   Sutton index of deaths: crosstabulations available at http://cain.ulst.ac.uk/sutton/
     crosstabs.html. Accessed 3 April 2018.

39   Dáil Debates, 290/1324–33 (13 May 1976).

40   Murray, The SAS in Ireland, p. 163.

41   Many of the most compromising government files on these atrocities were not handed
     over to the national archives but rather retained in large secret vaults. See Cobain,
     The History Thieves.

42   See comments of former Northern Ireland Minister, Michael Mates, during an
     interview as part of RTÉ's 2015 documentary, Collusion. Mates served for twenty
     years in the British Army, six of which were spent with the Royal Ulster Rifles.

43   NAUK FCO 87/294 (18 September 1974). Cadwallader, Lethal Allies, pp. 229–230.

44   'Note of a meeting between the Minister of State and a deputation led by [UVF
     leader] Hugh Smyth', NAUK CJ4/1919 and NAUK FCO 87/341; 'Talk with Mr
     Ken Gibson of the UVF', 21 May 1974, NAUK FCO 87/341; 'Meeting with UVF
     at Laneside', 27 May 1974, NAUK FCO 87/341. Meetings with UVF representative
     Ken Gibson took place on 9 April, 21 May, 27 May, 29 May, 26 June and 7 August
     1974. NAUK FCO 87/341 and FCO 87/342.

45   Urwin, State in Denial, p. 114.

46   See Ó Beacháin, Destiny of the Soldiers, p. 366.

47   Conor Cruise O'Brien has since written that it is 'not surprising' that some British
     army personnel saw loyalist paramilitaries as 'allies against a common enemy'. In
     her book on British Government collusion with loyalists in Ireland, Ann Cadwallader
     concludes that if Minister O'Brien knew, others in government did too and, in any
     case, 'it is indefensible for the Irish state to hold up its hands and say it didn't know
     … It was Dublin's responsibility to find out what the British state was up to in
     Northern Ireland'. Cadwallader, Lethal Allies, p. 365.

48   'Withdrawal from Northern Ireland – British intentions'. Not dated (9 September
     1974), NAI DT 2005/7/659.

49　'Report of Inter-Departmental Committee on implications of substantially increasing the numbers in the defence forces'. July 1974. Paragraph 1.2, NAI DT 2005/7/659.

50　This would approximate to about £2.1 billion in 2018.

51　'Report of Inter-Departmental Committee on implications of substantially increasing the numbers in the defence forces'. July 1974. Appendix 2, NAI DT 2005/7/659.

52　Report of Inter-Departmental Committee on implications of substantially increasing the numbers in the defence forces'. July 1974. Section 3.6, NAI DT 2005/7/659.

53　Report of Inter-Departmental Committee on implications of substantially increasing the numbers in the defence forces'. July 1974. Section 3.6, NAI DT 2005/7/659.

54　'Report of Inter-Departmental Committee on implications of substantially increasing the numbers in the defence forces'. July 1974. Section 3.6, NAI DT 2005/7/659.

55　Memorandum on a meeting between Taoiseach Liam Cosgrave and Prime Minister Harold Wilson in London, mainly discussing the Northern Ireland situation. 11 September 1974. NAI DT 2005/7/607.

56　Memorandum on a meeting between Taoiseach Liam Cosgrave and Prime Minister Harold Wilson in London, mainly discussing the Northern Ireland situation. 11 September 1974. NAI DT 2005/7/607.

57　'Dublin discouraged by Northern election results', 15 October 1974 (Dublin embassy), Wikileaks, 1974DUBLIN01459_b.

58　'Irish plans if British withdraw from EC', 22 July 1974, 11:00, (Dublin embassy), Wikileaks, 1974DUBLIN00962_b. See also *Irish Press*, 9 December 1974.

59　FitzGerald, 'The 1974–5 threat of a British withdrawal', p. 143.

60　FitzGerald, *All in A Life*, p. 255.

61　FitzGerald, *All in A Life*, p. 259.

62　FitzGerald, *All in A Life*, p. 259.

63　FitzGerald, *All in A Life*, p. 271.

64　See *Irish Times*, 30 October 1975.

65　*Dáil Debates*, 264/276 (29 November 1972).

66　*Hibernia*, 19 November 1976.

67　*Hibernia*, 17 October 1975.

68　*Hibernia*, 19 November 1976.

69　Letter from Conor Cruise O'Brien to Donal Ó Moráin, 21 March 1974. Garret FitzGerald Papers, UCDA P215/79.

70　Dunne and Kerrigan, *Usual Suspects*, p. 91.

71　Purcell, *Inside RTÉ*, p. 65.

72　Purcell, 'The silence in Irish broadcasting', p. 61.

73　See Purcell, *Inside RTÉ*, pp. 116–136.

74　*Hibernia*, 17 December 1976.

75　*Irish Press*, 9 September 1976.

76　*Irish Press*, 9 September 1976.

77　Smyth and Hazelkorn, *Let in the Light*, p. 151.

78　*Sunday Business Post*, 20 April 2003.

79   *Irish Times*, 11 October 1984.

80   Maillot, *New Sinn Féin*, p. 75.

81   *Irish Times*, 21 April 1986.

82   *Irish Independent*, 15 November 1973; *Irish Press*, 22 November 1973. The full title was *Up and Away (The Helicopter Song)*.

83   *Irish Press*, 21 September 1974.

84   McCartney's song was not only banned in Britain but broadcasters could not mention its title when reading out the charts.

85   Lyons, 'The meaning of independence', p. 223. Emphasis added.

86   *Irish Times*, 24 February 1972.

87   Quoted in Bradshaw, *'And so began the Irish Nation'*, p. 33.

88   For exploration of these issues see Regan, *Myth and the Irish State*.

89   *Hibernia*, 12 January 1973.

90   An estimated 30,000 people, for example, turned out for Sinn Féin's Wolfe Tone commemoration on 15 June 1975. *Hibernia*, 27 June 1975.

91   White, *Ruairí Ó Brádaigh*, p. 207.

92   See 'Frank Stagg: hunger strike and death 2 January 1976 to 10 March 1976', NAI DT 2006/133/707 and NAI DT 2007/116/771. An absorbing documentary, *Frank Stagg's Three Funerals*, produced by Liamy MacNally with Ronan Kelly, was broadcast on 4 November 2017 on RTÉ Radio 1 and is available at www.rte.ie/radio1/doconone/2017/1019/913540-frank-staggs-concrete-plot/. Accessed 3 April 2018.

93   Dillon, *The Shankill Butchers*.

94   See Cadwallader, *Lethal Allies*; Urwin, *A State in Denial*.

95   *Dáil Debates*, 292/120 (1 September 1976). The state of emergency declared in 1976 was rescinded in February 1995.

96   Quoted in Dunne and Kerrigan, *Usual Suspects*, p. 181.

97   Two years earlier Cruise O'Brien had proposed that Ireland's second TV channel should simply rebroadcast the British state channel, BBC1. White, *The Radio Eye*, p. 143.

98   *Irish Press*, 4 September 1976.

99   *Irish Press*, 4 September 1977.

100 *Irish Press*, 15 September 1976.

101 Corcoran and O'Brien, *Political Censorship and the Democratic State*, p. 56.

102 *Hibernia*, 10 September 1976.

103 See Conway, *Policing Twentieth Century Ireland*, pp. 138–151.

104 Dunne and Kerrigan, *Usual Suspects*, p. 185.

105 *Irish Times*, 16 February 1977.

106 *Irish Times*, 15 February 1977.

107 Kerrigan and Dunne, *Usual Suspects*, p. 188.

108 *Irish Times*, 14 February 1977.

109 O'Brien, *Memoir*, p. 355.

110 *Irish Times*, 1 June 1977.

111 *Irish Times*, 1 June 1977.

112 *Irish Times*, 11 June 1977.

113 *Irish Times*, 11 June 1977.

114 Letter from FitzGerald to Callaghan, 4 July 1977, NAUK PREM 16/1349. When he left office a decade later, in 1987, FitzGerald sent a similar letter to Callaghan's successor, Margaret Thatcher, in which he wrote that 'on a purely personal note … for Ireland's sake I hope you are returned to power'. Quoted in *Irish Times*, 29 December 2017.

115 British embassy (Haydon) telex dated 7 July 1977. NAUK PREM 16/1349.

116 See 'Meetings between the Prime Minister and the Taoiseach', NAUK FCO 87/610-613.

117 'Meeting between Prime Minister James Callaghan and Jack Lynch, the Taoiseach, Copenhagen, 7 April 1978', NAUK CJ 4/2392.

118 'Meeting between the Secretary of State and Mr O'Kennedy: Steering Brief' (n. d., 1978), PRONI CENT/1/7/6. Emphasis in original.

119 British embassy, Dublin confidential report. 10 August 1979. Robin Haydon, 'What is happening to Mr. Lynch's Government'. NAUK PREM 19/80.

120 See for example his interview with RTÉ's *This Week* programme, 11 January 1978.

121 *Magill*, July 1979, p. 22.

122 British embassy, Dublin confidential report. 10 August 1979. Robin Haydon, 'What is happening to Mr. Lynch's Government'. NAUK PREM 19/80.

123 Bowyer Bell, *The Irish Troubles*, pp. 570–575.

124 *Magill*, January 1980 p. 35.

125 Ryle Dwyer, *Charlie*, p. 124.

126 Cronin, *Washington's Irish Policy*, p. 316.

127 *Magill*, January 1980, p. 36.

128 *Irish Press*, 7 December 1979.

129 *Irish Independent*, 17 November 1979.

130 *Irish Independent*, 7 December 1979.

131 *Cork Examiner*, 7 December 1979.

132 *Irish Press*, 8 December 1979.

133 See interview with Síle de Valera in *Irish Independent*, 8 December 1979.

134 *Irish Times*, 8 December 1979.

135 *Irish Times*, 8 December 1979.

6

Totality of relationships, 1980–1992

Haughey and Northern Ireland, 1980–1981

From the beginning, Haughey had the difficult task of living up to the expectations of his forty-four parliamentary party followers who required him to be economically savvy and tough with the British on the North, while at the same time winning over the thirty-eight disappointed Colley supporters. Some of Haughey's allies expected a radical shift from Lynch's conduct of Northern Ireland policy. A British internal report on Haughey prepared on 9 April for the British Foreign Secretary and passed on to relevant parties suggested that the Whitehall mandarins were under no illusions as to whom they were now dealing with in Dublin:

> His predominant characteristic seems to be a calculating and ruthless ambition: there is no secret that the office of Taoiseach has been the overriding objective of his life. He seems to have few real friends but appears to surround himself with a close-knit and faithful coterie of associates, whom he dominates by force of character and some of whom, it is said, he has bought ... [He is a] tough, clever, wily man, no friend of ours, but not, perhaps, actively hostile. A charming, womanising, man who had made his fortune while minister for Finance and acquired a taste for the good things of life.[1]

Self-assured and with an eye for detail, Haughey brought a more presidential style of governance than his predecessor. To better coordinate and centralise policy he elevated the Department of the Taoiseach's status and role but, contrary to perception, he did not micro-manage ministries.[2] Haughey distanced himself from the Lynch administration's economic policies to the extent that his Government appeared as one that had 'just taken power from a rival at a general election rather than a successor Government from the same Party'.[3] As was the case with Lynch himself between 1966 and 1969, Haughey wielded power because he had won an internal party contest but he remained untested in a general election. Until he had secured his mandate from the electorate, he would be seen to be spending political capital accumulated by others.

Haughey's main priority would be to do enough – or be seen to do enough – to justify victory at the next election, which was due some time before June 1982. Success at the polls could be achieved by a breakthrough in the economy or the 'national question' but as prospects for the former were gloomy the electoral value of being seen to make major advances on Northern Ireland and Anglo-Irish relations became greater. It was also a matter of political survival. With almost half of the parliamentary party implacably opposed to his leadership and waiting for an opportunity to depose him, electoral success could provide the only effective protection from a heave.

On the economy, Haughey's strategy was to talk tough about the need for drastic cutbacks, thus appearing prudent and far-sighted (with the added bonus of disparaging his predecessor's profligacy), while doling out more money to key elements of the electorate, widening the budget deficit in the process. This was a policy tailored for elections rather than economists and the plan was to pursue it for a short enough period so that by the time voters had cottoned on Haughey would already have secured his mandate in an early snap election. His Northern Ireland policy involved talking up the prospects of an historic break-through while continuing with business as usual. A problem emerged when Thatcher called him to account for overselling the significance of their meeting in December 1980. After acquiring Thatcher's trust, Haughey ruined their budding relationship when he intimated to others that she was willing to go much further than was the case.

British Government secret reports on Haughey's first months as Taoiseach were initially positive. Haughey's remarks on Northern Ireland had 'not been as bad as some people had feared', concluded one confidential account.[4] Although he had largely dismissed the British-mediated conference of parties in the North,[5] he had not publicly resurrected the 1975 policy document that called for a British commitment to withdraw from Ireland. Moreover, he had condemned the IRA at his inaugural press conference and, by implication, during his ard fheis address. The British believed that Haughey would, at least initially, 'try to pursue a constructive policy on the North for the moment, hoping to capitalise electorally on any semblance of progress while remaining ready at any time to revert to a more Republican posture to satisfy the Party faithful'. While the report said that the British need not care about his electoral prospects, Haughey was considered 'the best placed to secure the agreement of the more Republican wing of his Party to any acceptable solution we can devise for the North'. Most important from the British perspective, Haughey's accession 'has not harmed security cooperation between the RUC and the Garda which seems, if anything, to have improved'. As for Haughey's 'real intentions and aims ... very little is known by the public and ... by top officials too ... The cards are held very closely to the chest.'[6]

According to the British embassy in Dublin's confidential briefing, Haughey's 'diplomatic initiative', aimed at informing countries with which Ireland enjoyed close diplomatic ties of the Government's position on Northern Ireland, had 'up to now ... caused us relatively little grief but keeps the faithful happy. They will be looking for more in due course.'[7] The paucity of results arising from the diplomatic initiative, though entirely predictable, accentuated Haughey's wish to have direct talks with Thatcher, and he publicly urged the two Governments to get together to solve the Northern Ireland problem. Prior to meeting Thatcher, Haughey's only substantive policy statement on the North as Taoiseach had been made during his ard fheis speech on 16 February when he described the search for a solution to the Northern Ireland problem as his 'first political priority'. Apart from the short-term political advantage that would follow a breakthrough on the North, Haughey also knew that it would cement his place in history. In April 1979, he had told a group of visiting British MPs that the man who solved the North would be viewed as a saint, adding that he 'rather fancied canonisation'.[8]

In the run-up to his first Anglo-Irish summit, which would take place on 21 May, Haughey tried to get the British to raise their sights. The Taoiseach told the Northern Secretary, Humphrey Atkins, that 'nothing was ruled out – not even the most revolutionary or radical solutions' and he emphasised that 'there was nothing restrictive, intransigent or inhibited' in his policy making on Northern Ireland. Haughey stressed that the 'important thing was to approach the whole problem in a broad historical context' and, no doubt trying to appeal to the legacy search that consumes most premiers, claimed that Thatcher now had the opportunity 'of achieving what no other prime minister had ever achieved'.[9]

Haughey's diplomatic offensive, Irish America and the Donlon Affair

The new Taoiseach did not trust officials within the Department of Foreign Affairs, whom he reportedly considered 'West Brits'.[10] As one of his advisors recalled, 'for the most part he regarded them as gin-swilling arrivistes with affected manners of speech and behaviour in whom he had very little confidence'.[11] Haughey had to engage warily with civil servants and political opponents alike.

Given the shadow of the arms trials, the new Taoiseach's adversaries harboured suspicions about how he would manage Northern Ireland policy and vigilantly patrolled his words and actions, seeking evidence of latent IRA sympathies or a break from how Lynch tackled Anglo-Irish relations. Consequently, the decision made at the end of June to move Seán Donlon from his position as Irish ambassador in Washington to the equivalent post as representative at the United Nations in New York provoked a disproportionate response.[12]

Rather than viewing the matter as a purely administrative one, there were many in London, Washington, on the opposition benches and in the media who interpreted the decision as emanating from a shift to a more hardline republican policy. In particular, the personnel change was portrayed by some as a rebuff to the influential 'four horsemen' (Senators Ted Kennedy and Daniel Moynihan, House Speaker Tip O'Neill and Governor of New York, Hugh Carey) in favour of groups that took a more stridently critical view of British governance in Northern Ireland. Donlon had cultivated powerful figures in the US political establishment to counteract active sections of Irish America that Dublin considered too sympathetic towards, or insufficiently critical of, the IRA. These included Irish Northern Aid (NORAID), the Irish National Caucus (INC) and prominent supporters of Irish republicanism such as Mario Biaggi, who during the 1970s had managed to enlist 130 of his fellow congressmen to a Northern Ireland action committee.

Successive British administrations had labelled as IRA supporters or sympathisers those in the US who offered a sustained critique of London's policies towards Northern Ireland. Donlon's detractors, some of whom had the Taoiseach's ear, believed that he had over-zealously allied himself with this practice. On the day of Haughey's election as Fianna Fáil leader, Neil Blaney was in the office of the Irish National Caucus. The INC had arranged for the influential republican congressman, Hamilton Fish[13] to meet with Fr. Raymond Murray who, along with Fr. Denis Faul, had spearheaded investigations into RUC brutality and SAS covert operations in Northern Ireland. According to INC leader Fr. Seán McManus, ambassador Donlon went 'berserk' and Fish told him that he had 'never been talked to in such a disrespectful fashion'. In a letter to Hamilton Fish, the Irish ambassador had tried to sabotage efforts to exonerate the Birmingham Six while endeavouring to discredit Fr. Raymond Murray.[14] When the content of the letter came to light in 1985 and was publicised in the *Sunday Press*, Donlon claimed that all actions had been taken on the instructions of the Irish Government. Michael O'Kennedy, Foreign Minister when the letter was written, rejected the claim and said that he had not authorised Donlon to act in this way.[15]

In so far as Haughey had a detailed Northern Ireland policy during those early months of 1980, an integral part of the strategy was to launch an international campaign to exert diplomatic pressure on the British Government to cooperate with Dublin in working for a settlement that might be presented to supporters as a step towards Irish unity. With this in mind, Haughey and Lenihan had briefings with officials from the departments of the Taoiseach and Foreign Affairs, together with the ambassadors to the US and UK in January 1980.

At the commencement of the briefing meetings, which took place over two days (22–23 January) in Dublin, Haughey said that this was his first opportunity for a discussion of Northern Irish policy since he had become Taoiseach six weeks earlier. While he had not yet taken a final decision on policy, he said that the objective should be 'to get the British to declare their interest in the unification of Ireland'.[16] The unionists would only move when confronted with pressure from London, Dublin and Washington acting together and therefore the Irish embassies in the US and UK would play an important role. The Taoiseach emphasised the need for unity among those in America who wished to help Ireland, including the 'four horsemen', Biaggi's congressional committee, the INC and NORAID, among others. Donlon countered by highlighting the difficulties and dangers in implementing such a policy and, according to him, was strongly supported by officials in the departments of the Taoiseach and Foreign Affairs. The discussion was apparently open, frank and without rancour with Haughey encouraging divergent views. As it ended, the Taoiseach announced that he might call another meeting, although this would be more to discuss the implementation of policy than debate its formulation. Donlon recalls that as he was leaving the room, Haughey took him aside briefly and 'asked me to bear in mind that the problem of Northern Ireland had been created by the British. The primary responsibility for dealing with the fallout in the US therefore rested with them and not with us. It was clear that he did not expect me to comment.'[17]

Throughout the first months of 1980, the Irish embassy in Washington sought without success to get the Government's official stance on Biaggi and the INC, who both repeatedly declared that they now were working closely with Dublin. Their position was, according to Donlon, 'exacerbated' when Foreign Minister Brian Lenihan met Biaggi at the White House for what he later described as a 'very friendly' discussion. On 1 April, a US Government Undersecretary of State privately met with Donlon and told him that there were indications that Biaggi and the INC were seeking to have him removed. According to the Undersecretary, Biaggi had informed US Secretary of State Cyrus Vance that the Irish Government was now working with the INC and had made a request for Donlon's removal on the grounds of actions incompatible with his diplomatic status. In his written response, Vance doubted the veracity of the claim, citing the previous Irish Government's doubts about the INC, which the State Department had no reason to believe had changed.[18]

Donlon travelled to Dublin for meetings with Lenihan and Haughey on 24 June. According to Donlon's contemporaneous note, Lenihan told him that Haughey had decided that he should leave Washington because of his 'involvement in US politics', but that as he had been performing well he would be promoted to the rank of Deputy Secretary with the possibility of choosing to become either Deputy Secretary at the Department of Foreign Affairs (DFA), the permanent representative to the UN in New York or ambassador to Germany. Lenihan asked Donlon to choose immediately as the Taoiseach, with whom Donlon would meet shortly, wished to know. Donlon said he regretted the decision on 'policy and personal grounds' and asked the Foreign Minister to elaborate on the accusation that he had become too involved in US domestic politics. Donlon recalls that:

> He said that I had been in contact with prominent US politicians on a frequent basis and that I had interfered with others, including Biaggi, who were genuinely interested in Irish affairs. I also had too high a profile in the US and this had become a disadvantage. I asked if there was any instance or series of instances which gave rise to the decision. Had I done anything contrary to instruction? Lenihan assured me that this was not the case. It would simply be better all round if I left Washington.[19]

Later that day, Donlon travelled to meet the Taoiseach and found him at his desk. The ambassador was not offered a seat and remained standing throughout what he described as 'a brief and cold' meeting. Haughey told Donlon he was to leave Washington in August to become permanent representative at the UN, an important position given that Ireland was about to take up a seat for two years on the UN Security Council. Donlon remonstrated with the Taoiseach:

> I said that the move would, however, be seen by the Four Horsemen and others as a snub. For the first time in history, a powerful Irish lobby had been created in the US. It appeared that it was now to be put at risk. Haughey made it clear that he did not wish for a discussion. He pointed to the door and I left.[20]

The ambassador's behaviour during the meeting had no doubt confirmed Haughey's suspicions. Donlon viewed himself as an indispensable instrument of Irish Government policy in the US due to his personal contacts and the alliances he had forged. The story of the impending transfer was picked up by the Washington correspondent of the *Daily Telegraph* and then amplified by the Irish papers. The plan quickly attracted the ire of influential US politicians, whom Donlon had engaged in battling the pro-IRA section of Irish America and who now enlisted to defend his ambassadorial post.[21] The 'four horsemen' consulted with Donlon on 8 July and proceeded to telephone Haughey, with a view to reversing the decision and establishing the policy implications of the proposed move. Labour TD Ruairí Quinn went so far as to declare that Donlon's removal would be seen as a victory for those in the US who supported violence in Ireland. Newspaper commentators took the view that the decision signified a shift in the Government's Northern Ireland policy. The Irish media also saw it as a sop to Blaney and a possible inducement to attract him back to the Fianna Fáil fold. Speculation that Haughey was moving Donlon at Blaney's behest was given credence when a Government spokesperson described the decision as akin to 'removing a pawn to gain a knight'.[22]

Haughey could have stuck to his guns, stating it was his prerogative to appoint ambassadors. Instead he folded and tried to backtrack. On 9 July, the Department of Foreign Affairs announced that Noel Dorr would be dispatched to the UN before stating that 'press speculation over recent days that the Irish Ambassador to the US, Mr Seán Donlon, was to be moved because of a change in Government policy on Northern Ireland is entirely without foundation. The Government [has] complete confidence in Mr Donlon as its representative in Washington.'[23] The pressure did not abate and there were renewed calls for Haughey to clarify his Government's position on Biaggi and the INC. Haughey ultimately caved in to the pressure and in a speech delivered on 27 July appealed to

> all in America who have the interests of Ireland at heart not to give this body [INC] any support . . . associations that exist between Noraid and the INC casts grave suspicions on the latter organisation . . . I say now to all supporters of the bodies I have mentioned [Noraid and the INC] that they should carefully consider whether the cause they profess to serve would not now be best served by uniting in firm support of the policy of the Irish Government.[24]

Realising that Haughey was now in full flight, FitzGerald pressed home his advantage by publicly releasing the letter he had sent to Haughey on 21 July:

> You will have seen that John Hume, Frank Cluskey and myself speaking independently ... urged on the 9 July, that you clarify at once your Government's position with respect specifically to Congressman Biaggi, and to organisations such as Northern Aid and Irish National Caucus ... Failure to re-state in unambiguous terms the position of three successive governments on this matter can only confuse the issue in the United States, as may be seen by the statement on an RTÉ news programme last week by the Rev. Seán McManus, speaking on behalf of the Irish National Caucus, that he presumed that they were 'right in thinking that there is a difference between the policies of Mr Haughey and Mr Lynch – it is our general impression and hope that Mr Haughey's policies will be quite different.'[25]

FitzGerald claimed credit for the u-turn. Haughey looked weak, indecisive, secretive and dishonest. Whatever hope the Taoiseach had entertained of wooing Blaney back to Fianna Fáil dissipated. 'He can't even change an ambassador now', Blaney opined to Pádraig Ó hAnnracháin, a Department of Foreign Affairs official with whom he was friendly.[26] According to Seán McManus, the Minister for Foreign Affairs told the INC, no doubt in jest, that 'maybe we will have another stab at Donlon and send him to Tehran', then undergoing a hostage crisis at the US embassy.[27]

The 'teapot summit' in Downing Street

When the Taoiseach and Prime Minister eventually met in Downing Street, on 21 May 1980, it was very much a *tour d'horizon* and designed to establish a rapport between the two leaders.[28] Northern Ireland was left to the end and the general discussion lacked detail or concrete proposals. Thatcher later recalled that the Taoiseach had repeatedly drawn parallels between the conflicts in Northern Ireland and Rhodesia (now Zimbabwe). The shift in British policy – from supporting a white minority regime to acknowledging the majority's right to self-determination – had given some Irish politicians hope for a similar *volte-face* in Ireland. While Thatcher, in her own words, found the parallel 'unconvincing', she couldn't determine 'whether this was Irish blarney or calculated flattery'.[29]

During this amicable meeting Haughey presented Thatcher with a Georgian-era silver teapot and she responded positively to his invitation to visit Ireland.[30] Noting that the UK already had regular and continuous meetings with Germany, France and Italy, Thatcher said it would be 'very nice' if similar arrangements could be made with the Republic. The joint communiqué that emerged from the meeting described, at Thatcher's suggestion, the relationship between the two countries as 'unique' and there was reference to enhanced cooperation in the economic, political and security fields.[31] Both Governments acknowledged that the constitutional position of Northern Ireland was based on the 'consent of the majority' but also acknowledged important differences: 'While agreeing with the Prime Minister that any change in the constitutional status of Northern Ireland would only come about with the consent of a majority of the people of Northern Ireland, the Taoiseach reaffirmed that it is the wish of the Irish Government to secure the unity of Ireland by agreement and in peace.'[32]

Irrespective of the paucity of tangible results that had emerged from the meeting, the early post-summit exchanges had the hallmarks of a political romance. The day after the meeting, the Irish ambassador, Eamon Kennedy wrote to Thatcher in gushing tones.[33] 'I hardly know how to thank you for yesterday's delightful luncheon', he began, '... we all felt that new and encouraging vistas of cooperation in friendship had been opened between us, and that the two islands were coming closer together.' Kennedy concluded by saying that he and his family were very much looking forward to seeing the Thatchers for a drink after the 'Trooping of the Colour' on 14 June. 'We feel quite overwhelmed by your kindness', he signed off. Thatcher responded to the Irish ambassador: 'Thank you so much for your letter and for the accompanying orchids. I am glad that you enjoyed the lunch. So did I. The orchids are quite lovely. I have had them brought down here to Chequers and they are by me as I write.'[34] The post-meeting telephone conversation between Haughey and Thatcher on 22 May was equally effusive.[35]

Haughey emphasised how impressed he had been by the relaxed and frank manner in which discussion had taken place over lunch. He said the meeting had gone much better than he had expected, before adding 'but we have to keep up the impetus'.[36] Both the British ambassador to Ireland, Robert Haydon, and Thatcher had explained to him why the constitutional guarantee could not be withdrawn but, according to Haydon, the Taoiseach had asked 'how was he ever going to manage to talk to Paisley with the guarantee behind him? Paisley would ignore him: yet it was important that he should talk to Paisley and others.' When Haydon suggested that perhaps with time such contacts could be developed, Haughey replied 'I haven't got any time!' and said that what was needed was something positive to parallel the guarantee to unionists. Haydon responded by saying that northern Protestants had genuine misgivings about what their role and position would be in a united Ireland and that, 'speaking as a Protestant', he could 'understand how they felt'. Haughey persisted. He was not a deeply religious man, he said, and did not mind if someone wished to 'worship Ali Baba and the Seven [sic] Thieves' but time was a problem for him. The meeting concluded with Haughey asking Haydon to suggest people from the North that he could invite to receptions. The British ambassador, who was making his farewell call to the Taoiseach, left with an impression of a man who wanted 'to achieve and be seen to achieve something on Northern Ireland, and, as he said to me, he has not much time'.[37]

As de Valera had done in 1938 during his negotiations with Neville Chamberlain, Haughey and his Foreign Minister, Brian Lenihan, dangled the carrot of some enhanced form of defence links by saying that they knew the British had concerns about security but that these would be fully incorporated into any new arrangement.[38] On 26 May, Haydon met with Lenihan, who spoke at length of how well the 21 May meeting had gone and spoke of his and Haughey's admiration for Thatcher. In his report of the meeting the British ambassador, who described the Minister for Foreign Affairs as 'his usual affable self', emphasised the positive 'vibes' felt after the Downing Street meeting and, 'not prompted by me', said Ireland would be prepared to participate in defence cooperation. When the ambassador asked whether this included possible NATO membership, Lenihan replied in the affirmative – in his view, Ireland's neutrality had been diminished from the moment it joined the EEC in 1973. Admitting that his views on neutrality and NATO might be in conflict with those of the electorate and some of his cabinet colleagues, the Minister noted optimistically that 'the public would have to be educated for the change which he was sure would come'.[39]

Haughey had dropped similar hints to the British ambassador regarding NATO membership[40] and, acknowledging British concerns, the Taoiseach assured Thatcher during the Dublin Castle summit that Ireland 'would never be used as a base for an attack on Britain'.[41] Without making a direct offer, Haughey intimated that Ireland would be willing to amend its traditional policy of military neutrality, even to the point of an Anglo-Irish defence pact or NATO membership, in the context of Britain facilitating a reunified Ireland. In this, the Irish Government overestimated how willing Thatcher was to rid herself of Northern Ireland and the desirability and utility of Ireland joining the NATO alliance.[42] Haughey and Lenihan may also have underestimated public and party attachment to neutrality. Not surprisingly, both men publicly denied that the issue had been discussed with the British.[43]

The 1980 hunger strikes

As had often been the case in the past, the designs of civil servants and their political masters risked coming undone by less savoury realities within Northern Ireland. The biggest threat to any Anglo-Irish initiative in 1980 came from the smouldering conflict within the prisons. As part of a three-pronged policy of 'Ulsterisation', 'normalisation' and 'criminalisation', the British Government had withdrawn, in March 1976, the special category status granted four years earlier in response to the hunger strike of IRA leader Billy McKee. As a result of this status, political prisoners had enjoyed a number of privileges, including the right to wear their own clothes. From 1 September 1976, IRA members were to be treated as common criminals within the prison structures. The first IRA prisoner jailed under the new regime, Kieran Nugent, refused to wear a prison uniform, donning a blanket instead. Following disagreements over washing facilities and 'slopping out', republican prisoners intensified their struggle so that in March 1978 the 'blanket protest' escalated to the 'dirty protest', with prisoners smearing excrement on the walls of their cells within the Maze prison complex (popularly known as the H-Blocks). While this had created miserable living conditions for the prisoners, it failed to arouse sufficient domestic and international attention to pressurise the British Government to reconsider its prisons policies.

Consequently, on 27 October 1980, seven republican prisoners refused food, and were soon joined by thirty others. The campaign focussed on five demands: the right to wear their own clothes, to abstain from prison work, to associate freely within their own particular prison confine, to use educational and recreational areas, and to full remission on their sentences for good behaviour. The anti-H-Block campaign avoided the terms 'prisoner of war' or 'political status', lest it prove an insurmountable obstacle for the British, preferring instead to emphasise the five demands. The British position that they could not concede the five demands on principle, implying that it was somehow unprecedented, contradicted the fact that special category status had been afforded to political prisoners by a previous Conservative Government and, indeed, there remained prisoners sentenced prior to March 1976 that maintained that status. On the eve of the hunger strike, Haughey wrote privately to Thatcher expressing 'very deep and serious concern' about how a hunger strike would affect 'our security'.[44] The Taoiseach warned that once a strike had started it would be almost impossible to end and would result in deaths. Claiming that 'the emotional impact on the public sympathies and attitudes throughout Ireland will be grave', the Taoiseach predicted a surge in IRA support, particularly in America, leading to increased arms and funds.[45]

Both sides realised that the hunger strikes had the potential to scuttle the Anglo-Irish talks process. Within days of the hunger strike commencing, Thatcher and her Northern Secretary, Humphrey Atkins, privately agreed that should developments within the prisons get to the point where the summit became inadvisable it would be cancelled.[46] Though from the beginning the hunger strikes were of vital importance for the Irish Government, they were initially of peripheral interest to the British. According to Haughey, Northern Ireland was, for Thatcher, a 'remote part of the United Kingdom and not an urgent central concern affecting the public in Britain'.[47] He might have added that there were no votes to be won or lost on the matter, given that the British Government's indifference was exceeded only by that of its electorate. As the Department of the Taoiseach described British policy towards the hunger strikes as 'clearly one of no compromise',[48] Haughey believed the most effective course might be to 'play the card of American public opinion', though he also suggested identifying an appropriate mediator. Cognisant of Thatcher's allergy to anything that smacked of political status, Haughey advised that any intervention or mediation should be on humanitarian grounds.[49]

The Donegal by-election, occasioned by the death of Fianna Fáil TD Joseph Brennan and scheduled for 6 November, would be Haughey's first electoral test and, mindful of how the loss of two Cork by-elections had provided ammunition for Jack Lynch's ouster, the new Taoiseach devoted huge time and resources to retaining the seat. In this most northerly of constituencies, connected to the Republic by a sliver of territory, Northern Ireland policy assumed a greater importance than for voters in most other parts of the state. Haughey's fear was that there would be sufficient support for the candidate representing Neil Blaney's Independent Fianna Fáil, which adopted a more stridently republican Northern Ireland policy, to win the seat or to take enough votes from the governing party to allow Fine Gael to slip in, though the latter party had only a third of the vote.

At the final Fianna Fáil rally in Letterkenny and on a podium containing several senior party figures, including Haughey and seven cabinet colleagues, Síle de Valera delivered a stinging personal attack on Margaret Thatcher and her handling of the hunger strike issue. Describing the current impasse as 'yet another example of bungling by the British Government when it comes to Irish affairs', she proceeded to attack Thatcher personally:

> As a woman, I am deeply shocked by Mrs Margaret Thatcher's lack of compassion on the issue of the H-Blocks ... the Iron Lady image of which the British Prime Minister seems so proud is little less than a mask for an inflexible and insensitive lack of common humanity.[50]

De Valera's comments undoubtedly reflected the views of many Fianna Fáil members, perhaps even the majority of grassroots opinion. As in the dying days of Lynch's premiership, she had proven to be an accurate barometer of party sentiment and a lightning rod for republican dissent. Her usefulness to Haughey, however, had evaporated the moment he had assumed office. De Valera had become a nuisance, all the more irritating for that she bore the name and blood of the party's founder (although few advertised that her illustrious grandfather had also, in his time, allowed republican prisoners to die on hunger strike rather than concede them political status).[51]

Haughey quickly attempted to distance himself from de Valera's comments. The Irish ambassador to the UK, Eamon Kennedy, was instructed to report to Thatcher that the Taoiseach was personally 'distressed by the incident'; that de Valera's views did not reflect those of Fianna Fáil and had been made without prior consultation.[52] 'The Taoiseach totally and without any ambiguity rejects what was said by the Deputy', Kennedy wrote to Thatcher.[53] Having staked his reputation on a by-election victory, devoting five consecutive weekends to canvassing in the constituency, Haughey was very relieved when Clem Coughlan comfortably won the seat.

The December 1980 Anglo-Irish summit

With the by-election behind him, Haughey could now give his undivided attention to the much-heralded Anglo-Irish summit, scheduled for 8 December. Two days before the meeting, a large crowd of several thousand from throughout Ireland marched towards the British embassy in solidarity with the hunger strikers. The Government deployed 2,000 Gardaí and 500 soldiers to ensure that there would be no repetition of the British embassy's torching eight years previously. The summit itself dripped with symbolism. This was the first official visit of a British Prime Minister to Ireland since the foundation of the state six decades before.[54] The location for the summit, Dublin Castle – the former bastion of British power in Ireland – and the calibre of Thatcher's team reinforced the impression that these were significant talks. Accompanying the Prime Minister was her Foreign Secretary, Lord Carrington, Secretary of State for Northern Ireland, Humphrey Atkins, and the Chancellor of the Exchequer, Geoffrey Howe, along with a bevy of influential mandarins from a variety of ministries. In addition to the small battalion of top civil servants supporting the Taoiseach during the meetings his ministers for Foreign Affairs and Finance, Brian Lenihan and Michael O'Kennedy, participated in the respective summit talks. Thatcher had thought that by bringing such a high-powered and diverse delegation she would divert the focus away from Northern Ireland and emphasise that a wide range of Anglo-Irish affairs were on the agenda.[55] However, the composition of the delegations, the location and duration of the discussions, and the context, which included the IRA hunger strikes entering a critical phase with seven men now forty-three days without food, all helped sustain Haughey's description of the summit as a 'historic breakthrough'.

During his private talk with Thatcher, Haughey argued that the two Governments should jointly approach resolving the Northern Ireland imbroglio. Were there 'some movement' on this, the Taoiseach said, he could 'come out for a crusade to end violence' – and muster considerable forces behind him. Moreover, he could argue that while the two Governments were jointly deliberating the future of the North 'violence should be ended to see if we could get anywhere through political argument and discussion'.[56] What Haughey had in mind was an inter-governmental conference in 1981 to 'review the totality of the relationship between the two countries'. Although Thatcher rejected the conference proposal, believing it to be 'a little soon yet', Haughey emphasised the need for direct government-to-government negotiations. As loyalists looked to London and nationalists to Dublin, the two Governments could together devise a solution to which both sides of the divide in Northern Ireland might relate. What was needed, according to Haughey, was 'a great historic move'.[57]

Haughey pressed throughout for joint studies to be commissioned as a basis for a future meeting, but while the Taoiseach envisioned wide-ranging discussions Thatcher spoke of cross-border initiatives and security. The Prime Minister was delighted with the level of cooperation between the Gardaí and the RUC, which 'seem[ed] to be working very well together – and actually enjoying it'.[58] Haughey returned to what he believed was the big picture. Important as security was, what he had in mind was a solution that could perhaps create a situation whereby a British prime minister could be escorted through Dublin city centre without extraordinary military protection. 'If we can get political movement going', he argued, 'we could make a major political initiative to end the violence.' There was some disagreement on where the violence originated. When Haughey expressed concern about the 'spillover of the effects of Northern violence down here', Thatcher replied that she believed that much of the violence came from the South. Haughey disagreed, claiming all his intelligence sources identified Belfast as the militant centre. 'We have locked up our own violent men. Down here they were isolated', Haughey boasted, 'what was important now was to isolate them in the North – leave them no basis, or no platform. This could be done if new political developments, to bring the two peoples together, were seen to be coming about.' Haughey said that the two Governments must provide a political basis that would make violence irrelevant. When Thatcher claimed that it was a 'tremendous advance' that the vast majority of people living in the Republic believed that violence would not achieve anything, Haughey said they harboured no illusions about the IRA. 'The Provos have spoken of an attack of both states', he reminded the Prime Minister, 'we were making a major effort on security and we believed that our Border security could not be better'. Thatcher concurred.[59]

A joint communiqué issued later said the next summit would consider 'the totality of relationships within these islands'. In the interviews following the summit, Haughey and Lenihan talked up the 'historic' importance of the 'breakthrough' achieved at the summit.[60] The 'totality of the relationships' was spun into something approaching an open-ended discussion on the constitutional future of Northern Ireland, for which the joint studies were upgraded from modest civil service recommendations to potential blueprints for fundamental change.[61] Brian Lenihan told the BBC that 'everything is on the table',[62] prompting the British Government to deny that constitutional issues were up for discussion. In her memoirs, Thatcher concluded that the summit had done 'more harm than good'[63] and reproved herself for not being sufficiently involved in the drafting of the communiqué to have 'allowed through' the commitment to review 'the totality of relationships' at the next Anglo-Irish summit. She blamed Haughey for overselling the summit at the press conference 'which led journalists to write of a breakthrough on the constitutional question. There had of course been no such thing.'[64]

The communiqué was notable too for its omission of the standard constitutional formula whereby the British Government affirmed and the Irish Government accepted that there could be no change to the status of Northern Ireland so long as the majority retained a wish to remain in the UK. As with the decision to bring a high-powered delegation to Dublin, this omission may have been motivated by a wish to take the focus away from Northern Ireland and on to Anglo-Irish relations generally but it only served to fuel the already combustible unionist paranoia. Paisley lost no time in declaring the summit a sell-out while his Westminster colleague Enoch Powell of the UUP described it as a 'mini-Munich'.[65] On 22 March, the Minister for Foreign Affairs Brian Lenihan upped the ante when, despite conceding that Northern Ireland's constitutional position was not under active discussion with the British, he claimed that the Anglo-Irish talks could lead to a united Ireland within ten years. Consequently, when Thatcher cornered Haughey during their subsequent meeting at the margins of an EEC summit, the British Prime Minister 'couldn't speak coherently, she was in such a rage' as she launched into 'a monologue, a diatribe'.[66] There is little doubt that the Irish Government's spin annoyed Thatcher and it certainly broke any tentative bonds of trust that had developed between the two Prime Ministers.

The 1981 hunger strikes

Negotiations between the British authorities and republicans intensified as the hunger strikers neared death. The prison authorities issued a detailed statement about what would happen after the prisoners ended their protest. Bobby Sands, the leader of the Republican prisoners, announced that this met their five basic demands and the hunger strike was called off on 18 December. According to the British Government's secret annual review of Irish politics, the ending of the hunger strike had been met with 'immense relief' and Dublin had been 'certainly very worried' of what might happen should a prisoner die.[67] The

British took succour from the fact that, contrary to expectations, Haughey had not taken a hard line on the North nor followed the 1975 Fianna Fáil policy statement that called for a British declaration of intent to withdraw from the North. Instead he had told his first ard fheis as Taoiseach that he sought an arrangement whereby 'Irish men and women on their own and without a British presence, but with active British goodwill, will arrange the affairs of the whole of Ireland in a constructive partnership within the EEC'. Haughey, the British ambassador maintained, was 'openly sceptical of our attempts to find a political basis for a devolved Government in Northern Ireland'.[68] Instead he claimed that no durable and equitable solution could be achieved that did not encompass the three dimensions (internal to Northern Ireland, North–South, Anglo-Irish). The summits of 21 May and 8 December, along with the Atkins–Lenihan meeting of 13 October, had given expression to the third dimension and the two Governments were about to embark on joint studies that encompassed citizenship, economic cooperation, security, mutual understanding and institutions. Northern Ireland had had a 'difficult year' but, the British government report concluded, 'at the end of 1980 we should be satisfied with the state of Anglo-Irish relations … the attitudes of both the British and Irish Governments have evolved considerably since the troubles started, just over ten years ago'.[69]

Before long it became apparent that the British proposals did not meet the H-Block protesters' five demands. Republican prisoners felt duped and immediately planned a second hunger strike. When on 1 March 1981, the fifth anniversary of the withdrawal of political status, the IRA's O/C in the Maze prison, twenty-six-year-old Bobby Sands, refused food, it was clear that the republicans had learned something from the winter 1980 strike. Prisoners would not embark on hunger strikes at the same time so as to avoid the pressure on the strongest to cut a deal when the weakest was close to death. Rather, the prisoners would begin their fasts at weekly or fortnightly intervals to maximise the effect and leverage.

Five days after Sands began his fast, Frank Maguire, the fifty-one-year-old Independent MP for Fermanagh-South Tyrone whose abstention during a vital Westminster vote had brought down the Callaghan Government two years earlier, died of a heart attack. In the resultant by-election on 9 April, Sands, still in prison on hunger strike, defeated the UUP candidate Harry West, taking more than 30,000 votes in a contest that attracted an 87 per cent turnout. Sands's election to Westminster transformed the profile of the hunger strikers and raised hopes of a resolution to new levels, the assumption being that Thatcher would not allow a fellow Member of Parliament to die when it was in her power to prevent it. According to the British ambassador in Dublin, Sands's election came as 'an unpleasant surprise'.[70] Consequently, the Representation of the

People (Amendment) Act, which would prohibit prisoners from running for Parliament, was speedily enacted.

On Easter Monday, 20 April, John O'Connell, Síle de Valera and Neil Blaney – all members of the Dáil and the European Parliament – were granted permission to visit Sands, now fifty-one days without food, in the Maze. O'Connell asked Sands to give up his hunger strike; it was right, he said, to fight for one's beliefs but little would be achieved by dying. O'Connell told Sands that he had made his point and promised that if he came off the strike they would fight to secure the prisoners' demands. O'Connell describes what happened next:

> He smiled at me silently. 'I knew you would say that', he said gently, and indicated that no, he would not be coming off the strike. Síle, who had watched my plea in silence although she would not have agreed with it, was clearly very moved and close to tears. She held him very gently, so as not to hurt his sore skin, and kissed him. Neil Blaney I had always seen as a strong man. He was very gentle on that occasion. You see a man in a different light when you see him supporting someone's republicanism, holding his hand gently, full of concern for him … Síle and Neil both told him he was a hero.[71]

During his hunger strike, Bobby Sands had five heart attacks and on Sunday, 3 May he went into a terminal coma. The following day Haughey's secretary requested Marcella Sands to make out a new complaint to the European Commission of Human Rights but, no longer trusting Haughey, she refused. With her brother having only hours to live, she believed that Haughey's gesture was too little and far too late. Bobby Sands died on 5 May after sixty-six days without food and his funeral, with over 100,000 mourners attending, was one of the biggest in Irish political history.

Sands's by-election victory and the mass support evidenced by the hunger strike campaign, especially at the funerals of the dead men, strengthened the arguments of those in the Sinn Féin movement eager to enter the electoral arena. Sands's death necessitated a by-election but as the British Government forbade another prisoner standing, his election agent, twenty-eight-year-old Owen Carron, was nominated to defend the seat. Three more hunger strikers, all in their early twenties, died in May.

When Francis Hughes died on hunger strike on 12 May, Dermot Nally from the Department of the Taoiseach telephoned Michael Alexander in Downing Street to communicate Haughey's concern that the population of County Fermanagh was 'completely under the control of the Provisionals' and that an early election in the Republic could see up to half a dozen IRA sympathisers elected and holding the balance of power.[72] That night a large crowd marched to the British embassy but they were dispersed by a Garda baton charge. Despite the domestic upheaval, Dublin did little to channel popular anger into public denouncements of the Thatcher administration. The British cabinet Secretary, Robert Armstrong, had correctly judged the mollifying effect of the joint studies and emphasised that their mere existence had 'no doubt contributed to the Irish Government's comparatively restrained behaviour over the Sands affair so far'.[73]

Haughey out, FitzGerald in

With the economy deteriorating and with no signs of immediate improvement, Haughey planned to call an early election in February but the Valentine's Day fire at the Stardust nightclub that left forty-eight youngsters dead prompted the cancellation of the party ard fheis and the election announcement. Eventually, 11 June was set as election day but by that stage the hunger strikes had intervened. Repeatedly heckled by supporters of H-Block prisoners, particularly in the border counties, Haughey emphasised his republican credentials. In Wexford he told a Fianna Fáil rally that Northern Ireland as a political entity had 'failed completely' and was 'no longer viable'. The only way forward, he said, was for the two sovereign Governments to come together and devise 'a solution which will ultimately lead to the unity of this country, North and South'.[74] Though the Taoiseach declared that he was calling the election because of 'the grave and tragic situation in Northern Ireland',[75] the state of the economy dominated much of the campaign.

Despite his relative unpopularity in the polls compared with his main rival Garret FitzGerald, Haughey ran a highly personalised election campaign encapsulated in Fianna Fáil's unofficial election anthem *Rise and Follow Charlie*.[76] Backbench fears were assuaged somewhat by the increase in Dáil seats from 148 to 166 but the party still lost half a dozen deputies. Standing in just nine of the state's forty-two constituencies and largely bereft of funding, organisation and, as a result of censorship laws, publicity, the H-Block candidates – all prisoners – garnered over 42,000 votes and two were elected to the Dáil: Paddy Agnew in Louth and Kieran Doherty in Cavan-Monaghan, both border constituencies. Joe McDonnell, a month into his hunger strike, came within 300 votes of depriving Fianna Fáil of a seat in Sligo-Leitrim. With seventy-eight Dáil seats to Fine Gael's sixty-five, Haughey was unlucky not to have obtained the necessary mandate to continue in power. Had he won ninety-four more votes in Wexford and 166 more in Dublin North, Fianna Fáil would have had eighty seats. Neil Blaney was anxious to see Haughey rather than FitzGerald in office and, despite his frequent trips to Brussels as an MEP, his vote in the

Dáil would have been assured. In such circumstances, it is difficult to see how FitzGerald could have cobbled a coalition together. Considering Fianna Fáil's electoral gloom in 1979, with only 34 per cent of the European election vote and the two by-election losses, Haughey had come closer to maintaining power than many had considered possible. Ultimately, the H-Block prisoners' intervention thwarted his ambitions.

On 30 June, Garret FitzGerald became Taoiseach at the head of an unstable Fine Gael–Labour coalition Government dependent on independents for survival. Prior to taking office, FitzGerald had visited the British ambassador and asked for an early meeting with Thatcher to try to end the hunger strike, which he said would be his 'top priority'. A fifth hunger striker, thirty-year-old Joe McDonnell, died on 8 July after sixty-one days without food. According to the British ambassador, 'the mood of the Irish Government was that they could ride out two or three deaths but more than that would radically alter the picture'.[77] That stage had now been reached and FitzGerald wasted no time.

Even had he not taken power in the midst of the H-Block debacle there is much to suggest that Northern Ireland would be high on FitzGerald's agenda. The new Taoiseach made much of his mixed religious parentage, which he believed provided him with special insights into the national question. Politically a radical republican, his mother Mabel McConnell was of northern Presbyterian stock, and had met her husband at an Irish-language seminar. Born and raised in London, his father, Desmond, had joined the Irish Volunteers and subsequently served as Minister for External Affairs (1922–1927) and Defence (1927–1932) in the Free State Government led by William Cosgrave. Garret FitzGerald's book, *Towards A New Ireland*, first published in 1972, was an innovative work brimming with ideas on how to ameliorate the Northern Ireland crisis, and a year later he had participated in the negotiations leading to the Sunningdale Agreement, which he ardently supported. FitzGerald was also a man of contradictions. Armed with a PhD in economics – no Taoiseach before or since has received a greater formal education – he presided over a ballooning national debt and the progressive degradation of the economy. Unemployment and emigration soared on his watch. His popular image as the absent-minded academic (encapsulated on the day when he publicly wore two odd shoes) belied a focus and determination without which he could never have risen to the top. Consistently more popular than Haughey in opinion polls, their rivalry would define Irish politics for much of the 1980s.

FitzGerald inherited the H-Block crisis at a time when it seemed impossible to de-escalate. In a secret letter written to Thatcher within days of taking office, FitzGerald wrote that Anglo-Irish relations and the stability of the state were jeopardised and that his Government's view of her handling of the H-Block crisis was beginning to converge with that of the IRA. While this was 'naturally the last position in which we would wish to find ourselves', the Fine Gael leader hinted that public opinion might force him to weaken security ties with the British. Unable to say or do anything to counter the lack of public confidence in the British approach to the crisis, FitzGerald warned that they were 'faced with the danger of a serious and progressive deterioration in bilateral relations'. Moreover, the Government's position that the prisoners should not be granted political status was becoming increasingly untenable.[78] In her response five days later – during which time Martin Hurson died after forty-six days without food – Thatcher threatened a 'sharp and bitter' response if there was any suggestion of less than full cooperation in fighting the IRA. 'I cannot believe your government will wish in any way to diminish the scale or intensity of the [security] co-operation', she wrote, and added that such a move would risk an 'adverse effect on wider Anglo-Irish relationships'.[79] On 18 July, two thousand Gardai assembled in Dublin ready to protect the British embassy from being destroyed for the second time in a decade. A march of ten thousand people in support of the hunger strikers descended into violent clashes between protesters and police, leaving two hundred people hospitalised.[80]

To augment the pressure on Thatcher, the Taoiseach also wrote to Ronald Reagan, then in the first few months of his presidency, to 'ask you to use your enormous influence with the British prime minister within the next 24 hours in the interest of averting a death which would inevitably increase support for the terrorists and further undermine the stability of our democracy in a dangerous way and can only harm the interests of the British, Irish and American govern-ments'.[81] Reagan did nothing and relations soured further when, on 25 July, Thatcher wrote a letter to the 'Friends of Ireland', a bipartisan group of influential US congressional leaders, in which she quoted FitzGerald as having accepted that the British 'were doing all they can to end the strike'. The Taoiseach upbraided the British ambassador to Ireland and issued a lengthy denial published in the Irish media on 29 July, along with a long message to the 'four horsemen' outlining his views.[82]

When the Government press Secretary Liam Hourican advocated a sharp public rebuke of the British Government,[83] cabinet Secretary Dermot Nally disagreed. Echoing the concerns that FitzGerald had communicated to Thatcher some days earlier, he warned that on the issue of republican prisoners the Irish Government's position now resembled that of the IRA to the point where they could not be distinguished. He cautioned against a major public row with London on the matter lest it endanger long-term Anglo-Irish relations. Nally could also foresee the problem of prison protests spreading to the South. 'What do we do if Portlaoise erupts?', Nally asked. The implication was clear. If Dublin supported

IRA prisoners in British prisons, how could they challenge republican prisoners in their jurisdiction?[84] In a memorandum prepared for the Government in August, David Neligan, assistant Secretary at the Department of Foreign Affairs, went further and argued that the British should be told to force-feed the prisoners to stop what he called their 'suicidal abstinence', although he acknowledged it would lead to 'much humanitarian protest'.[85]

The sharpest direct criticisms of Thatcher's policies came from Cardinal Tomas Ó Fiaich, the Crossmaglen-born Catholic Primate of All-Ireland. Referring to Ray McCreesh, the third striker to die and, like Ó Fiaich, a native of rural Armagh, the cardinal said publicly that he had 'no doubt that he [McCreesh] would have never seen the inside of a jail but for the abnormal political situation. Who is entitled to label him a murderer or a suicide?'[86] Accompanied by the Bishop of Kildare, Patrick Lennon, Ó Fiaich had a tempestuous meeting with the British Prime Minister during the night of 1 July during which, according to the report prepared by Irish Government officials, Thatcher 'reinforced the impression that she is insensitive and of an authoritarian disposition'. Thatcher 'lectured' Ó Fiaich, who before his appointment as cardinal had been professor of Irish history at Maynooth for fifteen years, and said that she 'had read all the documents about Northern Ireland and didn't need to be told what it was all about'. She then proceeded to negate this bold claim when she mused whether the motivation of the hunger strikers wasn't simply to demonstrate their virility. The Prime Minister said she 'could not understand the continued Irish animosity against the British considering that even the Germans were now willing to be friends', to which Ó Fiaich suggested that 'perhaps the reason the Germans were now friends with the British was that the British were no longer in occupation of Germany'.[87]

On 1 August, twenty-five-year-old Kevin Lynch died after seventy-one days without food and he was followed hours later by Kieran Doherty, also twenty-five, who had been elected to the Dáil seven weeks earlier. On the same day as Mickey Devine died after sixty days on hunger strike, Owen Carron successfully defended Bobby Sands's seat with an increased majority and, buoyed by these election victories, Sinn Féin announced that it would in future contest all elections in Northern Ireland.[88] As parents increasingly sanctioned medical intervention to revive their emaciated kin, the hunger strike ended on 3 October. Ten prisoners had died during the fast and sixty-nine people had lost their lives outside the prison walls. Three days after the termination of the strike, James Prior, who had replaced Humphrey Atkins as Secretary of State on 14 September, announced several changes to prison policy, including the right of prisoners to wear their own clothes at all times. In effect, the five demands were conceded and by the end of the month the blanket protest also came to an end. Thatcher's words and actions during the strike had reinforced her image as the immovable Iron Lady, but at a price. Radical militant republicanism in Northern Ireland had been reinvigorated and Sinn Féin would soon emerge as a major electoral force for the first time in decades. The prospect of Sinn Féin eclipsing the SDLP and becoming the largest nationalist party in the North troubled the Irish Government, as this would critically undermine their argument that the IRA represented a tiny minority.

The FitzGerald–Thatcher relationship

Apart from the ongoing Anglo-Irish talks process, FitzGerald's major Northern Ireland policy initiative was what was quickly dubbed the 'constitutional crusade'. In an RTÉ radio interview on 27 September 1981, the Fine Gael leader evoked the memory of Wolfe Tone and Thomas Davis, both Protestants who had taken up arms against British rule in Ireland, and proclaimed:

> I want to lead a crusade, a republican crusade to make this a genuine republic ... If I were a northern Protestant today, I cannot see how I could be attracted to getting involved with a state that is in itself sectarian – not in the acutely sectarian sense that Northern Ireland was ... [but] the fact is our laws and our constitution, our practices, our attitudes, reflect those of a majority ethos and are not acceptable to Protestants in Northern Ireland.[89]

FitzGerald told Thatcher that he had spoken from the heart 'because he felt passionately on the subject ... fully understood the position of Northern Protestants [and] had been full of suppressed fury since childhood at some of the attitudes adopted in the South'. The Taoiseach's basic aim was a constitution that would 'reflect the ethos of all the people of Ireland' and he claimed that this constituted the main reason he was in politics.[90] FitzGerald's initiative would come to little, however. A bitter and divisive referendum in 1983 paved the way for a constitutional prohibition on abortion. Even though abortion was illegal in Northern Ireland the fact that the Catholic Church played such a prominent role reaffirmed for some that home rule remained in fundamental aspects Rome rule, as did the comprehensive defeat of a referendum to introduce a modest form of marital divorce in 1986.[91]

The Fine Gael–Labour Government had hoped for an early Anglo-Irish summit in July but, at Thatcher's insistence, it was pushed back, and did not take place until November, after the hunger strikes had concluded. The main result of the FitzGerald–Thatcher meeting in London on 6 November was the decision to establish an Anglo-Irish inter-governmental council that would act as a forum for discussions between the two Governments. Thatcher feared misrepresentation of the joint studies, and claimed to have 'suffered a great deal from previous insinuations'.[92] Her suspicions were therefore aroused when the Irish team again devoted great attention to the choice of words that would emerge in the post-summit communiqué. In terms of fundamentals, the press release repeated the formula contained in Paragraph 5 of the Sunningdale Agreement that Northern Ireland's constitutional status could only be changed as a result of majority consent there and that the British Government would legislate for such a change should it be expressed. The Taoiseach 'affirmed' his Government's wish, and that of the great majority of Irish people, to secure the unity of Ireland 'by agreement and in peace'.[93] Unlike Sunningdale, however, there was little in the way of short- to medium-term political steps forward. The Irish Government had no formal role and the emphasis was on quashing violence and Sinn Féin. Reaction in Northern Ireland to the summit ranged from unionist rage that the meeting had taken place at all, through mild support from the SDLP, to criticisms from Haughey that the summit did not go far enough.[94]

The Government had little opportunity to develop its policies as it collapsed after just seven months in office and threw itself at the mercy of a disenchanted electorate. Fianna Fáil's election literature proclaimed that in pursuance of the party's 'fundamental national aim of unity', Haughey's December 1980 Anglo-Irish initiative had 'provided the only way forward', which he promised to continue if elected.[95] The election produced only modest change in seat numbers, with Fianna Fáil gaining three and Fine Gael losing two, but it was enough to tilt the parliamentary balance in Haughey's favour. Moreover, the controversial budget that had triggered the Government collapse had made the three deputies from Sinn Féin the Workers' Party (SFWP) and the new Independent TD Tony Gregory more amenable to Haughey's wooing. With their support, along with that of 'old reliable' Neil Blaney, Fianna Fáil was back in power, but only after Haughey had narrowly avoided a leadership heave. Northern Ireland, Haughey claimed, constituted 'the first national issue' and finding a peaceful solution would continue to be 'our first political priority'.[96]

Revolving door government and the Falklands Crisis

Primarily known as the 'GUBU government', Haughey's second term in office would be ill-fated and even shorter than his first.[97] However, it was long enough to drive a wedge in Anglo-Irish relations by virtue of the Government's stance on the conflict arising over the Argentinian invasion of the Falklands Islands on 2 April 1982. In a personal and confidential communication, the British Prime Minister wrote to Haughey saying she had been forced to turn to 'close friends' in Britain's hour of need, for she suspected the Soviet Union would scupper any attempt to impose UN sanctions. Claiming the Argentinean economy was vulnerable, Thatcher argued that measures to limit their access to markets and credit would 'hit them hard'. 'I now seek your personal help', Thatcher wrote to Haughey, 'to bring about the urgent introduction of economic and financial measures against Argentina, by national action co-ordinated among us.' Thatcher recognised that such sanctions would hurt the Irish economy as much as the Argentinean one but insisted that it would bring the South American Govern- ment 'to their senses'.[98] Whatever the merits of the dispute – and traditionally Irish Governments had favoured ceding sovereignty over the Falkland Islands to Argentina – the Department of Foreign Affairs recommended cooperation with Thatcher's request, predicting it would be to Ireland's long-term political and economic advantage. Ireland's embassy in London warned that non-compliance with the British request would lead to 'incalculable' effects on Anglo-Irish relations; the Irish community in Britain would be targeted and boycotts against Irish exports could not be ruled out. In his reply of 16 April, Haughey assured Thatcher of his Government's 'continuing readiness to help insofar as we can in advancing a resolution of the crisis and the achievement of an honourable and enduring settlement'.[99] Ireland did not impose any unilateral financial or trading embargo on Argentina but simply participated in those sanctions authorised by the EEC.

Irish policy changed on 2 May when a British submarine sank the Argentinian cruiser *General Belgrano* with the loss of 323 lives although it had been outside the maritime exclusion zone set by the UK Government only days earlier. The British privately recognised that the sinking of the *Belgrano* had provoked 'a wave of horror and revulsion' in Ireland but felt that Haughey's stance was greatly influenced by the need, given the parliamentary arithmetic, to keep Neil Blaney onside and to win the Dublin-West by-election scheduled for 25 May.[100] The British ambassador to Ireland, Leonard Figg, also told London that Haughey viewed 'Irish neutrality as a cloak for an anti-British attitude'.[101] The British embassy in Dublin believed that the Taoiseach was 'alone responsible for foreign policy'[102] and described the new Minister for Foreign Affairs, Gerry Collins, as 'only a cypher'.[103] Seán Donlon, now Secretary of the Department of Foreign Affairs, conceded to the British ambassador that since Haughey's resumption as Taoiseach neither he nor any of his officials in Iveagh House had had 'any meaning- ful talk' with him 'about Northern Ireland'.[104] Consequently, Haughey's return to power had not been welcomed by mandarins at the Department of Foreign Affairs, with one British source noting that 'DFA makes no secret of its view that his [Haughey's] return is a disaster, they are for the most part Fine Gael sympathisers'.[105]

The Fianna Fáil administration collapsed for much the same reasons as its coalition predecessor. Budget cuts triggered the withdrawal of support from the handful of left-wing TDs on which the Government depended. On 24 November 1982, the Republic's electorate again went to the polls. Apart from the economic situation, which remained dire, deteriorating Anglo-Irish relations – fuelled by the Government's policy on the Falklands War – played a substantial role in the election campaign. Though in their private conversations with British representatives Haughey and Lenihan had expressed a willingness to jettison Ireland's military neutrality, the Fianna Fáil leader now presented himself as a guardian of this policy and of maintaining Ireland's 'position in world affairs as a sovereign independent nation with her own policy on international issues'.[106] FitzGerald emphasised his ability to develop a good working relationship with Whitehall and promised a resumption of the Anglo-Irish summit meetings suspended during Haughey's second term of office. However, Fianna Fáil exploited FitzGerald's floating of an all-Ireland police force, which the Attorney-General dismissed as 'vague and improbable' and was presented in rural Ireland as something akin to a return of the Black and Tans. In some constituencies, leaflets were distributed asking 'do you want the RUC policing our streets?'[107] Matters were not helped when Secretary of State for Northern Ireland, James Prior made unguarded remarks while in the United States suggesting that he favoured FitzGerald and indicating that the Fine Gael leader would soon announce proposals for an all-Ireland court and police force.

Fianna Fáil decided to make Anglo-Irish relations a centrepiece of the election during the latter stages of the campaign and, in the words of one contemporary observer, 'maintained the Fine Gael leader was an instrument of British policy, in collusion and collaboration with the British government and that both the British government and the media were interfering in the election because they wanted Charles Haughey out'.[108] One of the more colourful accusations was that in meeting the Duke of Norfolk, FitzGerald, in the Taoiseach's words, had dined with 'a trained British spy', a reference to Norfolk's former (until 1967) position as head of intelligence at the British Ministry of Defence.[109]

At the third attempt, a general election finally produced a result that could facilitate stable governance. With a 2.1 per cent swing against Fianna Fáil, Fine Gael enjoyed its strongest performance since the party's foundation in 1933, coming within five seats of its historic rival (75 to 70) and outpolling Fianna Fáil in the capital. While turnout, at 72.9 per cent, was the lowest since 1961, it produced a two-seat majority for a Fine Gael–Labour coalition, which would endure for over four years.

The New Ireland Forum

British plans to restore a devolved administration in Northern Ireland centred on the idea of 'rolling devolution', which Jim Prior, Northern Secretary since September 1981, would be responsible for implementing. The plan was that an elected assembly would initially have only advisory and consultative roles but if it worked effectively on a cross-community basis then more powers, including executive ones, could be devolved in stages.[110] Assembly elections held in November 1982 saw the UUP and DUP take 53.7 per cent of the vote between them. The big surprise however was the performance of Sinn Féin, which took over 10 per cent of the vote and five seats compared with 18.8 per cent and fourteen seats for the SDLP. In their first electoral intervention as a party, Sinn Féin had attracted 35 per cent of the nationalist vote. Given that the Assembly was viewed as part and parcel of an internal Northern Ireland solution without an all-island 'Irish dimension', the 'rolling devolution' initiative lacked appeal for many nationalist voters. The SDLP attacked Prior's proposals for lacking a 'realistic Irish dimension' and, not wishing to be outflanked by Sinn Féin, boycotted the Assembly.

Sinn Féin came close to parity with the SDLP during the 1983 Westminster election. Fielding fourteen candidates, the republican party took 13.4 per cent of the vote compared with the 17.9 per cent garnered by the SDLP's seventeen candidates. As a result of the divided nationalist vote against solitary unionist candidates, the SDLP and Sinn Féin took one seat apiece (John Hume in Foyle and Gerry Adams in West Belfast). Danny Morrison – the man who had coined the 'armalite and ballot box' strategy – came within a whisker of taking a second seat for Sinn Féin in Mid-Ulster, losing out by just seventy-eight votes to the DUP's Rev. Willie McCrea. Sinn Féin's vote did not come at the expense of the SDLP, whose support remained solid, but resulted from the mobilisation of a section of the population hitherto uninvolved in elections.

Fearful that left unchecked Sinn Féin might overtake the SDLP electorally in the North, the Government devised a mechanism that would enhance the reputation of constitutional nationalism and, on 30 May 1983, inaugurated the New Ireland Forum.[111] The Forum was very much FitzGerald's brainchild; on bringing the proposal to cabinet he found that only two colleagues, Peter Barry and Michael Noonan, supported it while the other twelve ministers feared it would distract the Taoiseach from domestic concerns.[112] The SDLP, according to the Irish officials they met, were 'very depressed and gloomy' following Sinn Féin's election success. One future party leader, Alisdair McDonnell, for example, confided that the New Ireland Forum was 'the last chance for constitutional nationalism in Northern Ireland' and that if it failed, SDLP members like him would face 'the stark choice of continuing on the constitutional path or joining forces with Provisional Sinn Féin'.[113] With the advent of the New Ireland Forum, John Hume and his party acolytes would be transported from the periphery of British politics to the centre of Irish policy making on the national question, debating and negotiating on equal terms with the leaderships of the three larger parties in the Republic.

Though the Forum was designed ostensibly to alleviate nationalist alienation in Northern Ireland it explicitly excluded representatives of what was arguably the most disaffected section of northern society, those who had never voted before but in 1982 had cast a ballot for Sinn Féin. The credibility of the Government's Northern Ireland policy necessitated the marginalisation of Sinn Féin. With the SDLP in the ascendancy, Dublin could claim to be articulating the views of northern nationalists but should Sinn Féin overtake them the Taoiseach would be enunciating a position at odds with both the majority of unionists and the majority of nationalists in Northern Ireland. As the British ambassador to Ireland reported back to his superiors in London:

> I do not believe there is much instinctive horror of Sinn Féin outside sophisticated circles in the South, any more than there is in a wide range of the Northern Catholics. It is this range of feelings that inspires in the Irish Government the fear that Sinn Féin are set, both in the North and in the South, to achieve further political advances. If Sinn Féin were to get only 51% of Catholic votes in the North, the Irish Government's position as the spokesman of those voters would be intolerable.[114]

Between the Assembly election in November 1982 and the Westminster election of June 1983 the Sinn Féin vote had jumped from 35 per cent of the nationalist vote to 42 per cent; a mere 35,000 votes switching from the SDLP to its republican rival would trigger the nightmare scenario of Sinn Féin representing the majority of nationalists in Northern Ireland. On 17 April 1984, Peter Barry presented to the cabinet a report on the state of affairs in Northern Ireland. Reflecting the consensus of the Department of Foreign Affairs, it argued that, in the words of one of the ministers present, 'the Provos will, if nothing happens to stop them, get more than 50% of the nationalist vote in the May 1985 local elections', and painted 'a gradual slide down to the doomsday scenario'. Describing the situation as 'quite shocking', the minister believed that 'the only (rather dim) light is the feeling that Mrs Thatcher is finally beginning to grasp this reality also and is making certain moves in the right direction'.[115]

The Forum brought together representatives from 75 per cent of the island of Ireland and over 90 per cent of nationalist representatives. The volume of submissions to the Forum, written and in person from a diverse body of opinion, suggested that it had succeeded in stimulating discussion on what form a 'united Ireland' might take and identifying potential challenges. Given its purpose, tone and composition, the Forum had all the appearances of a nationalist think-in as it sought to provide evidence of momentum within constitutional nationalism. Regular set-piece news stories, based on the thirty-one submissions made in person and on the inter-party negotiations, kept the Forum centre-stage in the public mind. The final Forum report was published on 2 May 1984, just six weeks before the next big electoral contest between the SDLP and Sinn Féin.

Ultimately, the Forum came out decidedly in favour of a united sovereign independent Ireland as the preferred and best form of government, reflecting as it did the wishes of the vast majority of people living on the island. It was a 'major reality',[116] the final report declared, that Northern Ireland's existing structures had failed to provide peace, stability or reconciliation. The unionist veto (referred to as Section 1 of the 1973 Northern Ireland Constitution Act) had in its practical application inhibited the dialogue necessary for progress, and removed the incentive to seek a political solution. Consent was defined only in the context of negotiating a new agreed Ireland, which would take the form of a unitary state, and it would be for the two Governments to create the framework and atmosphere for these negotiations to take place. The unitary state would have a single legal and police system throughout the country and irrevocable guarantees to protect the unionist and nationalist identities.

The second option contained in the report – a federal or confederal state – would necessitate a new Constitution that would be formulated by an all-party constitutional conference convened by the two Governments. Each part of the federal/confederal unit would possess its own executive and Parliament with responsibility for most domestic issues with clearly defined powers reserved for central government and a rotating head of state. There would be a single supreme constitutional court for the island to protect citizen rights. The third option of joint sovereignty, which FitzGerald considered the most realistic in the short term, would involve authority being shared between London and Dublin, though provision was made for a local assembly and executive in Northern Ireland.

Elections to the European Parliament on 14 June 1984 provided tangible evidence that the New Ireland Forum had paid dividends and that the rise in support for Sinn Féin had been arrested. John Hume emerged as the leading figure from the nationalist community, taking 22 per cent of the overall vote compared with 13.35 per cent for Sinn Féin's Danny Morrison. While Sinn Féin was still taking a third of the nationalist vote, it seemed that an electoral ceiling had been reached. Sinn Féin also contested MEP seats in the Republic for the first time but, with 4.9 per cent of the vote, failed to win any of the fifteen seats available.[117]

Thatcher delayed meeting FitzGerald for five months, until March 1983, not least to demonstrate her priorities and to have established an internal solution – in the form of the Northern Ireland Assembly – before any resumption of an Anglo-Irish talks process. The Conservative Party's re-election victory in June 1983 has commonly and erroneously been attributed to Thatcher's military victory in the Falklands. However, the first-past-the-post electoral system skewed the result so that the Tories lost 700,000 votes but gained dozens of seats as the emergence of the SDP–Liberal Alliance disproportionately hit Labour, which recorded its worst result since 1918. Irish officials feared that – emboldened by her re-election – Thatcher would be in a mood of 'heady and reinforced certitude' and that it would be a 'daunting task' to try to influence her. In particular, they fretted that she would introduce hanging for terrorist offences, which would have a 'catastrophic effect' in both parts of Ireland.[118]

John Hume told Irish officials that nationalist alienation could only be reversed by having the Republic involved in security operations throughout the North, along with the British, which he called 'not Brits out, but Irish in'. For this the SDLP leader said he would be prepared to forgo his party's involvement in power sharing and concede majority rule to Unionists.[119] Such ideas confirmed FitzGerald's belief in joint sovereignty (or joint authority as it was commonly called to assuage British sensitivities) as the most effective means of ending nationalist 'alienation' from British rule in Northern Ireland. Not only did Thatcher refuse to consider 'joint authority' but she also rejected the term 'alienation'. 'I don't like that word', she told the Taoiseach and his officials, 'that's a Marxist word.'[120]

Out! Out! Out!

Thatcher never bothered to learn how to pronounce the names of her Irish counterparts. Haughey was pronounced 'Hockey' while Garret was frequently referred to in his presence as 'Gareth'.[121] FitzGerald's volubility did not endear him to the British Prime Minister and she had difficulty following his frequently inaudible rapid-fire speech. In her memoirs she expressed a preference for the comparatively taciturn Haughey, whom she described as 'tough, able and politically astute with few illusions and, I am sure, not much affection for the British … I found him easy to get along with, less talkative and more realistic than Garret FitzGerald.'[122] During one meeting with FitzGerald, Thatcher fell fast asleep soon after sitting down. FitzGerald looked at Thatcher's foreign policy aide, Charles Powell, to ask what they should do. 'Just keep talking', Powell replied, 'I'll write it all down.' Thereafter the 'meeting' continued with Powell noting all the points the Taoiseach wished to make before waking up the Prime Minister to brief her on what had been agreed for the joint press statement. Powell recalls that neither the Taoiseach nor his cabinet Secretary, Dermot Nally, who accompanied him, seemed to mind this arrangement.[123]

The IRA's attempt to assassinate Thatcher by bombing the Tory party conference in Brighton on 12 October 1984 only hardened her views on Ireland and she feared that any concessions to Dublin could be conceived as yielding to terrorism. She rejected the suggestion that the Irish Government might have a representative based in Belfast, asking rhetorically 'Why should the Irish have such a thing? How would you like it if there was a Russian representative in London who had to be consulted about everything?' David Goodall, one of the most senior British officials negotiating with the Irish Government, replied that Russians did not constitute 30 per cent of the UK population. Thatcher then proceeded to compare the Irish Government's view that they should have a say on Northern Ireland affairs to Nazi Germany's interest in the Sudetenland during the 1930s.[124] It was in this unpromising context that FitzGerald tried to push forward the Anglo-Irish process and impress on the British the importance of the New Ireland Forum Report.

As a result of heightened fears for Thatcher's safety, the scheduled Anglo-Irish summit of 18 November was shifted from Dublin to Chequers. When the British ambassador to Ireland, Alan Goodison, wrote that the Taoiseach could not afford to leave the summit empty-handed, Thatcher replied in the margin, 'That is not my problem'.[125] Throughout the summit meeting with Thatcher in Chequers, the Taoiseach emphasised the dangers posed by Sinn Féin's electoral rise, not just in Northern Ireland but also in the Republic as, according to FitzGerald, 'there were many soft-headed people in the country'.[126] After FitzGerald had departed, Thatcher spoke with officials. David Goodall recalled that Thatcher was wont to put forward various ideas about the North 'which everyone else tried to squash'. During a late-night conversation at Chequers, as she discussed Northern Ireland with James Prior and Foreign Secretary Geoffrey Howe, the Prime Minister began to float the idea of population displacement in Northern Ireland. As Goodall recalls:

> She said, if the northern [Catholic] population want to be in the south, well why don't they move over there? After all, there was a big movement of population in Ireland, wasn't there? Nobody could think what it was. So finally I said, are you talking about Cromwell, prime minister? She said, that's right, Cromwell.[127]

Her officials dissuaded Thatcher from this and other fleeting fantasies, such as redrawing the Irish border so that it would be easier to patrol.[128]

If Thatcher's late-night musings were a cause of concern to her inner circle, the Prime Minister's public utterances soon after sowed discord amongst the Irish political elite. At the press conference following the Anglo-Irish summit on 19 November 1984, Thatcher dismissed the Forum Report proposals:

> I have made it quite clear ... that a unified Ireland was one solution that is out. A second solution was confederation of two states. That is out. A third solution was joint authority. That is out.[129]

What became known as the 'out! out! out!' speech caused FitzGerald tremendous damage at home. Though in substance there was nothing new in Thatcher's response, it was the tone of her dismissal that caused most offence. Haughey smelt blood and sought to derive the maximum advantage from the debacle:

> I sought to warn the present Taoiseach about the dangers inherent in his approach and attitude to Anglo-Irish relations ... he engaged in an exercise of accommodation, undertaking a series of steps designed to inculcate an atmosphere of personal friendliness, helpfulness and acceptability ... international relations, international discussions, international negotiations are not kindergarten matters nor are they conducted as if they were some kind of amicable parlour game. The humiliation inflicted by the Taoiseach yesterday could have been foreseen ... you have led this country into the greatest humiliation in recent history. You have failed ignominiously in an area of vital national interest. Because of your incompetence, misjudgement and ineffectiveness you have done grievous damage to our national political interests and our pride.[130]

The Fianna Fáil leader used the period in opposition to build up his image as the only one capable of solving the national question. His collected speeches, many of which had been written by his key advisor Martin Mansergh, were published in a huge tome grandiosely entitled *The Spirit of the Nation*, edited by Mansergh himself. A lavish documentary entitled *Charles Haughey's Ireland*, starring and narrated by the Fianna Fáil leader and broadcast on the British television station, Channel 4, presented Haughey as a noble visionary. As he was filmed spending much of his time on his small island of Inishvickillane, he cut a Napoleonic figure temporarily confined on his Elba eagerly awaiting a return to former glories. Haughey's reference to FitzGerald as 'the present Taoiseach' chimed with how many in Fianna Fáil viewed modern Irish history, as one that was indistinguishable from Fianna Fáil's place as the 'natural party of government'. From this perspective, post-1932 Ireland had been characterised by long periods of strong, single-party Fianna Fáil government punctuated by mercifully brief interludes when Fine Gael had slipped into office only to be turfed out by the electorate at the first opportunity, allowing Fianna Fáil to return to the national rescue. An integral part of this belief system was the notion that only Fianna Fáil had the credentials, the leadership, the experience and the will to negotiate an agreement with Britain that would resolve the national question in a manner complementary to the party's first aim of securing a united Ireland as an independent republic. Bereft of these essential characteristics and disabled by shoneenism, Fine Gael, in this narrative, could never negotiate a durable settlement based on preserving the national interest. Thatcher's apparent dressing down of FitzGerald and her summary rejection of the New Ireland Forum Report confirmed this Fianna Fáil worldview. Thus, Haughey accused FitzGerald of reckless amateurism, of mistaking affability for acquiescence and of seeking to gain approval rather than results from the British Prime Minister.

FitzGerald braced himself for what would be the most difficult parliamentary party meeting of his career. The Taoiseach privately described Thatcher's behaviour as 'gratuitously offensive' and he expressed fears that the episode might promote a sharp rise in IRA membership, resulting in increased violence North and South. FitzGerald's essential point continued to be that constitutional politics had not only to work but be seen to work. Thatcher's comments had dealt that mission an almighty blow from which the process could either recover or succumb. It was at this time that the Irish Government sought to exploit its influence in the US to get the Reagan administration to pressure Thatcher back into constructive negotiations.

Conscious of the damage caused to Anglo-Irish relations, Thatcher's cabinet Secretary, Sir Robert Armstrong, gently suggested that she might write to the Taoiseach expressing regret 'if the manner in which what you said at your press conference was reported has created difficulties for him at home'. On the proposal itself, the Prime Minister wrote 'Certainly NOT. This whole proposal is too contrived and too apologetic. Why?' Instead, Thatcher's reply claimed that her words had been taken out of context. The pair revisited the topic when they met the following month at an EEC summit in Dublin (initially Thatcher had said she wouldn't visit Dublin on security grounds). When the Taoiseach broached the issue, the Prime Minister replied that she had communicated 'in her own style' and that 'nothing which she had said at the press conference should have surprised anyone ... one had to develop an extra sensitivity for commenting on the Irish problem.' The Taoiseach replied that 'after 800 years, extra sensitivity was indeed needed....'.[131]

FitzGerald had an opportunity to make a further impression on Thatcher at the margins of a European summit in Milan on 29 June 1985. Speaking with 'considerable emotion', the Taoiseach said he wanted the Prime Minister to understand that 'the Irish Government and people did not want a role in Northern Ireland'. FitzGerald said that he was regarded as eccentric because of the time and effort he was devoting to reach an agreement but 'he did so because he believed that otherwise Sinn Féin would gain the upper hand amongst the minority in the North, and provoke a civil war which would drag the Republic down as well'. He also tried to place Ireland in a larger context by arguing that 'there were people on the sidelines like Colonel Gaddafi ready to put up millions of pounds to achieve this aim'.[132] Thatcher had by now woken up to the threat that Gaddafi posed to British rule in Northern Ireland, though he had been supportive of the IRA since the early 1970s. As late as 1981, Thatcher was sending the Libyan dictator Christmas cards addressed 'To the Leader of the Great First of September Revolution'.[133] It was clear that FitzGerald was using the same tactic as he had employed ten years earlier during his meeting with James Callaghan, placing Ireland in a Cold War context and arguing that British inaction or mistakes could lead to the collapse of Ireland, north and south, with forces hostile to British interests filling the vacuum. 'For 800 years Britain had occupied Ireland to protect its flank', the Taoiseach pointed out. 'There was now a serious risk of ending up with what we [the British] had always tried to avoid, an Ireland under hostile and sinister influence.'[134]

In the British Government's account of the meeting, the Taoiseach is recorded as saying that all he wanted was 'minimal steps to protect the minority' and that he and Thatcher were the only two people able to reach an agreement. 'If they failed the opportunity would be lost, possibly forever. He was ready to take the risk whatever it might cost him personally and politically.' Thatcher could offer little to mollify the emotional Taoiseach. While the Prime Minister 'of course ... shared the Taoiseach's aim of preventing Ireland from coming under hostile and tyrannical forces' she 'did not want to mislead the Taoiseach into thinking that publicly announced steps of the sort he had described [such as joint courts] were in any way feasible'.[135]

As the months progressed, it was clear that Thatcher was reluctant to contemplate any major reforms, be they changes to the judiciary, the police or the army within Northern Ireland. In her minimalist approach she was supported by her private Secretary, Charles Powell, and newly appointed Northern Secretary, Tom King. Referring to media reports that suggested that there might be a defence element to any proposed agreement, the British ambassador assured Haughey in May 1985 that this was not the case, which the Fianna Fáil leader 'seemed to accept [readily]', but replied that 'this would not prevent him from talking about the threat to Irish neutrality in public'.[136] This opportunism was all the more remarkable given Haughey and Lenihan's offer of ditching neutrality when seeking to entice Thatcher in 1980.

Haughey confessed to deriving a certain *Schadenfreude* from the coalition's economic difficulties. While 'it was clear that nobody had any solution to the current economic problems of the Republic', Haughey told the British ambassador that he 'was content to let the Government bear responsibility'.[137] The Fianna Fáil leader understood FitzGerald's predicament better than most. Like Haughey in 1980, FitzGerald was constitutionally obliged to hold an election in two years, and faced with a deteriorating economy – one in six were out of work – the Fine Gael leader could only hope for a boost by delivering, or appearing to deliver, a breakthrough in Northern Ireland. Haughey was determined to deny him this life-line, not least because he knew that, after three unsuccessful leadership heaves against him, his own political survival depended on winning the 1987 general election. Indeed, the Fianna Fáil leader said that SDLP support for a new inter-governmental agreement would not deter him from opposing it. Liberated from the responsibilities of government, Haughey pandered to grassroots republicanism and sought to undermine or tarnish FitzGerald's initiatives. He told the British ambassador that eventually the British Government would have to stand up to the unionists and only then would they come to the negotiating table. When asked if he thought Thatcher was likely to do this, Haughey replied in the negative, saying that Anglo-Irish relations would have to await 'the right man' and none had emerged since William Gladstone.[138]

The Anglo-Irish Agreement and its aftermath

Pursuing the British for a deal on Northern Ireland had obvious risks for FitzGerald; a second rebuff from Thatcher could sink his administration. Influential actors in the US including the Reagan administration tried to assuage Thatcher's misgivings about an agreement and this, combined with gentle prodding from senior servants and the carrot of enhanced security cooperation against the IRA, encouraged her to relent.[139] On 15 November 1985, Thatcher and FitzGerald signed the Anglo-Irish Agreement (AIA) at Hillsborough Castle. From the Irish Government's perspective, the establishment of an Anglo-Irish Inter-governmental Conference composed of officials from both Governments was a major step forward. Though it had no decision-making powers, the Conference enjoyed a consultative role and could make proposals on matters that did not impinge upon the powers of a devolved administration in Northern Ireland, should one be constituted. The icing on the cake, however, was a permanent secretariat, which would include officials from the Department of Foreign Affairs and be based in Maryfield, on the outskirts of Belfast.

FitzGerald maximised the significance of the Agreement by saying that the commitment contained within Article 1 constituted the 'first clear affirmation in any binding Anglo-Irish agreement since 1921' that Britain has no interest in the continuing division of this island and that its presence in this island, undertaking the responsibility of government in Northern Ireland, continues solely because this is the wish of a majority of the people in that area'.[140] Although the British Government had agreed to a similar provision at Sunningdale in 1973, the Taoiseach's claim was based on the fact that whereas that agreement had never been registered at the United Nations the Hillsborough accord would be.

The Anglo-Irish Agreement, like its much more ambitious predecessor negotiated at Sunningdale, acknowledged that the Irish Government had a legitimate concern in the affairs of Northern Ireland. When it came to policy, however, the Irish Government could only propose whereas it was the British that would decide. The most the Irish Government could reasonably claim was that they had got their foot in the door, a fact most tangibly demonstrated by the existence of the Maryfield Secretariat. Dublin was entitled to be consulted on some matters but also retained its traditional right to be ignored. There was no mechanism whereby the Irish Government could seek to enforce its new 'powers'. The coalition Government understandably oversold its case to compensate for the major dilution of the Forum Report – purportedly the 'bottom line' of constitutional nationalism.

Public reaction to the Anglo-Irish Agreement in Northern Ireland differed significantly between the two communities. Fearing the Agreement was a device to facilitate creeping Dublin annexation of the North, unionists, in the words of one Irish minister, 'went bananas',[141] and pledged to mount an intensive campaign of street protests and non-cooperation with government institutions. Peter Robinson best exemplified the mix of disbelief and defiance when he claimed that loyalists were on 'the window ledge of the Union' but they were not going to jump off.[142] The Ulster Freedom Fighters (UFF) immediately declared that members of the Anglo-Irish Conference and Secretariat would henceforth be considered legitimate targets for assassination. Unionist MPs resigned their parliamentary seats at Westminster in protest, triggering fifteen by-elections fought under the banner of 'Ulster Says No'. All seats were predictably retained save that of Enoch Powell, who lost South Down to the SDLP's Eddie McGrady, mainly due to a drift in support from Sinn Féin to the SDLP. As in Fermanagh-South Tyrone and Mid-Ulster, South Down had previously returned a unionist to Westminster as the nationalist majority vote split between Sinn Féin and the SDLP. Overall the by-election results – and those obtained in the subsequent Westminster parliamentary elections in 1987

– suggested that the Agreement had achieved one of the Irish Government's core objectives – revitalising the SDLP while stymieing Sinn Féin's electoral advances.

The responses of the unionists and the Irish Government were mutually reinforcing. Michael Noonan's claim that Dublin had been given 'a major and substantial role in the day-to-day running of Northern Ireland' was extravagant and grist to the mill of the loyalist fear-merchants. Similarly, unionist apoplexy and protests merely confirmed to doubters in the Republic that something major had indeed been conceded. Loyalist protests also reassured northern national-ists, and assisted the SDLP in demonstrating the advantages of constitutional action.

Fianna Fáil's opposition to the Agreement brought the party into conflict with the SDLP leadership with whom they had closely cooperated during the New Ireland Forum deliberations. Haughey's stance on the Hillsborough Accord also put him on a collision course with the Agreement's influential backers in Irish America and the US Government. His argument that the Agreement 'copperfasten[ed] partition' found a receptive audience with many in the party and was bolstered by a series of statements made by the British negotiators seeking to allay unionist suspicions. Speaking in Brussels, Northern Secretary Tom King said that the British Government had secured a settlement in which the Taoiseach had 'accepted for all practical purposes and into perpetuity that there will never be a united Ireland'[143] and Thatcher asserted that the Agreement 'reinforce[d] the union'.[144] Several British Government representatives publicly emphasised that the pact was merely a mechanism for advancing security coopera-tion with Dublin.

The hunger strikes and resultant electoral triumphs had reinvigorated the republican movement, but had also tied it to judging advances and setbacks at least partially through the framework of elections. As the coalition Government was constitutionally obliged to hold a general election in 1987, the Sinn Féin leadership, increasingly a coterie of northerners close to party president Gerry Adams, dropped its traditional policy of refusing to take seats in Dáil Éireann. The proposal put to the party's ard fheis was not as sweeping as the 1970 conference motion, which had also advocated taking seats in Stormont and Westminster, and had resulted in a division into the Official and Provisional IRA. The Adams-led leadership had prepared party supporters to a greater degree than had been the case sixteen years earlier. Consequently, the new policy led to a splinter rather than a split, with veterans Ruairí Ó Brádaigh and Daithí Ó Conaill leading a walkout to establish a rival abstentionist party, Republican Sinn Féin. Though Sinn Féin did not have any representation in the Dáil and over a decade would pass before an election victory would see a

member take a seat in Leinster House, the move demonstrated signs of increasing
constitutionalism within the party leadership, which was now firmly wedded
to contesting elections. No longer would Sinn Féin pursue ad hoc electoral
interventionism and, accordingly, the leadership would become ever more sensitive to how the IRA's military endeavours impacted on the party membership
and vote.

The Hillsborough Agreement received overwhelming endorsement from
national and international media and there was little dissention within the coalition
Government. Mary Robinson, a future Irish President, resigned from the Labour
Party, claiming the imposed framework would inhibit political progress, and it
was known that former Labour Party leader Frank Cluskey and Fine Gael stalwart
Paddy Harte were similarly opposed. The dissenters constituted a tiny minority,
however. On the other side of the House, Mary Harney defected from Fianna
Fáil – citing Haughey's opposition to the AIA as the final straw – and joined
forces with other errant TDs to form the Progressive Democrats. North of the
border, Pascal O'Hare, who had participated in the New Ireland Forum, was
the most prominent of the small group of SDLP nonconformists. He resigned,
claiming that he could not 'live politically in a party who have accepted a few
crumbs falling from the British political table'.[145]

Haughey argued that the Agreement would 'lead the Irish Government into
an impossible political situation in which they will find themselves assuming
responsibility for actions and becoming involved in situations, particularly in
the security field, over which they have no control'.[146] Gerry Adams adopted a
similar line, claiming that 'far from ending the nightmare of the nationalist
people, the Dublin Government and the SDLP leadership have become part of
that nightmare'.[147] Haughey tabled a detailed amendment to the motion that
reflected traditional Fianna Fáil policy by citing Articles 2 and 3 of the Constitution, the 1949 all-party declaration and the New Ireland Forum Report. While
identifying the need to ameliorate the plight of the northern nationalist community
and welcoming any effective measures that might achieve that purpose, the
amendment repudiated 'any recognition of British sovereignty over any part of
the national territory' and called for a constitutional conference convened by
both Governments and representatives of all traditions in Ireland 'to formulate
new constitutional arrangements which would lead to uniting all the people of
Ireland in peace and harmony'.[148]

Haughey's reaction might have actually helped FitzGerald, though this was
hardly his intention. Had resistance to the Agreement come only from the
unionist side it would have enhanced the notion that this was a one-sided deal
that rewarded nationalists at the expense of northern loyalists. By providing
a nationalist critique of the Agreement, Fianna Fáil strengthened FitzGerald's

hand when dealing with the British. Unionist hostility by the same token insulated the Taoiseach from the charge of negotiating a sell-out of national interests.

Throughout 1986 the coalition disintegrated and limped towards an election, eventually called for 17 February 1987. The intervention of the newly formed Progressive Democrats party, founded by former veteran Fianna Fáil minister, Des O'Malley, deprived Charles Haughey of an overall majority when it took fourteen seats on its first electoral outing. The PDs had little to say about Northern Ireland policy but rather emphasised the economy, being a party that focussed on taxation reform. Labour lost almost a third of its electoral support and only four votes separated party leader Dick Spring from political oblivion, as he scraped home in his North Kerry constituency. Fine Gael losses were of a magnitude that made FitzGerald's resignation inevitable. Few could have imagined that it would be almost a quarter of a century before another Fine Gael-led coalition would win a general election.

The British administration worried that a Haughey-led Fianna Fáil Government would ditch the Agreement he had so vociferously condemned.[149] However, no sooner was Haughey back in office than he began to backtrack on his opposition to the AIA. Opinion polls had suggested that the electorate did not share Haughey's despondency, with opposition to the Agreement substantially below support for his party. What had been described as 'a sad day for Irish nationalism' in November 1985 was diluted a year later to a position whereby 'we would have to accept [the AIA] until such time as we were in a position to renegotiate the terms'.[150] According to senior Irish Government official Michael Lillis, Haughey remained 'strongly antipathetic to the idea of a longterm involvement of the Republic in a Northern Ireland still ultimately governed and administered by HMG'. Instead of a process 'which dribble[d] on' indefinitely, Lillis told the head of Northern Ireland's civil service, Ken Bloomfield, that Haughey thought the Governments should make a concerted effort to make progress on the main areas defined by the AIA. This would help 'clear the pitch' for a resolute bid to achieve a form of devolution that would confer the 'fullest powers possible', including law and order. Lillis thought the idea of 'Irishmen talking to Irishmen' would appeal to Haughey and that in such circumstances the inter-governmental conference could be sidelined and even the Maryfield Secretariat could possibly be dispensed with.[151]

As Fine Gael and Labour left office they had lobbed a ticking time bomb to the incoming Government in the form of the Extradition Bill, passed in the administration's dying days but which would not come into effect for a year. The case against extradition – that British and Northern Ireland systems of justice could not be relied upon in cases involving Irish republicans – proved particularly divisive within Fianna Fáil. According to one British report, extradition would be widely interpreted as 'handing our boys over to the vagaries, or worse, of British justice' and failure to reform Northern Ireland's judiciary fuelled distrust.[152] The same report argued that if Dublin delayed ratification of the Extradition Bill it 'could damage the whole future of the Agreement'. In the event, it was the IRA itself that eased the passage of the legislation with the bombing of a Remembrance Day commemoration in Enniskillen on 8 November 1987, killing eleven civilians. The Government reluctantly went ahead with the Extradition Act, but was disappointed a month later when the British Court of Appeal ruled that the convictions of the Birmingham Six were safe and satisfactory.

If 1987 had proved to be a difficult year in Anglo-Irish relations, 1988 saw the return of a level of animosity not witnessed since the Falklands war due to a series of damaging events, such as the Stalker–Sampson affair, which had confirmed high levels of collusion between British security forces and loyalist paramilitaries. The British Army embarked on a renewed offensive against the IRA. In May 1987, they had managed to ambush and kill eight IRA members and a civilian at Loughall and, throughout the following year, there were renewed accusations of a shoot-to-kill policy, most spectacularly when the SAS killed three unarmed IRA members in Gibraltar. The IRA in turn inflicted some notable blows during the summer of 1988. Six off-duty British soldiers were killed in June when their unmarked van was bombed not far from British military headquarters in Lisburn, while a huge bomb in Ballygawley two months later killed another eight British soldiers and injured over two dozen.

By 1988, it was clear that the AIA had failed to meet the expectations of both Governments. The lack of reform within Northern Ireland disappointed Dublin and northern nationalists while the British had anticipated greater security gains. The widening chasm was brought into sharp focus as the first three-year review of the Agreement approached in 1988. An opinion poll conducted throughout Northern Ireland in February 1988 found that whereas the overwhelming majority of Protestants (96 per cent) felt that the AIA had been of no benefit to them the same view was maintained by over four-fifths of Catholics.[153] A comprehensive poll conducted in Britain the following month found that only 27 per cent of the British electorate favoured Northern Ireland remaining within the United Kingdom.[154] The number of deaths resulting from the Troubles in 1988 was almost double that for 1985, when the Agreement was signed. In terms of the political process within Northern Ireland, much of the late 1980s and early 1990s was spent fruitlessly considering 'talks about talks'. It was during this period too that Haughey opened up secret indirect communications with the Sinn Féin leadership using intermediaries, such as Martin Mansergh and Fr. Alex Reid.

Buoyed by Fianna Fáil's rising status in the opinion polls, and despite a cooperative opposition, Haughey chose to call a snap election for June 1989. The gamble failed to pay off and, far from securing an overall majority, the party lost seats. Parliamentary arithmetic suggested a Fianna Fáil–Progressive Democrats Government as the two parties, with seventy-seven and six seats respectively, could muster the support of half of the Dáil's deputies. Party ideology, personality clashes and recent acrimonies suggested such an alliance would be unthinkable. Opposition to coalition government had been elevated from the realm of party policy to an integral part of Fianna Fáil's core dogma. During the six decades it had dominated Irish politics, Fianna Fáil had never shared power. The fact that the PDs were led in the main by those who had only recently defected from Fianna Fáil made the partnership seem all the more improbable. A survivor of multiple heaves, with a keen sense of his own vulnerabilities and an unrivalled will to power, Haughey went over the head of the party membership and his leadership colleagues and agreed to a coalition, which included two PD ministers. Despite being unloved by the grassroots and derided by senior party figures, the inter-party administration endured for over three years, not least because Haughey and O'Malley both wished to exercise power.

Haughey's replacement by Albert Reynolds in February 1992 quickly brought an end to what the new Fianna Fáil leader and Taoiseach had controversially described as a 'temporary little arrangement'.[155] The November 1992 election proved a mixed blessing for Reynolds. In what was the party's worst electoral performance since 1927, Fianna Fáil support dipped to 39.1 per cent. Despite this, Reynolds managed to stay in power by exchanging one awkward partner for another. While the PDs were dispatched to the opposition benches, an emboldened Labour Party, boosted by their best electoral outing, replaced them, with Labour leader Dick Spring becoming Tánaiste and Minister for Foreign Affairs. Fine Gael, which had ditched the conciliatory Alan Dukes for John Bruton, recorded its worst performance since 1948, garnering just over two-thirds of the vote achieved by Garret FitzGerald eight years previously. There had also been important changes in personnel on the British side. In November 1989 Northern Secretary Tom King made way for Peter Brooke and, more significantly, John Major replaced Margaret Thatcher as Prime Minister a year later. The relationship between Major and Reynolds would be a key component in establishing a viable peace process in the decade ahead.

Notes

1   Confidential report of British embassy on Charles Haughey, 9 April 1980. NAUK PREM 19/283.

2   See the memoirs of Haughey's (and Lynch's) press officer, Frank Dunlop, *Yes, Taoiseach*.

3   Confidential report of British embassy on Charles Haughey, 9 April 1980. NAUK PREM 19/283.

4   Confidential report of British embassy on Charles Haughey, 9 April 1980. NAUK PREM 19/283.

5   These talks, called by Secretary of State for Northern Ireland Humphrey Atkins, took place at Stormont between January and March 1980.

6   Confidential report of British embassy on Charles Haughey, 9 April 1980. NAUK PREM 19/283.

7   Confidential report of British embassy on Charles Haughey, 9 April 1980. NAUK PREM 19/283.

8   Confidential report of British embassy on Charles Haughey, 9 April 1980. NAUK PREM 19/283.

9   Transcript of meeting between Haughey and Atkins, 15 April 1980. NAI DT 2010/53/853.

10   See 'Anglo-Irish relations', 8 September 1982. NAUK CJ 4/4180.

11   Dunlop, *Yes, Taoiseach*, p. 199.

12   See 'Secretary of Department [Seán Donlon]: chronological file, 1981'. NAI DFA 2011/38/2.

13   Hamilton Fish was a great-grandson of the US Secretary of State (1869–1877) of the same name.

14   Letter from Donlon to Congressman Hamilton Fish dated 6 November 1979 as cited in McManus, *My American Struggle*, 164–165. See also Coogan, *The Troubles*, p. 412. 'Priest and ambassador in row over Birmingham Six', *Irish Independent*, 31 December 2010.

15   *Irish Press*, 5 November 1985.

16   Quoted in Donlon, 'Haughey bid to tighten grip on Northern policy derailed', Memoir Part 2, *Irish Times*, 28 July 2009.

17   Quoted in Donlon, Memoir Part 2, *Irish Times*, 28 July 2009.

18   Quoted in Donlon, Memoir Part 2, *Irish Times*, 28 July 2009.

19   Donlon, Memoir Part 2, *Irish Times*, 28 July 2009.

20   Donlon, Memoir Part 2, *Irish Times*, 28 July 2009.

21   See Joyce and Murtagh, *The Boss*, p. 155; McManus, *My American Struggle*, p. 164; Cronin, *Washington's Irish Policy*, pp. 318–319.

22   FitzGerald, *All in A Life*, p. 349.

23   *Irish Press*, 10 July 1980.

24   *Irish Times*, 28 July 1980.

25   Letter from FitzGerald to Haughey, 21 July 1980. NAI TSCH/2010/53/853. The letter was reprinted in the *Irish Times*, 28 July 1980.

26   Quoted in Dunlop, *Yes, Taoiseach*, p. 197.

27   McManus, *My American Struggle*, p. 145. Within a month of Haughey losing office in July 1981, the new Fine Gael–Labour Government led by Garret FitzGerald announced

that Seán Donlon would return from Washington to take charge of the Department of Foreign Affairs. Retiring from diplomatic life in 1987 for a career in private enterprise allowed Donlon to take up positions advising Fine Gael leaders John Bruton and Michael Noonan and to speak more freely on public affairs. He became a notable critic of the 'over-glorification' of historical figures such as 1916 rebellion leaders Pádraig Pearse and James Connolly and argued that the 'overly exuberant' state commemorations of 1966, celebrating as they did the military struggle for Irish freedom, had 'encouraged some of what happened in Northern Ireland subsequently'. Speech praising late-US Senator Ted Kennedy's contribution to the Northern peace process at the Parnell Summer School, 16 August 2013, as reported in the *Irish Independent*, 17 August 2013.

28   Record of a discussion between the Prime Minister and the Prime Minister of the Republic of Ireland, Mr Charles Haughey, at No. 10 Downing Street on 21 May at 1535. NAUK PREM 19/283.

29   Thatcher, *The Downing Street Years*, p. 388.

30   Record of summit meeting between Thatcher and Haughey, London, 21 May 1980. NAI DT 2012/59/1599.

31   Communiqué following meeting between Haughey and Thatcher, 21 May 1980. NAI DT 2012/59/1599.

32   Record of summit meeting between Thatcher and Haughey, London, 21 May 1980. NAI DT 2012/59/1599.

33   Letter from Eamon Kennedy to Margaret Thatcher, 22 May 1980. NAUK PREM 19/283.

34   Letter from Margaret Thatcher to Eamon Kennedy, 27 May 1980. NAUK PREM 19/283.

35   Prime Minister's telephone conversation with the Taoiseach, 22 May 1980. NAUK PREM 19/283.

36   Meeting between Haughey and Haydon, 23 May 1980. NAUK FCO 87/999.

37   'Farewell calls', 27 May 1980. NAUK PREM 19/283.

38   See for example 'Meeting between Haughey and [British ambassador] Haydon, 16 May 1980'. NAI DT 2012/59/1599.

39   'Record of meeting between Lenihan and Haydon, 26 May 1980'. NAUK FCO 87/999.

40   'Record of meeting between Haughey and Haydon, 23 May 1980.' NAUK FCO 87/999.

41   'Meeting between the Taoiseach and British Prime Minister, 8 December, 1980'. NAI DFA 2010/53/930.

42   See Justin Staples to M.J. Newington, 7 July 1980. NAUK FCO 87/1014.

43   See *Irish Times*, 17 December 1980.

44   Haughey to Thatcher, 23 October 1980. NAI DT 2010/53/928/1.

45   Haughey to Thatcher, 23 October 1980. NAI DT 2010/53/928/1.

46   Record of meeting between Thatcher and Atkins, 31 October 1980. NAUK FCO 87/1036.

47 'Main points emerging from meeting of 4 November', 5 November 1980. NAI DT 2010/19/1728.

48 'Effects of H-Block hunger strike on Anglo-Irish relations and on forthcoming meeting' (date omitted). NAI DT 2010/53/928.

49 'Main points emerging from meeting of 4 November' (5 November 1980). NAI DT 2010/19/1728.

50 *Irish Press*, 3 November 1980. *Irish Times*, 3 November 1980.

51 See Ó Beacháin, *Destiny of the Soldiers*, pp. 167–199.

52 Kennedy to Thatcher, 2 November 1980. NAUK FCO 87/1064.

53 Kennedy to Thatcher, 2 November 1980. NAUK FCO 87/1064.

54 Shortly after the summit Haughey described the delegation as the most important ever to visit the state. *Dáil Debates*, 325/6, 29 May 1980, cols 968–969.

55 Moore, *Not for Turning*, p. 601.

56 'Meeting between the Taoiseach and British Prime Minister, 8 December, 1980'. NAI DFA 2010/53/930. See also 'Record of conversation between the Prime Minister and the Taoiseach, Mr. Charles Haughey, in Dublin Castle on 8 December 1980'. NAUK PREM 19/507.

57 'Meeting between the Taoiseach and the British Prime Minister, 8 December, 1980'. NAI DFA 2010/53/930.

58 'Meeting between the Taoiseach and the British Prime Minister, 8 December, 1980'. NAI DFA 2010/53/930.

59 'Meeting between the Taoiseach and the British Prime Minister, 8 December, 1980'. NAI DFA 2010/53/930.

60 'Meeting between the Taoiseach and the British Prime Minister, 8 December, 1980'. NAI DFA 2010/53/930.

61 'Meeting between the Taoiseach and the British Prime Minister, 8 December, 1980'. NAI DFA 2010/53/930.

62 *Irish Times*, 31 December 2010.

63 Thatcher, *The Downing Street Years*, p. 390.

64 Thatcher, *The Downing Street Years*, p. 390.

65 *Irish Times*, 11 December 1980.

66 Quoted in McKittrick and McVea, *Making Sense of the Troubles*, pp. 186–187.

67 'Republic of Ireland. Annual review for 1980', dated 21 January 1981. PRONI CENT/1/10/13.

68 'Republic of Ireland. Annual review for 1980', dated 21 January 1981. PRONI CENT/1/10/13.

69 'Republic of Ireland. Annual review for 1980', dated 21 January 1981. PRONI CENT/1/10/13.

70 'The hunger strikes: view from the Irish Republic', 19 October 1981, PRONI NIO/12/202.

71 O'Connell, *Dr John*, pp. 152–153.

72 'Telephone conversation between No 10 Downing Street and the Taoiseach's Office', 12 May 1981. PRONI CENT/1/10/36A.

73   Armstrong minute to Thatcher ('Anglo-Irish joint studies'), 29 April 1981. NAUK PREM19/508.

74   'Taoiseach campaigns in border counties 1981'. Video available at www.rte.ie/archives/exhibitions/688-elections/694-general-election-1981/139433-taoiseach-campaigns-in-border-counties/?page=1. Accessed 8 April 2018.

75   Arnold, *Haughey*, p. 183.

76   The official name of the ditty, *Charlie's Song*, has been eclipsed by the rousing chorus encouraging supporters to 'rise and follow Charlie'.

77   'The hunger strikes: view from the Irish Republic', 19 October 1981. PRONI NIO/12/202.

78   Telegram No. 108 to Dublin, 13 July 1981. NAUK FCO/87/1261.

79   *Irish Times*, 30 December 2011.

80   *Irish Press*, 20 July 1981.

81   Letter to Ronald Reagan, 23 July 1981. NAI D/T 2011/127/1057. Some weeks later, US senator Ted Kennedy and seventeen colleagues wrote to Mr Reagan, seeking a meeting about the impact of the hunger strikes.

82   Letter to Horsemen, 28 July 1981. NAI D/T 2011/127/1057.

83   Liam Hourican to FitzGerald, 21 July 1981. NAI D/T 2011/127/1057.

84   Dermot Nally to FitzGerald, 21 July 1981. NAI D/T 2011/127/1057.

85   *Irish Independent*, 30 December 2011.

86   Cardinal Ó Fiaich's comment, 22 May 1981, as quoted in Beresford, *Ten Men Dead*, p. 166.

87   The cardinal had communicated details of his meeting with Thatcher in a private conversation with Carmel Heaney, the Consul General in Boston. *Irish Examiner*, 30 December 2011. 'Meeting with Cardinal O'Fiaich [sic]' (1 July 1981), [2 July 1981], PRONI NIO/12/121A.

88   Because of Section 31, RTÉ's camera crew at the polling station were not allowed to transmit any interview with Owen Carron but had to settle for broadcasting their meeting with the defeated unionist candidate. See Maillot, *New Sinn Féin*, p. 75.

89   *Irish Times*, 28 September 1981.

90   Note of a meeting held at 10 Downing Street on Friday 6 November 1981 [10 November 1981], PRONI CENT/1/10/93A. See also Record of meeting at the Foreign and Commonwealth Office, 6 November 1981 [11 November 1981], PRONI NIO/12/20.

91   For an overview of the constitutional crusade see Meehan, *A Just Society for Ireland?*, pp. 162–193.

92   Quoted in *Irish Times*, 30 December 2011.

93   *Irish Times*, 7 November 1981.

94   'Anglo-Irish Summit: local reactions', 9 November 1981, PRONI CENT/1/10/92A.

95   'We do a better job', election leaflet with message from Charles Haughey. Available at http://irishelectionliterature.wordpress.com/2009/09/10/fianna-fail-february-1982/. Accessed 8 April 2018.

96   *Dáil Debates*, 333/38 (9 March 1982).

97   GUBU is an acronym coined by Conor Cruise O'Brien derived from the words
     'grotesque', 'unbelievable', 'bizarre' and 'unprecedented' used by Charles Haughey
     during a press conference in 1982.

98   'Falkland Islands: economic measures against Argentina', 6 April 1982. NAUK
     PREM19/615.

99   Haughey to Thatcher, 16 April 1982. CAC THCR 3/1/20 (T75A/82). See also
     transcript of phone conversation between Haughey and Thatcher, 16 April 1982.
     NAUK PREM19/628.

100 'The Falklands Crisis and Anglo-Irish relations', 22 June 1982. NAUK PREM19/815.

101 'The Falklands Crisis and Anglo-Irish relations', 22 June 1982. NAUK PREM19/815.

102 'The Falklands Crisis and Anglo-Irish relations', 22 June 1982. NAUK PREM19/815.

103 'Meeting with HM ambassador to Dublin, Sir Leonard Figg, Stormont Castle 18
     June 1982', [21 June 1982], PRONI CENT/1/11/34A.

104 Record of conversation between Figg and Donlon, 23 March 1982. NAUK PREM
     19/815.

105 See comments by Figg, 'Anglo-Irish relations', 8 September 1982, NAUK CJ 4/4180;
     and *Irish Times*, 1 May 2014. The head of the Department of Foreign Affairs, Seán
     Donlon, told the British ambassador that much of Haughey's recent statements was
     merely 'verbal republicanism' and possibly necessary to keep Neil Blaney onside.
     He added that Haughey's remarks 'were a hang-over from electioneering and stimulated
     by the excitement of St. Patrick's Day and the visit to Ronald Reagan'. NAUK
     PREM19/815.

106 See Ó Beacháin, 'Elections and political communication', p. 29.

107 Penniman and Farrell, *Ireland at the Polls*, p. 49.

108 Penniman and Farrell, *Ireland at the Polls*, p. 48.

109 Quoted in Penniman and Farrell, *Ireland at the Polls*, p. 49.

110 Prior, 'Northern Ireland Assembly (Day of Election) Order 1982 – draft speech for
     House of Commons' (14 July 1982), PRONI CENT/1/11/37.

111 The British ambassador to Ireland noted that 'helping the SDLP was certainly an
     important motive in the establishment of the Forum'. 'The Republic of Ireland: Her
     Majesty's ambassador at Dublin to the Secretary of State for Foreign and Com-
     monwealth Affairs' (13 December 1983), PRONI CENT/1/13/17A, para. 21.

112 FitzGerald, *All in A Life*, pp. 464–465.

113 'Alleged shoot-to-kill policy of security forces in Northern Ireland', NAI DFA,
     2013/27/1479.

114 'The Republic of Ireland: Her Majesty's ambassador at Dublin to the Secretary of
     State for Foreign and Commonwealth Affairs' (13 December 1983), PRONI
     CENT/1/13/17A.

115 Hussey, *At the Cutting Edge*, p. 103.

116 *New Ireland Forum Report* Dublin: Stationery Office, 1984, chapter 5, section 1.

117 Sinn Féin garnered 6.82 per cent of the vote in Connacht-Ulster, 3.74 per cent in
     Munster, 5.17 per cent in Dublin and 4.32 per cent in Leinster. Fianna Fáil won
     eight seats, Fine Gael six and an independent took the remaining one.

118 'Meeting between Taoiseach and British Prime Minister', NAI DFA 2013/27/1501.

119 'Conversation with E1605 29 Sep 1983, Anglo-Irish Summit (draft programme) Secret: the Irish discussion, recent exchanges'. NAI DFA 2013/27/1589.

120 As recounted by Dermot Nally in BBC four-part documentary, *Endgame in Ireland* [part 1]. Video available at www.youtube.com/watch?v=cehznNljJLA. Accessed 8 April 2018.

121 Personal recollection and interview with Michael Lillis cited in Moore, *Everything She Wants*, p. 300.

122 Thatcher, *The Downing Street Years*, p. 388. See also Moore, *Everything She Wants*, p. 300.

123 Powell, *Great Hatred*, pp. 60–61.

124 Moore, *Everything She Wants*, p. 316.

125 Goodison, telegram no. 636, 12 November 1984. NAUK PREM 19/408. Emphasis in original.

126 'Meetings between the Taoiseach and British Prime Minister, Nov-Dec 1983'. NAI DFA 2013/100/1089.

127 *The Guardian*, 16 June 2001. Sir Charles Powell speaking to the BBC four-part documentary, *Endgame in Ireland* [part 1]. Video available at www.youtube.com/watch?v=cehznNljJLA. Accessed 8 April 2018.

128 Sir Charles Powell speaking to the BBC four-part documentary, *Endgame in Ireland* [part 1]. Video available at www.youtube.com/watch?v=cehznNljJLA. Accessed 8 April 2018.

129 'Thatcher rules out a unified Ireland 1984'. Video available at www.rte.ie/archives/2014/1118/660538-out-out-out/. Accessed 8 April 2018.

130 Mansergh (ed.), *The Spirit of the Nation*, pp. 874–880.

131 'Prime Minister's meetings with Taoiseach: Anglo-Irish relations; part 8', NAUK PREM 19/1549.

132 'Prime Minister's meetings with Taoiseach: Anglo-Irish relations; part 8', NAUK PREM 19/1549.

133 *The Guardian*, 17 March 2012. Iraqi dictator Saddam Hussein was also a recipient of Christmas cards at the time.

134 'Prime Minister's meetings with Taoiseach: Anglo-Irish relations; part 8', NAUK PREM 19/1549.

135 'Prime Minister's meetings with Taoiseach: Anglo-Irish relations; part 8', NAUK PREM 19/1549.

136 'Prime Minister's meetings with Taoiseach: Anglo-Irish relations; part 8', NAUK PREM 19/1549.

137 'Prime Minister's meetings with Taoiseach: Anglo-Irish relations; part 8', NAUK PREM 19/1549.

138 'Prime Minister's meetings with Taoiseach: Anglo-Irish relations; part 8', NAUK PREM 19/1549.

139 See Wilson, *Irish America and the Ulster Conflict*, chapter 9. Later she confided to the Conservative party treasurer, Lord McAlpine that: 'It was the pressure from the Americans that made me sign that agreement'. Quoted in Goodlad, *Thatcher*, p. 163.

140 *Dáil Debates*, 19 November 1985.

141 Hussey, *At the Cutting Edge*, p. 179.
142 *Northern Ireland Assembly Debates*, 118/127–8 (16 November 1985).
143 *New York Times*, 5 December 1985.
144 *Hansard*, House of Commons, 87/747–51 (26 November 1985).
145 *Irish Press*, 6 January 1986. Pascal O'Hare, interview with the author.
146 *Dáil Debates*, 361/2581, 19 November 1985.
147 *Irish Times*, 30 December 1985.
148 *Dáil Debates*, 361/2580–81, 19 November 1985.
149 'Doing business with Mr Haughey', 16 January 1987, PRONI CENT/3/83A.
150 'Handling Mr Haughey on Northern Ireland – tactics', February 1987. PRONI CENT/3/83A.
151 'Future of the Anglo-Irish Agreement', 6 April 1987, PRONI CENT/3/83A.
152 'Draft: Anglo-Irish relations – game plan', September 1987, PRONI CENT/3/83A.
153 Owen, *The Anglo-Irish Agreement*, p. 204. Commissioned by Ulster TV and *Fortnight* and conducted by Coopers and Lybrand, pollsters interviewed 1,000 people across Northern Ireland between 15 and 27 February 1988.
154 Owen, *The Anglo-Irish Agreement*, p. 209. Economist–MORI poll of a sample of 2,027 respondents aged over eighteen in 175 constituencies between 11 and 15 March 1988.
155 Quoted in Reynolds, *Autobiography*, p. 161. See also Murphy, *Electoral Competition in Ireland*, p. 40.

7

The age of consent, 1992–2018

Albert Reynolds's strategy for a peace process

On becoming Taoiseach, Albert Reynolds was a few months shy of his sixtieth birthday. A self-made businessman, he had come relatively late to national politics, being forty-four years old when elected in 1977 as part of Fianna Fáil's landslide majority. His intimate role as a member of the 'Gang of Five' that helped dislodge Jack Lynch in favour of Charles Haughey paid dividends; he was immediately promoted to ministerial rank after Haughey's election in December 1979, and by 1988 he held the Finance portfolio. Though previously a staunch Haughey supporter throughout the successive heaves against the party leader during the 1980s, disillusionment had set in and he opposed Haughey's unilateral abandonment of the party's 'no coalition' policy. Together with Pádraig Flynn, a fellow member of the so-called 'Country and Western' wing of the party, he resigned from the cabinet in November 1991 after a carefully choreographed motion of no confidence in Haughey's leadership was put down by a group of relatively young and junior Fianna Fáil deputies. Haughey survived until January and Reynolds decisively defeated Mary O'Rourke and Michael Woods in the subsequent leadership election on 6 February 1992, taking sixty-one of the seventy-seven votes.

Critical to the ease with which Reynolds swept to power was the decision of Haughey-loyalist Bertie Ahern not to contest the election. Though only forty years of age, Ahern was a veteran of six successful parliamentary election campaigns and had replaced Reynolds as Minister for Finance when he resigned from the cabinet to challenge Haughey. Ahern decided to master his newly acquired portfolio on the understanding that he would retain it under Reynolds's premiership and that he would contest the party leadership whenever Reynolds decided to step down.[1] Neither man knew how brief Reynolds's tenure as Taoiseach would be – little more than two years and nine months. However, during this time Reynolds would play a vital role in a series of major breakthroughs in Northern Ireland and in facilitating a peace process to take root. The new Taoiseach's proclamation that, along with the economy, Northern Ireland was his top priority surprised some. As one senior SDLP representative recalled at the time, Reynolds 'had never made a speech on Northern Ireland in his life that I'm aware of' but that lack, from a nationalist perspective, was potentially a plus as 'from a unionist point of view he had no baggage'.[2]

Reynolds's strategy to encourage a Northern Ireland peace process had three elements: direct and secret communications with republicans (and when possible and appropriate, less secret contacts with other parties in the North); ongoing discussions with the British Prime Minister, John Major; and, thirdly, exploiting the reservoir of goodwill in Irish America as well as the interest of the new US President, Bill Clinton. In terms of sequencing, Reynolds consistently emphasised that peace would have to come first, by which he meant a complete cessation of military actions by all parties. Inclusive talks that would include Sinn Féin would follow and these would lead to a comprehensive settlement that would be negotiated by, and acceptable to, political parties within Northern Ireland and the two Governments.

Central to this strategy was a positive relationship with his British counterpart, John Major. There had been an overlap during which Reynolds and Major had held their states' respective Finance portfolios but it was as Prime Ministers that their relationship blossomed. During Reynolds's premiership there was a tacit understanding between the two men that the Taoiseach would endeavour to bring the republicans and nationalists into the peace process and Major's task would be to keep the unionists onside. Via his secret talks with the Sinn Féin leadership and his support for the Hume–Adams dialogue, Reynolds sought to give the republican leadership enough to persuade their members that a political initiative aimed at securing national self-determination, and prosecuted by an alliance of Sinn Féin, the SDLP, the Irish Government and Irish America, could achieve far more than armed struggle. Such an alliance, frequently dubbed a 'pan-nationalist front' by those who opposed or feared it, would, its supporters maintained, provide the republican leadership with a cogent case for unarmed struggle.

Reynolds's concept of a peace process attracted vitriolic attacks from Ireland's largest-selling newspaper, the *Sunday Independent*. One columnist, Eoghan Harris, maintained that 'if we persist with the peace process it will end with sectarian slaughter in the North, with bombs in Dublin, Cork and Galway, and with the ruthless reign by provisional gangs over the ghettos of Dublin. The only way to avoid this abyss is to cut the cord to John Hume.'[3] Another weekly columnist,

Eamon Dunphy, claimed that Gerry Adams 'speaks for the barbarians', also describing John Hume as 'a political bomber flying over unionist heads trying to kill them'.[4] In the same paper, former Minister Conor Cruise O'Brien weekly prophesied civil war and called for the reintroduction of internment in Northern Ireland.[5] His position, as synopsised by McGarry and O'Leary, was that the peace process would culminate in 'a saga of catastrophe that included 500,000 refugees, 10,000 dead in a civil war which terminates with the construction of a smaller but ethnically homogenized Northern Ireland, a military coup in Dublin, and extensive explosions in British cities'.[6]

Despite such calumnies throughout the process, Reynolds remained confident in the virtues of his own approach. Peace was the prize, he repeatedly stressed, and his instincts, along with John Hume's imprimatur, suggested that Gerry Adams was sincere in his quest to move Northern Ireland beyond armed conflict. There was also the knowledge that the man seen to 'solve' the 'national question' would be remembered kindly by history, ticking the 'legacy' box as all prime ministers in a hurry seek to do. Reynolds was convinced that he needed to push rather than nudge Major in the right direction, and to persuade him that the peace process required speed and substance. The Taoiseach encountered the long-standing reality that Anglo-Irish relations were of far greater importance to Dublin than to London and that Northern Ireland, as a political problem, bore much heavier in the minds of Irish politicians than on their British counterparts, irrespective of the fact that the North was under Westminster's jurisdiction. Reynolds confided to his press secretary:

> If I have him [Major] on a one-to-one basis, I can talk sense to him. It's when these anti-Irish Tory headbangers and spymasters get to him that he weakens. I've told him the IRA have better intelligence than British Intelligence … I've told him that I won't see him wrong; that if I think they [the IRA] are not coming, I'll warn him even at the eleventh hour, but that he's got to trust me.[7]

In his 'Peace First' ard fheis speech delivered in November 1993, the Taoiseach told the party faithful that 'history will not forgive us if we waste this opportunity'. During subsequent interviews and visits to London aimed at applying pressure on Major he stressed that it was for the two Governments 'to run with the ball'.[8]

The greening of the White House

Reynolds was fortunate to have Bill Clinton in the White House from an early stage of the peace process. The young, energetic US president proved a valuable ally willing to intervene at key moments to break a logjam. Clinton's interest in Ireland was personal and political. As a Rhodes scholar at Oxford University during the late 1960s he had travelled to Ireland and taken an interest in the Northern civil rights movement. His knowledge of Irish affairs impressed all whom he encountered.[9] During his 1992 presidential election campaign Clinton had collaborated with influential Irish Americans and embraced much of their agenda. He promised to reverse the visa ban on Gerry Adams, and other senior Sinn Féin leaders, and to support the MacBride Principles, which promoted fair employment practices in Northern Ireland.[10] Clinton also promised that if elected president he would send a peace envoy to Northern Ireland. Considering him a threat, the British Government gathered intelligence on Clinton for use by the Bush administration during the election campaign, something he did not quickly forget.[11] London belatedly tried to patch up relations and to get Clinton to backtrack on his idea of a peace envoy. With the help of the Irish ambassador in Washington DC, Dermot Gallagher, Reynolds was determined to maximise US influence on any peace process that might take root.

An early opportunity for a meeting came on 17 March 1993, the first St. Patrick's Day of Clinton's presidency, when the President hosted an extravagant and well-attended ball for the Irish entourage. During their first formal meeting at the Oval Office the following day, Clinton introduced Reynolds to the soon-to-be US ambassador to Ireland, Jean Kennedy-Smith along with her brother, Senator Ted Kennedy. Unlike many of her predecessors, Kennedy-Smith was knowledgeable, active and interested in Irish affairs and she would play a significant role in guiding US policy towards the embryonic peace process.

When Clinton suggested US Senate majority leader George Mitchell as his special envoy to Northern Ireland, Reynolds cautioned that the timing was inappropriate. With local elections in Northern Ireland approaching in May, few parties would be in the right frame of mind for the initiative. Moreover, as the unionists would not meet with an envoy it would most likely be viewed as a failure and reflect badly on the Clinton administration. Reynolds was aware that those influential Irish-Americans that had campaigned and helped fund Clinton's election campaign were now seeking to recoup their investment but he advised Clinton to resist their petitions for now. Cognisant of his relationship with John Major, on which so much would depend if a peace process were to be established, he estimated that a US peace envoy would unnecessarily antagonise London. Thus, much to the disappointment of his Irish-American supporters, Clinton deferred the proposal to an unspecified future date.

Reynolds came away believing that Clinton would be a key player in the peace process. The Taoiseach had in his view forgone the short-term attraction of an envoy, which might jeopardise his relationship with Major, for the possibility of longer-term rewards that could promote a durable peace process: 'I finished by saying that I would come back to him and that when I did it would be with a very firm plan that I would need his assistance in implementing.'[12] While many explanations have been offered for Clinton's role in the evolving peace process, none enjoys greater cogency than that of John Dumbrell, who suggests that 'Clinton was attracted to Ireland by the relatively risk-free opportunity to secure a foreign policy breakthrough. With considerable intelligent foresight, the Clinton team discerned a real opportunity for peace in transformed conditions of war-weariness and an external environment where Dublin and London were at least showing signs of cooperation in the cause of a Northern Irish settlement.'[13]

Hume–Adams

The Sinn Féin leadership had given several signals, through carefully phrased public statements, that the IRA might be receptive to a plan that held out the prospect of a peaceful path to 'national self-determination'. Contrary to the celebratory militarism of the early 1970s and the patient long-war strategy of the latter part of that decade, Sinn Féin had been trying to devise ways of exiting the cycle of armed conflict. The seminal *Scenario for Peace* document published in 1987 and the Hume–Adams dialogue the following year had provided evidence of a rethink, though its political backing for the IRA campaign overshadowed this. Much of the Sinn Féin leadership's activities during the early 1990s was devoted to demonstrating the results and potential of political agitation. Not only would it be necessary to demonstrate to their republican support base that armed struggle was divisive, ineffectual and counterproductive but the leadership also had to convince them that an alternative non-violent path to national self-determination was open that enjoyed reasonable prospects of success.

During the first eighteen months of Reynolds's premiership there were several strands of talks between the conflicting sides, most of them completely unknown to the public and, quite often, to the parties themselves. Reynolds maintained and intensified the talks between Fianna Fáil and Sinn Féin using Fr. Alex Reid and Martin Mansergh as intermediaries, knowledge of which was confined to a handful of individuals. Whereas Haughey had been extremely cautious of contacts with republicans, Reynolds, unhampered by any political baggage, seized the initiative with both hands. Top-secret communications between the British Government and the republican movement were also taking place and leaked out at a critical stage of the process in November 1993. Finally, there were the bilateral talks sponsored by the British Government and overseen by the the Secretary of State for Northern Ireland, Patrick Mayhew. Highlighting the difference in negotiating with the Irish and British Governments, Adams commented that whereas the British had conceived and maintained partition, with Dublin 'we were never dealing with the enemy ... the most we were dealing with were maybe opponents'.[14]

Parallel to these talks were the secret meetings between Gerry Adams and John Hume, which came to light in April 1993 and whose series of public declarations thereafter became known in the public mind as the Hume–Adams initiative. The SDLP leader, who did not know of the republican lines of communication with Dublin and London, also came under immediate pressure from political figures and the media to explain himself. Hume saw no contradiction between his scathing criticisms of the IRA – he described them at the 1988 SDLP party conference as bearing 'all the hallmarks of undiluted fascism'[15] – and meeting with Gerry Adams in a bid to end the conflict. His rationale was that if his initiative failed no additional lives would be lost but were he successful the political situation would be transformed.[16]

On 23 April 1993, Hume and Adams issued the first of a series of joint statements. After some preliminary platitudes about the necessity of peace and the onus on all parties to end conflict, the two leaders stressed that 'an internal settlement is not a solution because it obviously does not deal with all the relationships at the heart of the problem'. They 'accepted' that the 'Irish people as a whole have a right to national self-determination' and highlighted that this was the majority view of the people living on the island, though not of all. How to exercise this right of self-determination would be 'a matter for agreement between the people of Ireland' and they were 'mindful that not all the people of Ireland share that view or agree on how to give meaningful expression to it'. Despite these differences, which extended to divergent views between their own parties, Hume and Adams pledged themselves to finding ways of securing agreement.[17] During subsequent months, the public was drip-fed cryptic press releases that hinted at opportunities for a major breakthrough but these statements were unaccompanied by concrete proposals.

A minor storm broke on 18 June 1993 when the Irish President, Mary Robinson, paid an unofficial visit to community groups in Belfast during which she shook hands with Gerry Adams. The visit took place despite the opposition of the British Government and the Northern Ireland Office (NIO), which apparently threatened to withdraw security for the occasion.[18] According to Albert Reynolds, his Tánaiste, Dick Spring, was 'incensed' at the announcement that Robinson would travel north and 'did his best to dissuade her'. During his meeting with Major in mid-June, the British Prime Minister 'insisted that the whole thing should be stopped' but Reynolds could see no reason to prevent the trip from taking place and believed that any attempt to do so would be counterproductive.[19]

It mattered little to her critics that Robinson had not travelled to Belfast for the purpose of meeting Adams, and had certainly not engaged in a tête-a-tête but rather exchanged greetings as he stood in line to meet her. The *Sunday Independent* produced a dozen critical articles in its subsequent edition with an editorial that proclaimed that: 'She should know that she has disgraced her office and tarnished her presidency beyond redemption. Mrs Robinson has shamed the people of this country gratuitously, unforgivably, indecently. She should now resign.'[20] Despite these attempts to whip up a reprisal, opinion polls indicated that Robinson's action was supported by over three-quarters of the republic's electorate.[21]

The Sinn Féin leadership, and Adams in particular, would spend much of 1993 and 1994 on what might be called a handshake offensive, whereby they would attempt to meet traditional foes or political luminaries and offer their hands for grasping. Several attempts to initiate physical contact with unionist and British representatives were rebuffed during this period, thus making Robinson's gesture all the more significant. Robinson took pride in her image as an inclusive public figure capable of reaching out to disparate communities. Given her resignation from the Labour Party in 1985 on the grounds that the Anglo-Irish Agreement had been negotiated without unionist input, she had been considered sensitive to loyalist concerns. Moreover, only three weeks before meeting Adams she had made history by visiting Queen Elizabeth II at Buckingham Palace, the first contact of its kind since the foundation of the Irish state.

Most of what was agreed between Hume, Adams and Reynolds was unexceptional considering that all parties shared a common nationalist outlook. The obvious difference was that Sinn Féin was signing up to a formula in which self-determination would be defined in such a way as to incorporate the hated loyalist veto, now repackaged as unionist consent. Secondly, the republican movement was now putting itself in a position whereby it was willing to accept the Irish Government negotiating with the British Government on behalf of a common nationalist alliance, of which Sinn Féin was a part.

Frustrated with what he perceived as a lack of momentum in the Anglo-Irish talks, John Hume phoned Reynolds in September 1993 to say that to move the situation forward he would issue another joint declaration with Adams saying that they had made considerable progress in their discussions and would now pass on the fruits of their endeavours to both Governments. Not least because he knew that such a move would taint the Anglo-Irish talks by giving the impression that they were somehow based on the Hume–Adams negotiations, the Taoiseach tried to dissuade Hume from this course of action.[22] Adams was also unenthusiastic about the idea and only agreed 'after great deliberation and considering all the issues involved'.[23] Despite this, the Hume–Adams joint statement of 25 September announced major advances and proclaimed that they had forwarded a report to Dublin with the understanding that 'the broad principles involved will be for wider consideration between the two governments'. To facilitate this, they had decided to suspend detailed discussions.[24] Anticipating Reynolds's discomfort, Adams wrote to him using, as always, Fr. Reid as the conduit. Now that the statement had been made, the Sinn Féin leader reasoned, Reynolds would be best advised to publicly welcome it and state that he would be taking up the matter with the British. After asking Reynolds to identify any ways he could help, Adams wrote that 'it is of vital importance that we seek through this development to advance our project and ensure that the onus is on the British – not you, John [Hume], or me!'[25]

Downing Street Declaration

The positions of the two Governments had converged sufficiently by 15 December for Reynolds and Major to issue what became known as the Downing Street Declaration (DSD). As part of this joint communiqué, Major reaffirmed that his Government would uphold the 'democratic wish of the greater number of the people of Northern Ireland on the issue of whether they prefer to support the Union or a sovereign united Ireland'. In a sentence designed to woo republicans, and that echoed the statement made by the then Northern Secretary Peter Brooke three years earlier, he maintained that his Government had 'no selfish strategic or economic interest in Northern Ireland'. The British Government's primary interest, according to the Declaration, was 'to see peace, stability and reconciliation established by agreement among all the people who inhabit the island'. In pursuit of this objective they would work together with the Irish Government and, borrowing a phrase from the 1980 Haughey–Thatcher summit, seek to facilitate an agreement that would 'embrace the totality of relationships'. The British Government would not act as persuaders for Irish unity, as Reynolds had initially hoped, but promised 'to encourage, facilitate and enable the achievement of such agreement over a period through a process of dialogue and cooperation based on full respect for the rights and identities of both traditions in Ireland'. In another passage designed to address the focus on Irish national self-determination that had been central to the Hume–Adams talks and Major's negotiations with Reynolds, the British Government declared that

> They accept that such agreement may, as of right, take the form of agreed structures for the island as a whole, including a united Ireland achieved by peaceful means on

the following basis. The British Government agree that it is for the people of the island of Ireland alone, by agreement between the two parts respectively, to exercise their right of self-determination on the basis of consent, freely and concurrently given, North and South, to bring about a united Ireland, if that is their wish. They reaffirm as a binding obligation that they will, for their part, introduce the necessary legislation to give effect to this, or equally to any measure of agreement on future relationships in Ireland which the people living in Ireland may themselves freely so determine without external impediment.[26]

'Constructive ambiguity' was a key feature of the DSD. For example, although the Declaration stated in its very first paragraph that 'the most urgent and important issue facing the people of Ireland, North and South, and the British and Irish Governments together, is to remove the causes of conflict' nowhere in the document were these causes explicitly identified.

While recognised as a significant development, the DSD, as with many compromises, generated little enthusiasm amongst the parties within Northern Ireland. In a letter to the Prime Minister, Ian Paisley adopted his standard accusatory tone. Describing the document as 'a tripartite agreement between Reynolds, the IRA and you', the reverend claimed that 'you have sold Ulster to buy off the fiendish republican scum'.[27] The UUP was far more restrained, not least because their leader, James Molyneaux, had been kept fully briefed by John Major and had contributed to the text, particularly in relation to 'consent'.[28]

Despite prodding from the Taoiseach, the British Government refused to entertain Sinn Féin's requests for 'clarification' of the Declaration, maintaining the details of the document were self-evident and unambiguous. The result was a war of words during the spring of 1994, which put the British Government and Sinn Féin centre-stage, sidelining other key players, including Dublin.[29] Reynolds again felt the need to develop a momentum. On 19 January 1994, he suspended the application of Section 31 of the Broadcasting Act so that interviews with Sinn Féin members could now be broadcast on radio and television for the first time in over two decades. The British broadcasting ban, introduced by the Thatcher administration in 1988, remained in place, however.

A week later the US Government issued a forty-eight-hour visa to Gerry Adams, reversing long-established practice.[30] For the Americans it was a win–win situation whereby Adams and Sinn Féin would either be drawn irrevocably into the democratic process or be exposed as frauds, permitting other parties to forge ahead without them. For the British, however, the decision to issue a visa had less to do with Adams per se than the very public demonstration of their limited influence on the Clinton administration. By his own admission, John Major's relationship with the US President at this time was 'frosty'[31] and, to add insult to injury, London was not informed officially of the visa decision but first learnt of it when it was published by Reuters news agency. For the Taoiseach, the visa furthered the strategy of shepherding Sinn Féin towards a position from which it would be difficult to withdraw.[32] Reynolds privately explained at the time that

> Sinn Féin will pay a price for going to Capitol Hill. A lot of powerful people went out on a limb for Adams. If he doesn't deliver they'll have him back in the house with steel shutters [Sinn Féin headquarters in Belfast] so fast his feet won't touch the ground. We're slowly putting the squeeze on them, pulling them in, boxing them in, cutting off their lines of retreat.[33]

On 19 May 1994, the Northern Ireland Office finally published a twenty-one-page clarification of Sinn Féin's questions arising from the Downing Street Declaration. Disheartened by the explanation – though most of it could not have come as a great surprise – the Sinn Féin leadership had a public airing of views at a special ard fheis in Letterkenny. While attempting to leave the door ajar for a new departure, the ard fheis criticised the 'negative and contradictory' aspects of the DSD but welcomed the acknowledgement that political and constitutional changes were necessary and resolved to pursue that change through what it called the 'Hume–Adams Irish Peace Initiative'.[34] This anti-climactic conference was followed by frenetic activity away from the public eye. At Reynolds's behest, Martin Mansergh met again in secret with Gerry Adams and Martin McGuinness and this was complemented when the Sinn Féin duo also participated in a clandestine meeting in Derry with Northern Secretary, Patrick Mayhew, and Michael Ancram, then Political Development Minister at the NIO.[35] On 26 August, an Irish-American delegation led by former Congressman Bruce Morrison travelled to Ireland for a three-hour meeting with Sinn Féin.[36]

In the face of British Government opposition, Reynolds employed his substantial leverage with Irish America – not least through the intervention of the US ambassador to Ireland, Jean Kennedy-Smith and Senator Ted Kennedy, to obtain a US visa for IRA veteran Joe Cahill.[37] Having been sentenced to death in 1942 along with the executed Tom Williams, Cahill had been a major figure in subsequent IRA campaigns and his mission to sell the idea of a ceasefire to the IRA's Irish-American supporters was seen as a vital piece of the jigsaw.[38]

The IRA ceasefire

Bringing weeks of speculation to an end, the IRA announced 'a complete cessation of military operations' effective from midnight, 31 August 1994. In what was immediately welcomed by the Irish Government as an historic announcement, the IRA stated their belief that 'an opportunity to secure a just and lasting settlement has been created' and that they were entering 'into a new situation … determined that the injustices which created this conflict will be removed'. In its announcement, the IRA noted that the DSD was 'not a solution', nor had it been presented as such by its authors, but that a settlement would only result from inclusive negotiations. While urging 'everyone to approach this new situation with energy, determination and patience' the statement claimed that the British Government had a duty to face up to its responsibilities.[39]

In a reversal of roles, the British Government now adopted Sinn Féin's stance after the DFD and demanded clarification of the IRA statement. Did the IRA mean that the cessation was 'permanent' and if so, why was it not explicit in the statement? Did it mean that the IRA would give up its weapons? In the House of Commons, Major spoke of a 'decontamination' period before Sinn Féin could expect even exploratory talks with British Government officials. If Major was cautious, the unionist parties were cynical. Quick to minimise the significance of the ceasefire, they sensed danger rather than opportunity. For Unionists, the IRA campaign had averted the need to deal with republicans or contemplate fundamental changes and shielded them from pressure to re-examine long-held beliefs. However, the Irish Government and northern nationalists argued that while unionists might be afforded a veto on constitutional change they could not expect others to concede to them an embargo on political, economic or social reforms.[40]

Reynolds appreciated the momentous character of the IRA ceasefire and knew first-hand what it had taken to deliver. Accordingly, he moved swiftly to publicly engage with Sinn Féin so that militant republicans could see the fruits of non-violent political action. A week after the IRA announcement, on 6 September 1994, Reynolds met with Hume and Adams at Government Buildings in Dublin. As the trio stood outside for the photo-shoot, Hume and Adams shook hands, at which point Reynolds grasped both hands, placing his own under and over them in the form of a cup. This highly significant gesture, described as 'one of the most iconic and symbolic handshakes of modern Irish political history',[41] was in marked contrast with the aloofness of the British administration (indeed, during his seven years as Prime Minister John Major would never meet Gerry Adams). After the summit, the three leaders issued a statement that sought to communicate the historic nature of what had transpired:

> We are at the beginning of a new era in which we are all totally and absolutely
> committed to democratic and peaceful methods of resolving our political problems.
> We reiterate that our objective is an equitable and lasting agreement that can command

the allegiance of all. We see the Forum [for Peace and Reconciliation] as a major instrument in that process. We reiterate that we cannot resolve this problem without the participation and agreement of the Unionist people. We call on everyone to use all their influence to bring this agreement about.[42]

Unionists attributed Reynolds's rush to meet with Adams to a shared republican-ism, all the more virulent for having joined forces.[43] According to this view, Reynolds and Adams, along with their respective parties, were divided not on ends but on means, and had now aligned forces to apply pressure on London to hand over Northern Ireland to the Republic.[44]

The Downing Street Declaration had made reference to a Forum for Peace and Reconciliation (FPR), which was described as an Irish Government initiative 'to enable democratic parties to consult together and share in dialogue about the political future ... to make recommendations on ways in which agreement and trust between both traditions in Ireland can be promoted and established'.[45] If the New Ireland Forum had been designed to engage the SDLP and to dem-onstrate the virtues of constitutional nationalism, the FPR a decade later was conceived for much the same reasons except it was Sinn Féin that needed to be engaged to show its supporters that their leadership's strategy was reaping divi-dends. Republican leaders would be chaperoned into mainstream politics, rubbing shoulders with other political parties and being afforded parity of esteem.[46] The Forum also underlined Sinn Féin's numerical inferiority. Of the forty delegates to the Forum, only three were from the Sinn Féin leadership. Despite the pomp associated with the high-level meetings in Dublin Castle, the Forum was a holding-exercise while waiting for the British Government to come round. Only two months after its establishment one long-time member of the SDLP, Brian Feeney, described the Forum as 'very much a sideshow and you can measure that by the [small] amount of time John Hume spends at it'.[47]

Whereas the New Ireland Forum had been about redefining nationalism and was exclusively composed of the main parties in Ireland that favoured, at least rhetorically, a united Ireland, the FPR included the bi-confessional Alliance Party of Northern Ireland along with Democratic Left, the PDs, the Workers Party, the Greens and independent members of the Dáil and Seanad. Unionist parties of all hues rebuffed invitations to attend; according to the Orange Order's Grand Master, Martin Smyth, the FPR was simply 'another Dublin Forum Mark 2 seeking to advance the cause of Irish unity'.[48]

Before Reynolds had time to consolidate and build on the ceasefire he was forced to relinquish office. Even at the time, the cause of his forced resignation seemed inconsequential, particularly when set against the gravity and uncertainty surrounding the embryonic peace process, now strengthened by the IRA and loyalist ceasefires. The Taoiseach's insistence in appointing Attorney-General Harry Whelehan to the position of President of the High Court, in the face of Labour Party hostility, proved his undoing. Reynolds resigned as Taoiseach and Fianna Fáil leader while power shifted to a 'rainbow coalition' of Fine Gael, Labour and Democratic Left without recourse to a general election. Never before or since has a new Government taken office without seeking a new mandate from the electorate. During the critical meeting of the Labour parliamentary party that decided the Government's fate, the peace process was cited as a reason for staying in coalition with Fianna Fáil but, according to the party's General Secretary 'the meeting was unconvinced that the retention or removal of the present Government would make much difference to the peace process now that it had been started'.[49] In this, they proved to be fundamentally wrong.

Many wondered whether momentum or, indeed, ultimate agreement, could be attained without Albert Reynolds at the helm given his central role in igniting the peace process.[50] However, as one senior SDLP source put it at the time, there were a number of ongoing underlying conditions – a rethink within the republican movement on the efficacy of armed struggle combined with ever-increasing cooperation between the two Governments – that were converging in a way that made a breakthrough likely. It might have taken some years more to mature 'but Reynolds helped them converge that bit earlier … because of the nature of who he was and the risks and the role that he was prepared to play'.[51]

The rainbow coalition

The new Taoiseach, John Bruton, was a very different individual and politician from Albert Reynolds. Born to a wealthy, Catholic landowning family with hundreds of acres devoted to beef and tillage in County Meath, Bruton's parents had spurned the local schools and had him educated at the exclusive private boarding school at Clongowes Wood. Not only did Reynolds and Bruton differ in terms of personality and background, but also their political origins and sympathies diverged greatly. In Bruton's worldview, the 1916 rising was a mistake that had damaged the Irish psyche and justified the Provisional IRA.[52] Over the new Taoiseach's office desk hung a portrait of arch-parliamentarian John Redmond. Bruton's reception of Prince Charles, who paid his first official visit to Ireland in 1995, was considered excessively fawning and the Taoiseach was reported to have described the occasion as the 'happiest day of his life'.[53] Even the London *Times*, traditionally more indulgent of deference to British royalty than most, described the Taoiseach's gushing tribute as 'embarrassingly effusive'.[54] In the words of former senior SDLP member, Brian Feeney, Bruton 'had been an opponent of the peace process at the beginning and remained a sceptic'.[55] While retaining a bipartisan approach to Northern Ireland policy generally, Fianna Fáil occasionally targeted what they perceived as Bruton's mishandling of the peace process, reflecting widespread grassroots sentiment in that party. Reynolds went so far as to describe his successor in the Dáil as – 'John Unionist'.[56]

Enjoying their first and only term in office, Democratic Left also brought with them a distinctive approach to the peace process. Born out of hostility to what became the Provisionals, antagonism towards Sinn Féin formed a major part of DL's identity. Party leader Proinsias de Rossa, himself a former IRA member, had been one of the most ardent critics of the Hume–Adams initiative and opposed Sinn Féin with the bitterness of an erstwhile comrade. As Foreign Minister, Dick Spring would provide vital continuity but his role had been secondary to Reynolds, for whom the peace process had become something of a personal obsession. As the Labour Party's General Secretary, Ray Kavanagh, pointed out, the coalition dynamic had changed in another important respect: 'With Fianna Fáil being nationalist, Spring was a more reasonable choice of partner for the moderate Unionist. Now with Fine Gael, which seemed more sympathetic to the Unionist position, he appeared to be in the Republican corner.'[57] When Reynolds had been at the helm, Dick Spring had spoken openly of the IRA handing over weapons but while Bruton's deputy his position changed to one of 'talks before guns'.[58]

When a Sinn Féin delegation met the Irish Labour parliamentary party, Gerry Adams argued that the kernel of the problem was the Major administration's refusal to move beyond the Downing Street Declaration. The British Government had yet to meet directly with Sinn Féin, let alone address substantive issues such as prisoner releases and police reform, which would influence opinion in the broader republican community. On decommissioning, Adams joked that perhaps they should ask Proinsias de Rossa about his experience, a reference to the fact that the Official IRA, from which Democratic Left could trace its political lineage, had never handed over their weapons after their 1972 ceasefire. Labour's General Secretary was 'surprised to find him [Adams] so charming and pleasant … it was a very credible performance and certainly broke the ice as far as the parliamentarians present were concerned'.[59]

Most of the positive aspects that bolstered the peace process during Bruton's incumbency had been set in train prior to his taking over. These included the Forum for Peace and Reconciliation, which met throughout 1995, the White House Conference for Trade and Investment in Ireland, which took place in Washington on 25–26 May 1995, and the visit of President Bill Clinton to Dublin and Belfast later that year, which injected optimism at a time when spirits had sagged. Bruton's lack of empathy with northern nationalists and, indeed, Irish nationalism generally, inhibited progress. When asked at one Fine Gael event about developments in Northern Ireland, Bruton told the reporter that he was 'sick of answering questions about the fucking peace process'[60] and at that stage he'd been a mere four months in the job. Major had kept his part of the bargain struck with Reynolds by keeping unionists sweet and, indeed, the survival of his Government now depended upon it. However, Bruton proved unable to keep the nationalist side on board, though British lethargy arguably played a greater role in disillusioning republican supporters of the peace process.

Almost six months after the IRA ceasefire, the two Governments finally produced the repeatedly delayed framework document that would provide a roadmap to inclusive all-party talks.[61] While reaffirming the three-stranded approach and the two Governments' central role in determining the structure and speed of negotiations, the framework document proved a false dawn. Another year would pass without significant movement and without inclusive all-party talks. Although the British Government could not force unionists to negotiate with Sinn Féin, their own engagement with the party was half-hearted at best. Eight months had passed since the IRA ceasefire before the Sinn Féin leadership was permitted to meet a British Minister and even then it was with junior Minister Michael Ancram and confined largely to superficialities. By the time Gerry Adams finally met with Patrick Mayhew, when both men were in Washington DC for the same event, he had already met with most of the Irish Government, President Bill Clinton, Nelson Mandela and other political luminaries. The British publicly opposed a US visa for Gerry Adams in March 1995, as they had done the year before and with the same result – failure.

On 7 March 1995, Mayhew enunciated three new preconditions which the IRA would have to embrace and carry out before Sinn Féin could be permitted to all-party talks: a new acceptance of decommissioning in principle, an understanding of what that involved in practice and 'the actual decommissioning of some arms'.[62] The conditions were quickly dubbed the 'Washington Three'. Making decommissioning the vital precondition for talks kept Sinn Féin centre-stage but acted as a brake on progress for the remainder of the year. As McKittrick and McVea have noted, the Irish Government's response to Mayhew's 'Washington Three' speech 'illustrated that Bruton's approach was very different from that of Reynolds'.[63] Whereas Reynolds had prioritised facilitating the entry of republicans into mainstream constitutional politics and applied pressure on the British to this end, his Fine Gael counterpart 'took a line closer to the British stance. Rather than opposing the new precondition, he called for a gesture on decommissioning, thus helping to establish Mayhew's stance as a position agreed by the two governments.'[64] It seemed that Mayhew's pronouncement on decommissioning reflected more his desire to show unionists he was articulating their concerns than a sincere evaluation of what was required before talks could take place. US deputy national security advisor, Nancy Soderberg, recalled that there was 'a complete disconnect' between what Mayhew had told US officials – that a handover of IRA weapons would not be a prerequisite for talks – and his more trenchant public pronouncement on decommissioning later the same day.[65] Former US congressman Bruce Morrison, a key intermediary in facilitating the IRA ceasefire, reflected that the British Government had been 'reeling' under the pressure to move the peace process forward; 'they told us privately they knew it [the demand for decommissioning prior to talks] was all nonsense and would have to be dropped. Then this guy [Bruton] came along ....'[66]

David Trimble and Ulster Unionism

In September 1995, the dour veteran UUP leader, Jim Molyneaux, stepped down from the party leadership and made way for David Trimble. Trimble's earliest political affiliation had been with the Vanguard movement, led by the charismatic demagogue, Bill Craig, who, like his then rival Ian Paisley, loitered on the periphery of paramilitarism. Impressed by Craig's dedication to the Union and his resolute leadership, Trimble participated in the 1974 Ulster Workers Council strike that doomed the power-sharing institutions established under the Sunningdale Agreement. Trimble joined the UUP in 1990 and was elected to represent the Upper Bann constituency at Westminster, but it was his much-publicised support of the Orangemen at Drumcree that brought him to national prominence. The Orange Order had a bloc vote within the Ulster Unionist Council and was instrumental in getting 'their' man elected. This was to be the zenith of Trimble's popularity within the broad unionist political family.

During the dying days of the Major administration, Trimble and his nine-member UUP parliamentary party exerted an influence on the Prime Minister greatly disproportionate to their numbers, but this would disappear when Tony Blair was elected Labour Prime Minister with a huge majority. Like most unionists, Trimble had been unsure of how to react when their political enemies, the IRA, announced a ceasefire. International commentators had looked for a Gorbachev or a de Klerk to reform Ulster Unionism and bring them into negotiations with their republican opponents. Trimble had no intention of emulating either of these individuals in the sense that both had brought ruin to their respective parties. Rather, he would seek to cut a deal for unionism that would secure peace with stability and ensure that Northern Ireland would remain within the United Kingdom. He did not enter negotiations with Sinn Féin because he wanted to but rather because he knew it was necessary, and only on condition that republicans fulfilled a number of criteria. The key issues identified by Trimble as central to Ulster Unionism included the decommissioning of IRA weapons. For Trimble this would be the crucial confidence-building measure without which the majority of unionists would not consent to share power with Sinn Féin.

The end of the IRA ceasefire

As the first anniversary of the IRA cessation of military operations approached, Albert Reynolds proclaimed that 'it's almost 12 months since we had an IRA ceasefire followed by loyalist ceasefires, and it's not unreasonable to expect that we would have passed the point where people would have been sitting down to talks. Nobody should be afraid of peace, nobody should be afraid of talking about peace. It's time to start the talks process.' The former Taoiseach said he would never have signed the Downing Street Declaration had decommissioning of IRA weapons been made a precondition for Sinn Féin participation in negotiations.[67] Sinn Féin had persuaded the IRA that a ceasefire would lead to a pan-nationalist effort to push for Irish unity at all-party talks. Bruton, however, had replaced Reynolds and republicans believed that due to his vulnerable parliamentary majority, John Major was supporting unionist efforts to stall the establishment of all-party negotiations.

The international decommissioning body established by both Governments reported in January 1996 and recommended that all-party talks and decommissioning occur simultaneously. This amounted to a rejection of the British Government insistence of prior disposal of IRA weapons. John Major effectively binned the report and instead called for elections as an entry mechanism into all-party talks. The IRA now calculated that the Major Government was unwilling or unable to address its concerns and, consequently, it called off its ceasefire on 9 February 1996, bombing London's financial district at Canary Wharf. Writing in the *Irish Times* a week after the collapse of the IRA ceasefire, the paper's political correspondent, Geraldine Kennedy, wrote that

> an irreparable mistake was made by Mr Bruton last March when he implicitly accepted the Washington 3 test … Bruton said he would be telling President Clinton that they had to see some movement on the arms question so that talks could begin between British Ministers and Sinn Féin. He made statement after statement implicitly supporting Sir Patrick's [Mayhew's] position in the US and at home … Either inadvertently – or worse knowingly – Mr Bruton underwrote the British demand for Washington 3, a decommissioning gesture prior to talks. He helped place it at the top of the Anglo-Irish agenda. It has dominated the agenda at heads of government, ministerial and official level ever since.[68]

The decommissioning of IRA weapons was likely to become an integral part of any final settlement and, by itself, would constitute an important – if symbolic – confidence-building measure to assuage unionist fears. Making it a precondition for talks, as the British Government did throughout 1995, risked derailing the whole process. All-party talks were aimed at addressing the causes of conflict and establishing sustainable and inclusive political institutions but to elevate decommissioning of IRA weapons above all other issues induced intransigence and lethargy amongst the unionist parties while making a return to armed conflict more likely. There had been no reference to decommissioning in the Downing Street Declaration and certainly no assertion that it would be a *sine qua non* for all-party talks.[69]

Tensions surrounding unionist marches through nationalist areas and the release of paramilitary prisoners also undermined attempts to foster agreement on political structures for governing Northern Ireland. The 1995 Orange Order parade forced down the Garvaghy Road in Portadown had climaxed with Ian Paisley and David Trimble triumphantly holding hands in the air, and was widely interpreted as an attempt to humiliate republicans. Unionists refused to consider agreeing to the release of republican prisoners, though when safely ensconced in a one-party Government at Stormont the UUP had given an amnesty to IRA prisoners following the end of the border campaign in 1962.

The rainbow coalition survived the collapse of the IRA ceasefire by sixteen months, during which time it never looked likely that it would be restored. Bertie Ahern's two and a half years as opposition leader had provided the opportunity to prepare him and Fianna Fáil for power. The 1997 election had been largely bereft of a Northern Ireland dimension as each side contented themselves with economic manifestos that focussed on tax reductions. Running under the slogan 'People before Politics', Ahern outflanked the coalition, and Fianna Fáil returned to power allied with the much smaller Progressive Democrats party led by Mary Harney. The 1997 election also provided evidence that Sinn Féin's rising support in the North was being mirrored on a smaller scale in the Republic. Elected to represent the border constituency of Cavan-Monaghan, Caoimhghín Ó Caoláin became the first TD elected under the Sinn Féin banner since 1957, but unlike his predecessors he took his seat in Leinster House. The Labour Party lost almost half its seats, a haemorrhaging partially offset when it absorbed Democratic Left, now reduced to four TDs, the following year.[70]

A new partnership: Bertie Ahern and Tony Blair

During the summer of 1997, the Irish and British Governments were transformed. Eighteen years of Conservative Party rule were decisively brought to an end on

1 May when the 'New Labour' party led by forty-four-year-old Tony Blair won a landslide victory with 418 MPs, providing a majority of 179. The new Prime Minister presided over a largely inexperienced cabinet; Blair himself had never held government office. One month later, forty-five-year-old Bertie Ahern became the youngest Taoiseach ever when Fianna Fáil took an additional ten seats and joined with the four Progressive Democrats TDs and a small assortment of independents, many from the Fianna Fáil political gene pool.

Ahern's rise to the top was remarkable given its speed, ease and lack of obstacles. For years, he had navigated the stormy waters of Fianna Fáil's internal politics without making enemies. His was the first united Fianna Fáil cabinet since 1966. Moreover, the new Taoiseach possessed rare conciliatory talents, honed in particular as chief whip in a bitterly divided Fianna Fáil parliamentary party and five years as Minister for Labour in strike-prone Ireland. As Minister for Labour he had earned a reputation as a conciliator, a listener, a man who could win the confidence of conflicting sides and nudge them towards an agreement. Though from a republican family background, he came, by his own admission, with no ideological or historical baggage, and despite being twenty years in the Dáil was not noted for any strong views on Northern Ireland. Ahern also represented a new generation in Irish politics (being nineteen and twenty-six years younger than Reynolds and Haughey respectively) and was an ideal match for the energetic Tony Blair, whose relative youth was underlined when in 2000 he became the first Prime Minister since Lord John Russell in 1849 to father a child in office.

From Sinn Féin's perspective the replacement of Major's Conservative Government was a positive development. Enfeebled by scandal, entrenched by eighteen years in power and dependent for survival on the pleasure of the Unionist parties at Westminster, the Tories were seen as a barrier to progress. The Sinn Féin leadership had already told the Irish Government that they believed they could get a ceasefire within seven to ten days if the new British administration could guarantee they would be brought quickly into all-party talks.[71] The rainbow coalition's replacement on 26 June 1997 with an administration dominated by Fianna Fáil and led by Bertie Ahern was the final piece of the jigsaw that allowed the Sinn Féin leadership to persuade the IRA that the time was propitious for a new ceasefire, which was duly announced on 20 July.[72]

The contrast between Blair's 'New Labour' administration and Major's Conservative Government was stark. Within a month of the IRA reinstating their ceasefire, Gerry Adams had met with the new Secretary of State for Northern Ireland, Mo Mowlam, and substantive political negotiations between the parties began on 15 September under the chairmanship of George Mitchell.[73] Weeks later a Sinn Féin delegation had met with Prime Minister Blair and before Christmas they had been received for talks at No. 10 Downing Street.

Realising the mistake his predecessor John Major had made in keeping Sinn
Féin at arm's length after the August 1994 ceasefire, Tony Blair had agreed to
a speedy meeting. On 13 October, a British Government team led by the Prime
Minister met with a Sinn Féin delegation composed of Adams, McGuinness, Pat
Doherty and Siobhán O'Hanlon. Adams presented Blair with a small harp made
of Irish bog wood and added jokingly that he hoped it would be the only part
of Ireland he would keep. Though historic, the meeting produced little beyond
pleasantries.[74] Conscious of previous splits within the republican movement,
the Sinn Féin leadership preferred to demur rather than accept a pact they
felt was premature or could not be sold to the broader republican movement.
The Sinn Féin position, which was shared by the Irish Government, was that
the problem was at its core a political rather than a security one and had to be
addressed accordingly. As Secretaries of State for Northern Ireland, one could
not imagine a greater contrast between the aloof and haughty Patrick Mayhew
and the earthy, dynamic Mo Mowlam. Dick Spring made way for Ray Burke in
Foreign Affairs, though the latter's forced resignation in October following charges
of corruption led to the reappointment of David Andrews (Andrews had held the
brief for eleven months during 1992–1993). Junior Minister for Foreign Affairs,
Liz O'Donnell, would represent the Progressive Democrats at the Stormont
talks.

Blair had set about discarding Labour's policy on Ireland, which had supported,
albeit weakly and even hypocritically, Irish unity. On becoming party leader in
1994, he had dropped Kevin McNamara, a bête noire for unionists, as shadow
spokesman for Northern Ireland. Blair's first visit outside of London as Prime
Minister was to Northern Ireland, where he delivered a speech designed to
assuage unionist fears that, as Tory election posters had warned, new Labour
meant new dangers. Blair had given a draft of his speech to the Irish and US
Governments beforehand and Paddy Teahon, Secretary-General at the Taoiseach's
Department, was unhappy with the sentence 'none of us in the hall today, even
the youngest, is likely to see Northern Ireland as anything but part of the United
Kingdom', but Blair insisted that it stay in the script.[75] Other parts of the speech
were equally unattractive to Irish nationalist ears:

> My agenda is not a united Ireland. Northern Ireland is part of the United Kingdom
> alongside England, Scotland and Wales. The union binds four parts of the United
> Kingdom. I believe in the United Kingdom. I value the union … Any settlement
> must be negotiated not imposed; it must be endorsed by the people of Northern
> Ireland in a referendum; and it must be endorsed by the British parliament. So
> unionists have nothing to fear from a new Labour government. A political settlement
> is not a slippery slope to a united Ireland. The government will not be persuaders
> for unity.[76]

According to Blair's advisor Jonathan Powell, 'the pro-Union tone of the speech upset the Irish [Government] and unsettled the republicans [but] it served the primary purpose of reassuring unionist voters and winning over David Trimble'.[77] Blair's speech supported what republicans referred to as the unionist veto and dismissed a central plank of the pan-nationalist consensus that the British Government should act as persuaders for unity.

For a political community that ostentatiously proclaimed their democratic credentials, unionists had great difficulty cultivating allies and generating sympathy for their case in the democratic world. They had tended to identify themselves with settler communities that had lost power, as in South Africa, or embattled Israelis in the Middle East. It was difficult if not impossible to persuade most unionists that the manner in which Northern Ireland had been established and the way in which unionists had governed the region for decades had been anything other than democratic. Considering their rationale for partition and one-party rule, unionists were instinctively ill-disposed towards sharing power with nationalists or permitting a role for Dublin as, for them, it undermined Northern Ireland's very *raison d'être*. However, unionist political impotence combined with a sense that Britain's commitment to the union was dutiful rather than enthusiastic and the knowledge that they were losing the demographic war all provided rational grounds for negotiations. Inertia, some feared, would merely facilitate the further erosion of their position. Despite the tenacity with which they defended their position within Northern Ireland, unionists rarely went beyond the UK to argue their case. Republicans, by contrast, often enjoyed more popularity abroad, particularly in the US, than at home, though this support was frequently soft core. Bertie Ahern would initially find it very difficult to strike up any kind of a rapport with David Trimble. The Taoiseach's successful technique had always been to identify the interests of the other and to find common ground. He could, however, offer little to satisfy Trimble's love for canals and knew even less about his other great passion – opera.[78]

The Good Friday Agreement

Following the establishment of a Scottish Parliament and Welsh Assembly, approved by referenda in both countries, devolution became easier in theory for unionists to digest. No longer did it necessarily signify that Northern Ireland was a place apart worthy of exceptional treatment but rather it could be presented as part of an ongoing process of decentralisation within the United Kingdom. Moreover, the objection in principle to an international chair for internal UK negotiations had been nullified by the acceptance of former Australian

Governor-General Ninian Stephen presiding over the ill-fated talks initiated by then Northern Secretary Peter Brooke in 1991. Although the UUP, along with the two small loyalist parties, the Progressive Unionist Party (PUP) and Ulster Democratic Party (UDP), entered into talks on 17 September it would take some time before they would agree to be in the same room as Sinn Féin and longer again before they would countenance direct talks with them. The UUP leadership's instinctive caution was nurtured by the knowledge that the DUP and UKUP remained outside the process waiting to capitalise on any perceived betrayal of the unionist cause.

Decommissioning of IRA weapons was imbued with symbolism for all sides. As Blair and Ahern realised, getting the republican movement to sign up to the principle of unionist consent (hitherto referred to by republicans as the unionist veto) was far more significant in the long term than dispensing with its armoury. Weapons were easy to procure and decommissioned weapons could be replaced. Far more difficult to acquire was the degree of trust and cooperation necessary to push militarism to the periphery. The decommissioning of weapons could be a technical and momentary process but the decommissioning of mindsets would take much longer and would ultimately be the only guarantee for progress in the long term.

Unionists, however, could not understand why the IRA (whom they assumed, at least for public consumption, were one and the same as Sinn Féin) should wish to hold on to their weapons if they had renounced the use of force for political ends once and for all. Either the IRA commitment to non-violence was insincere, unionists suspected, and republicans retained an open mind on resuming an armed offensive at some point in the future, or they wished to use the threat of violence as leverage during the negotiations, which would give them an unfair advantage. The image regularly conjured up by unionist spokesmen was that of a negotiating process with one side holding a gun under the table. The fate of Terence O'Neill and Brian Faulkner was always in the background, as was Ian Paisley, who had felled both of these men and their projects of compromise.

When it came to the issue of weapons, republicans sought a demilitarisation of society, which suggested a parity of responsibility between the British armed forces in Northern Ireland and the IRA to put weapons aside, rather than a unilateral decommissioning of weapons held by republicans. As a minority within Northern Ireland, republicans were inclined to view IRA weapons as primarily defensive and argued that with a successful peace process the need for weapons would wither away. The IRA had never before destroyed its weapons, let alone handed them over. Rather it had, as in 1923 and 1962, dumped arms. Unilaterally destroying weapons smacked of surrender and would be very difficult to sell to many IRA members, particularly those of the younger generation. For the

Sinn Féin leadership, decommissioning wasn't just about what was desirable but what was politically possible. The overriding objective was to keep the republican movement intact; otherwise the Governments would find themselves some years hence negotiating with a new splinter group that had eclipsed the current leadership, in much the same way as they, the Provisionals, had outflanked the Official IRA almost three decades earlier.

After weeks of exhaustive talks under the chairmanship of Senator George Mitchell, an inter-party agreement, guaranteed by both Governments, was successfully negotiated on 10 April 1998. Quickly dubbed the 'Good Friday Agreement' (GFA), the pact secured the assent of the SDLP, the UUP, Sinn Féin, Alliance, the Northern Ireland Women's Coalition and the small loyalist parties (the PUP and UDP) while the DUP and UKUP opposed the pact. The opening section of the GFA, which dealt with vital constitutional issues, copy-pasted much of what had been agreed in the Downing Street Declaration. The participants endorsed the two Governments' commitment to respect the constitutional choice of Northern Ireland's electorate, though this was, as in previous inter-governmental agreements, narrowed down to just two options – remaining within the UK or a sovereign united Ireland. Significantly, Sinn Féin now accepted what had previously been depicted as the unionist veto. The following section of the Agreement repeated the unwieldy formula that it was for the Irish people alone, by agreement between the two parts respectively and without external impediment, to exercise their right of self-determination but reiterated that a six-county majority consent was a prerequisite. The third section acknowledged that a majority of people on the island of Ireland wished for a united Ireland, and that this included a substantial section within Northern Ireland, but emphasised that the current desire of a majority in the six counties, freely exercised and legitimate, was for no change. In deference to nationalist aspirations, it was affirmed that should the people of Northern Ireland opt for a united Ireland it would be a binding obligation on both Governments to introduce legislation to give effect to that wish. Parity of esteem and equality of political, civil, social and cultural rights were guaranteed. The birthright of all of Northern Ireland's people to identify themselves as Irish, British or both was recognised and this right could not be affected by any change to the constitutional status of the North. Furthermore, the two Governments undertook to propose and support changes in, respectively, the Irish Constitution and in British legislation relating to the constitutional status of Northern Ireland. In the Irish case this involved changes to Articles 2 and 3 of Bunreacht na hÉireann.

Strand 1 of the talks had resulted in agreement on internal political structures for Northern Ireland. There would be a 108-member Assembly elected from the eighteen Westminster constituencies with powers to pass legislation, though only within clearly defined parameters and while being subordinate to Westminster. Legislation would be passed either by the parallel consent of a majority of unionists and nationalists or a weighted majority (60 per cent) including at least 40 per cent of each of the representatives of the two communities. All Members of the Legislative Assembly (MLAs) would commit themselves to the principles of democracy and non-violence and ministers would be appointed using the d'Hondt system. At the apex of the Assembly would be a First Minister and Deputy First Minister. Though in theory a partnership government in which power was shared, unionists had insisted on a hierarchy of titles for the first ministers. The position of Secretary of State for Northern Ireland would remain and continue to be a member of the British cabinet in London. A toothless Civic Forum would be formed to consult on social, economic and cultural issues.

Strand 2, which had proved so contentious and provoked numerous clashes, ended up being a list of innocuous areas for North–South cooperation that would be natural between any two neighbouring states. Strand 3 was largely designed to take the sting out of Strand 2 and to quash the impression that North–South cooperation was a vehicle to trundle unionists into a united Ireland. With its British-Irish Inter-governmental Conference and British-Irish Council, which would encompass Ireland, the devolved assemblies within the United Kingdom and the UK Crown dependencies of Guernsey, Jersey and the Isle of Man, along with an expanded British-Irish inter-parliamentary body, it facilitated cooperation between Ireland and the various parts of the United Kingdom and its dependencies.

Much of the publicity surrounding the referenda necessitated by the Belfast Agreement gave the impression that the people of the Republic of Ireland were, along with their counterparts in the North, voting on the pact. In fact, the twenty-six-county electorate were being asked to approve amendments to Bunreacht na hÉireann changing the wording of Articles 2 and 3. The fact that both parts of Ireland were being asked to vote on the same day – 22 May 1998 – was another example of 'constructive ambiguity', a hallmark of the Agreement. The SDLP had long argued that there was a need to replace the last act of self-determination exercised by the people of Ireland when, during the 1918 general election, they had returned an overwhelming majority of separatists and nationalists. Republicans had constantly referred to this election as demonstrating how the will of the Irish people for a united, independent Ireland had been stymied and that until this preference was respected the institutions arising from partition lacked legitimacy. The SDLP had argued that referenda conducted concurrently in both jurisdictions could be considered to be an act of self-determination by the Irish people and this idea had gained currency among many in the Irish political elite. In Northern Ireland a clear majority of 71.1 per cent (676,966 votes to 274,979) endorsed the Agreement and this mandate was underpinned by a high turnout of 81.1 per cent. In the Republic of Ireland an overwhelming 94.39 per cent voted in favour of the constitutional changes on a 56.26 per cent turnout, constituting a majority of the electorate. The referenda gave an early fillip to the peace process and helped maintain momentum.

Elections to the new Northern Ireland Assembly on 25 June demonstrated that despite the UUP and SDLP leading the way in negotiations the DUP and Sinn Féin were increasingly snapping at their heals electorally. Although the SDLP emerged with the largest share of the vote, they secured four seats fewer than the UUP (twenty-four to twenty-eight). The DUP and Sinn Féin took twenty and eighteen seats (18.1 per cent and 17.6 per cent of the vote respectively). With only five candidates returned, the Alliance Party had a disappointing outing.[79] On 1 July, the Assembly met in 'shadow' form (as powers had not yet been devolved) and the cabinet included some of those who had opposed the Good Friday Agreement. David Trimble was elected 'First Minister Designate' of the new Assembly and, though John Hume remained SDLP party leader, his second-in-command, Seamus Mallon, was elected 'Deputy First Minister Designate'. Things soon began to unravel.

The ceasefires and the Good Friday Agreement had reduced the level of violence in Northern Ireland but had not eliminated it. The enormity of the Omagh bombing on 15 August – with twenty-nine fatally injured as a result of the blast – initially appeared to be an opportunity to cement the alliance between those parties committed to the power-sharing pact. The 'Real IRA', a breakaway group responsible for the bombing, announced a suspension of 'all military operations' on 18 August and the INLA called a ceasefire four days later, although the other republican splinter organisation, the Continuity IRA, did not follow suit. In the three years following the GFA, loyalists killed over thirty people, including human rights lawyer Rosemary Nelson and Martin O'Hagan, a journalist with the Dublin-based *Sunday World* newspaper. The Secretary of State, John Reid, declared on 12 October 2001 that the ceasefires of the Ulster Defence Association, the UFF and the Loyalist Volunteer Force had ended and that the organisations 'seem[ed] determined to spurn the opportunity – given to them by the people – to make the transition from violence to democracy'.[80] Such killings contributed to republican fears that decommissioning, in the absence of an acceptable police force, might lead to the increased exposure of nationalist communities.

Paramilitary prisoners were released from jails within the two-year time frame laid down in the Good Friday Agreement and the process would be completed on 28 July 2000. However, the pace of demilitarisation disappointed many in the nationalist community. British troop levels remained stubbornly high and most of the military infrastructure (e.g. watchtowers, barracks, etc.) had stayed in place. Opposing protagonists engaged in a circular argument whereby continued British army operations were used by the IRA to justify a leisurely approach to decommissioning whereas this in turn was cited as a reason for maintaining a substantial British military presence.

Gerry Adams and David Trimble only consulted face to face on 10 September 1998, the first meeting between leaders of Sinn Féin and Ulster Unionism since the formation of Northern Ireland. The announcement in October 1998 that the Nobel Peace Prize for that year would be awarded to John Hume and David Trimble also provided a welcome boost. While the peace prize might quite justifiably have been awarded to Tony Blair and Bertie Ahern, officials and political elites blanched at the prospect that it might be conferred on John Hume and Gerry Adams.[81] In December 1998, six new North–South administrative bodies and ten ministries in Northern Ireland were finally agreed between the Northern parties. The six North–South bodies would cover inland waterways, agriculture, trade and business development, the Irish and Ulster-Scots languages, European Union funding programmes and food safety. However, by the end of 2000 Trimble had not nominated representatives to attend North–South Ministerial Council meetings.

No executive was established during the eighteen months following the Belfast Agreement as deadlines came and went. Eventually, on 2 December 1999, some key aspects were triggered. Within twenty-four hours, direct rule formally came to an end as powers were devolved to the Northern Ireland Assembly. The North–South Ministerial Council, the British-Irish Ministerial Council, and the revised Articles 2 and 3 of the Irish Constitution all came into effect. The Northern Ireland executive assembled for the first time with representatives of the UUP, SDLP and Sinn Féin while the DUP boycotted the meeting. Finally, the IRA announced that they would be sending a representative to meet the decommissioning body chaired by Canadian General John de Chastelain. In welcoming these breakthroughs, the Minister for Foreign Affairs, David Andrews, spoke as if the process were reaching a conclusion – 'this is indeed a red-letter day'[82] – but it would prove to be another false dawn.

Decline of the UUP and the SDLP

Since the abolition of the Stormont Government in the 1970s, unionists had sought to regain devolution for Northern Ireland. But when it was eventually delivered it came in a form that many found hard to accept. The prospect, for example, of Martin McGuinness being responsible for educating their children proved particularly difficult to swallow. Northern Ireland had, after all, been established to keep Catholics and nationalists out of government and it was hard for many to accept the legitimacy of any arrangement that afforded them such a role. The feeling that nationalists were in the ascendant made unionists particularly sensitive to any indications that their position was being eroded. The 'Siege of Drumcree' therefore became a lightning rod for unionist dissent and a microcosm for the loyalist struggle within Northern Ireland. Orange Order leaders with unionist political allies made inflammatory speeches while paramilitaries led the disruption throughout Northern Ireland. The Orange Order opted to make their annual celebration of Catholic defeat and disenfranchisement into a litmus test to determine whether they still were top dog. Consequently, local disputes such as those at Drumcree or in Ardoyne were elevated into inter-communal tugs-of-war.

In July 2000, Northern Ireland experienced the worst violence for some years when the Orange Order renewed attempts to force its parade down the Garvaghey Road and when marches were re-routed in Derry and Belfast. Trimble would be haunted by his own association with the Drumcree march, torn between his duties as putative First Minister and his attachment to the Orange Order. Unionists had refused to accept the ruling of the newly established Parades Commission that a march could not be permitted unless local assent was secured. Within three months of the Good Friday Agreement, loyalists had blocked roads throughout Northern Ireland as part of the traditional marching season and attacked Catholic homes and businesses, culminating on 12 July when three pre-teen brothers were killed when their home in Ballymoney was set ablaze. The Orange Order rebuffed calls to end their demonstration and maintained a symbolic protest until the following year when the battle to march through the Garvaghey Road was enjoined anew. Another loyalist protest that involved the intimidation of young girls travelling to a Catholic primary school in north Belfast grabbed world headlines and reinforced the view that, irrespective of the peace process, Northern Ireland remained a society in conflict.[83]

While nationalists of all hues, bar the electorally insignificant dissident republicans, were united in favour of the general thrust of the peace process, unionism was divided throughout and this continually acted as a brake on momentum. Sinn Féin had prepared supporters for compromise and the party leadership united behind Adams and McGuinness. Trimble by contrast had not done the groundwork and was beset by internal sniping, sabotage and attempted coups. Moreover, whereas Sinn Féin's main electoral rival, the SDLP, ardently supported the GFA, Trimble's competitors in the DUP encamped themselves on the rejectionist extreme of the political spectrum from where they sought to undermine the GFA and the UUP. Trimble had to contend with constant attacks from within his party. In May 2000, the Ulster Unionist Council only narrowly – by 459 votes to 403 – supported a proposal to re-enter the power-sharing executive with Sinn Féin under certain conditions.

As a result of the Assembly elections of 26 November 2003, the DUP's five years of trying to outflank Trimble finally paid off when the party overtook the UUP. The difference in the party vote (25.7 per cent v. 22.7 per cent) and distribution of seats (thirty v. twenty-seven) was not huge but nonetheless Paisley and his leadership colleagues were now enthroned as the majority unionist voice, and while Trimble remained leader of the UUP his effective career had finished before the inglorious and decisive loss of his Upper Bann Westminster seat to the DUP eighteen months later. To exacerbate Trimble's predicament, his party was also outpolled by Sinn Féin, whose vote increased by 6.8 per cent to come within 15,000 votes of being the largest party in Northern Ireland. The surge was at the expense of the SDLP, which was now on a downward slide that seemed impossible to arrest. Previously, all agreements and declarations between the two Governments had been based on the premise that, while the 'extremes' would be offered the prospect of inclusion, the bedrock of the institutions would be a coalition of the centre 'moderate' forces within nationalism and unionism. A new reality faced them now; any new deal would have to be based on an agreement between the DUP and Sinn Féin, a prospect that seemed improbable. Most fears focussed on Paisley's legendary obduracy. Whereas Sinn Féin had been electorally rewarded for moving to the centre, stealing much of the SDLP's policy positions in the process, the DUP had profited from their negativity and for condemning Trimble's willingness to engage.

Once the UUP and DUP switched places in the hierarchy of parties, they also traded political stances. Now potentially in the driving seat during any forthcoming negotiations, the DUP were at pains to appear reasonable so as not to provide the two Governments with an opportunity to undermine them. They refused to be 'Trimbled', to 'jump first' to revive the peace process, and exuded confidence and flexibility at the very time the UUP began to implode. In February 2004, John Taylor and David Burnside attempted a heave against Trimble to install Reg Empey, while the party position became more intransigent than that of the DUP. When the DUP leadership met Blair on 5 February and 3 March 2004, it said the party would be willing to share power with Sinn Féin if the IRA decommissioned (the so-called 'Blair necessities'). Paisley was transformed from being a pariah to a pivotal player in the peace process. Speaking at one rally he proclaimed: 'isn't it remarkable what a difference a year makes. Last year the [US] President [George W. Bush] was told by his friend Tony Blair not to speak to that man Paisley. This year the President telephones me to my home.'[84] The 2005 Westminster election completed the UUP meltdown, with the party winning a solitary seat (Sylvia Hermon in North Down) and Trimble exiled to the House of Lords and political oblivion.

The peace process also witnessed the progressive marginalisation of the SDLP, particularly after the 2001 elections to Westminster, when they lost the mantle of being Northern Ireland's largest nationalist party. This loss of ascendancy coincided with the retirement of veteran party leader John Hume and Deputy First Minister Seamus Mallon, with Mark Durkan filling both positions. Although Durkan managed to cultivate a better working relationship with Trimble than Mallon had, the 2001 elections, in which Sinn Féin's vote surpassed that of the SDLP, hobbled his status of Deputy First Minister from the beginning. Sinn Féin eclipsed the SDLP within the Assembly in 2003 and during the following year the party won the European Parliament seat held by John Hume since 1979. The SDLP had always defined itself by opposition to violence but was increasingly dismissed as male, old and predominately rural. While the Good Friday Agreement seemed like a mission accomplished from an SDLP perspective, Sinn Féin by contrast presented it as a stepping-stone to greater things. At election time, it took ownership of the 'hope' and 'change' mantras so vital to keeping party membership energised. Because the peace process delivered the type of political regime the SDLP had advocated, the party was sometimes taken for granted by the two Governments. Whereas Sinn Féin could at least promise to use their influence on the IRA, the SDLP could do little in this respect. Some SDLP leaders ultimately became embittered and felt the Governments and the electorate had cast them aside despite years of loyal patient work in favour of late converts to constitutional politics.

As Fianna Fáil ushered Sinn Féin through the peace process it also nurtured an electoral foe. However, while Sinn Féin enjoyed the greatest percentage boost of any party during the Republic's 2002 general election, it remained transfer toxic for other party supporters, with the result that even though it received over one and a half times the vote of the Progressive Democrats, the latter party took over a third more seats. Fine Gael suffered its worst election since its rock-bottom performance of 1948, losing twenty-three seats including several members of the front bench.[85] The Fianna Fáil–PD coalition reaped electoral dividends from unprecedented national prosperity and in 2002 they became the first Government since 1969 to be re-elected. Buoyed by a booming economy, the Government had delivered increased spending combined with tax cuts. Unemployment had dropped from 10 to 4 per cent between the elections while GDP growth – at 8.5 per cent between 1996 and 2000 – compared favourably with an EU average of 2.3 per cent.

Unlike Tony Blair, Bertie Ahern did not have the luxury of administering a single-party Government. Though his coalition partners, the Progressive

Democrats, constituted a tiny fraction of the Fianna Fáil component, they were afforded disproportionate representation and certainly could not be ignored. Moreover, the PD leaders had different views on Northern Ireland. Mary Harney had resigned in protest against Fianna Fáil's opposition to the Anglo-Irish Agreement. As a columnist in the virulently anti-republican *Sunday Independent* newspaper, Michael McDowell had been an early and bitter opponent of the Hume–Adams discussions, maintaining they had 'set back the inter-community peace process very significantly' and were 'doomed to failure'.[86] He had opposed the lifting of Section 31, the granting of a US visa to Gerry Adams, whom he called a 'fascist',[87] and regularly castigated Albert Reynolds's Government for its gestures to republicans. Having lost his Dáil seat in 1997, McDowell had joined the cabinet as Attorney-General two years later before regaining his seat in 2002 and being appointed Minister for Justice, Equality and Law Reform. He replaced Mary Harney as PD leader and Tánaiste in 2006 but lost his seat the following year, the first Tánaiste in Irish electoral history to suffer this fate.

The devil is in the decommissioning

Sinn Féin and republicans generally resented the unionist fixation on decommissioning to the extent that it eclipsed all other issues, including good governance.[88] Armed conflict, they argued, was a product and not the cause of the deep divisions in society and only maintaining a sustainable and inclusive government could help banish the gun from Irish politics. Moreover, the Sinn Féin leadership had devoted huge political capital and innumerable meetings to convincing the IRA that politics should replace armed struggle as a means of effective action. The failure of this promise to materialise had been the main reason for the collapse of the ceasefire in February 1996 and disagreement on the issue now inhibited the implementation of the Good Friday Agreement. When Sinn Féin's electoral vote surpassed that of the SDLP in 2001 it strengthened the argument that republicans should be engaged on the basis of their electoral mandate and not because of their perceived influence over the IRA. Bertie Ahern provided unionists with an additional rationale for not sharing power with Sinn Féin when he claimed that he would not consider a coalition with Sinn Féin in the Republic until the IRA had disbanded. He argued, however, that whereas the state he governed was a consolidated democracy, the Northern Ireland administration was an experiment in conflict resolution.[89]

Against the Irish Government's strongly expressed wishes, Northern Secretary Peter Mandelson suspended the newly devolved Government (Assembly, executive and other related institutions) on 11 February 2000 and reintroduced direct rule. It followed reports from the Independent International Commission on Decommissioning that it had 'received no information from the IRA as to when decommissioning will start'.[90] Unionists threatened to walk. After the IRA undertook, on 6 May, to open some of its arms dumps for inspection and declared its willingness to 'initiate a process that will completely and verifiably put IRA arms beyond use',[91] the British Government restored devolution and the RUC disclosed that five military installations were to close. The IRA proceeded to open some of its arms dumps for inspection by the independent weapons inspectors, former African National Congress Secretary-General Cyril Ramaphosa and former Finnish President Martti Ahtisaari. At this critical juncture the process lost the highly engaged Bill Clinton, who in January 2001 was replaced as US President by George W. Bush, and nine months later the attacks on New York and the Pentagon made the White House even less sympathetic to non-state actors engaged in armed struggle for political ends.

Once the DUP replaced the UUP as the largest unionist party it refused to meet either the Irish Government or Sinn Féin during bilateral talks, which got bogged down on how the IRA would prove that their weapons had been decommissioned. It became apparent that the IRA was unlikely to decommission unilaterally if it were interpreted to be at the request of the British Government but might relent if the process were the product of negotiations with unionists. This would conform to republican ideology as it could be presented as an agreement between Irish people without British interference. The trouble was that the DUP wanted decommissioning not so much because it aided conflict resolution (arms could be obtained at any time) but as a way of demonstrating that republicanism had been defeated. In particular, the DUP sought photographs, and was supported by the British Government, which even presented it as a deal-breaker to Sinn Féin. Whatever chance this demand had of being met evaporated on 27 November 2004 when, in a speech to constituents, Paisley said 'The IRA needs to be humiliated. And they need to wear their sackcloth and ashes, not in a backroom but openly.'[92] Having framed decommissioning in terms of surrender and humiliation, Paisley had eliminated the possibility, however remote it had been, of a public decommissioning of weapons captured on camera and disseminated via the media.

There was further pressure for decommissioning when a robbery at the Belfast headquarters of Northern Bank on 20 December 2004, which netted over £26 million, was attributed to the IRA. As Sinn Féin attempted damage limitation their case was debilitated further when, on 31 January 2005, IRA members killed a civilian, Robert McCartney, during an altercation in a Belfast pub. McCartney's fiancée and sisters undertook a highly publicised campaign for justice and Bertie Ahern introduced them to George Bush at the White House on St Patrick's Day. Adams and McGuinness had always feared a major split within the republican movement and had striven to minimise defections, but by 2005 it was clear that both Governments had lost patience and demanded a formal dissolution of the IRA, not least to rob unionists of their key objection to coalescing with Sinn Féin in government. Elections to Westminster held on 5 May 2005 further confirmed the enthronement of the DUP and Sinn Féin as the two main parties. With a third of the vote, the DUP took half of the eighteen Westminster seats. The SDLP retained three seats, losing Seamus Mallon's Newry and Armagh seat to Sinn Féin while taking South Belfast for the first time following the retirement of the UUP's Rev. Martin Smyth. Whereas less than a decade earlier Sinn Féin did not have a single Westminster MP, on this occasion the party took five seats with a quarter of the overall vote. Similar victories for the DUP and Sinn Féin were recorded in the local elections held on the same day.[93] When, on 26 September 2005, General de Chastelain announced that all IRA weapons had been put beyond use the impact was underwhelming and anti-climactic. Coming over a decade after the IRA's ceasefire of August 1994, the long wait had killed the enthusiasm. It was, nonetheless, historic.

Policing

With decommissioning seemingly put to bed, there was an urgent need to resolve the policing issue for, as Blair's Chief of Staff, Jonathan Powell, noted, 'the IRA couldn't police the community any more, yet they wouldn't let the police do so either'.[94] Chris Patten, a former senior Conservative Party figure and the last Governor of Hong Kong, was entrusted with the task of chairing the commission to review the future of the Royal Ulster Constabulary.[95] Ahern had emphasised to Patten the importance of significant reform to make the police force acceptable to both communities in the North and Patten's report, published on 9 September 1999, recommended a radical overhaul of the composition, ethos, training and structure of the police.[96] While the RUC should not be disbanded, the report recommended it be re-named the Northern Ireland Police Service. Half of all new recruits would be drawn from the Catholic community with the aim of eventually reaching parity. The report recommended that the Gaelic Athletic Association repeal Rule 21, which prohibited members of the British Army or police forces from joining the Association, an action taken two years later despite opposition from most six-county members.[97] A new Policing Board and District Policing Partnership Boards, drawn from both communities, would be established, and the report recommended the creation of a police ombudsman along with a complaints tribunal. Patten and his supporters sought to facilitate a move away from policing during a state of armed conflict to a form of community policing with a strong emphasis on impartiality and human rights.

The report also addressed the problem of contested symbolism. The police service should 'adopt a new badge and symbols which are entirely free from any association with either the British or Irish states'.[98] The report also recommended that the Union flag should no longer be flown from police buildings and that on those occasions when it might be appropriate to fly a flag, that of the Northern Ireland Police Service should be used, which would be free from associations with any state. In sum, the report was guided by the objective of depoliticising the police force but this appalled unionist leaders and their supporters. Trimble described it as 'the most shoddy piece of work I have seen in my entire life',[99] and there were strong objections from rank-and-file RUC officers. The SDLP and Sinn Féin expressed a willingness to engage with the recommendations and were prepared to view the document positively.

The Northern Secretary Peter Mandelson watered down the proposals but the revised Patten Report published on 17 August 2001 was rejected by the DUP for going too far and by Sinn Féin for not going far enough, with the UUP and SDLP reserving immediate judgement. While the Irish Government called on both Sinn Féin and the SDLP to support the implementation plan, only the latter obliged. Explaining their stance, the SDLP noted that policing had been 'at the very heart of the political fault-line in our society' since 1920 and that 'no issue has been more difficult, more divisive and more controversial in the history of the north of Ireland'.[100] The party had been unable to support Mandelson's Police Bill in May 2000, which had so greatly diluted the Patten Report, but they had since noted ninety-four positive changes to the Bill. John Hume announced that his party would reverse its traditional policy of withholding support and, instead, encourage membership of the reformed police force.[101] The Police Service of Northern Ireland (PSNI) came into being on 4 November 2001 but when the new Policing Board formally met for the first time two days later Sinn Féin refused to take its seat. Gerry Adams said that Nationalist recruits to the new PSNI would be 'accorded exactly the same treatment the republican movement accorded to the RUC'.[102]

St Andrews Agreement

As 2007 beckoned, it became clear that Blair would be stepping down as Labour Party leader and British Prime Minister. That an Irish election was also expected within the year injected urgency, as there was a general appreciation, not least amongst Northern Ireland's party leaders, that this would be the last chance to do a deal under their stewardship. Following multi-party talks held in St Andrews in Scotland from 11–13 October 2006, an agreement was reached between the two Governments and the North's political parties which seemed to establish a timeframe for the restoration of the Northern Ireland Assembly, the formation of a new Northern Ireland executive and a decision by Sinn Féin to support the PSNI.

Sinn Féin wouldn't support a new policing regime unless it was under the control of the elected Assembly and the Executive, which Sinn Féin co-governed. That way it could be sold to supporters that control of the security forces had been devolved to the Irish. An IRA Army Convention followed by a Sinn Féin ard fheis in January backed the proposals but the two Governments feared the DUP would find a way to avoid going into an executive within the agreed timeframe. Two days after the Sinn Féin ard fheis, Blair made clear that if power sharing was not established by 26 March the process would be 'over' and the two Governments would devise a new partnership arrangement and, without using the phrase, hinted at joint sovereignty.[103] Elections to the Northern Ireland Assembly on 7 March 2007 confirmed the DUP's and Sinn Féin's political ascendancy, and two weeks later Ian Paisley and Gerry Adams finally met face to face to arrive at an agreement to re-establish the power-sharing executive with their respective parties at the helm.

The DUP had wanted to have themselves and Sinn Féin seated opposite each other to present the image of adversaries whereas the republican leadership sought to have each side seated beside each other to signal partnership. The organisers displayed considerable ingenuity in accommodating both perspectives by placing Adams and Paisley at either side of the table corner so that they sat simultaneously beside and across from each other. The footage of the two leaders sitting together (for what was their first face-to-face encounter) was transmitted throughout the world and suggested that Northern Ireland had indeed entered a new phase. On 4 April 2007, another symbolic breakthrough was captured on camera when Paisley publicly shook Bertie Ahern's hand for the first time.[104]

The new Assembly met on 8 May and an executive was formed with Ian Paisley and Martin McGuiness as First Ministers. Bertie Ahern and Tony Blair sat in the front row of the gallery. Others present included the Minister for Foreign Affairs, Dermot Ahern, Attorney-General Rory Brady and former Taoiseach Albert Reynolds, as well as members of the IRA Army Council.[105] The two First Ministers as well as Blair and Ahern addressed the Assembly while the oath of office taken by Paisley and McGuinness included promises that ministers would 'prevent discrimination', support 'non-violence and exclusively peaceful means' and 'uphold the rule of law ... including support for policing and the courts'.[106] Even though Paisley had ruled out a public handshake between himself and Martin McGuinness the photo that was transmitted around the world to indicate the beginning of a new era was of the two men laughing together. Consequently, the duo were quickly dubbed the 'chuckle brothers'. Four days after the establishment of the executive, the Sinn Féin ard chomhairle nominated three party MLAs to take their seats on the Policing Board. The following month, on 27 June 2007, Tony Blair stepped down as Prime Minister after over a decade at the helm, handing over the reins to his long-time Chancellor, Gordon Brown.

Capitalising on positive media coverage arising from the breakthrough in Northern Ireland, Ahern called an election, which was held on 24 May. Sinn Féin had hopes of making further inroads into the politics of the Republic but despite an increased vote they lost one of their five Dáil seats. Against the trend of pre-election polls, Fianna Fáil's vote remained solid. However, Ahern's junior coalition partner, the Progressive Democrats, lost six of their eight seats including that of newly elected party leader, Michael McDowell. While Ahern retained the support of the PD rump (the party dissolved soon after) he reached out to the six Green Party TDs to secure a parliamentary majority. With their support and that of a few independent TDs, Ahern was comfortably re-elected Taoiseach for a third consecutive five-year term on 14 June 2007, making him the most electorally successful party leader since Eamon de Valera. The irregularities in Ahern's personal finances, which had surfaced prior to the 2007 election, continued to dog him and, consequently, on 2 April 2008, the Taoiseach announced that he would resign on 6 May. Before stepping down he embarked on an impressive lap of honour including an address to both Houses of the US Congress.

Finance Minister and party stalwart, Brian Cowen replaced Ahern as Taoiseach. Dermot Ahern, who had retained the Foreign Affairs portfolio following the 2007 election, was moved to the Department of Justice and Law Reform and replaced by Micheál Martin. Cowen had solid experience of the Northern Ireland brief, having held the Foreign Affairs portfolio between 2000 and 2004. However, the new formation had little time to settle in to their roles. Cowen's administration would be confronted and overwhelmed by the global economic crisis, which placed the Government in survival mode for the remainder of its tenure. The Hillsborough Castle Agreement, signed on 5 February 2010, was the most notable achievement of the Cowen administration relating to Northern Ireland. Amongst other things, the accord facilitated the devolution of policing and justice powers to the Northern Ireland executive.

New executive, old problems

The administration of Northern Ireland was now, under the tutelage of the British Government, left in the hands of the DUP–Sinn Féin power-sharing Government. The two parties that had been the bulwark of the power-sharing Government established by the Good Friday Agreement, the SDLP and UUP, were left out in the cold. Paisley had little time to enjoy the position he had so long coveted. During the spring of 2008, he was persuaded to step aside in favour of his long-time lieutenant, Peter Robinson, who also took over leadership of the DUP. As Peter Robinson and Martin McGuinness moved their parties towards the centre they increasingly mopped up the support of their electoral adversaries. Indeed, their centrist positioning brought the *raison d'être* of the SDLP and UUP into question. This occasionally left the SDLP and UUP trying to outflank their foes by adopting more purist or less pragmatic stances, which only further eroded their core support base.

The composition of the Anglo-Irish partnership that fostered the peace process, based on cooperation between the governing parties of Fianna Fáil in Ireland and Labour in Britain, fundamentally changed in 2010–2011. An election in May 2010 in the UK, and in Ireland the following February, created a new dynamic, with a Tory-led Government in Britain under the leadership of David Cameron while Fine Gael revived their pact with Labour to win their first general election since 1982. Fianna Fáil's vote collapsed. In 2007, the party had won seventy-seven seats; three and a half years later and it had been reduced to twenty. Fine Gael and Labour's combined parliamentary majority was the largest in Irish electoral history, as was the margin (ninety votes) that secured Enda Kenny's election as Taoiseach. Labour Party leader Eamon Gilmore was appointed Tánaiste and Minister for Foreign Affairs and Trade.

As First Ministers, Peter Robinson and Martin McGuinness broke new ground, symbolically. Robinson attended his first Gaelic football match in January 2012, while Martin McGuinness recorded an historic handshake with Queen Elizabeth II during her visit to Belfast in June of that year. The cross-community photo opportunities camouflaged the dearth of legislation the two leaders managed to steer through the Northern Ireland Assembly. Only five Bills were passed during 2012, for example.

Sectarianism remained a distinct feature of life in Northern Ireland. These tensions came to the surface when, on 3 December 2012, Belfast City Council voted to limit the occasions that the Union flag flies from Belfast City Hall to eighteen days a year, bringing it in line with the rest of the United Kingdom. Uniting all strands of unionism, both legal and illegal, the resultant 'flag protests' continued well into 2013 and drifted into the summer marching season. Days and weeks of violent clashes between loyalists and the PSNI followed a decision by the Parades Commission to deny the Orange Order permission to march by the nationalist Ardoyne region of North Belfast. For many unionists the fate of the flag mirrored their own loss of status and prestige. When City Hall was completed in 1906, Catholics made up only a quarter of Belfast's population, whereas now nationalists constituted the greater number, reflected by Sinn Féin's position as the largest party on the city council. The Northern Ireland census results, released at the end of 2012, confirmed that the unionist demographic superiority that had justified the creation of Northern Ireland in 1920 was dissolving. For the first time since the establishment of Northern Ireland, those from a Protestant background no longer constituted a majority of the population (48 per cent compared with 45 per cent from a Catholic background).

For the remaining years before the 2015 Westminster elections Martin McGuinness and Peter Robinson remained locked together in a loveless political marriage, only seen together for carefully choreographed appearances to dispel rumours that they had split up, or when soliciting investment. For the most part the two First Ministers, veterans of 'Smash Sinn Féin' and 'Smash Stormont' campaigns respectively, avoided direct confrontation with, or criticism of, each other. The Northern Ireland executive became gridlocked, however, with the abuse of the 'petition of concern' mechanism, built into the Good Friday Agreement, being a major cause for stalemate. This mechanism had been established to allow either the nationalist or unionist community to block measures believed to undermine their fundamental interests, but it was regularly used to stymie inconsequential Assembly motions enacted by 'the other side'.

False and fresh starts

The North drifted without political agreement on fundamental issues and confronted crises and legacies of the conflict without the necessary mechanisms to defuse them. In July 2013, Richard Haass – President of the Council on Foreign Relations in New York and an envoy to Northern Ireland from 2001 to 2003 – was invited to chair all-party talks on flags, emblems and the past. Recriminations dominated five months of excruciatingly detailed talks amongst the Assembly parties, and despite numerous dilutions and amendments, the two unionist parties rejected Haass's recommendations. Many believed that the DUP and UUP's reluctance to embrace the proposals was in large part due to fears of being outflanked in the May 2014 European and local elections by the Traditional Unionist Voice, a splinter party led by former DUP MEP,

Jim Allister. In the Republic, these elections proved calamitous for Labour, forcing the resignation of party leader and Tánaiste Eamon Gilmore and his replacement by Joan Burton. The Foreign Affairs portfolio was assigned to Charles Flanagan, the first Fine Gael member to hold the position since Peter Barry (1982–1987) and a surprise choice given that he had only a few weeks' ministerial experience under his belt.

Flanagan had to find his feet quickly and on 23 December, after eleven weeks of talks and twenty-six hours of continuous negotiations, the two Governments facilitated the fourteen-page, seventy-five-point Stormont House Agreement, which the five main parties in Northern Ireland signed up to with varying degrees of enthusiasm. The main proposals included the creation of a Historical Investigations Unit to inquire into killings that took place during the Troubles,[107] an oral history archive where experiences of the conflict could be shared[108] and a commission to enable people to learn privately how their loved ones were slain.[109] Responsibility for parades was taken from the independent Parades Commission – a bête noire for unionists given its occasional rulings to re-route a contentious parade away from a nationalist district – and devolved instead to the gridlocked Northern Assembly.[110] The Northern executive secured a spending package to the value of almost £2 billion in loans and grants over the following decade from the UK Government, and in return the executive would have to present a balanced budget for 2015/16 and agree to a major programme of public sector reform.[111]

Soon after the ink was dry the British Government accused Sinn Féin of welching on the deal, with the Northern Secretary Theresa Villiers claiming that the party would have to 'get to grips' with welfare cuts as the British Government would not pay for a more generous system in Northern Ireland than existed elsewhere in the United Kingdom. Without a budget acceptable to Westminster, Villiers argued, Northern Ireland's political institutions would become increasingly dysfunctional to the point where they might 'jeopardise their credibility and even their sustainability'.[112] Although Minister for Foreign Affairs Charlie Flanagan maintained that the Irish Government could not support 'in any circumstances' such a 'departure from devolution',[113] Villiers repeated her threat of a return to direct rule when she addressed the Conservative party conference later that year.[114]

On 17 November 2015, after ten weeks of intensive negotiations, the British and Irish Governments, the DUP and Sinn Féin signed off on a sixty-seven-page document entitled *Fresh Start: The Stormont House Agreement and Implementation Plan*. A joint task force, comprising the Garda Síochána, the PSNI, and the British and Irish revenue commissioners, would be set up to deal with para-militarism and cross-border crime while a newly established international body would implement and monitor the disbanding of paramilitary organisations.[115] A new group, similar to the disbanded Independent Monitoring Commission, would be established to adjudicate on the status of paramilitaries. The British Government committed £500m to tackle issues 'unique to Northern Ireland', including £60 million over five years for 'confidence building measures' such as the removal of Belfast's so-called peace walls.[116] On the key sticking point of welfare reform, London also promised £585 million over four years to mitigate the effects of welfare cuts, an increase on the £565 million over six years contained in the Stormont House Agreement.[117] In an attempt to attract more jobs and investment, corporation tax in the North would be reduced from 20 per cent to 12.5 per cent by April 2018 so that it converged with the rate in the Republic.[118] The new agreement again kicked to touch 'legacy' issues such as flags, emblems and parades.

Despite the 'Fresh Start' title, most of what was agreed had also been proposed in the failed Richard Haass deal of Christmas 2013 and the abortive Stormont House Agreement of Christmas 2014. Thus, the agreement was 'about as fresh as twice-reheated turkey'.[119] This was in fact the fourth pact in a decade negotiated by the two Governments and the major parties in Northern Ireland. Indeed, the abundance of formal agreements resulted from the ongoing quarrels within the executive and within Northern Ireland society generally.

Transformations within the DUP and Sinn Féin

The St Andrews Agreement had not arrested fragmentation within Northern Ireland's unionist political elite. First Minister Peter Robinson presided over a divided party, making agreements with his coalition partners difficult. At the beginning of 2014 the founder of the DUP, and Robinson's predecessor as First Minister, Ian Paisley, gave a controversial, and occasionally surreal, interview to journalist Eamonn Mallie, in which he and his wife, Eileen, took several swipes at the DUP leadership. These grudges were taken to the grave. Following Paisley's death on 12 September 2014 several senior DUP figures were not invited to the memorial service, including deputy party leader Nigel Dodds MP, Gregory Campbell MP, Jeffrey Donaldson MP and Lord Morrow. Their absence was all the more remarkable considering that invited attendees included not only the former IRA leader Martin McGuinness, but also former Taoiseach Bertie Ahern and former Fianna Fáil ministers Éamon Ó Cuív and Mary Hanafin. Not a single Fine Gael or Labour Party representative, either from the incumbent Government or previous administrations such as the rainbow coalition of the mid-1990s, were invited. Arlene Foster's appointment as DUP party leader in

December 2015, replacing Peter Robinson, and as First Minister a month later, provided an opportunity to heal the rift, though divisions remained.

Unlike the DUP, for Sinn Féin the Republic is a major political focus. In Northern Ireland, Sinn Féin can lead a regional administration with limited powers; in the Republic they can be a decisive factor in influencing the policies of a sovereign state, not least in its strategies towards Northern Ireland. Sinn Féin on both sides of the table at talks between the executive and Irish Government is perhaps the worst-case scenario for unionists. With Sinn Féin's position in Northern Ireland's administration virtually institutionalised, the party increasingly diverted its energies to expanding its support base in the Republic. At the beginning of 2010, Sinn Féin had only four seats in the Dáil. Six years later and in a shrunken legislature (reduced from 166 to 158 TDs) its parliamentary representation had jumped to twenty-three. In the 2014 elections to the European Parliament Sinn Féin won more votes than any other party on the island of Ireland.

Sinn Féin's popularity in the Republic prompted frequent references to their performance in Stormont by other party leaders in Dublin, particularly to highlight the divergence between articulating an anti-austerity agenda in the Republic while implementing cuts in Northern Ireland. Sinn Féin's rise in the Republic has prompted a major shift in the dynamics of Irish government policy towards Northern Ireland. Whereas twenty years ago, Sinn Féin did not pose an electoral threat to the governing parties in Dublin, by 2014 it had become a major force. This complicated interaction between the Northern executive, which Sinn Féin jointly led, and the Irish Government, composed of two of Sinn Féin's chief adversaries in the Republic.

The peace process brought an end to the IRA's campaign, which had been so prominent a feature of the Troubles. It didn't disappear, however. A three-strong expert group, utilising PSNI and MI5 files, concluded in 2015 that while the seven-strong IRA army council still operated, it did so generally with benign intent, such as to prevent defections to dissident organisations, and had an entirely political focus. [120] According to former Tánaiste and Minister for Justice, Michael McDowell, the Governments that negotiated the Belfast and St Andrews Agreements had always intended to allow the Provisional IRA to continue as an 'unarmed and withering husk' rather than risk a vacuum emerging that could be filled by a dissident group hostile to the peace process.[121] The analogy used at the time, according to the former Progressive Democrats leader, was that of the 'Old IRA', which had been 'a harmless grouping'. Former Taoiseach Bertie Ahern concurred with this assessment and claimed that what had been envisaged was similar to 'what happened in the old days in the IRA' when these erstwhile militants had, without causing offence, 'continued on commemorating things until 60 years after'.[122]

Brexit

The Scottish Parliament's decision to hold a referendum on independence in 2014 had ramifications for Northern Ireland. Ulster unionists understood that a United Kingdom without Scotland could only weaken their position and UUP leader Tom Elliott decried the Scottish National Party as 'a greater threat to the union than the violence of the IRA'.[123] Few doubted that Sinn Féin would be buoyed by a vote for Scottish independence and the party argued that, irrespective of the outcome, the vote would have 'huge implications' for Ireland.[124] The Scottish drive for a referendum also prompted Sinn Féin to push for a poll in Northern Ireland which, under the terms of the Good Friday Agreement, the British Secretary of State for Northern Ireland has the power to initiate, on whether the electorate there favoured the status quo or a united Ireland.[125]

The Irish Government maintained a studious silence throughout the referendum campaign lest they be accused of unwarranted interference.[126] When the Scots narrowly rejected independence after promises of enhanced powers, the Taoiseach said his Government would be closely watching 'the changes likely to take place following the referendum, particularly in terms of devolution of powers'.[127] The Scottish referendum had all the appearances of being the end of a chapter rather than the finale of the story.

David Cameron's pledge that a Conservative Government, if elected in 2015, would hold an 'in/out' referendum on EU membership presented Dublin with a much greater challenge. Devised with a view to seeing off an incipient challenge from the right-wing Eurosceptic United Kingdom Independence Party (UKIP), and placating influential elements within the Tory Party, the decision represented a high-risk gamble that failed to make allowance for the profound impact a British departure from the EU (popularly known as 'Brexit') would have on both parts of Ireland. Symptomatic of this indifference was the decision of the Secretary of State for Northern Ireland, Theresa Villiers, to campaign for the 'leave' side. The Irish Government maintained that Brexit would be damaging for Europe, for Northern Ireland and for cooperation between the two parts of Ireland.[128]

That nightmare scenario came to pass on 23 June 2016 when 52 per cent of the UK electorate voted to leave the European Union, a decision that dramatically reopened the constitutional debate. While there were clear majorities in favour of Brexit throughout most of England, with the important exception of London, both Scotland (62 per cent) and Northern Ireland (56 per cent) voted to remain part of the EU. Within the North, the DUP alone campaigned for the 'leave' side, receiving, it later transpired, about half a million euro for that purpose from the Constitutional Research Council, a shadowy pro-Union group. Areas west of the river Bann, along with most of Belfast, where nationalists predominated, voted by significant majorities to stay in the EU while unionist-dominated areas east of the Bann mainly voted to leave.

Brexit immediately raised several important questions regarding Northern Ireland's status within the UK and its relationship with the rest of the island. As the EU treaties of Rome, Maastricht and Lisbon underpinned the foundations of the GFA and its successor pacts, many feared that Brexit would undermine the work of reconciliation and destabilise the region. Consent was at the heart of the Good Friday Agreement, particularly the principle that there could be no change in the constitutional status of Northern Ireland without a majority there agreeing to such a change. Brexit now threatened to fundamentally alter Northern Ireland's status against the explicit wishes of the majority that had indicated a wish to stay in the EU.[129]

With the weekly value of British–Irish trade of goods and services surpassing €1 billion, along with over €65 billion directly invested in each other's economy and exports sustaining 200,000 jobs, predictions of how Brexit would affect Ireland were almost universally negative. There was little evidence, however, that the British Government or electorate had considered Brexit's impact on Ireland, north or south. The Irish Government sought the softest Brexit possible but, as with the plebiscite itself, Dublin's role was largely reactive. When David Cameron's successor as Prime Minister, Theresa May, opted for a 'hard' Brexit, leaving the EU single market and customs union, Taoiseach Enda Kenny appealed to the EU to help alleviate the 'asymmetric shock' that Brexit represented for Ireland.[130] The Irish Government described its priorities as protecting all provisions of the GFA, maintaining EU support for the peace process, and avoiding the imposition of a hard border on the island while supporting continued north–south cooperation.[131]

Northern Ireland's geographical and political peripherality suggested that the impact of Brexit would be calamitous.[132] EU funding had helped finance numerous cross-border and cross-community initiatives; at the time of the Brexit vote, Northern Ireland received over half a billion euro annually from the EU.[133] Once the most militarised in Europe, the Irish border had virtually disappeared for an entire generation and almost two million trips were made across the frontier every month. Reinstating a physical boundary would have negative consequences, particularly on cross-border communities. Former Taoiseach

Bertie Ahern argued that such a move would have a 'destabilising effect', stoking anger within the northern nationalist community who had seen the Good Friday Agreement as a way of 'integrating the island'.[134] The future of cross-border services in health, education, business, agriculture – all predicated on being part of a single European market – was also rendered uncertain by the Brexit vote.[135]

The Good Friday Agreement, which the Irish and British Governments had registered at the United Nations, incorporated the legal relationships of the signatories with the EU and was based on the European Convention of Human Rights and European Court of Human Rights, both of which Britain was determined to leave as part of the Brexit process. In the absence of a written British constitution and no external recourse to the EU, Brexit jeopardised rights guaranteed in the GFA.[136]

It also coincided with a period of instability within the Irish Government. The February 2016 general election produced an unstable and greatly weakened Fine Gael-led Government reliant on independent TDs, who were offered cabinet positions, and Fianna Fáil's conditional support from the opposition benches. Dublin hosted multiple all-island civic dialogues to discuss the impact of Brexit but the DUP refused to participate. To add to the international uncertainty, Donald Trump, a vocal Brexit supporter, was elected US President in November 2016 on a ticket promoting economic protectionism and diplomatic isolationism.

Against the backdrop of Brexit, Northern Ireland went to the polls on 2 March 2017. The collapse of power sharing overlapped with Martin McGuinness's retirement from politics on health grounds (he died shortly afterwards) and his replacement by Michelle O'Neill as Sinn Féin's leader at Stormont. Reflecting Northern Ireland's demographic changes, Unionists held only four of the fifteen Assembly seats in Fermanagh and Tyrone and took a solitary seat in the Derry City-based constituency of Foyle. Only in Antrim and Down did unionists constitute solid majorities but in Belfast they took a mere six of the regional capital's twenty seats. In sum, the election returned forty Unionists (twenty-eight DUP, ten UUP, two Others) and thirty-nine Nationalists (twenty-seven Sinn Féin and twelve SDLP). Emboldened by its electoral strides north and south, Sinn Féin repeated its call for a border poll. Within days of the Northern election, Fianna Fáil announced plans to publish a White Paper on a united Ireland that envisaged the Northern Ireland Assembly remaining but all powers reserved for Westminster being transferred to Dublin. The Taoiseach and the President of the European Commission, Jean-Claude Juncker, jointly agreed that, in the event of Irish reunification, the North would be able to re-join the EU, in a manner similar to East Germany's accession in 1990.

Prime Minister Theresa May's decision to announce a snap general election for 8 June 2017 added to the volatility and uncertainty that had followed the Brexit referendum. As an attempt to enhance the Tories' parliamentary majority, divide the opposition, and strengthen her hand within the Conservative Party and in negotiations with the EU, the election spectacularly backfired. Despite UKIP's electoral collapse, the Conservative Party lost thirteen seats and with it their parliamentary majority. Labour increased its representation to 262 MPs but it was not enough to form a Government even had they been able to secure the combined support of the Scottish National Party (thirty-five seats) and the Liberal Democrats (twelve seats). With ten seats – its best performance ever – the Democratic Unionist Party was catapulted centre-stage, being quickly wooed by a Conservative Government eager to retain office.

Given that the DUP had campaigned for Brexit and was eager to demonstrate its fidelity to the British Government it should have been a good match. DUP support, however, ultimately came with a price tag of £1 billion in additional spending in Northern Ireland and there were several controversial aspects to the deal. The Tories – now repeatedly referred to as 'the Conservative and Unionist Party'– stated in the agreement that they would 'never be neutral in expressing its support' for the Union. Furthermore, the deal proclaimed that there could be no Irish border poll without the 'consent of the people', which suggested that there should be a 'referendum on whether to hold a referendum' whereas the GFA left a decision to organise a plebiscite at the discretion of the Secretary of State for Northern Ireland. As for the implementation of the legacy bodies established under the Stormont House Agreement, the UK Government promised that they would 'not unfairly focus on former members of the armed forces or police' while in the next sentence of the agreement both parties reiterated their 'admiration for the courage and sacrifice of the police and armed forces in upholding democracy and the rule of law and will never forget the debt of gratitude that we owe them'.[137] This stance reinforced fears that the British Government would seek to avoid detailed scrutiny of killings carried out by its armed forces during the Troubles or collusion with loyalist paramilitaries.

The pact rehabilitated Arlene Foster, whose leadership had been questioned after the 'cash for ash' debacle, a failed renewable energy incentive scheme overseen by her ministry that had cost the exchequer up to half a billion pounds and had precipitated the collapse of the executive. Indeed, the DUP's centrality in propping up the Conservative Government obscured the performance of Sinn Féin, which had enjoyed its best ever Westminster election in Northern Ireland with its parliamentary representation jumping from four to seven seats. The party's success came at the expense of a complete wipeout of the SDLP. It meant that for the first time in five decades there would be no Irish nationalist voice at Westminster as the electorate opted for abstentionist candidates.[138]

The British general election coincided with a Fine Gael leadership contest to replace Enda Kenny who stepped down on 14 June after six years as Taoiseach. In the subsequent party leadership battle Leo Varadkar defeated Simon Coveney in a two-horse race, and Coveney's decision to seek the Foreign Affairs portfolio dislodged Charlie Flanagan at a critical juncture in terms of Brexit and talks in Northern Ireland. The Conservative–DUP pact placed the new Dublin cabinet in a difficult position. As the British Government's survival now depended on maintaining DUP support it undermined London's ability to be 'rigorously impartial' in its dealings with Northern Ireland, as required by the Good Friday Agreement. This, in turn, complicated Dublin's interaction with the North and the Brexit negotiations. An unprecedented co-ordination committee comprising senior Conservative and DUP figures would monitor and vet laws before they were put to Parliament, giving the DUP enormous leverage on the British Government. It was assumed that much of what had been tacitly settled between the two party leaderships had not been included in the formal agreement, such as the location of the additional British government investment, which many believed would be focussed on the interests and constituencies of DUP MPs.[139] The deal with the British Government also made the DUP less likely to modify its refusal to introduce an Irish Language Act, which emerged as a key obstacle in efforts to resuscitate power-sharing institutions.[140]

The DUP quickly exercised their newfound political clout. In December 2017, Theresa May was forced to temporarily withdraw from a vital agreement with the EU, which allowed the UK to progress to the second stage of Brexit negotiations, because of DUP reservations on the provisions relating to Ireland.[141] Two months later, Arlene Foster backed away from a pact with Sinn Féin that would have restored the power-sharing administration, after she encountered hostility to the deal from within her party.[142] Given the parliamentary arithmetic at Westminster, the Tories were disinclined to push the DUP to reconsider. For the DUP, sharing power with Sinn Féin was unlikely to be as attractive as the dividends derived from its 'confidence and supply arrangement' with the British Government. Better at this stage to enjoy power without responsibility, as had been afforded by its alliance with the Conservatives, than responsibility without much power (further diluted by having to share it with Sinn Féin), which was the prize of any resurrected administration at Stormont.

When pressed by Brussels and Dublin to demonstrate how exiting the European single market and customs union could be reconciled with maintaining a friction-less border and existing levels of North–South cooperation, London presented aspirational proposals that lacked cogency.[143] Moreover, in their rush to leave the EU, many Brexiteers dismissed all obstacles as irrelevancies or, worse, conspiracies, even seeking to jettison the Good Friday Agreement once it became clear that it might impede a hard Brexit.[144] Some of them suggested that the EU was using Ireland as a pawn in a much larger game designed to thwart British ambitions.[145] Others maintained that Dublin was using the EU to attain a united Ireland by stealth or to outflank Sinn Féin.[146] Brexit polarised relations between the EU and the UK, between Britain and Ireland, and within Northern Ireland by fuelling debates about identity and sovereignty that common membership of the supranational body had de-emphasised over the years. The peace agreements that had been painstakingly negotiated, and which followed decades of deadly conflict, could not be taken for granted.

An end to partition?

The prospect of a Brexit re-energised debate on the constitutional future of the UK and Ireland; within weeks of the British referendum, Taoiseach Enda Kenny announced that in the upcoming Brexit negotiations the EU would need to 'prepare for a united Ireland'.[147] In August 2017, the Oireachtas Joint Committee on the Implementation of the Good Friday Agreement published a detailed 452-page report entitled *Brexit and the Future of Ireland: Uniting Ireland & Its People in Peace & Prosperity*, which included eighteen core recommendations. The German reunification process was repeatedly cited as a model for how a united Ireland could be accommodated within the EU with a minimum of disruption. The report recommended the establishment of a second New Ireland Forum to 'set a pathway to achieve the peaceful reunification of Ireland' and urged the Government to carry out an audit in relation to the legal and constitutional changes pre- and post-unification. It also emphasised that lessons needed to be learned from the failed referenda in Quebec and Scotland so that 'the Irish government fulfils its constitutional obligations of achieving its main aim of the peaceful reunification of Ireland'.[148] Commenting on the committee's endeavours, its rapporteur, Fianna Fáil Senator Mark Daly, claimed that Brexit had made a poll on a united Ireland inevitable.[149]

Any border poll result will be largely influenced by Northern Ireland's demographic composition. The 2011 census[150] showed that the six-county population had increased by 7.5 per cent since 2001, to 1.8 million, the highest figure since the post-famine census of 1851, and provided fresh evidence that the numerical gap between Catholics and Protestants was narrowing. Protestants, or those brought up as Protestants and other non-Catholic Christians,[151] constituted a minority of the population (48 per cent) for the first time, compared with 45 per cent of the population who indicated that they were Catholic or had been brought up as Catholics. This demographic trend showed no sign of being arrested. From nursery schools to university, Catholics now constituted the greater number. Almost 55 per cent of Northern Ireland's school-goers were Catholic and 49 per cent of college students (compared with 35 per cent Protestant). Moreover, the Protestant population was aging and more prone to emigration. For the first time, the census asked a question on national identity, and of those who answered 40 per cent described themselves as British only, a quarter as Irish only and 21 per cent as Northern Irish only. The issue of constitutional preferences is less clear-cut, however, and has been complicated, perhaps decisively, by Brexit. As one unionist writer pointed out, 'a post-Brexit Border poll would centre around a very different question [from that posed pre-Brexit]: do you support a united Ireland (inside the European Union, protective of a multiplicity of identities and supported by the Republic's political/business establishment) or do you support the union (outside the EU, possibly diminished by the departure of Scotland, and with the rise of a new form of English nationalism which will have no interest in the Celtic fringes)?'[152] While most unionists might remain unconvinced, a combination of nationalists (including those previously inclined towards accepting the status quo), soft unionists and those self-defined as 'others', who constitute an increasing proportion of the electorate, could produce the numbers required to vote for a united Ireland.[153]

Following the Brexit referendum, there were high-profile political interventions that maintained that, even should a majority in Northern Ireland opt for reunifica-tion, it could not be countenanced, being contrary to unionist wishes. In October 2017, for example, John Taylor, a former deputy leader of the UUP, stated that 'if Ireland was reunited by a narrow margin in a border poll, then it would spark a civil war'. Maintaining that 'you cannot force Northern Ireland out of the UK by a one per cent majority', he asked rhetorically, 'can you imagine the loyalists in Belfast taking it quietly? I couldn't.'[154] Using the threat of loyalist violence to inhibit debate on a united Ireland is a well-worn tactic and there is little to suggest that Taylor's views are anything but mainstream unionism. A major opinion poll published within days of Taylor's statement indicated that whereas 99 per cent of nationalists sought a border poll (the overwhelming majority wanting one within five years), a majority of unionists (53 per cent) preferred that a plebiscite never be held. Moreover, only 16 per cent of unionists favoured a 50 per cent +1 formula, with a majority preferring a threshold of above 70 per cent.[155] For many unionists the question is not, therefore, Northern Ireland's right to self-determination but rather a permanent right for their sup-porters never to be subjected to majority rule anywhere on the island of Ireland. From this perspective, unionist preferences would always trump concurrent majorities in the United Kingdom, Ireland and Northern Ireland that favoured a united Ireland. When it comes to unionist definitions of 'majority rule', such elasticity is hardly novel. When Northern Ireland voted against Brexit, for example, the DUP pointed out that it mattered little because Northern Ireland was part of the UK, which had voted to leave the EU. For decades, however, unionists argued that, although majorities in the UK consistently favoured an end to British rule in Northern Ireland, these preferences should be ignored because of the six-county regional majority favouring the status quo.

Taoiseach Leo Varadkar bolstered the unionist position when he claimed that Irish reunification could not come about as a result of a small majority, as specified in the Good Friday Agreement. A united Ireland, he maintained, 'must' be preceded by unity amongst the people of Northern Ireland and contended that 70 per cent would constitute a better threshold than a simple majority for changing Northern Ireland's constitutional position.[156] 'Bouncing Ulster Protestants into a unitary Irish state against their will would', the Taoiseach argued, 'be as grievous a wrong as was abandoning a large Catholic minority in the North on partition.' Worse, it risked unionist 'alienation and even a return to violence'.[157]

In blurring the line between 'majority' and 'unionist' when it comes to consent, Varadkar moved the goalposts set down in the Good Friday Agreement in a very fundamental sense. The GFA's success was in large part due to republicans agreeing to accept Northern Ireland as a unit for self-determination. A crucial component too was the provision for a border poll, committing both Governments in an internationally binding agreement to legislate for reunification if a simple majority of Northern Ireland's electorate voted in favour. Dismissing such a core feature of the GFA subverts the peace process it was designed to sustain. Indeed, rejecting the principle that a majority should decide the constitutional status of Northern Ireland undermines the legitimacy of the status quo given that four of the six counties are majority nationalist, along with the North's two largest cities, Belfast and Derry. Invoking the spectre of loyalist violence is, moreover, the argument that justified partition in the first place. Assuming that majority unionist agreement is unlikely to precede a united Ireland, Varadkar's argument came perilously close to presenting a rationale for permanent partition.

Notes

1   Ahern, *Autobiography*, pp. 136–137.
2   Joe Hendron MP, interview with the author.
3   Quoted in *Irish Times*, 6 October 2015.

4   *Sunday Independent*, 8 August 1993.
5   See for example, *Sunday Independent*, 12 September 1993.
6   McGarry and O'Leary, *Explaining Northern Ireland*, p. 395.
7   Quoted in Duignan, *One Spin*, p. 119.
8   Duignan, *One Spin*, p. 119.
9   Reynolds, *Autobiography*, p. 240.
10 See McNamara, *The MacBride Principles*, pp. 129–164.
11 O'Clery, *Greening of the White House*, pp. 24–26.
12 Reynolds, *Autobiography*, pp. 244–245.
13 Dumbrell, *Clinton's Foreign Policy*, p. 91.
14 Quoted in Reynolds, *Autobiography*, p. 286.
15 Murray, *John Hume and the SDLP*, chapter 9.
16 Duignan, *One Spin*, p. 98.
17 John Hume/Gerry Adams statement 23rd April 1993. Quoted in Adams, *Free Ireland*, p. 188.
18 O'Dowd, 'Mary Robinson and Gerry Adams – her finest hour', *Irish Central*, 9 April 2009.
19 Reynolds, *Autobiography*, p. 273.
20 Quoted in Mallie and McKittrick, *The Fight for Peace*, p. 184.
21 Reynolds, *Autobiography*, p. 274.
22 Reynolds, *Autobiography*, p. 265.
23 Letter from Adams to Reynolds dated 24 September 1993. Reprinted in full in Reynolds, *Autobiography*, pp. 266–267.
24 Quoted in Sinn Féin, *Setting the Record Straight*, p. 33.
25 Reynolds, *Autobiography*, p. 266.
26 Downing Street Declaration, paragraph 4.
27 Quoted in Cochrane, *Unionist Politics*, p. 318.
28 McDonald, *Trimble*, pp. 133–134.
29 O'Day, *Political Violence in Northern Ireland*, p. 39.
30 See Lynch, 'The Gerry Adams visa in Anglo-American relations'.
31 Major, *Autobiography*, p. 497.
32 See Clancy, *Peace Without Consensus*, p. 65.
33 O'Clery, *Daring Diplomacy*, p. 111.
34 Coogan, *IRA*, p. 654.
35 The Sinn Féin–British Government talks, which took place on 16 August 1994, did not become public knowledge until almost a year later (24 July 1995).
36 Bruce Morrison's role and that of the Clinton administration are considered in detail in Rhodeen, *Peacerunner*.
37 *The Independent* (UK), 31 August 1994.
38 Anderson, *Joe Cahill*, pp. 344–351.
39 Irish Republican Army (IRA) ceasefire statement, 31 August 1994. The statement is quoted in full in Cox et al., *A Farewell to Arms?*, p. 494.
40 Brian Feeney, interview with the author.

41   *The Argus*, 30 August 2014.

42   *Irish Times*, 7 September 1994.

43   Martin Smyth, interview with the author.

44   Martin Smyth, interview with the author.

45   According to the terms of reference the Forum was established 'to consult on and examine ways in which lasting peace, stability and reconciliation can be established by agreement among all the people of Ireland, and on the steps required to remove barriers of distrust, on the basis of promoting respect for the equal rights and validity of both traditions and identities'. Paragraph 11 of DSD.

46   As Brian Feeney put it at the time (November 1994): 'they get parity of esteem like all political parties and they are treated the same as everyone else. All that's important to get them involved in the political process and to say to them that we regard you the same as any other party.' Brian Feeney, interview with the author.

47   Brian Feeney, interview with the author.

48   Martin Smyth, interview with the author.

49   Kavanagh, *Spring, Summer and Fall*, p. 160.

50   As Sinn Féin's Director of Publicity put it shortly after the IRA ceasefire was announced: 'Reynolds did it! Reynolds did the necessary public things to move the peace process to a stage where it was a viable proposition. And that's the difference between him and former Taoisigh.' Rita O'Hare, interview with the author.

51   Alex Atwood, interview with the author.

52   *Irish Times*, 1 July 2014.

53   *Belfast Telegraph*, 12 July 2010.

54   Quoted in *Irish Times*, 8 June 1995.

55   Feeney, *A Short History of the Troubles*.

56   *Irish Independent*, 21 August 2014.

57   Kavanagh, *Spring, Summer and Fall*, p. 169.

58   Smith, *Making the Peace in Ireland*, pp. 188, 190–191.

59   Kavanagh, *Spring, Summer and Fall*, p. 169.

60   *Herald Scotland*, 18 April 1995.

61   'A new framework for agreement: a shared understanding between the British and Irish Governments to assist discussion and negotiation involving the Northern Ireland parties' (22 February 1995). Available at http://cain.ulst.ac.uk/events/peace/docs/fd22295.htm. Accessed 12 April 2018. The framework document was supplemented by a British Government position paper, 'Framework for accountable government in Northern Ireland', which dealt with Strand 1. See also O'Leary, 'Afterword: what is framed in the Framework Documents?'.

62   O'Clery, *Greening of the White House*, p. 189.

63   McKittrick and McVea, *Making sense of the Troubles*, p. 204.

64   McKittrick and McVea, *Making sense of the Troubles*, pp. 204–205.

65   Quoted in Cox, 'Rethinking the international', p. 419.

66   Coogan, *IRA*, p. 682.

67   Weiss, *Peace in Their Time*, p. 154.

68　*Irish Times*, 17 February 1996.

69　Paragraph 9 of the Downing Street Declaration had stated that 'the achievement of peace must involve a permanent end to the use of, and support for, paramilitary violence'.

70　Democratic Left TDs Pat Rabbitte and Eamon Gilmore would go on to serve as Labour party leaders.

71　Powell, *Great Hatred*, p. 13.

72　Bertie Ahern had met Gerry Adams many times when leader of the opposition, including shortly before and after he was elected Taoiseach in the run-up to the second IRA ceasefire. Ahern, *Autobiography*, pp. 195–196.

73　Though Blair stated that such talks would take place with or without Sinn Féin, the SDLP was reluctant to participate without Sinn Féin, and talks without either the SDLP or Sinn Féin would have deprived negotiations of the vital cross-community basis.

74　See Blair, 'How we agonised over shaking hands with Gerry Adams in 1997', *Evening Standard*, 27 June 2012; Powell, 'A moment in history: sitting down to talk with Adams and McGuinness', *The Guardian*, 17 March 2008.

75　Powell, *Great Hatred*, p. 11.

76　Address by the Prime Minister Mr. Tony Blair at the Royal Agricultural Society Belfast, 16 May 1997. Available at http://cain.ulst.ac.uk/events/peace/docs/tb16597.htm. Accessed 12 April 2018.

77　Powell, *Great Hatred*, p. 13.

78　Bertie Ahern interview with Katie Hannon. See *Village*, 22 May 2007. Available at http://politico.ie/archive/village-interview-bertie-ahern. Accessed 12 April 2018.

79　Other parties that secured representation in the Assembly were the United Kingdom Unionist Party (UKUP) 5, PUP 2, Northern Ireland Women's Coalition 2, Independent Unionist 3.

80　*The Guardian*, 12 October 2001.

81　Powell, *Great Hatred*, p. 141.

82　*Irish Times*, 3 December 1999.

83　See Cadwallader, *Holy Cross*; and Troy, *Holy Cross*.

84　Extracts from speech by Ian Paisley at the North Antrim DUP Association Annual Dinner, 27 November 2004. Available at http://cain.ulst.ac.uk/issues/politics/docs/dup/ip271104.htm. Accessed 12 April 2018.

85　See Gallagher, 'Stability and turmoil'; Doyle and Connolly, 'Foreign policy and domestic politics'.

86　*Sunday Business Post*, 27 February 2005.

87　*Sunday Business Post*, 27 February 2005. See also *Irish Independent*, 8 March 2004.

88　For an overview of the decommissioning issue see O'Kane, 'Decommissioning and the peace process'.

89　Powell, *Great Hatred*, p. 208.

90　Quoted in O'Kane, *Britain, Ireland and Northern Ireland*, p. 165.

91　Quoted in Maillot, *New Sinn Féin*, p. 41.

92　Extracts from speech by Ian Paisley at the North Antrim DUP Association Annual Dinner, 27 November 2004. Available at http://cain.ulst.ac.uk/issues/politics/docs/dup/ip271104.htm. Accessed 12 April 2018.

93　'The 2005 local government elections in Northern Ireland'. Available at http://www.ark.ac.uk/elections/flg05.htm. Accessed 12 April 2018.

94　Powell, *Great Hatred*, p. 275.

95　See Doyle, *Policing the Narrow Ground*.

96　*A New Beginning: Policing In Northern Ireland: The Report of the Independent Commission On Policing For Northern Ireland* [Patten Report] (HMSO 1999).

97　See Hassan, 'The Gaelic Athletic Association, Rule 21, and police reform in Northern Ireland'.

98　Patten Report, para. 17.6.

99　Quoted in Doyle, 'The transformation of policing in post-conflict societies', p. 160.

100　*Irish Times*, 21 August 2001.

101　*Irish Times*, 20 August 2001.

102　*Irish Times*, 22 September 2001.

103　Transcript of press conference with Tony Blair and Bertie Ahern following the publication of the Thirteenth Report of the Independent Monitoring Commission (IMC), Downing Street, London (30 January 2007). Available at http://cain.ulst.ac.uk/issues/politics/docs/pmo/tbba300107pct.htm. Accessed 12 April 2018.

104　Paisley had shaken Ahern's hand in private at the conclusion of the St Andrews Agreement talks the previous October. During their first face-to-face meeting at the Irish embassy in London in January 2004 Paisley had specifically requested a hard-boiled egg when offered food for, in his own words, it would be difficult to poison. *Irish Times*, 5 March 2008.

105　Details gleaned from main British and Irish newspapers dated 7 May 2007.

106　The Sinn Féin MLAs who took the pledge of office began their statements in the Irish language.

107　Stormont House Agreement, paragraphs 30–40.

108　Stormont House Agreement, paragraphs 22–25.

109　Stormont House Agreement, paragraphs 41–50.

110　Stormont House Agreement, paragraphs 16–20.

111　Stormont House Agreement, paragraphs 3–8.

112　*Irish Times*, 11 May 2015.

113　*Irish Times*, 7 September 2015.

114　*Irish Times*, 7 October 2015.

115　*Fresh Start: The Stormont House Agreement and Implementation Plan*, pp. 14–18.

116　*Fresh Start*, p. 8.

117　*Fresh Start*, p. 22.

118　*Fresh Start*, p. 21. See also *Irish Examiner*, 17 November 2015.

119　Emerson, 'Fresh start for North in 2016 looks predictable', *Irish Times*, 1 January 2016.

120 'NI paramilitary report: does IRA army council still exist?', BBC, 20 October 2015. Available at www.bbc.com/news/uk-northern-ireland-34577864. Accessed 12 April 2018.

121 McDowell, 'Abolition of Provisional IRA was never on the cards', Irish Times, 26 August 2015.

122 Irish Times, 27 August 2015.

123 Irish Times, 9 September 2014.

124 Irish Times, 11 September 2014.

125 Good Friday Agreement. Constitutional Issues Section. Annex 1. Irish Times, 7 March 2015; Irish Times, 26 January 2015.

126 According to an internal Department of Foreign Affairs brief, the Government had to be 'very careful to avoid expressing views' on the question of Scottish independence. Irish Times, 22 July 2014.

127 'Statement from the Taoiseach Enda Kenny T.D., on outcome of the Scottish referendum'. Available at www.taoiseach.gov.ie/eng/News/Taoiseach's_Press_Releases/Statement_from_the_Taoiseach_Enda_Kenny_T_D_on_outcome_of_.html. Accessed 12 April 2018.

128 Government of Ireland, Draft National Risk Assessment, 10. Available at www.taoiseach.gov.ie/eng/Publications/Draft_National_Risk_Assessment_2014.pdf. Accessed 12 April 2018. See also address by the Taoiseach to the Institute of European Affairs on 'Ireland at the heart of a changing European Union', Dublin, 15 February 2017. Available at www.iiea.com/eu-affairs/ireland-at-the-heart-of-a-changing-european-union/. Accessed 12 April 2018.

129 As a result of the GFA, and irrespective of Brexit, the population of Northern Ireland are entitled to Irish citizenship, and therefore the rights attached with possessing an EU passport.

130 Irish Times, 16 February 2017.

131 Brexit: Ireland's Priorities, p. 6.

132 NERI, Economic Implications of Brexit, p. 3.

133 It was allocated to receive in excess of €3 billion in EU funding, from 2014 to 2020. Irish Congress Trade Unions, The Case Against Brexit, p. 9.

134 The Observer, 11 February 2017.

135 Lissek et al., Brexit, pp. 23–24.

136 However, as the Vienna Convention on international treaties precludes a party to a treaty changing it as a result of amending domestic legislation, the British Government cannot unilaterally alter the GFA unless the Irish Government agrees.

137 The deal can be accessed at www.gov.uk/government/publications/conservative-and-dup-agreement-and-uk-government-financial-support-for-northern-ireland/uk-government-financial-support-for-northern-ireland; and www.gov.uk/government/uploads/system/uploads/attachment_data/file/621794/Confidence_and_Supply_Agreement_between_the_Conservative_Party_and_the_DUP.pdf. Accessed 12 April 2018.

138   In the immediate aftermath of the election, Sinn Féin came under pressure from some political parties in the Republic, particularly Fianna Fáil, to take their seats in Westminster.

139   Feeney, 'DUP/Tory deal is horribly bad for Sinn Féin', *Irish News*, 28 June 2017.

140   The St Andrews Agreement of 2006 states: 'The [British] Government will introduce an Irish Language Act reflecting on the experience of Wales and Ireland and work with the incoming Executive to enhance and protect the development of the Irish language' (Annex B). Speaking in Belfast during the 2017 impasse, Tony Blair's Chief of Staff, Jonathan Powell, said: 'I know how vexed a political point that is here now, but I'd have to say that my memory of the negotiations is very clear that we, the Government had agreed to the Irish language issue. Now the DUP will have to interpret what happened in the negotiations in their way, but it was very clear what was agreed there as far as we were concerned', *Belfast Telegraph*, 2 October 2017.

141   'DUP wrecks May's Brexit deal', *The Guardian*, 5 December 2017. The DUP would continuously flex its muscles during subsequent months when efforts to achieve a breakthrough in Brexit negotiations reached critical junctures. See for example 'DUP threatens to pull plug on May after hints of Border compromise', *Irish Independent*, 26 April 2018.

142   The 'Draft Agreement Text' passed from the DUP to Sinn Féin on 9 February can be accessed at http://eamonnmallie.com/2018/02/full-draft-agreement-text/. Accessed 20 February 2018.

143   *Northern Ireland and Ireland Position Paper*, 2017. See also O'Toole, 'The UK government's border proposals for Ireland are absurd', *The Guardian*, 16 August 2017. 'British Government's Irish border proposals "comprehensively" rejected by EU', *Belfast Telegraph*, 20 April 2018; 'Government urges Britain to think again on Brexit problems', *Irish Examiner*, 20 April 2018. For the Irish Government's position see *Ireland and the Negotiations on the UK's Withdrawal from the European Union: The Government's Approach*, 2017.

144   O'Toole, 'The Belfast Agreement was not a bribe', *Irish Times*, 24 February 2018.

145   'Northern Ireland is not the EU's pawn', *Telegraph*, 19 April 2018.

146   See, for example, the comments of former Conservative Party leader Iain Duncan Smith in a BBC interview, as reported in 'Iain Duncan Smith blames imaginary election for Irish Brexit difficulties', Inews, 6 December 2017. Available at https://inews.co.uk/news/politics/iain-duncan-smith-blames-imaginary-election-irish-brexit-difficulties/. Accessed 27 April 2018. See also 'Dublin using North for its own ends on Brexit, claims Foster', *Irish Times*, 21 November 2017; 'Brexiter Tories back DUP position on Irish border issue', *The Guardian*, 4 December 2017.

147   Joint Committee on the Implementation of the Good Friday Agreement, *Brexit and the Future of Ireland: Uniting Ireland & Its People in Peace & Prosperity*, p. 189.

148   Joint Committee on the Implementation of the Good Friday Agreement, *Brexit and the Future of Ireland*, Summary of recommendations, pp. 14–15.

149 'United Ireland referendum is inevitable after Brexit, says Irish parliamentary report author', *Independent* (UK), 2 August 2017.

150 The census was carried out on 27 March 2011 but the results were only released in December 2012.

151 The biggest of these were Presbyterians (19 per cent), Church of Ireland (14 per cent), and Methodist (3 per cent). 5.8 per cent described themselves as 'Christian or Christian-related denominations'. Data taken from the Northern Ireland Statistics and Research Agency.

152 Kane, 'Brexit challenges the identity of Ulster unionism', *Irish Times*, 14 April 2017. Kane is a former Director of Communications for the Ulster Unionist Party.

153 See O'Leary, 'Brexit or UKExit? Twelve predictions about Northern Ireland's future', *Irish Times*, 14 April 2018.

154 'Unionist peer Kilclooney says small majority vote for united Ireland would cause civil war', *Belfast Telegraph*, 18 October 2017; 'Peer: tiny majority for united Ireland would spark civil war', *Derry Journal*, 18 October 2017.

155 LucidTalk poll: 'Should there be a referendum on Irish unity?', 26 October 2017. Available at www.northernslant.com/lucidtalk-poll-should-there-be-a-referendum-on-irish-unity/. Accessed 13 April 2018.

156 Emerson, 'Leo Varadkar courting trouble over Border poll', *Irish Times*, 19 October 2017.

157 'Sinn Féin's push for border poll "alarming", says Varadkar', *Irish Independent*, 2 April 2017.

Conclusion

Despite the centrality of Northern Ireland in recent Irish history, no book until now has focussed exclusively on Dublin's Northern Ireland policies from the foundation of the state until the present day. In an effort to make an original contribution to our understanding of Anglo-Irish relations over the last century, this work has sought to provide an accessible, comprehensive and up-to-date overview of how political leaders in Dublin have struggled to adapt to partition. This concluding chapter will highlight some important themes essential to appreciating the context in which Irish Governments have devised and implemented policies towards Northern Ireland.

Getting used to partition

It took some time for Dublin's political elite to grasp that partition was not a transient aberration. When the Boundary Commission failed to dismember Northern Ireland, the Irish Government was bereft of a policy and, by signing the tripartite agreement in 1925, it agreed to respect the border between Northern Ireland and the Free State. President W.T. Cosgrave's decision to set aside the last tenuous link connecting the two parts of the country – the Council of Ireland – in return for a verbal agreement that the two Governments would 'meet together, as and when necessary, for the purpose of considering matters of common interest'[1], proved an extraordinarily inept move. Cosgrave believed that this verbal declaration of amity surpassed the 'cold power contained in a statute'.[2] In fact, not only would Cosgrave and Craig never see each other again but there would be no meeting between premiers representing North and South for another four decades. With the unionist Government entrenched, and supported by Westminster, Cosgrave's administration focussed on the affairs of the new Irish Free State.

Established in the wake of the Boundary Commission report, Fianna Fáil harried the minority Cumann na nGaedheal Government for the remainder of its time in office and regularly charged it with having deserted their northern kin. De Valera, however, was also vague when it came to specific policy proposals. Fianna Fáil contented itself with highlighting Government inadequacies and confidently asserting that, given the calibre and convictions of its leadership, partition would be effectively challenged once the party achieved office. Significantly, unlike the Sinn Féin party from which they had split, Fianna Fáil did not organise in Northern Ireland.[3]

During the first years of its rule, Fianna Fáil focussed on achieving the maximum level of political independence, triggering a six-year economic war with Britain. Simultaneously holding both the position of Prime Minister and the Foreign Affairs portfolio, de Valera controlled the Government's Northern Ireland policy. An opportunity for a breakthrough presented itself in 1938, when top-level and comprehensive Anglo-Irish negotiations took place with Neville Chamberlain's Conservative Government. The agreement that resulted from these deliberations ended the economic war and, by removing British naval bases, facilitated Ireland's military nonalignment during the Second World War. While this neutrality would be considered the ultimate proof and symbol of Irish independence, it also increased Britain's reliance on Northern Ireland as a strategically important military asset, with post-war consequences. By concluding these negotiations, de Valera had distilled contentious Anglo-Irish disputes down to the issue of partition alone.

When, in 1940, the British Government dangled the prospect of reunification in return for Ireland abandoning its military neutrality, the Fianna Fáil cabinet demurred. Some ministers believed that Britain was on the verge of defeat while others doubted its sincerity. Many too remembered the fate of John Redmond, whom they had outflanked during the previous world war when he decided to trade a promise of home rule for supporting the British war effort.

During the early decades of independence, the Government's Northern Ireland policies were predicated on some fundamental assumptions. These included the belief that the people resident on the island of Ireland constituted a single Irish nation that had been artificially divided by the British Government to further its own selfish ends. Unionists in this scenario were victims of false consciousness, willing pawns in an imperial chess game, unable to identify their true interest in aligning themselves with their (predominantly Catholic) fellow countrymen. Consequently, they were frequently spared the type of animosity reserved for successive British Governments. As dupes of a manipulator, they did not, according to this view, merit odium but could also never be rationally convinced of their true destiny until liberated from British influence. This in turn meant that Irish

Government policy should not be overly concerned with establishing contact
with unionists in advance of Irish unification. Reconciliation would, according
to this view, follow reunification rather than precede it.

The assumption that only the British Government could dismantle partition
led Dublin to deprioritise or exclude other policy options. Accordingly, no
consistent strategy existed of establishing or maintaining contact with the Northern
Ireland Government or with the unionist community generally. It is only fair
to note that even the most sophisticated political microscope could not detect
any enthusiasm from unionist administrations to cooperate. Stormont's policies
towards the Catholic minority under its jurisdiction demonstrated that regime's
deep hostility to any and all manifestations of Irish nationalism or unification
with the rest of Ireland.

Drifting to war

During the 1950s, there was a small but perceptible reappraisal of some traditional
assumptions.[4] Initially considered a transient abomination established unjustly
and maintained through coercion, Northern Ireland had now been in existence
for over three decades. An entire generation had grown up with the North as
a fixed reality and there were few signs, except for the desperately optimistic,
that suggested the six-county state was withering away as nationalists had
prophesised. Bolstered by increased subsidies from Britain, Northern Ireland
had, if anything, become more entrenched. Moreover, the provision of free
health care and education, combined with comparatively generous social welfare
allowances introduced by the post-war British Labour Government, had widened
the gap between the quality of life enjoyed by six-county unionists and their
neighbours in the Republic. This had not stopped the Stormont Government,
unbeknownst to the public, from initially attempting to block these benefits
from being extended to Northern Ireland, as they feared that Catholics would
be the main beneficiaries. While attachment to superior economic conditions
confirmed to many nationalists that Stormont's supporters were 'loyal to the
half-crown rather than the Crown', it remained an undisputable fact that unionists
would have had to endure a radical reduction in power, prestige and standards
of living should they have opted for a united Ireland.

Partition deprived Governments of first-hand knowledge of Northern Ireland
at ministerial or even parliamentary party level. With the passing of the revolutionary generation no minister born and raised in the six counties served in
cabinet, indicating 'growing localism and actual separation from the North'.[5]
That said, the participation of Northerners in Governments dominated by the
revolutionary generation did not impinge greatly on policies relevant to

North—South relations. Irrespective of origin, none of the ministers who served in a Dublin cabinet had experienced life in Northern Ireland after partition. In this regard Northern members of Dublin cabinets had more in common with their Southern colleagues than they had with those living under Stormont's control. The experience of ministers such as Frank Aiken, Ernest Blythe, Joe Connolly, Patrick McGilligan, Eoin MacNeill and Seán MacEntee, all of whom were from pre-partition Northern Ireland, bear this out.[6] A real difference in the thinking of the Dublin cabinet could only have conceivably come about with the inclusion of ministers who had lived in Northern Ireland for a considerable period after partition and had experienced the vicissitudes of life under the Stormont regime. This never transpired.

Successive Governments ruled out institutional links to Northern Ireland that it was within their power to establish. Elected nationalist representatives from Northern Ireland, for example, petitioned for a right of access to the Oireachtas – either in the form of actual representation or a mere right of audience – to demonstrate to their electorate the fruits of constitutional politics, only to be consistently rebuffed.[7] Suggestions that those political parties active in the Republic should also organise in Northern Ireland, while attractive from an ideological perspective, were similarly rejected on the grounds that such endeavours would encourage confusion and disunity.[8] Dublin found it difficult to maintain a unified and definite policy of how best to interact with northern nationalists and their representatives. During the mid-1920s and, again, during the mid-1960s, Irish Governments recommended that Nationalist MPs take their seats at Stormont but advocated a policy of abstentionism for most of the intervening period. Despite such advice, Dublin declined to defray the costs of abstentionism by contributing to the salaries, expenses or constituency offices of northern nationalist public representatives.

The belief that, in contrast to authentic nationalist separatism, loyalist sentiment was a false consciousness that could be remedied, led to some contradictory positions. To its own supporters, the Government portrayed free trade and occasional North—South summitry as stepping-stones to a united Ireland when unionists, at most, were willing to countenance what they called 'neighbourly cooperation' based on mutual common interest. The very cautious acceptance by some unionists of the potential virtues arising from functional cooperation was often presented as movement towards eventual reunification. And yet, when Seán Lemass enthusiastically sought a free trade agreement with Britain, it did not prompt Government members to suggest that it presaged Ireland's return to the United Kingdom.

While Seán Lemass was not the first to depict the problem as one internal to Ireland and the solution, therefore, as one to be devised between Irishmen, he was the first Taoiseach for whom this came to be seen, briefly at least, as the main plank of his Northern Ireland policy. With the zeal of converts, the Irish Government went from one extreme to the other during the 1960s. Before the *rapprochement* with Terence O'Neill, Dublin spoke almost exclusively (if only occasionally and dutifully) to northern nationalist representatives. The new policy of functional cooperation involved bypassing nationalist representatives and reaching out to the Unionist Party. In the interests of establishing a cordial relationship with Stormont, the one issue that was to dominate politics during the coming years and fundamentally change the political landscape in Northern Ireland – civil rights – was never discussed during inter-governmental summits between Dublin and Stormont. Northern nationalists quickly discovered that they had no place in this new era of détente. When, in December 1967, the Nationalist Party leader, Eddie McAteer, travelled to Dublin to make known his views on the drift between the Irish Government and the six-county minority, he was unable to secure a meeting with Taoiseach Jack Lynch and had to content himself with confessing to a civil servant that nationalists now felt they were 'nobody's children'.[9] A new generation of activists soon pushed aside McAteer along with other spurned petitioners, and insisted on being heard.

Coping with the Troubles

Widely perceived as a compromise candidate, Jack Lynch presided over a cabinet divided on Northern Ireland policy and which contained powerful, charismatic ministers of differing outlooks and ideological beliefs. There were those who, like Lynch, attributed the rising tensions to anti-Catholic discrimination and saw cooperation with Stormont as the most effective way of remedying the political ills that had brought the civil rights movement into existence. Others ascribed the strife to partition and favoured bilateral talks with the British Government to confront them with their responsibility for dividing the country and to seek a declaration of their intent to withdraw from Northern Ireland. Lynch's desire to avoid confrontation and achieve consensus was, depending on the times, his greatest political asset but also his Achilles heel. When the Troubles erupted, Lynch's lack of firm leadership, and his delegation of responsibility to subordinates, sowed confusion. Lynch's titular position of political supremacy disguised his lack of rootedness in the party organisation and it was only after the resignations, suspensions and expulsions that followed the Arms Crisis that he began to emerge as an undisputed leader of his party and, indeed, the state.

Notwithstanding his internal party triumph, Lynch struggled to get the measure of British Prime Minister Ted Heath during a sequence of one-sided military attacks on the nationalist community in Northern Ireland. These included the

Falls Road Curfew (July 1970), the introduction of internment (August 1971) and Bloody Sunday (January 1972), all of which at critical junctures signified a major escalation of the conflict. Instead, Lynch repeatedly expressed confidence in the good intentions and bona fides of the Stormont regime and its backers in London, despite compelling evidence to the contrary. His criticism of the Falls Road Curfew emphasised its partiality not its brutality[10] and shortly afterwards Lynch told the UN General Assembly that he '[did] not question the honesty of purpose of the [Northern Ireland] Prime Minister [Chichester Clark], nor of his predecessor [Terence O'Neill]'.[11] Lynch's condemnation of internment in Northern Ireland was fundamentally undermined by the fact that only months earlier he had threatened to introduce it in the Republic to see off a much smaller challenge.[12] At times, the tone of his approach could be excessively deferential, as when he apologised to Heath for calling him so late on the night of Bloody Sunday.[13]

A more consistent Irish approach to Northern Ireland evolved following the abolition of Stormont by the British Government in March 1972, and was largely maintained for most of the two decades preceding the Downing Street Declaration of December 1993, regardless of who wielded power in Dublin. A key part of this approach was consistent opposition to the IRA campaign. Dublin shared an interest with the British in quashing armed republicanism and, with varying degrees of enthusiasm, cooperated with London to achieve that end, and to ensure that violence did not 'spread' south. Sinn Féin's decision following the 1981 hunger strikes to contest elections on an ongoing basis, as opposed to ad hoc interventions, prompted intensified Irish Government efforts to convince London to devise mechanisms that could erode republican electoral support by addressing 'nationalist alienation'. Rewarding the exertions of moderate nationalists with tangible improvements for their constituents could also help justify anti-republican security offensives. Allied with the policy of crushing the IRA was an acceptance that a united Ireland could only take place if the consent of a majority within Northern Ireland could be secured. Occasionally this argument was employed to suggest that the two Governments could not pursue political projects without unionist endorsement.

A third central plank of Irish Government policy was the claim that Dublin had a vital role to play in any solution designed to resolve the conflict. While the Government occasionally asserted the right to speak on behalf of all Irish people, north and south, unionist and nationalist, in practice it mainly contented itself to pushing for greater recognition of northern nationalists' rights. This was done in large part because of a conviction that enhanced rights for the six-county minority and participation in the organs of government could reduce support for the IRA. Stemming from this was Dublin's preference for a comprehensive settlement based on power sharing between representatives of the two communities and guaranteed by both Governments, the better to assuage the fears of nationalists and unionists within Northern Ireland. The Government also highlighted the need for some kind of institutional arrangements between north and south (the so-called Irish Dimension) and frequently maintained that there could be no purely internal solution to Northern Ireland's strife.

The British Government contained the conflict at huge financial and military cost. Dublin's speedy realisation that it could not sustain such a burden tempered any predilection towards maximalist policies. Whatever could be said about the appetite for unity in the Republic it was unclear whether 900,000 unionists could be digested. Unity involving a large number of militant loyalists might destabilise the Irish state, and whereas the North constituted only about 2 per cent of the UK population, it would have made up well over a quarter of the population of a united Ireland. Policies had to be tailored to meet these realities and, after the 1974 collapse of the Sunningdale power-sharing agreement, influential members of the Irish Government reappraised core questions. Partition was no longer considered the primary problem for which Irish unity was the obvious and only solution. Rather, violence was deemed the evil and a British military, political and economic presence in Northern Ireland would have to be part of the solution for the foreseeable future, if not indefinitely.

During the 1980s, it was popular to contrast the actions and motivations of Garret FitzGerald and Charles Haughey, the leaders of Fine Gael and Fianna Fáil respectively. This focus on personality also coloured perceptions of their policies.[14] However, these rival Taoisigh arguably converged on policy fundamentals and merely diverged on style. If anything, the real disharmony was between Haughey the Taoiseach and Haughey the opposition leader. Determined to regain power, Haughey opposed all government initiatives, however obscure, and irrespective of whether he had endorsed them in the past or would promote them in the future. Critics who believed that Haughey's hostility to the Anglo-Irish Agreement was opportunistic felt vindicated when he swiftly accepted it on taking office and implemented the controversial extradition agreement his party had excoriated while in opposition.

Sometimes progress fell foul of the different electoral cycles in Ireland and Britain. When Jack Lynch returned to power in 1977 with a huge majority that made a full term likely, he was faced with a minority Labour administration that, dependent on unionist votes and in the twilight of its term in office, was determined to avoid discussing Northern Ireland with Dublin. When Charles Haughey took office in January 1980, he was a man in a hurry who believed a breakthrough in Anglo-Irish relations would distract voters away from the deteriorating economy long enough to facilitate an early election. Margaret

Thatcher, by contrast, enjoyed a commanding majority and was in no particular rush to involve the Taoiseach in discussions about the future of Northern Ireland. The prospects were better for the Fine Gael–Labour coalition Government. Within months of their November 1982 election victory, Thatcher came back with a renewed mandate. Both Governments could look forward to an extended term in office and both went to the electorate within months of each other in 1987. This provided the necessary time and space to work on what ultimately became the Anglo-Irish Agreement.

Northern Ireland policy on an international stage

Given London's reticence, occasionally bordering on outright hostility, to countenance any Irish Government involvement in what it perceived to be the 'internal affairs of the United Kingdom', Dublin occasionally sought to internationalise the Northern Ireland question. However, the relative weakness of the Irish state compared with its British counterpart imposed limitations on Dublin's realistic strategic choices. For most of the period covered in this book, the UK had a population fifteen times that of Ireland and was one of the top five world economies. This also impacted on Dublin's ability to get its case across internationally. In addition to having only a small diplomatic network at its disposal, traditional networks and global influence always favoured the UK, a disparity all too clear when Ireland launched periodic international anti-partition initiatives.

After a sterling performance at the League of Nations, Ireland found itself excluded from its successor, the United Nations, for a decade. A convention within Irish government and diplomatic circles was established that attempts to involve largely indifferent foreign Governments in the Anglo-Irish dispute were counterproductive as they alienated the key player that had to be persuaded: the British Government. The brief experiment carried out by the inter-party Government of 1948–1951, whereby Irish Government officials raised the partition issue at multiple international bodies, confirmed rather than disproved this assumption. By the 1960s, the Department of External Affairs – never a large ministry – was focussing on the UN. Anglo-Irish relations were increasingly seen through the prism of closer economic ties with the UK and monitoring British attempts to join the EEC. Ireland's veteran Foreign Minister, Frank Aiken, exemplified this focus, spending several months every year in New York. Ireland's small diplomatic staff played little role in foreign policy development, with much of the responsibility for developing Anglo-Irish relations falling to the departmental Secretary.[15]

Though Ireland had joined the United Nations in 1955, it never formally raised partition before 1969. Ireland could hope for the support of the communist bloc and recently decolonised developing nations but it would have been difficult to muster support amongst Western states. Frustration and lack of options prompted Patrick Hillery's missions to the UN in 1969, after the Troubles erupted, and again in 1972, in the immediate aftermath of Bloody Sunday. However, these international initiatives, which included visits to a small number of Euro-Atlantic capitals, represented brief deviations from long-established practice and were not, as some suspected at the time, new departures. Indeed, the primary audience to be impressed was not the UN but Irish domestic opinion. Spontaneous street demonstrations that included the burning of the British embassy in Dublin indicated that the Government had to find a way of being seen to respond to popular anger or risk becoming a target of that wrath.

Taking the long view, however, successive Irish Governments consistently demurred from confronting their British counterparts on the global stage. Disputes, when possible, were raised inter-governmentally rather than internationally. Dublin realised that for any progress to occur along the lines it desired, cooperation with London would be necessary. Attacking the British Government internationally might win some plaudits at home but risked making London less inclined to listen to Dublin's concerns. Consequently, it was the Anglo-Irish dimension that took precedence. Even when evidence of collusion between British military forces and loyalist paramilitaries was damning, or when Dublin's pride was slighted as when Margaret Thatcher made her dismissive 'out! out! out!' speech, the Anglo-Irish process was considered to be the only realistic game in town.

The USSR and satellite communist regimes in Eastern Europe actively backed Ireland's 'anti-colonial struggle for self-determination' but successive administrations in Dublin refused to harness this support, even when Anglo-Irish relations were rock bottom. Antagonism towards communism trumped any temptation to gain short-term political advantage by encouraging the Soviet Union to push Northern Ireland higher up the international agenda. Moreover, it was generally believed that Moscow's critical stance towards British rule in Northern Ireland was motivated more by animosity towards Western powers than love of Ireland. Unsolicited Soviet interest in Northern Ireland peaked during the early Troubles when fatalities soared, and in the late 1970s to counteract Western criticisms of Soviet human rights abuses following Moscow's signing of the CSCE's Helsinki Final Act. The belief that Moscow was, directly and indirectly, a key supplier of weapons to the IRA accentuated Dublin's weariness of Kremlin support. Indeed, in times of acute desperation, Irish Governments, particularly those involving Garret FitzGerald, clumsily tried to plant the idea in the minds of senior British and American politicians that the conflict should be viewed through the prism of the Cold War by arguing that the USSR or Libya would fill the vacuum in the event of a British withdrawal from Northern Ireland.

European integration enhanced Ireland's status and put it on a more level footing with the UK.[16] Before it joined the EEC in 1973, Ireland was a small player in the large and rapidly expanding UN General Assembly while the UK was one of the five permanent members of the Security Council with veto powers. In the expanded EEC of just nine members, however, Ireland had a seat on the Council of Ministers on an equal basis with the UK. Representation in the other institutions, such as the European Commission, Parliament and Court of Justice, was also weighted to favour small states. Moreover, Britain frequently needed Irish support 'in Europe' to advance its interests. Regular European summits meant that the British Government could not simply avoid coming into contact with Irish leaders as they had often tried to do during the early stages of the Troubles and, indeed, during preceding decades. Better still, Anglo-Irish meetings could take place at the margins of EEC summits, thus reducing publicity and moderating expectations.

But while the growing web of institutional engagements, characterised by the transition of the EEC to the EC and later to the EU, enhanced opportunities for dialogue between the two Governments, the ability of European institutions, or, indeed, their inclination, to play a major role in resolving the conflict was modest.[17] Because of the EU's limited role, Irish diplomacy primarily directed itself towards the United States. This involved persuading various US Government institutions and political notables to persuade Britain to sympathetically act on Dublin's concerns. It also involved disavowing some Irish-American organisations – even those with substantial political influence, membership and financial resources – that Dublin believed to be supportive of the IRA and/or causes associated with militant republicanism in Ireland. During the early years of the Troubles, the US had been the major source for arms and funds destined for Irish republicans. Dublin could not, for example, bring itself to fully and consistently endorse the MacBride Principles, devised by former Irish Foreign Minister Seán MacBride to discourage US investment in companies with discriminatory hiring practices in Northern Ireland. While the campaign united large sections of Irish America, becoming law in eighteen states and in over forty major cities, the fact that the Irish National Caucus spearheaded the campaign inhibited active support from Dublin. This resulted in the Irish Government frequently aligning itself with the British position more than with Irish-Americans concerned about injustices in Northern Ireland. Despite privately acknowledging that the levels of pervasive anti-Catholic employment discrimination had remained largely unchanged over decades, the British Government invested major resources to thwart the campaign, and highlighted Dublin's indifference to buttress its case.[18]

Bill Clinton's administration took an active interest in the early stages of the peace process and was willing at crucial moments to favour Dublin over London, as when, in 1994, it approved the issuing of a visa to Gerry Adams, facing down hostility from John Major's Government and the US State Department. It was significant too that it was the US, rather than the EU or UN, that played a vital mediating role in the Good Friday Agreement, not least in the form of George Mitchell, who chaired the negotiations.

Responding to public opinion

Government composition remained remarkably stable for most of the twentieth century with Fianna Fáil predominating for eight decades and a Fine Gael-led coalition, which always included Labour, usually constituting the only alternative. The revolutionary generation was extraordinary, not only for its longevity but also for its dynastic successions, all the more peculiar for being effected by a political elite that had cast off British rule for a republic. Following the 1923 election, for example, William Cosgrave headed the Government and was ably assisted by his Minister for External Affairs, Desmond FitzGerald, and Attorney-General, John A. Costello. Fifty years later, following the 1973 election, a new administration came to power led by Liam Cosgrave, son of William, and flanked by Foreign Minister Garret FitzGerald, son of Desmond, and Attorney-General, Declan Costello, son of John A. Their political challenges remained much the same as those confronted by their fathers a half century earlier; both administrations had to contend with a state under siege and the North in turmoil. During critical periods, political parties – particularly Fianna Fáil – diverted popular emotion away from militant agitation by providing an outlet where spontaneous outrage could be harnessed and given a political platform. Moreover, as ordinary activists were more committed on core policy issues than the wider public, party leaders frequently used the Northern Ireland issue to animate grassroots sentiment.

The potential of popular opinion to influence Irish government policy was limited by a number of factors. While a substantial majority of the electorate consistently favoured a united Ireland it was for most people, most of the time, understood as a long-term objective – a low-intensity aspiration that had little relevance for day-to-day life. In this sense, attachment to a united Ireland resembled affection for the Irish language, which also remained consistently high despite the unwillingness of the population to use it. Proposals to end the teaching of

Irish as an essential subject in primary and secondary schools were consistently rebuffed in a manner similar to suggestions to formally abandon Irish unity as government policy. Statements favouring a united Ireland, or the restoration of Irish, were as much a reflection of national identity as an indicator of daily action or political priorities. Genuflections affirming their importance became standard fare, obliged little remedial action and, unlike unfulfilled promises to increase employment and salaries, cost little in terms of votes.

Before the Troubles, pressure on the Government to 'do something' peaked in the late 1940s, following Westminster's retaliatory passing of the Ireland Act, and again in the mid-1950s during the initial phase of the IRA's border campaign. Throughout these decades, Governments did not gauge popular sentiment via opinion polls but had to estimate attitudes from less scientific but nonetheless illuminating phenomena such the atmosphere at party conferences or levels of attendance at republican funerals or commemorations. Indeed, up to and including the 1977 general election, politicians and media commentators did not consider opinion polls to be a vital barometer of public sentiment.[19]

Fluctuations in popular sentiment occasionally dictated Dublin's reactions to particular events. In 1969 and 1972, public opinion in large part compelled the Government to embark on international tours, including half-hearted initiatives at the United Nations, to highlight the injustices associated with unionist misrule and British army atrocities in Northern Ireland. Arguably, the 1981 hunger strike was the last major event that intensified public awareness of the conflict and enhanced pressure for government action.[20] That no event since then has triggered a popular reaction of similar proportions can be explained by two factors. First, blame for these events (internment, Bloody Sunday, hunger strikes) was placed on the British Government and inter-governmental action deemed appropriate. While the IRA also committed atrocities, these generally did not result in large-scale public demonstrations to force a Government response. Secondly, demands for action, however imprecise or ill-defined, occurred when there was a vacuum in Anglo-Irish relations and when there was no effective institutionalised mechanism for communicating and addressing Dublin's concerns. Once an Anglo-Irish inter-governmental process was established and became entrenched, 'leaving it to the Government' became a viable option for some who might otherwise have been inclined towards protest.

While the opinions of certain people and groups remained constant throughout the conflict, the attitudes of others fluctuated. Some of those animated by spontaneous empathy with the plight of northern nationalists during the early phase of the Troubles would subsequently adopt more dispassionate positions as a result of changed circumstances and/or advancing years. How else can we explain people who – archival records document – badgered the Irish Government for weapons during the early stages of the Troubles, but subsequently adopted mainstream political positions and, when interviewed years later, strongly denied any dalliances with militancy? Popular and individual attitudes towards the North meandered over time, sometimes evolving, other times reverting to earlier positions. It was also possible to hold conflicting emotions simultaneously – for example, a desire for security and prosperity co-existing with a need to actively resist injustice. A similar dichotomy frequently occurred amongst those living within Northern Ireland.

Over the years, the Government refined legislation to deter support for causes directly or indirectly associated with militant republicanism in Northern Ireland. Secret police made their presence felt at public meetings devoted to topics related to the North, and harassed attendees in an effort to isolate the curious from the hard-core. This often had the effect of delegitimising civil/human rights causes or individual activists. Fear of how public opinion might react to events in Northern Ireland led the Government in 1972 to activate Section 31 of the Broadcasting Act. Amended and expanded in 1975, Section 31 prohibited not only members of the IRA from speaking on television and radio but also ordinary members of Sinn Féin, irrespective of the topic under discussion, and despite it being a legal political party throughout the Troubles. By the time Section 31 was suspended in 1994, a generation had grown up without ever hearing the voices of republican representatives such as Gerry Adams or Martin McGuinness on radio or television. Censorship was also extended to entire communities within Northern Ireland and perspectives on the conflict that challenged the government narrative. Fear of the present and future also extended to the past and to popular culture. As history became a proxy battleground for contemporary disputes, commemorations became contested sites with state tributes to major historical events such as the Easter Rising being downplayed or prohibited altogether.

For many years Ulster unionists could point to the Catholic Church's elevated status as a reason to reject an enhanced political relationship with the Republic. The argument was that the civil liberties enjoyed by the Protestant-dominated North would be jeopardised by association with the priest-ridden South. During the last quarter century, however, an undeclared but nonetheless comprehensive and deep-rooted societal change has occurred in Ireland, reflected in fundamental changes in attitudes towards, for example, religion, censorship, marriage, divorce and sexuality. This has resulted in a reversal of roles, whereby it is now the DUP and its allies in Northern Ireland which consistently block the relaxation of religiously inspired legislation. During the same year that Ireland voted by referendum to enshrine marriage equality in the Constitution, the DUP vetoed a Sinn Féin motion – the fifth in three years – designed to legalise same-sex marriage, which had secured a slender majority in the Northern Assembly.[21] Asked the extent to which 'faith and church should influence the party' on a 0 (not at all) to 10 (maximum) scale, the then DUP leader and First Minister Peter Robinson scored 'faith' at 10, while his private Secretary, Paul Girvan MLA, claimed that 'if you use the Ten Commandments, you can formulate almost every law you need.'[22] The challenge in the twenty-first century, therefore, is not potentially how to absorb hundreds of thousands of liberal unionists into a Catholic-dominated republic but, more, how to accommodate religious conservatives, accustomed to political dominance, in a comparatively secular, liberal-democratic unitary state.

In recent decades, opinion polls have provided some indication of popular sentiment for a united Ireland but these are very much influenced by the wording of the questions asked and the political environment in which the propositions are put. The same voter might find themselves rejecting proposals to *abandon* the right of the Irish people to *self-determination* while agreeing that the *consent* of a majority in Northern Ireland must be a prerequisite for Irish unity. When that same 'consent' was framed as a 'unionist veto', enthusiasm understandably diminished. Moreover, support for unification has tended to be far less solid when linked to the proposition that additional taxes might be necessary to fund it. The complexities involved, combined with an appreciation that the electorate's approach to the issue is fragmented, have given the Government considerable leeway when it comes to negotiating agreements with the British. Voters have also demonstrated that they are willing to accept solutions that fall far short of unity if persuaded that they guarantee peace, and do not explicitly exclude unity as a possible eventual outcome.

The peace process and Brexit

Northern Ireland retains the scars of prolonged misrule. Societal segregation persists in the most fundamental of ways – geographically, educationally, religiously – down to what newspapers people read or sports they play. The negotiated agreements have respected the integrity of the conflict by institutionalising it; it is impossible to form an administration that is not a coalition of opposites composed of unionists and nationalists who have little in common beyond a mandate to govern bestowed by the peace accords. As the two largest parties in Northern Ireland, entrusted with the task of sharing power, Sinn Féin and the DUP remain locked in a loveless political marriage. A stalemate at Stormont co-exists with societal tumult just beneath the surface. The photo opportunities showing former adversaries smiling together have disguised a lack of a genuine cooperative spirit within the Northern executive and Assembly. Choreographed levity, while of symbolic value, has proved an unsatisfactory substitute for constructive legislation.

While the Northern Ireland Troubles can finally be referred to in the past tense, complacency is ill-advised. Until the 1970s, the Troubles referred to an earlier Anglo-Irish war and Bloody Sunday was dated to 1920. Too often in the past the 'Irish Question', as British politicians liked to call it, was consigned to history, only to re-emerge with a vengeance, in large measure because of London's wilful indifference. The Good Friday and St Andrews Agreements institutionalised a peace process that has fundamentally altered day-to-day life in Northern Ireland. Violence has abated and erstwhile antagonists have shared power. But while unquestionably a successful attempt at conflict management, it is perhaps too big a leap to say that what has been achieved is conflict resolution, let alone conflict transformation.

Of all regions within the EU, Northern Ireland is the most distinctly affected by Brexit. When Ireland and the UK joined the EEC in 1973 there was a hope that common membership of this supranational community would over time erode borders and reduce animosities within Ireland and between Ireland and Britain. With Brexit, many of the old certainties and assumptions on which Irish government policies were predicated evaporated overnight. Brexit has introduced profound uncertainty into Anglo-Irish relations. It will take many years before the full effects are felt and can be properly assessed.

Notes

1   Section 5 of Agreement Amending and Supplementing the Articles of Agreement for a Treaty between Great Britain and Ireland to which the force of law was given by the Irish Free State (Agreement) Act, 1922, and by the Constitution of the Irish Free State (Saorstát Éireann) Act, 1922, London, 3 December 1925.

2   Treaty (Confirmation of Amending Agreement) Bill, 1925—Second Stage (Resumed). *Dáil Debates*, 13/15 (8 December 1925). Labour leader Thomas Johnson provided a particularly withering critique of the ungrounded optimism presented in defence of the pact (col. 1465ff).

3   De Valera had previously been MP for Down between 1921 and 1929 but with the sole exception of de Valera's acceptance of an invitation to stand in South Down in 1933, Fianna Fáil did not contest any of the six-county elections.

4   A prominent example is Donal Barrington's article 'Uniting Ireland', published in *Studies* in 1957.

5   Cohan, *The Irish Political Elite*, p. 48.

6 Ernest Blythe wrote almost exclusively under the Irish-language form of his name, Earnán de Blaghd. Almost two decades after losing office he wrote, in 1955, *Briseadh na Teorann* (*Breaking the Border*). Its publication in the Irish language limited its potential readership. See also Ó Corráin, '"Ireland in his heart north and south"'.

7 See Ó Beacháin, *Destiny of the Soldiers*, pp. 225–230.

8 See for example de Valera's response to an ard fheis motion suggesting Fianna Fáil extend to Northern Ireland (*Irish Independent*, 16 June 1949) and his contribution during a Dáil debate in which he argued that the proposal 'would lead to antagonisms'. *Dáil Debates*, 126/2283 (19 July 1951).

9 See Ó Beacháin, *Destiny of the Soldiers*, pp. 260–264.

10 Lynch, *Speeches and Statements*, pp. 20–21.

11 *Irish Times*, 23 October 1970.

12 See Ó Beacháin, *Destiny of the Soldiers*, pp. 309–311. *Dáil Debates*, 250/485–94 (9 December 1970).

13 *Irish Times*, 2 January 2003.

14 Long after the pair had departed from politics, the broadcaster and historian, John Bowman, rhetorically asked 'were there ever two rivals for the office of Taoiseach who had such different approaches to Northern Ireland policy as Charles Haughey and Garret FitzGerald?' *Irish Times*, 30 December 2011.

15 Craig, *Crisis of Confidence*, pp. 8–10. On the preoccupations of the Irish embassy in London during this period see Hugh McCann to J.G Molloy, 21 October 1967. NAI DFA 96/3/216.

16 Mansergh, 'The new context of British–Irish relations', p. 97.

17 John Hume was instrumental in securing the European Parliament's Haagerup Report into the conflict in Northern Ireland. Though the report said little that was remarkable, and achieved even less, it did establish the important precedent of international scrutiny of political and economic affairs in Northern Ireland, despite British Government hostility (the Thatcher administration condemned the initiative, depicting it as an interference in the UK's internal affairs). The report can be accessed at http://cain.ulst.ac.uk/issues/europe/docs/haagerup84.pdf. Accessed 15 April 2018.

18 See for example J.M. Lyon, 'Disinvestment from the USA' (11 February 1985) [PRONI CENT/3/31A; A.J. Merrifield, 'Employment Opportunities' (11 February 1985) [PRONI CENT/3/31A; A.J. Merrifield, 'Disinvestment from the USA' (14 February 1985) [PRONI CENT/3/31A; D. Chesterton, 'Paper to be put to the Irish on MacBride Principles' (2 April 1987) [PRONI CENT/3/83A]. See also McNamara, *The MacBride Principles*.

19 Ó Beacháin, 'Elections and political communication', p. 34.

20 The protests in 1981 were on a substantially smaller scale than in 1972 and protesters were more politicised.

21 The DUP vetoed the legislation using the 'petition of concern' mechanism contained in the Belfast Agreement. See Ó Beacháin, 'Ireland's foreign relations in 2015', p. 238.

22 Quoted in Tonge et al., *The Democratic Unionist Party*, p. 144.

Appendix 1
A century of government in Ireland, 1919–2018

CnG = Cumann na nGaedheal
DL = Democratic Left
FF = Fianna Fáil
FG = Fine Gael
IND = Independent
LAB = Labour
PD = Progressive Democrats
SF = Sinn Féin

Table A.1: Government in Ireland during the revolutionary period, 1919–1923

	Government	Taoiseach or functional equivalent	Party	Minister for Foreign Affairs	Party
1919–1921	Sinn Féin majority	Cathal Brugha (1919) Eamon de Valera (1919–1921)	SF	George Noble Plunkett	SF
1921–1922	Sinn Féin majority	Eamon de Valera	SF	Arthur Griffith	SF
1922	Pro-Treaty Sinn Féin	Arthur Griffith, Michael Collins, William Cosgrave	SF	George Gavan Duffy, Arthur Griffith, Michael Hayes, Desmond FitzGerald	SF
1922–1923	Pro-Treaty Sinn Féin CnG minority	William Cosgrave	SF CnG	Desmond FitzGerald	SF CnG

Table A.2: Government in Ireland during the post-civil war period, 1923–1969

	Government	Taoiseach or functional equivalent	Party	Minister for Foreign Affairs	Party
1923–1927	CnG minority	William Cosgrave	CnG	Desmond FitzGerald	CnG
1927	CnG minority	William Cosgrave	CnG	Kevin O'Higgins	CnG
1927–1932	CnG minority	William Cosgrave	CnG	Patrick McGilligan	CnG
1932–1933	Fianna Fáil minority	Eamon de Valera	FF	Eamon de Valera	FF
1933–1937	Fianna Fáil majority	Eamon de Valera	FF	Eamon de Valera	FF
1937–1938	Fianna Fáil minority	Eamon de Valera	FF	Eamon de Valera	FF
1938–1943	Fianna Fáil majority	Eamon de Valera	FF	Eamon de Valera	FF
1943–1944	Fianna Fáil minority	Eamon de Valera	FF	Eamon de Valera	FF
1944–1948	Fianna Fáil majority	Eamon de Valera	FF	Eamon de Valera	FF
1948–1951	Fine Gael–Labour–Clann na Poblachta, National Labour, Clann na Talmhan	John A. Costello	FG	Seán MacBride	Clann na Poblachta
1951–1954	Fianna Fáil minority	Eamon de Valera	FF	Frank Aiken	FF
1954–1957	Fine Gael–Labour	John A. Costello	FG	Liam Cosgrave	FG
1957–1959	Fianna Fáil majority	Eamon de Valera	FF	Frank Aiken	FF
1959–1961	Fianna Fáil majority	Seán Lemass	FF	Frank Aiken	FF
1961–1965	Fianna Fáil minority	Seán Lemass	FF	Frank Aiken	FF
1965–1966	Fianna Fáil majority	Seán Lemass	FF	Frank Aiken	FF
1966–1969	Fianna Fáil majority	Jack Lynch	FF	Frank Aiken	FF

Table A.3: Government in Ireland during the Troubles, 1969–1994

	Government	Taoiseach	Party	Minister for Foreign Affairs	Party
1969–1973	Fianna Fáil	Jack Lynch	FF	Patrick Hillery	FF
1973–1977	Fine Gael–Labour	Liam Cosgrave	FG	Garret FitzGerald	FG
1977–1979	Fianna Fáil	Jack Lynch	FF	Michael O'Kennedy	FF
1979–1981	Fianna Fáil	Charles Haughey	FF	Brian Lenihan	FF
1981–1982	Fine Gael–Labour minority	Garret FitzGerald	FG	John Kelly (1981–1982)	FG
				James Dooge (1982)	FG
1982	Fianna Fáil minority		FF	Gerry Collins	FF
1982–1987	Fine Gael–Labour	Garret FitzGerald	FG	Peter Barry	FG
1987–1989	Fianna Fáil minority	Charles Haughey	FF	Brian Lenihan	FF
1989–1992	Fianna Fáil–PD	Charles Haughey	FF	Gerry Collins	FF
1992–1994	Fianna Fáil–Labour	Albert Reynolds	FF	David Andrews (1992–1993)	FF
				Dick Spring (1993–1994)	LAB

Table A.4: Government in Ireland during the peace process, 1994–2018

	Government	Taoiseach	Party	Minister for Foreign Affairs	Party
1994–1997	FG–LAB–DL	John Bruton	FG	Dick Spring	LAB
1997–2002	Fianna Fáil–PD	Bertie Ahern	FF	Ray Burke (1997)	FF
				David Andrews (1997–2000)	
				Brian Cowen (2000–2002)	
2002–2007	Fianna Fáil–PD	Bertie Ahern	FF	Brian Cowen (2002–2004)	FF
				Dermot Ahern (2004–2007)	
2007–2008	FF–Greens–PD	Bertie Ahern	FF	Dermot Ahern	FF
2008–2011	FF–Greens–PD	Brian Cowen	FF	Micháel Martin	FF
2011–2016	FG–Labour	Enda Kenny	FG	Eamon Gilmore (2011–2014)	LAB
				Charles Flanagan (2014–2016)	FG
2016–2017	FG–IND minority	Enda Kenny	FG	Charles Flanagan	FG
2017–	FG–IND minority	Leo Varadkar	FG	Simon Coveney	FG

Appendix 2
Key personalities

Adams, Gerry (1948–) President of Sinn Féin 1983–2018; MP for West Belfast 1983–1992 and 1997–2011; TD for Louth 2011–

Ahern, Bertie (1951–) Taoiseach 1997–2008

Aiken, Frank (1898–1983) Chief of Staff of the IRA 1923–1925; Minister for Defence (1932–1939), Coordination of Defensive Measures (1939–1945), Finance (1945–1948), Foreign Affairs (1951–1954 and 1957–1969); Tánaiste 1965–1969

Barry, Peter (1928–2016) Minister for Foreign Affairs 1982–1987

Blair, Tony (1953–) British Prime Minister 1997–2007

Blaney, Neil (1922–1995) Fianna Fáil TD 1948–1970; Independent TD 1970–1995; Minister for Local Government (1957–1966), Agriculture and Fisheries (1966–1970)

Blythe, Ernest (1889–1975) Minister for Finance 1922–1932; Vice-President of the Executive Council 1927–1932

Boland, Kevin (1917–2001) Minister for Defence (1957–1961), Social Welfare (1961–1965), Local Government (1965–1970)

Brooke, Basil (1888–1973) Prime Minister of Northern Ireland 1943–1963. Appointed 1st Viscount Brookeborough in 1952.

Brooke, Peter (1934–) Secretary of State for Northern Ireland 1989–1992

Bruton, John (1947–) Leader of Fine Gael 1990–2001; Taoiseach 1994–1997

Callaghan, ('Jim') James (1912–2005) British Home Secretary 1967–1970; Prime Minister 1976–1979

Cameron, David (1966–) British Prime Minister 2010–2016

Chamberlain, Neville (1869–1940) British Prime Minister 1937–1940

Chichester-Clark, James (1923–2002) Prime Minister of Northern Ireland 1969–1971

Churchill, Winston (1874–1965) Member of British Government team during Treaty negotiations 1921; British Prime Minister 1940–1945, 1951–1955

Clinton, ('Bill') William (1946–) President of the United States of America 1993–2001

Colley, George (1925–1983) Minister for Finance 1970–1973, 1977–1979 and Tánaiste 1977–1981. Twice defeated for Fianna Fáil leadership (1966 and 1979)

Collins, ('Gerry') Gerard (1938–) Minister for Foreign Affairs March–December 1982 and 1989–1992

Collins, Michael (1890–1922) Minister for Finance, Director of Information and TD in the First Dáil of 1919; Adjutant General, Director of Intelligence and Director of Organisation and Arms Procurement for the IRA; President of the Irish Republican Brotherhood 1920–1922; member of the Irish delegation during the 1921 Anglo-Irish Treaty negotiations; Chairman of the Provisional Government and Commander-in-Chief of the National Army at the time of his assassination in August 1922

Cooney, ('Paddy') Patrick (1931–) Minister for Justice 1973–1977

Corish, Brendan (1918–1990) Labour Party leader 1960–1977; Minister for Social Welfare, 1954–1957; Tánaiste, 1973–1977

Cosgrave, Liam (1920–2017) Leader of Fine Gael, 1965–1977; Minister for Foreign Affairs 1954–1957; Taoiseach 1973–1977

Cosgrave, William T. (1880–1965) President of the Executive Council of the Irish Free State 1922–1932

Costello, John A. (1891–1976) Attorney-General 1926–1932; Taoiseach 1948–1951 and 1954–1957

Cowan, Brian (1960–) Minister for Foreign Affairs 2000–2004; Taoiseach 2008–2011

Craig, James (1871–1940) Prime Minister of Northern Ireland 1920–1940. Appointed Viscount Craigavon in 1927.

de Valera, Éamon (1882–1975) President of (unrecognised) Irish Republic, 1919–1921; Taoiseach (or functional equivalent) 1932–1948, 1951–1954, 1957–1959. President, 1959–1973; founded Fianna Fáil in 1926

Devlin, ('Paddy') Patrick (1925–1999) Stormont MP 1969–1972; SDLP member of Northern Ireland executive January–May 1974

Durkan, Mark (1960–) Leader of SDLP 2001–2010; Deputy First Minister of Northern Ireland 2001–2002

Faulkner, Brian (1921–1977) Prime Minister of Northern Ireland 1971–1972; Chief Executive of Northern Ireland executive January–May 1974

Fitt, ('Gerry') Gerard (1926–2005) Leader of the SDLP 1971–1979; Deputy Chief Executive of the Northern Ireland executive January–May 1974

FitzGerald, Desmond (1888–1947) Minister for Foreign Affairs 1922–1927; Minister for Defence 1927–1932

FitzGerald, Garret (1926–2014) Minister for Foreign Affairs 1973–1977;
Taoiseach 1981–1982 and 1982–1987

Flanagan, ('Charlie') Charles (1956–) Minister for Foreign Affairs 2014–2017

Foster, Arlene (1970–) Leader of the DUP, 2015–; First Minister of Northern
Ireland 2016–2017

Gilmore, Eamon (1955–) Leader of the Labour Party 2007–2014; Minister
for Foreign Affairs 2011–2014

Griffith, Arthur (1872–1922) Founded Sinn Féin in 1905; President of Dáil
Éireann, January–August 1922; Chairman of the Irish delegation at the Treaty
negotiations in 1921

Haughey, Charles (1925–2006) Minister for Justice 1961–1964, Agriculture
1964–1966, Finance 1966–1970, Health and Social Welfare 1977–1979;
Taoiseach 1979–1981,1982,1987–1992

Healy, Cahir (1877–1970) MP 1922–1965 in Stormont and Westminster
legislatures (frequently an abstentionist)

Heath, Edward (1916–2005) British Prime Minister 1970–1974

Hillery, Patrick (1923–2008) Minister for Foreign Affairs 1969–1973; President
1976–1990

Hume, John (1937–) Member of the Northern Ireland executive January–May
1974; Leader of the SDLP 1979–2001; MP 1983–2005; MEP 1979–2004

Kenny, Enda (1951–) Leader of Fine Gael 2002–2017; Taoiseach 2011–2017

Lemass, Séan (1899–1971) Taoiseach 1959–1966

Lenihan, Brian (1930–1995) Minister for Foreign Affairs January–March
1973, 1979–1981 and 1987–1989

Lloyd George, David (1863–1945) British Prime Minister 1916–1922

Lynch, Jack (1917–1999) Taoiseach 1966–1973 and 1977–1979

MacBride, Seán (1904–1988) Chief of Staff of the IRA 1936–1937; Founder
of Clann na Poblachta 1946; Minister for Foreign Affairs 1948–1951

MacEntee, Seán (1889–1984) Minister 1932–1948, 1951–1954, 1957–1965;
Tánaiste 1959–1965

MacNeill, Eoin (1867–1945) Irish Free State representative on the Boundary
Commission 1924–1925

Maffey, John (1877–1969) British civil servant and diplomat who was a key
figure in Anglo-Irish relations during the Second World War

Major, John (1943–) British Prime Minister 1990–1997

Mallon, Seamus (1936–) SDLP MP 1986–2005; Deputy First Minister of
Northern Ireland 1999–2001

Mason, Roy (1924–2015) Secretary of State for Northern Ireland 1976–1979

May, Theresa (1956–) British Prime Minister 2016–

Mayhew, Patrick (1929–2016) Secretary of State for Northern Ireland 1992–1997

McAteer, Eddie (1914–1986) Leader of the Nationalist Party in Northern Ireland 1964–1969

McDowell, Michael (1951–) Attorney-General 1999–2002; Minister for Justice, Equality and Law Reform 2002–2007; leader of the Progressive Democrats 2006–2007; Tánaiste 2006–2007

McGuinness, Martin (1950–2017) Deputy First Minister of Northern Ireland 2007–2017

Mitchell, George (1933–) United States Senator 1980–1995; Chairman of Northern Ireland peace talks 1996–1998

Molyneaux, ('Jim') James (1920–2015) Leader of UUP 1979–1995

Mowlam, ('Mo') Marjorie (1949–2005) Secretary of State for Northern Ireland 1997–1999

Mulcahy, Richard (1886–1971) Chief of Staff of the IRA during the War of Independence; Commander-in-Chief of the new Free State Army after the death of Michael Collins; leader of Fine Gael 1944–1959; Minister in various administrations from 1920s to 1950s

Ó Brádaigh, Ruairí (1932–2013) President of Sinn Féin 1970–1983; President of Republican Sinn Féin 1986–2013

O'Brien, Conor Cruise (1917–2008) Labour Party TD and Spokesperson on Northern Ireland 1969–1977; Minister for Posts and Telegraphs 1973–1977

O'Duffy, Eoin (1890–1944) Pro-Treaty Chief of Staff of the IRA in 1922; Commissioner of the Irish police force (An Garda Síochána) 1922–1933; established the Army Comrades Association (also known as the 'Blueshirts') in 1932; first leader of Fine Gael, 1933–1934

O'Higgins, Kevin (1892–1927) Vice-President of the Executive Council and Minister for Justice 1922–1927

O'Kennedy, Michael (1936–) Minister for Foreign Affairs 1977–1979

O'Neill, Michelle (1977–) Leader of Sinn Féin in Northern Ireland 2017–

O'Neill, Terence (1914–1990) Prime Minister of Northern Ireland 1963–1969

Paisley, Ian (1926–2014) Leader of the DUP 1971–2008; DUP MP 1970–2010; DUP MEP 1979–2004

Prior, ('Jim') James (1927–2016) Secretary of State for Northern Ireland 1981–1984

Rees, Merlyn (1920–2006) Secretary of State for Northern Ireland 1974–1976

Reynolds, Albert (1932–2014) Taoiseach 1992–1994

Robinson, Peter (1948–) Deputy Leader of the DUP 1979–2008; leader of the DUP 2008–2015; First Minister of Northern Ireland 2008–2016

Sands, ('Bobby') Robert (1954–1981) IRA prison leader; hunger striker March–May 1981; Anti-H-Block MP April–May 1981

Spring, ('Dick') Richard (1950–) Leader of Labour Party 1982–1997; Tánaiste 1982–1987 and 1993–1997; Minister for Foreign Affairs 1993–1997

Thatcher, Margaret (1925–2013) British Prime Minister 1979–1990

Trimble, David (1944–) UUP MP 1990–2005; Leader of UUP 1995–2005; First Minister of Northern Ireland 1999–2001 and 2001–2002

Varadkar, Leo (1979–) Taoiseach 2017–

Villiers, Theresa (1968–) Secretary of State for Northern Ireland 2012–2016

Wilson, Harold (1916–1995) British Prime Minister 1964–1970 and 1974–1976

Bibliography

Primary sources

Interviews

Gerry Adams (Sinn Féin President 1983–2018)

David Alton (British Liberal Party MP 1979–1997)

Alex Atwood (SDLP Assembly Member 1998–2017)

Tony Benn (British Government Minister 1964–1970, Chair of British Labour Party 1971–1972)

Kevin Boland (Irish Government Minister 1957–1970, Founder of Aontacht Éireann, 1971)

Roy Bradford (UUP Stormont MP 1965–1973, Northern Ireland Government Minister 1969–1972, Member of Sunningdale power-sharing executive 1974)

Seán Clancy (East Clare Brigade IRA 1918–1919, Dublin Brigade IRA 1919–1921, Irish Defence Forces, reaching position of Commanding Officer Fifth Infantry Battalion 1922–1959)

Bob Cooper (Deputy Leader of Alliance Party, Member of Sunningdale power-sharing executive 1974)

Jeremy Corbyn (British Labour MP 1983–, Labour Party leader 2015–)

Paddy Devlin (Stormont MP 1969–1972, SDLP co-founder 1970, Member of Sunningdale power-sharing executive 1974)

Brian Feeney (SDLP Belfast city councillor 1977–1993, author, columnist)

Joe Hendron (SDLP MP 1992–1997)

John Kelly (Chairman of Central Citizens Defence Committee, Arms Trial defendant, Leader of Belfast Provisional IRA 1970–1972)

Pascal O'Hare (SDLP Representative in Northern Ireland Assembly 1973–1974, Northern Ireland Assembly 1982–1985, Belfast City Council 1977–1985)

Rita O'Hare (Sinn Féin Director of Publicity 1990–1998, Representative to
   the United States 1998–2018, General Secretary, 2007–2009)
Des O'Malley (Minister for Justice (1970–1973), Industry and Commerce
   (1977–1981, 1989–1992) Trade, Commerce and Tourism (1982). Leader of
   Progressive Democrats (1985–1993)
Patrick Mayhew (British Conservative Party MP, Secretary of State for Northern
   Ireland 1992–1997)
Richard McAuley (PA/Press Officer to Gerry Adams, early 1990s to 2018)
Jim McDaid (Fianna Fáil TD 1989–2010 and Minister 1991, 1997–2002)
Laurence McKeown (IRA hunger striker, went seventy days without food, 1981)
Mitchel McLaughlin (General Secretary of Sinn Féin, MLA 1998–2016, Speaker
   of Northern Ireland Assembly 2015–2016)
Oliver Napier (Leader of the Northern Ireland Alliance Party 1972–1984,
   Member of Sunningdale power-sharing executive 1974)
Michael Ritchie (Research Officer at Committee for the Administration of
   Justice, 1989–1995, Director, 2007–2011)
Martin Smyth (Grand Master, Grand Orange Lodge of Ireland, 1971–1996,
   Ulster Unionist Westminster MP 1982–2005)

Archives

Churchill Archives Centre (CAC), [Cambridge], Winston Churchill Papers,
   Margaret Thatcher Papers (many available at www.margaretthatcher.org/)
Éamon Donnelly Collection at Newry and Mourne Museum, Eamon Donnelly
   Papers
National Archives [Dublin], Department of the Taoiseach (D/T), Department
   of Justice (D/J), Department of Foreign Affairs (D/FA)
National Archives [London], Foreign and Commonwealth Office (FCO), Cabinet
   Papers (CAB), Home Office (HO), Prime Minister's Office (PREM)
National Library of Ireland [Dublin], Frank Gallagher Papers, Joseph McGarrity
   Papers
UCD Archives (UCDA; University College, Dublin):
   Frank Aiken Papers
   Ernest Blythe Papers
   Colonel Dan Bryan Papers
   Clann na Poblachta Papers
   Cumann na nGaedheal and Fine Gael Party Papers
   Éamon de Valera Papers
   Fianna Fáil Party Papers
   Garret FitzGerald Papers

Seán MacEntee Papers
Mary MacSwiney Papers
Patrick McGilligan Papers
Richard Mulcahy Papers
George Noble, Count Plunkett, Papers
Conor Cruise O'Brien Papers
Ernie O'Malley Papers
Wikileaks

Parliamentary sources

Hansard British House of Commons Parliamentary Debates
Parliamentary Debates: Dáil Éireann: Official Report
Parliamentary Debates, Northern Ireland House of Commons
Parliamentary Debates: Seanad Éireann: Official Report

Reports

*A New Beginning: Policing In Northern Ireland: The Report of the Independent Commission
    on Policing For Northern Ireland* [Patten Report], 1999
Brexit: Ireland's Priorities, 2017
Dáil Éireann, *Correspondence of Mr. Éamon de Valera*, 1922
Department of Finance, *Economic Development*, 1958
Fresh Start: The Stormont House Agreement and Implementation Plan, 2015
Independent Commission of Inquiry into the Dublin and Monaghan bombings [The Barron
    Report], 2003
*Ireland and the Negotiations on the UK's Withdrawal from the European Union: The
    Government's Approach*, 2017
Joint Committee on the Implementation of the Good Friday Agreement, *Brexit
    and the Future of Ireland: Uniting Ireland & Its People in Peace & Prosperity*, 2017
New Ireland Forum Report, 1984
Northern Ireland and Ireland Position Paper, 2017
Stormont House Agreement, 2014
The Future of Northern Ireland: A Paper, 1972
The Hillsborough Castle Agreement, 2010

Periodicals

An Phoblacht
Belfast Telegraph

Clonmel Nationalist
Combat
Cork Examiner
Dublin Review of Books
Evening Press
Fermanagh Times
Fortnight
Herald Scotland
Hibernia
Honesty
Irish Central
Irish Examiner
Irish Independent
Irish Post
Irish Press
Irish Times
Limerick Leader
Magill
New York Times
Northern Ireland Progress
Sunday Business Post
Sunday Independent
The Argus
The Guardian
The Independent
The Nation
The Observer
The Star
Tipperary Star
Ulster Herald
Ulster Review
United Irishman
Village
Voice of Labour
Western People

Secondary sources

Adams, Gerry. *Free Ireland: Towards a Lasting Peace*. Roberts Rinehart, 2000 (first
    edition Brandon, 1995).

Adams, Gerry. *Hope and History: Making Peace in Ireland*. Hardie Grant, 2004.

Ahern, Bertie. *Autobiography*. Random House, 2009.

Anderson, Brendan. *Joe Cahill: A Life in the IRA*. O'Brien Press, 2012.

Anderson, Don. *Fourteen May Days: The Inside Story of the Loyalist Strike of 1974*. Gill and Macmillan, 1994.

Arnold, Bruce. *Haughey: His Life and Unlucky Deeds*. HarperCollins, 1993.

Baker, Joe. *The McMahon Family Murders and the Belfast Troubles 1920–1922*. Revised International Edition, Glenravel Local History Project, 1993.

Barrington, Donal. 'Uniting Ireland.' *Studies: An Irish Quarterly Review* 46.184 (1957): 379–402.

Beresford, David. *Ten Men Dead: The Story of the 1981 Hunger Strike*. Grafton Books, 1989.

Bew, Paul (ed.). *David Gray: A Yankee in De Valera's Ireland*. Royal Irish Academy, 2012.

Bew, Paul and Henry Patterson. *The British State and the Ulster Crisis: From Wilson to Thatcher*. Verso, 1985.

Bew, Paul, Ellen Hazelkorn and Henry Patterson. *The Dynamics of Irish Politics*. Lawrence and Wishart, 1989.

Boland, Kevin. *We Won't Stand (Idly) By*. Kelly Kane, 1971.

Boland, Kevin. *Up Dev!* K. Boland, 1976.

Boland, Kevin. *The Rise and Decline of Fianna Fáil*. Mercier, 1982.

Bowman, John. *De Valera and the Ulster Question, 1917–1973*. Clarendon Press, 1982.

Bowyer Bell, J. *The Secret Army: The IRA, 1916–1979*. Poolbeg, 1989.

Bowyer Bell, J. *The Irish Troubles*. Gill and Macmillan, 1993.

Bradshaw, Brendan. *'And so began the Irish Nation': Nationality, National Consciousness and Nationalism in Pre-modern Ireland*. Routledge, 2015.

Brady, Séamus. *Arms and the Men: Ireland in Turmoil*. S. Brady, 1971.

Bruce, Steve. *The Red Hand: Protestant Paramilitaries in Northern Ireland*. Oxford University Press, 1992.

Buckland, Patrick. *The Factory of Grievances: Devolved Government in Northern Ireland, 1921–1939*. Gill and Macmillan, 1979.

Cadwallader, Anne. *Holy Cross: The Untold Story*. Brehon Press, 2004.

Cadwallader, Anne. *Lethal Allies: British Collusion in Ireland*. Mercier, 2013.

Callaghan, James. *A House Divided: The Dilemma of Northern Ireland*. Harper, 1973.

Canning, Paul. *British Policy towards Ireland, 1921–1941*. Oxford University Press, 1985.

Chubb, Basil. '"Going about persecuting civil servants": the role of the Irish parliamentary representative.' *Political Studies* 11.3 (1963): 272–286.

Chubb, Basil. *Cabinet Government in Ireland*. Institute of Public Administration, 1974.

Chubb, Basil. *The Government and Politics of Ireland*. Longman, 1982.

Clancy, Mary Alice C. *Peace Without Consensus: Power Sharing Politics in Northern Ireland*. Ashgate, 2010.

Coakley, John. 'Minor parties in Irish political life, 1922–1989.' *Economic and Social Review* 21.3 (1990): 269–297.

Coakley, John. 'The election and the party system.' In Michael Gallagher, Michael Marsh and Paul Mitchell (eds), *How Ireland Voted 2002*. Palgrave Macmillan, 2003, pp. 230–246.

Coakley, John. 'Adjusting to partition: from irredentism to "consent" in twentieth-century Ireland.' *Irish Studies Review* 25.2 (2017): 193–214.

Cobain, Ian. *The History Thieves: Secrets, Lies and the Shaping of a Modern Nation*. Portobello Books, 2016.

Cochrane, Feargal. *Unionist Politics and the Politics of Unionism since the Anglo-Irish Agreement*. Cork University Press, 1997.

Cohan, Al. *The Irish Political Elite*. Gill and Macmillan, 1972.

Connolly, Eileen and John Doyle. 'Ripe moments for exiting political violence: an analysis of the Northern Ireland case.' *Irish Studies in International Affairs* 26 (2015): 147–162.

Conway, Vicky. *Policing Twentieth Century Ireland: A History of An Garda Síochána*. Routledge, 2014.

Coogan, Tim Pat. *The IRA* (second edition). Fontana, 1980.

Coogan, Tim Pat. *Michael Collins: A Biography*. Hutchinson, 1990.

Coogan, Tim Pat. *The Troubles: Ireland's Ordeal 1966–1995 and the Search for Peace*. Random House, 1996.

Cooney, John. *John Charles McQuaid: Ruler of Catholic Ireland* (second edition). O'Brien Press, 2003.

Corcoran, Mary P. and Mark O'Brien. *Political Censorship and the Democratic State: The Irish Broadcasting Ban*. Four Courts, 2005.

Coulter, Carol. *Ireland: Between the First and the Third Worlds*. Attic Press, 1990.

Cox, Michael. 'Rethinking the international: a defence.' In Michael Cox, Adrian Guelke and Fiona Stephen, *A Farewell to Arms? Beyond the Good Friday Agreement*. Manchester University Press, 2008, pp. 427–442.

Cox, Michael, Adrian Guelke and Fiona Stephen. *A Farewell to Arms? Beyond the Good Friday Agreement*. Manchester University Press, 2008.

Craig, Tony. *Crisis of Confidence: Anglo-Irish Relations in the Early Troubles*. Irish Academic Press, 2010.

Crawford, Robert George. *Loyal to King Billy: A Portrait of the Ulster Protestants*. Hurst and Company, 1987.

Cremin, Con. 'Northern Ireland at the United Nations August/September 1969.' *Irish Studies in International Affairs* (1980): 67–73.

Cronin, Seán. *Washington's Irish Policy, 1916–1986: Independence, Partition, Neutrality.* Anvil, 1987.

Crossman, Richard Howard Stafford (ed.). *The Diaries of a Cabinet Minister: Secretary of State for Social Services, 1968–1970.* Vol. 3. Holt, Rinehart and Winston, 1976.

Curran, Frank. *Derry: Countdown to Disaster.* Gill and Macmillan, 1986.

Curran, Joseph M. *The Birth of the Irish Free State, 1919–23.* University of Alabama Press, 1980.

Daly, Mary E. *Industrial Development and Irish National Identity, 1922–1939.* Syracuse University Press, 1992.

De Blaghd, Earnán. *Briseadh na Teorann.* Sáirséal agus Dill, 1955.

Desmond, Barry. 'A Larkinite in power.' *Dublin Review of Books,* Issue 83 (November 2016).

Devlin, Paddy. *The Fall of the Northern Ireland Executive.* Published by the author, 1975.

Devlin, Paddy. *Straight Left: An Autobiography.* Blackstaff, 1993.

Dillon, Martin. *The Shankill Butchers: A Case Study of Mass Murder.* Random House, 1990.

Dorr, Noel. *Ireland at the United Nations: Memories of the Early Years.* Institute of Public Administration, 2010.

Dorr, Noel. *A Small State at the Top Table: Memories of Ireland on the UN Security Council, 1981–82.* Institute of Public Administration, 2011.

Doyle, John. '"Towards a lasting peace"? The Northern Ireland Multi-Party Agreement, referendum and assembly elections of 1998.' *Scottish Affairs* 25.1 (1998): 1–20.

Doyle, John (ed.). *Policing the Narrow Ground: Lessons from the Transformation of Policing in Northern Ireland.* Royal Irish Academy, 2010.

Doyle, John. 'Irish Government Policy on the Northern Ireland Conflict'. Dublin City University, Centre for International Studies, Working Papers in International Studies, No. 10, 2011.

Doyle, John. 'The transformation of policing in post-conflict societies.' In Timothy J. White (ed.), *Lessons from the Northern Ireland Peace Process.* University of Wisconsin Press, 2014, pp. 148–172.

Doyle, John. 'Brexit and the Northern Irish Question.' In Federico Fabbrini (ed.), *The Law and Politics of Brexit.* Oxford University Press, 2017, pp. 139–162.

Doyle, John and Eileen Connolly. 'Foreign policy and domestic politics: a study of the 2002 election in the Republic of Ireland.' *Irish Studies in International Affairs* (2002): 151–166.

Duignan, Seán. *One Spin on the Merry-go-Round.* Blackwater, 1995.

Dumbrell, J. *Clinton's Foreign Policy: Between the Bushes, 1992–2000*. Routledge, 2009.

Dunlop, Frank. *Yes, Taoiseach: Irish Politics from Behind Closed Doors*. Orbit Books, 2004.

Dunne, Derek and Gene Kerrigan. *Round Up the Usual Suspects: Nicky Kelly and the Cosgrave Coalition*. Gill and Macmillan, 1984.

Ervine, St. John Greer. *Craigavon, Ulsterman*. Allen and Unwin, 1949.

Fanning, Ronan. *The Irish Department of Finance 1922–58*. Institute of Public Administration, 1978.

Fanning, Ronan. 'The United States and Irish participation in NATO: the debate of 1950.' *Irish Studies in International Affairs* 1.1 (1979): 38–48.

Fanning, Ronan, *Independent Ireland*. Helicon, 1983.

Fanning, Ronan. *Éamon de Valera: A Will to Power*. Faber and Faber, 2015.

Fanning, Tim. *The Fethard-on-Sea Boycott*. Collins Press, 2010.

Farrell, Brian. *Chairman or Chief? The Role of Taoiseach in Irish Government*. Gill and Macmillan, 1971.

Farrell, Michael. *Northern Ireland: The Orange State* (second edition). Pluto, 1980.

Farrell, Michael. 'How Cumann na nGael [sic] sold out on the border for gold.' *Magill* August (1981).

Farrell, Michael. *Arming the Protestants: The Formation of the Ulster Special Constabulary and the Royal Ulster Constabulary*. Pluto, 1983.

Farrell, Michael. *Sheltering the Fugitive? The Extradition of Irish Political Offenders*. Mercier, 1985.

Faulkner, Brian. *Memoirs of a Statesman*. George Weidenfeld and Nicholson, 1978.

Feeney, Brian. *A Short History of the Troubles*. O'Brien Press, 2014.

Ferriter, Diarmaid. *Judging Dev: A Reassessment of the Life and Legacy of Eamon de Valera*. Royal Irish Academy, 2007.

Fisk, Robert. *The Point of No Return: The Strike which Broke the British in Ulster*. Times Books/Deutsch, 1975.

Fisk, Robert. *In Time of War: Ireland, Ulster, and the Price of Neutrality, 1939–45*. A. Deutsch, 1983.

FitzGerald, Garret. *Towards A New Ireland*. Torc, 1972.

FitzGerald, Garret. *All in A Life: Garret Fitzgerald, an Autobiography*. Gill and Macmillan, 1991.

FitzGerald, Garret. 'The 1974–5 threat of a British withdrawal from Northern Ireland.' *Irish Studies in International Affairs* (2006): 141–150.

FitzGerald, Garret. *Just Garret: Tales from the Political Front Line*. Liberties Press, 2014.

Forester, Margery. *Michael Collins: The Lost Leader*. Sphere, 1972.

Foster, Roy. *Modern Ireland 1600–1972*. Penguin, 1988.

Gallagher, Michael. *Political Parties in the Republic of Ireland.* Manchester University Press, 1985.

Gallagher, Michael. 'Stability and turmoil: analysis of the results.' In Michael Gallagher, Michael Marsh and Paul Mitchell (eds), *How Ireland Voted 2002.* Palgrave Macmillan, 2003, pp. 88–118.

Gallagher, Michael. 'The Oireachtas: president and parliament.' In John Coakley and Michael Gallagher (eds), *Politics in the Republic of Ireland* (fifth edition) Routledge, 2010, pp. 198–229.

Garvin, Tom. 'Political cleavages, party politics and urbanisation in Ireland: the case of the periphery-dominated centre.' *European Journal of Political Research* 2.4 (1974): 307–327.

Gilbert, Martin. *World in Torment: Winston S. Churchill, 1917–1922.* Minerva, 1990.

Goodlad, Graham. *Thatcher.* Routledge, 2015.

Griffith, Kenneth and Timothy O'Grady. *Curious Journey: An Oral History of Ireland's Unfinished Revolution.* Mercier Press, 1998.

Hand, Geoffrey. 'Introduction.' In Irish Boundary Commission, *Report of the Irish Boundary Commission, 1925.* Irish University Press, 1969, pp vii–xxii.

Hand, Geoffrey. 'MacNeill and the Boundary Commission.' In F. X. Martin, with John Francis Byrne (eds), *The Scholar Revolutionary: Eoin MacNeill, 1867–1945, and the Making of the New Ireland.* Irish University Press, 1973, pp. 201–275.

Hanley, Brian and Scott Millar. *The Lost Revolution: The Story of the Official IRA and the Workers' Party.* Penguin, 2010.

Hannon, Philip (ed.). *Taking the Long View: 70 Years of Fianna Fáil.* Blackwater, 1996.

Harkness, David W. *Northern Ireland since 1920.* Helicon, 1983.

Hassan, David. 'The Gaelic Athletic Association, Rule 21, and police reform in Northern Ireland.' *Journal of Sport and Social Issues* 29.1 (2005): 60–78.

Hennessey, Thomas. *The Northern Ireland Peace Process.* Gill and Macmillan, 2001.

Hennessey, Thomas. *Northern Ireland: The Origins of the Troubles.* Gill and Macmillan, 2005.

Hennessey, Thomas. *Hunger Strike: Margaret Thatcher's Battle with the IRA, 1980–1981.* Irish Academic Press, 2013.

Hennessey, Thomas. *The First Northern Ireland Peace Process: Power-Sharing, Sunningdale and the IRA Ceasefires 1972–76.* Springer, 2016.

Hepburn, A.C. *The Conflict of Nationality in Modern Ireland.* Edward Arnold, 1980.

Holland, Jack. *Hope Against History: The Course of Conflict in Northern Ireland.* Henry Holt, 1999.

Hopkinson, Michael. *Green Against Green: The Irish Civil War*. Dublin: Gill and Macmillan, 1988.

Hopkinson, Michael. 'The Craig–Collins pacts of 1922: two attempted reforms of the Northern Ireland government.' *Irish Historical Studies* 27.106 (1990): 145–158.

Hussey, Gemma. *At the Cutting Edge: Cabinet Diaries 1982–1987*. Gill and Macmillan, 1990.

Irish Boundary Commission and Geoffrey J. Hand. *Report of the Irish Boundary Commission, 1925*. Irish University Press, 1969.

Irish Congress of Trade Unions. *The Case Against Brexit*. ICTU, 2016.

Ivory, Gareth. 'Fianna Fail, constitutional republicanism, and the issue of consent: 1980–1996.' *Éire-Ireland* 32.2 (1997): 93–116.

Ivory, Gareth. 'Revisions in nationalist discourse among Irish political parties.' *Irish Political Studies* 14.1 (1999): 84–103.

Ivory, Gareth. 'Fianna Fáil, Northern Ireland and the limits on conciliation, 1969–1973.' *Irish Political Studies* 29.4 (2014): 522–546.

Jones, Thomas and Keith Middlemas. *Whitehall Diary: Volume III: Ireland, 1918–1925*. Oxford University Press, 1971.

Joyce, Joe and Peter Murtagh. *The Boss: Charles J. Haughey in Government*. Poolbeg, 1983.

Kattan, Victor. 'Self-determination during the Cold War: UN General Assembly Resolution 1514 (1960), the prohibition of partition, and the establishment of the British Indian Ocean Territory (1965).' *Max Planck Yearbook of United Nations Law Online* 19.1 (2016): 419–468.

Kavanagh, Ray. *Spring, Summer and Fall: The Rise and Fall of the Labour Party 1986–1999*. Blackwater, 2001.

Keane, Elizabeth. *An Irish Statesman and Revolutionary: The Nationalist and Internationalist Politics of Sean MacBride*. I.B. Tauris, 2006.

Keatinge, Patrick. *The Formulation of Irish Foreign Policy*. Institute of Public Administration, 1973.

Keatinge, Patrick. *A Place among the Nations: Issues of Irish Foreign Policy*. Institute of Public Administration, 1978.

Kee, Robert. *Ourselves Alone*. Vol. 3. Penguin, 1989.

Kelly, Stephen. 'A policy of futility: Eamon de Valera's anti-partition campaign, 1948–1951.' *Études irlandaises* 36.2 (2011): 1–13.

Kelly, Stephen. 'Fresh evidence from the archives: the genesis of Charles J. Haughey's attitude to Northern Ireland.' *Irish Studies in International Affairs* (2012): 155–170.

Kelly, Stephen. *Fianna Fáil, Partition and Northern Ireland, 1926–1971*. Irish Academic Press, 2013.

Kelly, Stephen. 'A Failed Political Entity': Charles Haughey and the Northern Ireland Question, 1945–1992. Merrion Press, 2016.

Kennedy, Michael. Ireland and the League of Nations. Irish Academic Press, 1996.

Kennedy, Michael. Division and Consensus: The Politics of Cross-border Relations in Ireland, 1925–1969. Institute of Public Administration, 2000.

Kennedy, Michael and Deirdre McMahon (eds). Obligations and Responsibilities: Ireland and the United Nations, 1955–2005. Institute of Public Administration, 2005.

Keown, Gerard. First of the Small Nations: The Beginnings of Irish Foreign Policy in Inter-war Europe, 1919–1932. Oxford University Press, 2015.

Kiberd, Declan. 'The elephant of revolutionary forgetfulness.' In Máirín Ní Donnchadha and Theo Dorgan (eds) Revising the Rising. Field Day, 1991, pp. 1–20.

Kiberd, Declan. Inventing Ireland. Harvard University Press, 1997.

Kirchheimer, Otto. 'The transformation of the Western European party systems.' In J. LaPalombara and M. Weiner (eds), Political Parties and Political Development. Princeton University Press, 1966, pp. 177–200.

Laffan, Michael. The Partition of Ireland, 1911–25. Dundalgan Press, 1983.

Lee, Joseph. Ireland, 1912–1985: Politics and Society. Cambridge University Press, 1989.

Lee, Joseph and Gearóid Ó Tuathaigh. The Age of De Valera. RTÉ, 1982.

Liggett, Michael. A District Called the Bone: A Brief History of the 'Marrowbone' Area of Belfast. Glenraval Local History Project, 1994.

Lissek, Ralf, Brian Murphy and Volker Treier. Brexit – a View from the Chambers in December 2016. German-Irish Chamber of Industry and Commerce, 2016.

Livingstone, Peadar. The Fermanagh Story (third edition). Watergate Press, 1977.

Lynch, Jack. Speeches and Statements on Irish Unity, Northern Ireland, Anglo-Irish Relations, August 1969 to October 1971. Government Information Bureau, 1971.

Lynch, Timothy J. 'The Gerry Adams visa in Anglo-American relations.' Irish Studies in International Affairs (2003): 33–44.

Lyons, F.S.L. 'The meaning of independence.' In Brian Farrell (ed.), The Irish Parliamentary Tradition. Gill and Macmillan, 1973, pp. 223–233.

Mac Flynn, Paul. The Economic Implications of Brexit for Northern Ireland. NERI (Nevin Economic Research Institute), 2016.

Macardle, Dorothy. The Irish Republic. Irish Press, 1951.

MacMillan, Gretchen. State, Society and Authority in Ireland: The Foundation of the Modern State. Gill and Macmillan, 1993.

Maillot, Agnès. New Sinn Féin: Irish Republicanism in the Twenty-First Century. Routledge, 2004.

Maillot, Agnès. In the Shadow of History: Sinn Féin, 1926–70. Manchester University Press, 2015.

Mair, Peter. *The Changing Irish Party System: Organisation, Ideology and Electoral Competition*. Frances Pinter, 1988.

Major, John. *John Major: The Autobiography*. HarperCollins, 2013.

Mallie, Eamonn and David McKittrick. *The Fight for Peace: The Secret Story behind the Irish Peace Process*. Heinemann, 1996.

Mannix, Patrick. *The Belligerent Prelate: An Alliance Between Archbishop Daniel Mannix and Eamon de Valera*. Cambridge Scholars Publishing, 2011.

Mansergh, Martin (ed.). *The Spirit of the Nation: The Speeches and Statements of Charles J. Haughey*. Mericer, 1986.

Mansergh, Martin. 'The new context of British–Irish relations.' In Ben Tonra and Eilís Ward (eds), *Ireland in International Affairs*. IPA, 2002, pp. 93–103.

McCarthy, John F. 'Ireland's turnaround: Whitaker and the 1958 Plan for Economic Development.' In John F. McCarthy (ed.), *Planning Ireland's Future: The Legacy of T.K. Whitaker*. Glendale, 1990, pp. 11–74.

McCullagh, David. *A Makeshift Majority: The First Inter-party Government, 1948–51*. Institute of Public Administration, 1998.

McCullagh, David. *The Reluctant Taoiseach: A Biography of John A. Costello*. Gill and Macmillan, 2010.

McCullagh, David. *De Valera: Rise, 1882–1932*. Gill, 2017.

McDonald, Henry. *Trimble*. Bloomsbury, 2001.

McGarry, John and Brendan O'Leary. *Explaining Northern Ireland: Broken Images*. Wiley-Blackwell, 1999 (1st edition 1995).

McKittrick, David and David McVea. Making Sense of the Troubles: The Story of the Conflict in Northern Ireland. New Amsterdam Books, 2002.

McMahon, Deirdre. *Republicans and Imperialists: Anglo-Irish Relations in the 1930s*. Yale University Press, 1984.

McManus, Seán. *My American Struggle for Justice in Northern Ireland*. Collins Press, 2011.

McNamara, Kevin. *The MacBride Principles: Irish America Strikes Back*. Liverpool University Press, 2010.

McNay, John T. *Acheson and Empire: The British Accent in American Foreign Policy*. University of Missouri Press, 2001.

Meehan, Ciara. *A Just Society for Ireland? 1964–1987*. Palgrave Macmillan, 2013.

Moore, Charles. *Margaret Thatcher: The Authorized Biography, Volume One: Not for Turning*. Penguin UK, 2013.

Moore, Charles. *Margaret Thatcher: The Authorized Biography: Volume Two: Everything She Wants*. Penguin UK, 2015.

Moynihan, Maurice. *Speeches and Statements by Éamon de Valera 1917–1973*. Gill and Macmillan, 1980.

Murphy, Brian. *Forgotten Patriot: Douglas Hyde and the Foundation of the Irish Presidency*. Collins Press, 2016.

Murphy, Gary. *Electoral Competition in Ireland since 1987: The Politics of Triumph and Despair*. Manchester University Press, 2016.

Murray, Gerard. *John Hume and the SDLP: Impact and Survival in Northern Ireland*. Irish Academic Press, 1998.

Murray, Raymond. *The SAS in Ireland*, Mercier, 1990.

Neeson, Eoin. *The Civil War, 1922–23*. Poolbeg, 1989.

Nelson, Sarah. *Ulster's Uncertain Defenders: Protestant Political, Paramilitary and Community Groups and the Northern Ireland Conflict*. Appletree Press, 1984.

Norton, Christopher. 'The internment of Cahir Healy M.P., Brixton Prison July 1941–December 1942.' *Twentieth Century British History* 18.2 (2007): 170–193.

Ó Beacháin, Donnacha. *Destiny of the Soldiers: Fianna Fáil, Irish Republicanism and the IRA, 1926–1973*. Gill and Macmillan, 2010.

Ó Beacháin, Donnacha. '"Slightly constitutional" politics: Fianna Fáil's tortuous entry to the Irish Parliament, 1926–7.' *Parliamentary History* 29.3 (2010): 376–394.

Ó Beacháin, Donnacha. 'Elections and political communication.' In Mark O'Brien and Donnacha Ó Beacháin (eds), *Political Communication in the Republic of Ireland*. Liverpool University Press, 2014, pp. 25–44.

Ó Beacháin, Donnacha. 'Ireland's foreign relations in 2013.' *Irish Studies in International Affairs* 25 (2014): 259–301.

Ó Beacháin, Donnacha. 'Ireland's foreign relations in 2014.' *Irish Studies in International Affairs* 26 (2015): 275–320.

Ó Beacháin, Donnacha. 'The dog that didn't bark: Southern Unionism in pre- and post-revolutionary Ireland.' *History Ireland* 23.4 (2015): 44–47.

Ó Beacháin, Donnacha. 'Ireland's foreign relations in 2015.' *Irish Studies in International Affairs* 27 (2016): 235–278.

Ó Corráin, Daithí. '"Ireland in his heart north and south": the contribution of Ernest Blythe to the partition question.' *Irish Historical Studies* 35.137 (2006): 61–80.

Ó Drisceoil, Donal. 'When Dev defaulted: the land annuities dispute, 1926–38.' *History Ireland* 19.3 (2011): 42–45.

O'Brien Conor Cruise. *The United Nations: Sacred Drama*. Simon and Schuster, 1968.

O'Brien, Conor Cruise. *Memoir: My Life and Themes*. Poolbeg, 1998.

O'Brien, Justin. *The Arms Trial*. Gill and Macmillan, 2000.

O'Brien, Mark and Donnacha Ó Beacháin (eds). *Political Communication in the Republic of Ireland*. Liverpool University Press, 2014.

O'Clery, Conor. *The Greening of the White House: The Inside Story of how America Tried to Bring Peace to Ireland*. Gill and Macmillan, 1996.

O'Clery, Conor. *Daring Diplomacy: Clinton's Secret Search for Peace in Ireland*. National Book Network, 1997.

O'Connell, John. *Dr John: Crusading Doctor and Politician*. Poolbeg, 1989.

O'Connor, Fionnuala. *In Search of a State: Catholics in Northern Ireland*. Blackstaff, 1993.

O'Day, Alan. *Political Violence in Northern Ireland: Conflict and Conflict Resolution*. Greenwood Publishing Group, 1997.

O'Donnell, Catherine. *Fianna Fáil, Irish Republicanism and the Northern Ireland Troubles, 1968–2005*. Irish Academic Press, 2007.

O'Halloran, Clare. *Partition and the Limits of Irish Nationalism: An Ideology under Stress*. Gill and Macmillan, 1987.

O'Kane, Eamonn. 'Decommissioning and the peace process: where did it come from and why did it stay so long?' *Irish Political Studies* 22.1 (2007): 81–101.

O'Kane, Eamonn. *Britain, Ireland and Northern Ireland since 1980: The Totality of Relationships*. Routledge, 2012.

O'Kane, Eamonn. 'The perpetual peace process? Examining Northern Ireland's never-ending, but fundamentally altering peace process.' *Irish Political Studies* 28.4 (2013): 515–535.

O'Leary, Brendan. 'Afterword: what is framed in the Framework Documents?' *Ethnic and Racial Studies* 18.4 (1995): 862–872.

O'Leary, Brendan and John McGarry. *The Politics of Antagonism: Understanding Northern Ireland*. Bloomsbury, 2016.

O'Mahony, T.P. *Jack Lynch: A Biography*. Blackwater, 1991.

O'Neill, Terence. *Ulster at the Crossroads*. Faber, 1969.

O'Neill, Terence. *The Autobiography of Terence O'Neill*. Rupert Hart-Davis, 1972.

O'Shiel, Kevin R. 'The problem of partitioned Ireland.' *Studies: An Irish Quarterly Review* XII.48 (December 1923): 625–638.

Owen, Arwel Ellis. *The Anglo-Irish Agreement: The First Three Years*. University of Wales Press, 1994.

Penniman, Howard R. and Brian Farrell. *Ireland at the Polls 1981, 1982, and 1987: A Study of Four General Elections*. Duke University Press, 1987.

Phoenix, Eamon. *Northern Nationalism: Nationalist Politics, Partition and the Catholic Minority in Northern Ireland, 1890–1940*. Ulster Historical Foundation, 1994.

Powell, Jonathan. *Great Hatred, Little Room: Making Peace in Northern Ireland*. Random House, 2008.

Purcell, Betty. 'The silence in Irish broadcasting.' In Bill Rolston (ed.), *The Media and Northern Ireland: Covering the Troubles*. Palgrave, 1990, pp. 51–68.

Purcell, Betty. *Inside RTÉ: A Memoir*. New Island, 2014.

Rafter, Kevin. *Neil Blaney: A Soldier of Destiny*. Blackwater, 1993.

Raymond, J. 'John Cudahy, Eamon de Valera, and the Anglo-Irish negotiations in 1938: the secret dispatches to Washington.' *International History Review* 6.2 (1984): 232–264.

Regan, John M. *The Irish Counter Revolution*. Gill and Macmillan, 1999.

Regan, John M. *Myth and the Irish State: Historical Problems and Other Essays*. Irish Academic Press, 2013.

Reynolds, Albert. *Albert Reynolds: My Autobiography*. Random House, 2010.

Rhodeen, Penn. *Peacerunner*. BenBella Books, 2016.

Rose, Peter. 'Labour, Northern Ireland and the decision to send in the troops.' In Sean McDougall and Peter Catterall (eds), *The Northern Ireland Question in British Politics*. Palgrave Macmillan, 1996, pp. 88–101.

Rumpf, Erhard and A.C. Hepburn. *Nationalism and Socialism in Twentieth-Century Ireland*. Liverpool University Press, 1977.

Ryle Dwyer, T. *Michael Collins and the Treaty: His Differences with de Valera*. Mercier, 1981.

Ryle Dwyer, T. *Charlie: The Political Biography of Charles J. Haughey*. Gill and Macmillan, 1987.

Sacks, Paul Martin. *The Donegal Mafia: An Irish Political Machine*. Yale University Press, 1976.

Schwelb, Egon. 'Northern Ireland and the United Nations.' *International and Comparative Law Quarterly* 19.03 (1970): 483–492.

Short, Con. *The Ulster GAA Story, 1884–1984*. Comhairle Uladh, C.L.G., 1984.

Sinn Féin, *Setting the Record Straight*. Sinn Féin, 1994.

Skelly, Joseph Morrison. *Irish Diplomacy at the United Nations, 1945–1965: National Interests and the International Order*. Irish Academic Press, 1997.

Smith, Jeremy. *Making the Peace in Ireland*. Routledge, 2014.

Smyth, Patrick and Ellen Hazelkorn. *Let in the Light: Censorship Secrecy and Democracy*. Brandon, 1993.

Staunton, Enda. 'The Boundary Commission debacle 1925: aftermath & implications.' *History Ireland* 4.2 (1996): 42–45.

Sunday Times Insight Team. *Ulster*. Penguin, 1972.

Taylor, Peter. *States of Terror: Democracy and Political Violence*. BBC, 1993.

Thatcher, Margaret. *The Downing Street Years*. HarperCollins Publishers, 1993.

Tonge, Jonathan, Maire Braniff, Thomas Hennessey, James McAuley and Sophie Whiting. *The Democratic Unionist Party: From Protest to Power*. Oxford University Press, 2014.

Tonra, Ben. *Global Citizen and European Republic: Irish Foreign Policy in Transition*. Manchester University Press, 2006.

Tonra, Ben and Eilis Ward (eds). *Ireland in International Affairs: Interests, Institutions and Identities*. Institute of Public Administration, 2002.

Tonra, Ben, Michael Kennedy, John Doyle and Noel Dorr (eds). *Irish Foreign Policy*. Gill and Macmillan, 2012.

Trimble, David. 'The foundation of Northern Ireland (part III).' *Ulster Review: The Journal of the Young Unionist Council* No. 10: 20.

Troy, Aidan. *Holy Cross: A Personal Experience*. Currach Press, 2005.

Urwin, Margaret. *A State in Denial: British Collaboration with Loyalist Paramilitaries*. Mercier, 2016.

Valiulis, Maryann Gialanella. 'The "army mutiny" of 1924 and the assertion of civilian authority in independent Ireland.' *Irish Historical Studies* 23.92 (1983): 354–366.

Walsh, Dick. *The Party: Inside Fianna Fáil*. Gill and Macmillan, 1986.

Walsh, John. *Patrick Hillery: The Official Biography*. New Island, 2008.

Weiss, Ruth. *Peace in Their Time: War and Peace in Ireland and Southern Africa*. I.B. Tauris, 2000.

Whelan, Noel. *A History of Fianna Fáil: A Biography of the Party*. Gill and Macmillan, 2011.

Whitaker, T.K. 'Economic development 1958–1985.' In Kieran A. Kennedy (ed.), *Ireland in Transition*, Mercier, pp. 10–18.

White, Terence de Vere. *Kevin O'Higgins*. Anvil, 1966.

White, Jerry. *The Radio Eye: Cinema in the North Atlantic, 1958–1988*. Wilfrid Laurier University Press, 2009.

White, Robert W. *Ruairí Ó Brádaigh: The Life and Politics of an Irish Revolutionary*. Indiana University Press, 2006.

White, Robert W. *Out of the Ashes: An Oral History of the Provisional Irish Republican Movement*. Merrion, 2017.

Williamson, Daniel C. 'Taking the Troubles across the Atlantic: Ireland's UN initiatives and Irish–US diplomatic relations in the early years of the conflict in Northern Ireland, 1969–72.' *Irish Studies in International Affairs* (2007): 175–189.

Williamson, Daniel C. *Anglo-Irish Relations in the Early Troubles*. Bloomsbury, 2016.

Wilson, Andrew J. *Irish America and the Ulster Conflict, 1968–1995*. Catholic University of America Press, 1995.

Wilson, Tim. 'Ghost provinces, mislaid minorities: the experience of Southern Ireland and Prussian Poland compared, 1918–23.' *Irish Studies in International Affairs* 13 (2002): 61–86.

Younger, Calton. *Ireland's Civil War*. Fontana, 1970.

Index

Note: 'n.' after a page reference indicates the number of a note on that page